THE ANTHROPOLOGY OF HEALTH

THE ANTHROPOLOGY OF HEALTH

ELEANOR E. BAUWENS, R.N., Ph.D.

Associate Professor of Nursing
University of Arizona
Tucson, Arizona

Illustrated

THE C. V. MOSBY COMPANY

SAINT LOUIS   1978

The C. V. Mosby Company
11830 Westline Industrial Drive, St. Louis, Missouri 63141

Library of Congress Cataloging in Publication Data

The anthropology of health.

　　Includes bibliographies and index.
　　1.　Medical anthropology—Addresses, essays,
lectures.　I.　Bauwens, Eleanor.　[DNLM: 1.　Ethnic groups.　2.　Anthropology, Cultural.
3.　Delivery of health care.　4.　Food habits.
5.　Aging.　WA300 A631]
GN296.A56　　　362.1　　　78-6776
ISBN 0-8016-0516-4

GW/M/M　9　8　7　6　5　4　3　2　1

CONTRIBUTORS

Agnes M. Aamodt, R.N., Ph.D.
The University of Arizona
College of Nursing, Tucson, Arizona

Anita L. Alvarado, R.N., Ph.D.
The University of New Mexico
Department of Anthropology
Albuquerque, New Mexico

Sandra Anderson, R.N., M.S.
The University of Arizona
College of Nursing
Tucson, Arizona

Jan R. Atwood, R.N., Ph.D.
The University of Arizona
College of Nursing and
Arizona Health Sciences Center
Tucson, Arizona

Eleanor E. Bauwens, R.N., Ph.D.
The University of Arizona
College of Nursing, Tucson, Arizona

Thomas G. Betz, M.D.
Austin, Texas

Molly Dougherty, R.N., Ph.D.
The University of Florida
The J. Hillis Miller Health Center
College of Nursing
Gainesville, Florida

Glenn Friedman, M.D.
Pediatric Associate
Papago Butte Medical Center
Scottsdale, Arizona

Gail Harrison, Ph.D., R.D.
The University of Arizona
College of Medicine
Department of Family and Community Medicine
Tucson, Arizona

Shirley M. Johnson, M.P.H., Ph.D.
Michigan State University
Department of Family Medicine
East Lansing, Michigan

Margarita Kay, R.N., Ph.D.
The University of Arizona
College of Nursing
Tucson, Arizona

Kathyrn Kolasa, Ph.D.
Michigan State University
College of Human Ecology
Department of Food Science and Human Nutrition
East Lansing, Michigan

Lynn L. Krause, M.A.
Arizona State University
College of Education
Tempe, Arizona

Carolyn Lackey, Ph.D.
Michigan State University
College of Human Ecology
Department of Food Science and Human Nutrition
East Lansing, Michigan

Barbara Myerhoff, Ph.D.
Professor and Chairperson
Department of Sociology and Anthropology
The University of Southern California
Los Angeles, California

Cheryl Ritenbaugh, Ph.D.
Michigan State University
Department of Anthropology
East Lansing, Michigan

William L. Roberts, M.S.W.
The University of Arizona
College of Medicine
Department of Family and Community Medicine
Tucson, Arizona

Nadine H. Rund, Ph.D.
Health Program Systems Center
Indian Health Services
Tucson, Arizona

Clarissa S. Scott, M.A.
The University of Miami
School of Medicine
Department of Psychiatry
Miami, Florida

Loudell F. Snow, Ph.D.
Michigan State University
Department of Anthropology
East Lansing, Michigan

Anita M. Stafford, M.D.
The University of Arizona
College of Medicine
Department of Pediatrics
Tucson, Arizona

Marie Tymrak, M.P.H., R.D.
Papago Butte Medical Center
Scottsdale, Arizona

Christine S. Wilson, Ph.D.
The University of California
George Williams Hooper Foundation
San Francisco, California

PREFACE

Several related influences have prompted me to organize a group of papers concerning the place and relationship of anthropology within the broad spectrum of the behavioral and health sciences. My experience with the difficulty involved in finding an adequate book for both students and colleagues is the most immediate influence. The growing importance about the desirability and necessity of incorporating anthropological concepts within other disciplines such as medicine, nursing, and public health reflects a need for a volume such as this.

There is an increasing need to communicate to a broader audience the many facets of anthropology. Members of the health professions are beginning to extend their knowledge about health beliefs, practices, and needs of individuals from different cultures. As these professionals take a more active part in providing health care to people from diverse cultures, it becomes essential that they attempt to increase their understanding about these cultural groups.

The purposes of this volume are to contribute to the educational process of preparing more individuals for specialized work in the field of medical anthropology, to contribute to the development of literature in medical anthropology, and to introduce behavioral science to medical, nursing, and other health professions.

This volume includes original research and theoretical papers that attempt to bridge anthropological and medical perspectives and methods contributing to a science of illness and health care. Included are discussions of how the concept of culture is operationalized in anthropology and the health sciences. Chapters are organized into four sections: (1) Clinical Anthropology, the relation and application of anthropological principles to health care; (2) Strategies for Health Care, the attempts to relate medicine to culture, society, and health care programs; (3) Nutritional Anthropology, the discussion of the sociocultural value attached to various foods by various groups and the concern with changing the food habits in different cultural settings; and (4) Anthropological Perspectives on Aging and Dying, the discussion of the sociocultural aspects of aging and dying.

For help in locating authors and for various suggestions regarding the book, I should like to express my gratitude to Margarita Kay, Loudell Snow, and Jane Underwood. In addition, I should like to thank both Margarita Kay and Michael Rich for reading portions of the manuscript and for sharing with me their critical comments.

I should like to offer my appreciation to Ada Ann Sotelo for her dedicated labors in typing the manuscript.

Finally, to Maurice Bauwens, my husband, I am indebted for persevering with me during the completion of this project.

Eleanor E. Bauwens

CONTENTS

PART ONE

CLINICAL ANTHROPOLOGY

Chapter 1 explores clinical anthropology, which is the application of principles of anthropological theory to the practice of patient care. The principal message of medical anthropology has been that medical culture patterns are not isolated, but rather integrated into a complex network of beliefs and values that are part of the culture of each society. Prevention, diagnosis, and treatment of illness follow more or less directly from beliefs about causation. Thus the anthropologist has tried to learn what people know, believe, and do with their lives in order to discover the logic underlying health and illness behavior. However, clinical anthropology requires more, for health care behavior may be determined by the relationship of individuals to the social structure of the dominant society, their economic positions, and biological factors.

Chapter 2 illustrates how clinical anthropology can be the bridge between traditional methods of treatment and folk medicine. This chapter presents a case history of abdominal pain in an 11½-year old Mexican-American female.

Chapter 3 is a selected review of the literature of interest to both anthropologists and health professionals. Chapter 4 examines the cultural dimension of the concept of care and suggests alternative strategies for research. The assumption is made that all cultures provide a system of rules for caring for oneself and/or others, and that health specialists can advance health and patient care when they understand these rules.

Chapter 5 focuses on a study done in a prenatal clinic with a multi-ethnic low income clientele. The women informants document the reasons why they have been unable to prevent their pregnancies.

Chapter 6 discusses an adaptive strategy utilized by women for dealing with their dissatisfaction with hospital births and hospital maternity care in general. Home births have been chosen as a way to reduce the dissonance that occurs with hospital births.

Chapter 7 looks at the health and healing practices among five ethnic groups residing in Miami, Florida. Patterns of use of both orthodox and traditional healing systems among these groups are discussed. The goal is to develop models for more appropriate health care delivery.

CHAPTER 1

Clinical anthropology

Margarita Kay

1. Mrs. Jackson is black. Let's see her about root medicine.
2. You can give them the best diagnostic work-up and treatment, but they won't even come back to cooperate.
3. You can't teach them prevention, not of babies or of disease. They are fatalistic, you know, they're in the culture of poverty.
4. We've got some Papago blood samples left over from that diabetes study. Why don't we just send them in to the laboratory to see if they have antibodies to Chagas disease?
5. The man in room 7 is refusing to let the student nurse bathe him. How can we give good care if we let patients make decisions about what we do?
6. Mrs. Begay hasn't come into the intensive care nursery once to visit her baby. It sounds like she is rejecting him.

The above statements may appear to be egregious cases of cultural ignorance. In fact, they are typical of occurrences that may take place daily in any medical facility. They are examples of why clinical anthropology, the study of anthropology applied to patient care, should be offered to health care workers. The first statement illustrates the misconception that any member of an ethnic group is expert in all aspects of that culture, and that anyone can do an anthropological study without special training. Furthermore, the statement ignores the possibility that an individual might be reluctant to discuss something so easily misunderstood as root medicine with an outsider. It ignores personal interest and other differences, such as social class and education, which might make Mrs. Jackson ignorant of root medicine.

The second statement is common. Why don't people comply with carefully designed courses of diagnosis and treatment? The reasons are legion, but the most common is lack of communication between health care provider and client.

The third statement ascribes social reasons for cultural phenomena. Although culture and life-style are often treated as if they were identical, there is more than a theoretical distinction between the two categories. The life-styles of people in poverty are varied, with economics the only factor held in common. Thus social scientists have discarded the idea of a single culture of poverty as an explanation for health-seeking behavior. But there has been a continued uncritical use of this concept, probably stemming from frustration at noncompliance. Such action by some health care professionals has distorted the organization of clinics and other health services and wasted the time and money of all.

The fourth statement is an example of how two cultures can view the same entity—blood samples—in two distinct ways. To the physician, the blood is simply laboratory material, conveniently available for study. To the Papago, the blood represents individual people who cannot benefit from learning about a disease that gives them no symptoms.

In example five, the nurse assumes that the phenomenon of care is the same for all people. The nurse assumes that touch, space, motion, soap, and water have the same meaning and the same effect on everyone.

The sixth example might reflect an accurate appraisal of a specific individual. However, the chances are great that the statement simply reflects cultural ignorance, a lack of knowledge of a different mode of nonverbal communication, which is another dimension of care.

3

Examples such as these pointed up the need for a class designed to apply principles of anthropology to the practice of patient care. This chapter will describe my experience in teaching a course called clinical anthropology, cross-listed for students in anthropology, family and community medicine, and nursing, which is the home department. Students also come from nutrition, physical therapy, occupational therapy, pediatrics, gerontology, and other health fields. Similar courses are offered in many other colleges and universities, but none has been described in the literature for comparison, emulation, or criticism.

THE CLASS

In my course that portion of anthropology that is immediately relevant to health care in the southwestern United States is surveyed. Thus clinical anthropology is not the same as medical anthropology, for topics such as paleopathology, primitive medicine, biological adaptation, and sexual selection are omitted because they are not obviously germane.

Many health care providers have stated the need to take cultural factors into consideration in health care. These commendable but vague statements are not put into action very often, because the scholars of culture have given little practical help. The goal of my course is to show how the nebulous ideal of "taking into account the patient's culture" may be met. There is an attempt to introduce applied anthropology.

Shiloh (1977:444) states that "too much of applied anthropology is still dilettante do-gooding, too much of action anthropology is still underdog advocacy, and too much of medical anthropology continues to be Naive Victoriana," and suggests a new role for the anthropologist, that of a private practitioner of therapeutic anthropology. Even without developing a new professional in health care, it is beneficial to help existing providers of care to remove their cultural blinders. Many know only the ethnocentric medical model that represents Western science today.

The heterogeneous composition of the class is believed by all members to be beneficial. At first, undergraduate nursing students are timid to find themselves as classmates of practicing physicians, and require encouragement not to drop out. The physi-

cians in turn may be concerned about handling cultural data that they find to be unfamiliar, ambiguous, and "soft." The class variation immediately provides an opportunity to illustrate that what is commonly called "the" health system is in fact not shared culture. Caste relations, minority behavior, and different cultural knowledge can be explored as each health care giver learns what the other knows.

Students are told that the purpose of the course is to give training to professional health care workers and anthropologists in topics of mutual interest. In order to solve clinical problems that are not primarily biological in nature, lectures are addressed to questions such as:

1. Who are the people seeking health care in the Southwest?
2. What does one need to know about a people in order to assist them in health care?
3. Which methods are most useful for learning aspects of life-style and culture that influence health behavior?
4. How may elements be organized into a model for studying any medical system?

It is expected that the students' objectives reflect their own professional needs. Physicians should be aware of cultural factors if they are to prevent as well as diagnose and treat disease. Nurses need to know cultural factors to understand health-seeking behavior and learn culturally appropriate ways to assist patients who cannot care for themselves. Anthropologists need to know official scientific medicine's point of view as well as how to apply anthropological theory and data to health problems.

At the beginning of the course certain theories that have proved useful in clinical anthropology are presented. Each is illustrated by studying one or more groups living in the greater Southwest, and the method by which the anthropologist obtained and analyzed the data is also presented. The models that are used are (1) a medical system, (2) biological and cultural response to ecology, and (3) healing as an aspect of religion.

Little time is spent on the equally important models from law and economics, since there are other courses available that concentrate on the contributions of those disciplines to the anthropology of health and illness. More time is devoted to the differences among the concepts of race, culture, ethnic identity, life-style, and social class. These anthropological categories are often misused in studies of disease distribution and in epidemiology. Advanced anthropology students are assigned *Ethnic Identity in the Southwest* by Spicer (1972). For students in the health care fields, the lectures covering these concepts are usually sufficient; if they are not, ethnology courses such as "Indians of the Southwest," "Peoples of Mexico," and "Mexican-American Culture" are recommended as well as introductory courses in physical anthropology.

The history and geography of the greater Southwest are surveyed, because an historical experience, real or in myth, contributes to an identity system. Also, roots in the land may be an important element in this history.

Ethnographic maps that locate the following Southwestern people are distributed to class members: Navajo, western and eastern Apache, Havasupai, Hualapi, Yavapi, Pima, Papago, eastern and western Pueblo, Yaqui, and Yuman linguistic groups. The exploration of these areas, the establishment of missions, and the settlement of these lands by Spanish, English, Chinese, Mormons, blacks, and others are briefly reviewed in lectures.

The concept of system (Malinowski's institution) is then introduced. It is described as an organization of elements, factors, or parts. The most fundamental property of a system is the interdependence of its parts or variables. This interdependence is shown in the relationships among the parts, and in the order among the components that enter into a system. This approach is, of course, structural-functional.

Medical system model

From the concept of system, we proceed to the idea of a medical system, using the definitions by writers such as Clark (1970) and Weaver (1970). Weaver states that a medical system in its entirety includes "the whole complex of a people's beliefs, attitudes, practices, and roles associated with concepts of health and disease, and with patterns of diagnosis and treatment" (p. 141). Thus the components of a health care system

model are ideas, roles, and materials. Each of these elements will be discussed.

The principal message of medical anthropology has been that medical culture patterns are not isolated, but rather integrated into a complex network of beliefs and values that are part of the culture of each society. Each health care system is based on a philosophy of what constitutes health and what constitutes illness. It is the group's theory of medicine. This theory consists of propositions formulated from the group's answers to such questions as: "What is illness?" "What causes illness?" "How may illness be prevented?" "How may illness be treated?" The sources of this theory are beliefs about causation.

Another element in a medical system is social role. What kinds of people are needed to do the different tasks of health and healing? And how do societies select people for these roles in a health system? Are individuals found suitable to occupy a specific status because of their achievements, because they have had certain training and a certain initiation such as graduation, or are they given their status by a supernatural power? Is the role inherited, or revealed in a wish or dream? What is the comparative hierarchy of diagnostician, curer, therapist, and care giver?

The third component of a medical system is material. What kinds of equipment are required to make diagnoses and to give treatment? Some of the same materials are used by all systems. For example, many believe that body parts or excreta are extensions of an individual. Thus such remainders are used for diagnostic or therapeutic or witchcraft purposes in every system. Other materials are medicines to swallow, to rub in, to fix on, to irrigate with, or to anoint with.

The Southwest, like other regions, has many medical systems that exist either parallel with or alternative to the official medical system. To illustrate different kinds of medical systems, students in the class are assigned to read Scott's (1974) "Health and Healing Practices Among Five Ethnic Groups in Miami, Florida," which appears on pp. 61 to 70 of this text. These five ethnic groups are Bahamian, Cuban, Haitian, Puerto Rican, and southern U.S. black. Maps from the National Geographic Society and discussion of social stratification further clarify Scott's material.

For a required text we use *Ethnic Medicine in the Southwest* (Spicer, 1977), which details the health culture of urban blacks, Mexican-Americans, Yaquis (Mexican migrant Indians), and lower income Anglos. Some of the material is summarized in Snow's (1974) "Folk Medical Beliefs and Their Implications For Care of Patients," which is assigned for discussion. Stafford in Chapter 2 discusses an example of a patient's simultaneous use of several parallel medical systems. This will also be used in the future. As a principal text, we have used the book edited by Lynch (1966), *The Cross Cultural Approach to Health Behavior*, since it includes so many of the classic articles in medical anthropology that deal with people of the greater Southwest.

Culture, Disease and Healing, edited by Landy (1977), contains excellent readings for students with advanced knowledge in anthropology. One book of readings especially addressed to nurses is Brink's (1976) *Transcultural Nursing*. Branch and Paxton (1976) have compiled *Safe Nursing Care for Ethnic People of Color*. This last text reflects these authors' concern that the entire nursing curriculum should integrate knowledge about groups defined as ethnic people of color, that is, American Indians, Blacks, Chicanos, and Orientals. All of these books contain valuable essays from cultural and physical anthropology.

After the medical system model of clinical anthropology is outlined, the class is introduced to concepts of the epidemiology of disease, defined in terms of the culture of Western scientific medicine. The distinction between disease and illness is clearly explained by Fabrega (1975). Now the health professionals are on more comfortable ground, and the anthropologists less secure. The works of Alexander Alland, for example, *Adaptation in Cultural Evolution: An Approach to Medical Anthropology* (1970), are recommended to those students with a limited background in medicine and parasitology. Hughes' (1961) paper, "Public Health in Non-Literate Societies," presents a model for the influences of life-style and culture on health. Collections such as Rabin et al. (1972), *Health Problems of U.S. and North American Indian Popula-*

tions, articles found in the *Index Medicus*, the *Social Sciences Index*, and computer retrieval systems help the students to ferret out medical research relevant to clinical anthropology.

Ecology model

The second principal model in clinical anthropology is ecology. Ecology is given three definitions: biological (that branch of biology that deals with the relations of organisms and their environment), social (the relations of people and institutions and their interdependence), and cultural (the relation of culture and environment, which includes the other cultures and societies that are in the environment). The Navajo are used to illustrate ecology because they have been studied extensively from all three standpoints. Assignments are made from the Lynch reader as well as a newer summary in *Science* (McDermott and coworkers, 1972).

Ecological determinants of disease distribution are demonstrated not only by the Navajo, but also the Apache and Papago peoples. Guest anthropologists illustrate their lectures with slides of the desert, its life forms, and the life-styles that developed in response to the ecological system. One guest lecturer speaks to the class specifically about the work of a clinical anthropologist in the Indian Health Service.

Indian patients are challenging to health care workers at local hospitals. Communication, both verbal and nonverbal, is a principal difficulty. Sections in *The People's Health* (Adair and Deuschle, 1970), a summary of the Cornell project for the Navajo not included in the Lynch reader, are particularly helpful in suggesting some of the linguistic sources of difficulty. The writings of Hall (1959, 1969) are useful for conveying those aspects of nonverbal communication that particularly affect patient care. Kay's (1977) *Southwestern Medical Dictionary* illustrates the differences among scientific, lay, and folk vocabularies.

The geography and history of the Navajo are presented in lecture and further illustrated by a film, "The Navajo Way."* Some Navajos object to this film, which makes it

---

*This CBS documentary may be obtained from Navajo Community College, Tsaile Az 86556.

useful for stimulating a classroom discussion of the problems of stereotype and the use of old people as principal informants. The film also evokes argument about the role of culture in definitions of problems, suggested by the film's depiction of Navajo drinking. Some students insist that alcoholism is a problem to the white man, not to the drinking Navajo. Others point to Navajo membership in the Native American Church, which forbids alcohol, to show that Navajo do see alcohol as a problem.

Religious model

Traditional Navajo medicine is an aspect of religion. Disease is explained as the result of imbalance between the individual and the total physical and social environment. In this system, the Navajo find no significant distinction between mind and body.

If health and illness come from God, as many people believe, then religion is an important part of the anthropology of health. However, one person's religion is another's magic, witchcraft, or superstition. Traditionally a fascination of anthropologists and folklorists, the study of religion, magic, and witchcraft is difficult for health professionals to see as directly relevant to their practice. It is equally difficult for them to realize that for some groups religion is an equivalent of science. We start the course by reading Miner's (1956) classic, "Body Ritual of the Nacerima," returning periodically to discuss various procedures and therapies of the health professions that appear to be more magical than scientific.

There are several good ethnographic films to illustrate religion as a model for clinical anthropology. I have used "The Holy Ghost People," a film about southern white American Pentecostalists, and "Dream Dances of the Kashia Pomo," both of which may be rented from the Extension Media of the University of California at Berkeley. The University of Arizona purchased "We Believe in the Niño Fidencio." This film is about the cult that has grown around a charismatic healer who lived in Zacatecas, Mexico, in the early part of this century. The film shows a pilgrimage to the place where the Niño lived and cured.

There are several opportunities for clinical anthropology students to observe and per-

haps participate in religious ceremonies of health. The feast of St. Francis Xavier is celebrated on October 4 at Magdalena del Kino, site of a mission established by Father Kino at the end of the 17th century. Magdalena is 60 miles south of the border, or 120 miles from Tucson. Festivities extend through the weekend that is nearest to this date. People go to the feast of St. Francis seeking recovery from illness or to petition for continued health and good luck. Papago, Yaqui, and Mexican-Americans go from the United States, celebrating the festival in quite different ways. Mexican people from as far away as Yucatan may come to fulfill a vow by dancing and making music. All can buy herbs or amulets, and join the throng waiting to kiss the statue of St. Francis.

Clinical anthropology students who cannot make the trip to Mexico may see abbreviated versions of the same celebration at the nearby Mission of San Xavier del Bac. In the spring, they may observe the Lenten cycle of dances of the Yaqui, whose dancers have generally joined their societies in gratitude for a cure. Students have gone on invitation to participate in Sufi, Kundalini Yoga, Christian Science, and laying-on-of-hands by members of various cults.

Medical decision-making model

Two other models are discussed. One is medical decision making. I argue the validity of the concept of the culture of poverty, since it has been a popular, if mindless, explanation for why poor people do not go to the doctor. Alternative possibilities are also discussed, such as the theories of structural or behavioral integration, illustrated by the use of family planning agencies. The various reasons individuals do or do not want to have a child are explored, as is these individuals' cultural knowledge of fertility regulation.

Folklore model

Folklore was long ago the dominant model for medical anthropology. Fraser's (1890) and Sumner's (1906) monumental works are known today only by scholars of literature and a few psychoanalysts. I try to present folklore as a scientific model for clinical anthropology, teaching it by readings and field method instruction when there is interest.

Careful recording and filing of materials are demonstrated. The use of the camera and the tape recorder for data collection is encouraged. Class members discuss technical problems associated with these methods. I demonstrate collecting, preserving, and mounting botanical specimens of medicinal herbs and indicate available sources for botanical identification.

STUDENT RESEARCH

The main way that students begin to learn clinical anthropology is through their own research. Each student selects a problem based on his or her interest. For a surprising number of students, this is a first experience in field work. A few others have already done field work but lack a frame of reference either in anthropology or in health care for selecting data to use and analyze.

Selection of a problem that is small enough to investigate during one semester is the first task. Clinical anthropology is not reductionist but holistic. Which of the various possible determinants of health behavior should be covered? Which method of data collection is most appropriate for the problem? Reading assignments are made in textbooks of field methods such as Brownlee's (1978) *Community, Culture, and Care* and Crane and Angrossino's (1974) *Field Projects in Anthropology*.

The population studied may be one of the groups already identified, such as Mexican-American, Navajo, or Anglo. Any group to which the student has access is used. Thus students have written papers on the medical systems of Greek-Americans, Vietnamese refugees, Cubans, urban black migrants, American blacks, Mormons, Pentecostalists, Chinese-Americans, Christian Scientists, middle class Anglos, and neo-Orientals (for example Zen Macrobiotic). Some students may use the opportunity of the project to discover ethnic roots.

These beginning students face the problems of all field workers. Should ethnographies of the people to be studied be read prior to starting their research? If field workers do not read first, they may merely rediscover the same elements that have already been found and described. On the other hand, too much time in the library may so prejudice their observations that the students are oblivious to cultural or social change. Field workers who already know what they will see might as well stay home.

Selection of informants is the next problem. Do aged women who remember old healing practices or young people enculturated to the medical system of the dominant society make the best representatives of a medical culture? To what extent is a particular aspect of a culture shared? Students may find wide discrepancies among their few informants, and this diversity may cause them to question the validity of anthropological technique or even to reject the concept of culture. How does one know that the total variation in a society will be represented from only a few informants? Indeed, the problems of diversity plague many anthropologists, and these are serious problems in applied anthropology.

A related problem is that of stereotype. Anthropology looks at patterns, standards, or norms. Students who have only a superficial acquaintance with the anthropology that comes from popular literature or only a brief academic introduction followed by cursory research may come to conclusions such as "Navajos do not believe in germs"; "Blacks will not accept surgery"; "All Mexicans prefer herbs to synthetic medicines"; and so on. I believe that the seminar design of the class, with forthright challenges of ideas may lessen the tendency to stereotype since the utility of the concept of culture is not rejected.

Students must then get permission to do their research, both from their informants and from the committee to protect human subjects. Our students are required to submit their protocols to the College of Nursing Ethical Review Committee, which judges if subjects are at psychological, social, or biological risk. The College of Nursing committee then passes the protocol and their recommendations to the University committee. This is an excellent exercise for the student, as well as a way to prevent abuse of research. It provides an opportunity to discuss in class the implications of "informed consent," what is meant by risk, and other ethical issues. It is also very time consuming for the faculty. At present, the interpretation of the Privacy Act (1974) by some institutions is making it harder and harder to get permission to do research that otherwise appears to offer no risk to a subject. It may eventually preclude using hospitalized patients. For the study of health and wellness, this very limitation may turn out to be advantageous (see Chapter 7).

Obtaining tribal permission for research is generally not possible, because of the length of time required for such permission. Authorization is occasionally given for studies that have a very apparent and immediate use to the people, and reports of findings to the tribal council are required.

Anthropologists such as Firth, Eggan, and Spicer consider the training of people to be their own anthropologists as an ultimate goal. Branch and her coworkers (1976) see this goal to be more urgent and immediate, and question the validity of anthropologists who are not members of the culture they study. I maintain that even group members must first get training in clinical anthropology to realize their potential contribution.

Students are introduced to the differences among social science research techniques, using Spradley and MacCurdy's (1972) example of the "scientists from Mars" studying the game of checkers. These writers explain differences implied by the terms "respondents" to questionnaires, "subjects" of experiments, and ethnographic "informants." The method for collecting and recording the data comes, of course, from the problem to be studied. Questionnaires are popular when culture is shared by both field worker and respondent. (Unfortunately, they are also popular when this criterion is not met, especially when culture is assumed to be shared because informants use the same language.) In such cases, students may get enough respondents for statistical manipulation of data. Sampling techniques must then also be explained. However, unless a student has already spent considerable time prior to taking the course in research of his or her problem, the student is not considered ready to administer a questionnaire.

Students may do interviews in depth, which they are taught to record by field notes or tape recorder, to be transcribed as soon as possible. They then must learn to manipulate the bulky data. Categorizing continuous ideographic ideas is a science that in part depends on the general intellectual skill and humanistic background of the students as well as their level of training.

Other techniques for collection of data are taught. I have used videotaped interviews to demonstrate different concepts of disease. We have tapes of a Navajo informant whose mother was a hand trembler and father a singer, and of several Mexican-American *curanderas*. I have also interviewed in class demonstration a black informant who uses ethnic terms for illness in order to demonstrate that English words may have foreign meanings (e.g., a "rizin" is a furuncle).

Kleinman (1977) states that "clinically oriented anthropologists . . . have concentrated their investigations on psychiatric problems, while leaving general medical disorders virtually unexamined" (p. 12). Students in my course, however, have spent more time on general medical disorders, especially those students who apply the epidemiological-ecological model. Students also are interested in variants of official medicine. The differences in the systems of allopathy, homeopathy, osteopathy, and chiropractic are discussed using readings from Inglis (1964) *The Case for Unorthodox Medicine* and Kruger's (1976) *Other Healers, Other Cures.* Students of psychiatry and of mental health nursing are especially interested in the newly labeled "holistic medicine." Lectures by chiropractors, touch-healers, reflexologists, or other folk curers demonstrate the variety of roles within Anglo medical culture. Many students do their research about these alternatives to Western scientific medicine, because informants are easily available and offer no great language barrier. Informants tend to be pleased by the interest, and some of them even hope to make converts to their beliefs. (None has yet succeeded.)

All of these variants compete with Western scientific medicine, especially when patients are not satisfied with previous treatment. Scientific technology is most successful for certain categories of illness, such as infection and traumatic injury. But successful therapy for emotional illness tends to be ethnic or class specific. Thus there is interest in non-Western therapy.

The social anthropological aspects of medical anthropology are also discussed. Students are introduced to M.A.N. (*Medical Anthropology Newsletter*), the Society of Medical Anthropology, and its specialist groups such as nutritional anthropology, ethnopharmacology, committee on nursing and anthropology, and the like. They became familiar with the growing literature of medical anthropology. Students have read papers at anthropology meetings and articles or chapters prepared for the course have been published. Several students have been referred to graduate programs in medical anthropology at other universities to pursue master's or doctoral programs. Some are assisted in preparing medical anthropology as a major or minor focus for examinations preliminary to doctoral candidacy at the University of Arizona.

SUMMARY

The course is not static. It changes, depending on which approaches have been most successful. For example, because I believe history is relevant, I used to present a survey of the history of medical anthropology, reading from writers such as Herodotus, Aristotle, Chaucer, and Clements. The students were not interested and so the lecture was dropped. I have had to limit ethnographic films because there is no money to pay for rent. This is unfortunate. Finally, I spend increasing time on field methods, since it is a first experience in field work for many students, including advanced graduate students. I have two written examinations in order to motivate the students to read the assignments in time to make their research easier to do.

Because my course in clinical anthropology can only survey part of the field of the anthropology of health, I have recently added another course, "The Anthropology of Childbearing." In this class students study different beliefs and practices in the reproductive cycle, and consider these to be determined not only biologically but also structurally, the result of the status of women in a particular society. The role of women is studied as an aspect of the political, religious, and economic systems of the society. Since the field guide produced by the Human Relations Area Files for the study of human reproduction (Ford, 1964) is limited by the social perspectives of reproduction offered by medicine (for example, discussions of the "dangers" of contact with menstrual blood), I have developed a new "Notes and Queries" for the

study of the anthropology of childbearing. This is a very active field, with a literature of reproductive behavior from a holistic, anthropological framework beginning to appear. This literature is supplemented by lectures from anthropologists, who, as women, are interested and able to obtain data by participant observation. Societies that have been studied include those of the Kalapalo Indians of central Brazil, Yap Islanders, Sicilian peasants, Ibo tribeswomen, urban Japanese, and peasant and elite Pakastani. The students themselves have written ethnographies of the childbearing culture of Mexican-Americans, Apaches, Mormons, Hawaiian Philippinos, Samoans, and Free Clinic activist women.

These courses in clinical anthropology are presented because they give students a better understanding of their own system, their own "folk medicine." The courses provide insights for the application of Western science to health care problems. They offer an introduction to what is now possible and what is not possible in the immediate application of anthropology. And because they are about all of us, they are interesting.

REFERENCES

Alland, A. 1970. Adaptation in cultural evolution: An approach to medical anthropology. Columbia University Press, New York.

Adair, J., and Deuschle, K. W. 1970. The people's health. Appleton-Century-Crofts, New York.

Brown, A. 1978. Community, Culture, and Care. The C. V. Mosby Co., St. Louis.

Branch, M. F., and Paxton, P. P. 1976. Providing safe nursing care for ethnic people of color. Appleton-Century-Crofts, New York.

Brink, P. 1976. Transcultural nursing. Prentice-Hall, Englewood Cliffs, N.J.

Crane, J. G., and Angrosino, M. V. 1974. Field projects in anthropology. A study handbook. General Learning Press, Morristown, N.J.

Fabrega, H. 1975. The need for an ethnomedical science. Science **189**:969-975.

Frazer, J. G. 1890. The golden bough. Macmillan, London.

Hall, E. T. 1959. The silent language. Fawcett Publications Premier Book, Greenwich, Conn.

Hall, E. T. 1969. The hidden dimension. Doubleday & Co., Inc. Anchor Books, Garden City, N.Y.

Hughes, C. C. 1961. Public health in non-literate societies. In I. Galdston, ed. Man's image in medicine and anthropology. International Universities Press, Inc., New York.

Inglis, B. 1969. Fringe Medicine. Putnam, New York.

Kay, M. 1977. Southwestern medical dictionary. English-Spanish, Spanish-English. University of Arizona Press, Tucson, Arizona.

Kleinman, A. 1977. Lessons from a clinical approach to medical anthropological research. Medical Anthropology Newsletter 8(4):11-15.

Kruger, H. 1975. Other healers, other cures. A guide to alternative medicine. Bobbs-Merrill, Indianapolis.

Landy, D., ed. 1977. Culture, disease, and healing. Studies in medical anthropology. Macmillan Publishing Co., Inc., New York.

Lynch, L. R. 1969. The cross cultural approach to health behavior. Fairleigh Dickinson University Press. Rutherford, N.J.

McDermott, W., Deuschle, K. W., and Barnett, C. R. 1972. Health care experiment at Many Farms. Science 175(4017):23-31.

Miner, H. 1956. Body ritual among the Nacerima. American Anthropologist 58:503-507.

Rabin, D. 1972. Health problems of the U.S. and North American Indian populations. MSS Information Corp., New York.

Shiloh, A. 1977. Therapeutic anthropology: The anthropologist as private practitioner. American Anthropologist 19(2):443-446.

Spicer, E. H. 1975. Plural society in the Southwest. In E. H. Spicer and R. H. Thompson, eds. Plural Society in the Southwest. University of New Mexico Press, Albuquerque.

Spicer, E., ed. 1977. Ethnic medicine in the Southwest. University of Arizona Press, Tucson, Arizona.

Spradley, J., and McCurdy, D. 1972. The cultural experience. Ethnography in complex society. Science Research Associates, Chicago.

Sumner, W. G. 1906. Folkways. Ginn and Company, Boston.

Weaver, T. 1970. Use of hypothetical situations in a study of Spanish-American illness referral systems. Human Organization 29:140-154.

CHAPTER 2

The application of clinical anthropology to medical practice: case study of recurrent abdominal pain in a preadolescent Mexican-American female

Anita M. Stafford

In the relationship between health care provider and patient certain crucial elements must exist if the patient's problem is to be managed successfully. The provider must be able to obtain accurate information from the patient, assess correctly the nature of the problem, and establish a treatment plan with which the patient will comply. Such a relationship requires trust and mutual cooperation. When both patient and provider are from same socioeconomic and sociocultural background, there is likely to be a high degree of congruence between their respective beliefs about the nature of illness and appropriate modes of therapy, and their expectations of the therapeutic relationship. When, however, the patient and provider are from differing backgrounds there may be considerable divergence in these beliefs and expectations.

It is pertinent to distinguish between disease and illness. "Disease" is a term used to describe a process in the patient that is open to objective description and definition. An example would be coronary artery disease in which narrowing of the major blood vessels supplying the heart muscle can be demonstrated by special radiographic technique. "Illness" is a term that denotes the patient's perception of a health problem and is therefore more subjective. These terms are often used interchangeably when there is agreement between provider and patient as to the nature of the problem. When views diverge, however, it is important to perceive the nature of the illness through the eyes of the patient in addition to defining the disease process. It is the patient's perception

of the illness that governs his or her behavior.

Knowledge and beliefs about health and illness are frequently agreed upon by individual members of a cultural group. These beliefs influence the patient's recognition of illness, the selection of a health care provider, the expectations of the provider-patient encounter, and the attitudes toward professional institutions and social agencies in whom medical care is invested. In addition to cultural factors, the choice of medical care is influenced by economic factors and by the availability and accessibility of health care.

The health beliefs and practices of many cultural and socioeconomic groups have been studied in detail. Such knowledge, developed through the discipline of cultural anthropology, can be of considerable help to the health care provider both in the management of individual patients and in the planning of health care delivery to specific cultural and social groups. It should be axiomatic that in any patient encounter, the patient can be viewed as an individual and, as such, unique with his or her own personality and belief system. Yet knowledge of cultural norms enhances the ability of providers to understand patients' problems in the context of their sociocultural setting. Failure to achieve this understanding results in frustration for both patients and providers. At worst, the patient's problems remain unresolved. Frequently, patients will then seek alternative methods of health care.

These principles can be illustrated by discussion and analysis of a single case history.

The problem is one of recurrent abdominal pain in an 11½-year-old Mexican-American girl. It is well established that the majority of children with this diagnosis have pain of psychogenic origin (Green, 1967; Apley, 1964). Although the pain experienced is real, it originates in a disturbance of emotional homeostasis rather than in organic disease. Although in this instance there was delay in recognizing the true nature of the child's pain, even when an accurate assessment was made, traditional Anglo, medical, and psychotherapeutic approaches were unsuccessful. Unknown to the physicians, the patient was receiving additional treatment common to the Mexican-American healing tradition. Not until a treatment plan was devised that reconciled these alternative systems and was acceptable within the belief system of the family was there successful resolution of the problem and relief of symptoms.

CASE HISTORY

Celia* was the second of four children born to a Mexican-American family in Tucson, Arizona. The father's family originated from Hermosillo and the mother was third generation Mexican-American. The parents divorced when Celia was 2 years old but continued to live together in a stormy relationship on and off for 8 years. The family home was a modest, single story, adobe dwelling typical of the Mexican-American community in which it was situated. The mother worked from time to time as a maid and the father was employed in construction. The maternal grandmother, Mrs. H., lived adjacent to the family home and spoke no English. Mrs. M. and all her children were bilingual.

Celia was born in a hospital and received the full complement of immunizations from the well-baby clinics run by the Public Health Department. At 13 months, she had a febrile convulsion and was admitted to the Pima County General Hospital where a urinary tract infection was diagnosed and treated. Subsequently, she was treated in the outpatient clinic of the Pima County Hospital on numerous occasions for a variety of common childhood illnesses such as respiratory infections, impetigo, and insect bites. Prominent among the symptoms were gas-

trointestinal complaints dating from infancy, including intermittent constipation and episodes of diarrhea and vomiting, which were mostly self-limited and treated symptomatically. The medical records show that since Celia was 6 years old she made a number of visits for treatment of abdominal pain occasionally accompanied by fainting spells. These symptoms caused the child to miss school although never for more than 1 or 2 days. There is record of one severe episode, however, which precipitated Celia's admission to the hospital with suspected appendicitis. The symptoms subsided spontaneously after 24 hours, and she was discharged with a diagnosis of "mesenteric adenitis." Psychogenic abdominal pain was considered by at least one resident physician according to the notes on the medical records, but this possibility was not pursued following discharge, and Celia was not seen again until May 1972 when she was sent directly to the clinic from school again with abdominal pain and vomiting. On this occasion the medical record revealed that physical examination was unremarkable and the primary diagnostic considerations were acute infectious illness including hepatitis, urinary tract infection, and gastroenteritis. A series of tests was ordered but Celia failed to return for follow-up. Attempts to encourage follow-up through routine clinic reappointments were unsuccessful.

In January 1973 she was referred back to the clinic by the school nurse for medical evaluation because of frequent absences from school over a period of a month. The absences were said to be caused by "stomach pains" often accompanied by vomiting, which developed prior to Celia's departure for school in the mornings, or had their onset during the school day. During this period the mother described Celia as being unusually listless and inactive, "just sitting around the house all day doing nothing" and being "very fussy about food." Tests were performed to evaluate the child but while these were in progress Celia came to the emergency room one evening with a different kind of abdominal pain, colicky in nature and associated with severe diarrhea. Given the prolonged nature of the complaints and absence of definite diagnosis, Celia was admitted to the hospital. Investigations performed while she was an inpatient

---

*To preserve anonymity, fictitious names have been used throughout this description.

CASE PRESENTATION

Celia M.
  Aged 11 yrs; date of birth 1/3/61
  Bilingual; English and Spanish
  Family resident in Southwest for 20 years

Family structure

Mother
  Five siblings;
    family from
    Hermosillo and
    central Arizona

Father
  Seven siblings;
    family from
    Hermosillo

Medical history

Legend

  ◯ Female

  ▢ Male

Celia

Pregnancy and delivery—spontaneous vaginal delivery in hospital in Tucson; no complications in pregnancy
Growth and development—within normal limits; prepubertal
Immunizations—complete

Past medical history

1962 Age 12 months: admitted to hospital with convulsion thought to be febrile in origin; urinary tract infection diagnosed and treated.
1969 Age 8 years: admitted to hospital for investigation of recurrent urinary tract infections: no congenital abnormality found; discharged on Furadantin.
1970 Age 9 years: admitted to hospital as possible appendicitis; symptoms resolved within 24 hours; discharge diagnosis "mesenteric adenitis."
1973 Age 11 years: admitted to hospital for investigation of recurrent abdominal pain.

included examination of the urinary tract for evidence of congenital anomaly or infection; tests of liver function; examination of the stools for blood, parasites, and bacteria; X-ray studies of the entire gastrointestinal tract; and an electroencephalogram (EEG) to look for "abdominal migraine." The results of all of these tests were within normal limits.

A social worker evaluated the child and mother and felt that there was sufficient evidence of disturbance in family dynamics to account for Celia's symptoms. Celia was discharged from the hospital after 6 days and referred to a mental health clinic, La Fron-

tera, which is primarily set up to serve the Mexican-American community in which it is located. The clinic psychologist and the psychiatrist who evaluated Celia through interview and psychological testing were, however, both Anglo. The reports of their evaluation were detailed and thorough. The two major diagnostic categories considered were: (1) psychophysiologic reaction, gastrointestinal type (given the prolonged history of gastrointestinal complaints), and (2) school phobia.

It was noted that the father had remarried several weeks prior to the onset of the symptoms and had ceased to visit the family. Celia

*History of abdominal pain**

	USE OF "SCIENTIFIC" MEDICINE	USE OF ALTERNATIVE SYSTEM
1961-1968	Numerous visits to clinic for constipation; as infant treated with formula change; as toddler with suppositories, enemas, etc.	Use of herbal teas such as *manzanilla* and *yerba buena*.
1970	Seen in outpatient clinic for fever and abdominal pain: admitted as above.	
1972	May: Seen in outpatient department with abdominal pain and vomiting; tests ordered but C. failed to return. August: Seen in outpatient department for "tonsillitis."	May-July: Visit to black healer, given "pills" for pain and treated with massage; also used proprietary medicine. October-November: Visit to "Amalia"; diagnosis of *susto* and treated with garlic cloves.
1973	January: Sent to outpatient department by school nurse for evaluation of abdominal pain; tests ordered in outpatient department February 2: Arrived at emergency room with colicky, abdominal pain: admitted. February 12 and 20: Seen at La Frontera Clinic for evaluation; mother did not return after second visit. April 25: Returned to Dr. S. in outpatient department for advice of pediatric resident. April 28: Returned to school; follow-up by phone and visit scheduled for 2 months.	Treated by Amalia for *empacho* March: Consulted a physician in Hermosillo, Sonora; parasitism diagnosed and treated with drugs. April: Visit to Yaqui healer; diagnosed as *histerica*. Treatment was with sage and rosemary baths. Continued visits to Yaqui healer.
1974	July: Mrs. M. and C. interviewed for follow-up.	

*Data obtained from Mrs. M. and Celia; charts at Pima County Hospital and Arizona Health Sciences Center; La Frontera Mental Health Clinic; school nurse and school counselor. No direct data obtained from "Amalia," Yaqui healer, or physician in Hermosillo.

had always been in competition with the father for the mother's attention and had stepped into the void to fill the emotional needs of the mother. Although the mother expressed desire to improve her life status, she was clearly ambivalent about Celia's return to school. The basic therapeutic problem to be resolved was described as the independence-dependence conflict between Celia and her mother. The therapeutic plan included: (1) prompt return of Celia to school; (2) treatment of the gastrointestinal symptoms with Compazine; and (3) instruc-

tions to the mother not to reward the "staying home" behavior. Mrs. M. recently had begun a General Education Development Program to attempt to improve her employment capabilities and she was encouraged to continue this. Following the evaluation, however, Mrs. M. failed to keep any further appointments, discontinued the medication, and was lost to follow-up.

In May 1973 when there was still no resolution to the problem and Celia remained out of school, Mrs. M. discussed her problems with a pediatric resident with whom she had a trusting relationship and for whom she worked as a maid. The resident recognized that Mrs. M. had been using a number of alternative healing practices and was sensitive to the real nature of the problem. The resident encouraged her to return to the Pima County Clinic to be seen by a physician who was knowledgeable about Mexican-American health practices.

In two lengthy interviews with Mrs. M., it became apparent that she had little confidence in the Pima County Hospital or the mental health clinic to help resolve the current problems of her child. She felt that the treatment the child received at the clinic for illnesses was effective but that in this instance no treatment was being offered that provided any help. For this reason she had failed to return to the clinic in May 1973. When asked directly about the use of healing practices known to be common among Mexican people, she volunteered at length that she had sought help from a variety of sources and had employed a number of herbal remedies known both to herself and her mother. Frequently, these alternative treatments were being administered concurrently with her visits to the clinic.

In May 1972 Mrs. M. visited a black healer who, although primarily a voodoo and spiritualist healer, has a large clientele of Mexican-American patients and had been consulted by Mrs. M. on previous occasions for other ailments. The healer treated Celia with massage and herbal remedies with some temporary relief of symptoms. These treatments continued on and off until late fall when an incident occurred that led Mrs. M. to consider consulting a more traditional Mexican healer or *curandera*. Celia was informed one day in the street by a friend that her father had remarried and she arrived home looking pale and shocked and she remained listless for several days. The healer made a diagnosis of *susto*. This illness belongs to a group of folk illnesses loosely categorized as "Mexican illness," largely because Anglo physicians have no belief in them. *Susto* develops when the patient experiences a frightening event that is thought to cause the soul to leave the body. This results in a feeling of weakness and loss of energy. Treatment must be applied by a knowledgeable Mexican-American healer

and includes, among other things, the insertion into the rectum of garlic cloves soaked in olive oil daily for 9 days. The rapid disappearance of the garlic clove following insertion is said to confirm the diagnosis. This did not occur with Celia and her symptoms continued, suggesting to the healer that *susto* was not a correct diagnosis.

At about this time, Celia had been sent back to the Pima County Hospital by the school nurse. In addition to keeping appointments at the clinic, Mrs. M. consulted with the *curandera*. Continuation of the symptom of abdominal pain led to consideration of a second folk illness, *empacho*. This condition is thought to be caused by undigested food attaching itself to the wall of the stomach or intestine where it molds. It is dislodged by vigorous massage, and its passage is achieved by the administration of purges. Crushed bluing (anil) is administered in oil and at the end of the third day castor oil is given. Not infrequently this purgative causes colicky, abdominal pain, and diarrhea. The occurrence of these symptoms prompted the visit to the emergency room, which led to admission to the Arizona Health Sciences Center in January 1973.

Mrs. M. did not share with the physicians the treatment that the child had received from the *curandera* because, in her previous experience, such information had been met with scorn and derision. Mrs. M.'s response to the psychiatric evaluation was well represented in a note that appeared on the medical record, which stated that "the mother is disgusted, confused, angry, defensive, frustrated, and guilty. She is trying to improve her own life status and Celia is interfering with this. The mother has tried a number of home remedies and chiropractic and nothing seems to help."

Mrs. M. resented what she considered as an invasion of her privacy when questions were asked concerning her marriage and family life. She considered all of this irrelevant to the current problem. She also considered the use of a drug that she knew to be a tranquilizer to be inappropriate and very quickly stopped the Compazine therapy.

Mrs. M. remained convinced that the symptoms had a physical cause, and, in desperation, followed a route not uncommon for Mexican-Americans, even third generation citizens; namely, she undertook a trip to Hermosillo, approximately 200 miles south in the state of Sonora, to consult with a Mexican physician. The Mexican physician essentially repeated the examination and tests that had been done in the medical facilities in Tucson, with the single exception that he identified intestinal parasites. The mother returned to Tucson convinced that she had finally found the solution but was dismayed to find that the abdominal pain persisted even after the course of therapy for parasites was completed. At this time, yet another healer was selected, a Yaqui Indian woman, who diagnosed a condition known as *histerica*. She said that Celia was about to menstruate and that the menstrual contents were accumulating within the uterus and the resultant pressure was leading to abdominal pain. A regimen of treatments of olive oil massage and sitz baths in rosemary water was instituted. Celia was still receiving these treatments at the time she was interviewed once more at the Pima County Hospital. She had then been out of school for almost 4 months.

Although the psychiatric evaluation performed at La Frontera was not immediately available, from a review of all the available data, it was judged that school avoidance was a central issue in Celia's problems. The symptoms allowed Celia to remain at home with her mother and grandmother, both of whom were ambivalent about her return to school. Prompt return to school was, therefore, set as the primary goal of initial management. It was arranged that Celia would not be allowed to return home or to the clinic even in the presence of symptoms and that the school nurse was free to call the physician before calling the child's mother if advice was needed. Arrangements were made with the school teacher for Celia to make up her missed school work. Celia was encouraged to remain in the classroom despite abdominal pain and within a short time the symptoms disappeared.

Secondary management goals were directed toward Mrs. M. and her mother. Mrs. M. was encouraged to resume her General Educational Development classes and to become involved in specific community activities that necessitated her being away from home during the school day. Celia's

grandmother was included in the discussions to enlist her cooperation in Celia's return to school.

A crucial component of the management was a continued dialogue with Mrs. M. to discuss the measures she thought helpful and to incorporate them whenever possible. For example, since Mrs. M. considered that the treatments administered by the Yaqui healer were beneficial and since they did not appear to be harmful, she was encouraged to continue with them. Although attempts to contact the Yaqui healer were made on a number of occasions by phone and house call, the healer was not willing to cooperate directly. Within several days, Celia's enthusiasm for school returned. She caught up with her school work and, a year later, was in regular attendance. Although largely symptom free, she occasionally experienced some gastrointestinal complaints for which she usually sought relief symptomatically. Some time later Mrs. M. developed a new relationship which subsequently led to remarriage.

Some months after my initial encounter with Mrs. M., I interviewed her at home, for the purpose of clarifying the various treatments that she had sought and her beliefs about Celia's problems. It emerged for the first time that Mrs. M. had come to believe that the real cause of her daughter's pain was witchcraft. Although Mrs. M.'s marriage had always been stormy and ridden with conflict, the relationship deteriorated prior to her husband's remarriage. This change coincided with the exacerbation of Celia's symptoms. Mrs. M. considered that the new spouse's family had used witchcraft to "win her husband into the relationship" and also had placed a hex on Celia to "cause trouble" for Mrs. M. Since the Yaqui healer also was knowledgeable about witchcraft and considered this in her treatment of Celia, Mrs. M. remained convinced that the Yaqui healer was primarily responsible for the cure of Celia's symptoms and that the return to school was an incidental occurrence.

Given the reluctance of people to discuss their beliefs about witchcraft, the Yaqui healer's unwillingness to cooperate becomes understandable. Interestingly, Celia was uncomfortable with the notions of witchcraft and ambivalent about belief in its powers. She was able to see a connection between her reluctance to attend school and her symptoms, and she believed that going back to school was more helpful than seeing the Yaqui healer.

DISCUSSION

To interpret the many features of interest in this case, it is necessary to go beyond the bounds of the traditional medical history, physical examination, and consideration of family dynamics. Since Mrs. M. was offered ample opportunity for medical care but failed to follow through, it would be easy to dismiss her as a difficult patient or one who shows poor compliance. Such is frequently the lament of health care providers in their management of low income patients. Yet there is no question that Mrs. M. showed considerable persistence in attempting to find a solution for her daughter's problem. It is only when her behavior is viewed in the context of her social and cultural milieu that her actions can be understood.

Celia is a member of a family in cultural transition. A superficial encounter with Mrs. M. would suggest that she is well assimilated into the values of the predominant Anglo culture. Her family name is Anglo (Scots-Irish), she is a third generation resident, has good command of English, and seems to aspire to Anglo middle class values in her manner of dress, her acquisition of material possessions, and her wish for a college education for her son. She uses the hospital for medical care and has had all of her children immunized against common childhood diseases. A more penetrating interview, however, reveals that Mrs. M. has beliefs at variance with scientific medicine and more typical of traditional Mexican culture. Thus she uses herbal remedies extensively for the cure of minor illnesses, retains a belief in concepts of Mexican folk illness, and, although reluctant to admit it, has a strong belief in witchcraft. Since these beliefs influence Mrs. M.'s behavior, it is pertinent to examine their origins and the reasons for their persistence in a third generation American citizen.

For many immigrant groups, contact with the parent culture was ruptured by geographical distance and limited communications. Assimilation of the beliefs and values of the predominant Anglo culture was effected within one or two generations and often fostered by parents who saw their adoption as the route to economic and social success. For several reasons, Mexican-Americans have retained stronger ties with the parent culture. Historically, the territory of Arizona belonged to Mexico until the Gadsden purchase of 1856. Mexican labor was employed in the ranching and mining industries, which dominated the early economic development of the state. Among the early settlers were immigrants of Scots-Irish origin. These immigrants often married Mexican women who raised their children in the tradition of Mexican family culture. Such was the case with Mrs. M.'s great grandfather.

The typical Mexican family is a closely knit unit, and relationships with the extended family are close and often heavily proscribed so that an individual looks to family members for most social contact. Elder family members are respected and influence the behavior of the younger members. Ties with the community are strong. Catholicism is the predominant religion and frequently families are large. Since 1856, migration of Mexicans and Mexican-Americans to and fro across the border has been a continuous process, fluctuating according to the political and economic forces affecting the neighboring states of Arizona and Sonora. Geographically, these states are similar in their climate, terrain, and ecology. Because of the strong nature of family ties, movement across the border is frequent to visit relatives. Thus it has been said that for many Mexican-Americans the border hardly exists except as a political entity (Kay, 1972).

The geographical proximity, the nature of family ties, and the frequent contact with Mexican relatives have led to the retention of a stronger identity with the original culture than has been possible for other immigrant groups in the United States. For a given individual, the extent to which the values and attitudes of Mexican culture persist seems to depend upon the size of and the person's relationship to the Mexican-American community, the frequency of contact with Mexican relatives, and the degree of exposure to Anglo culture. Poorer individuals tend to remain, as elsewhere, alienated from the mainstream of American life. Education promotes awareness of alternative life-styles, and younger individuals are questioning the old ways.

Thus we find in Mrs. M.'s family of three generations a rather typical constellation. The family name derives from a Scots ancestor who mined in an area northwest of Tucson. Mrs. M.'s mother speaks no English and retains strong ties to Mexican culture, frequently visiting relatives on both sides of the border. She has never worked outside of the home. She is consulted by Mrs. M. on many family matters, especially concerning health, and has strong opinions about the appropriate behavior of her grandchildren. In contrast, Mrs. M.'s children are frequently in open conflict with many of the traditional Mexican beliefs and values. They attend schools in which the teachers are predominantly Anglo, they have frequent exposure to Anglo television, and, although bilingual, they usually converse among themselves in English. They have many friends outside the extended family. Mrs. M. herself occupies a position intermediate not only in age but also in her beliefs and values between her mother and her children. This is seen particularly in her perceptions of illness where she draws on knowledge from several sources.

Concepts of disease and illness among Mexican-Americans have been extensively studied (Rubel, 1960; Clark, 1959). Among the classical studies is that of Saunders (1954: 141) who, writing about the Mexican-American population in Colorado and the Rio Grande valley, notes:

In varying degree, depending upon who he is and where he lives and what his personal experience has been, the Spanish speaking individual draws his knowledge of illness and its treatment from four widely separated sources; (1) from the folk medical lore of medieval Spain as refined in several centuries of relative isolation from the source; (2) from the culture of one or more American Indian tribes; (3) from Anglo folk medicine as practiced in both rural and urban areas, and (4) from "scientific" medical sources. In any given instance of illness, elements from any or all of the four sources may be utilized in any sequence that may seem appropriate to the individual or to those who may advise or otherwise try to help him.

It is interesting that although it was written over 20 years ago, this paragraph describes Mrs. M.'s behavior rather accurately.

Mrs. M. has delivered her babies in the hospital, has accepted immunizations, and has taken her children to the hospital for many illnesses. In this she, like many Mexican-Americans, has been quick to see the value of Western methods. However, in general she is suspicious of Anglo doctors. Whereas she sees the black healer as "kind and loving," she feels many Anglo physicians to be "cold and distant"; private doctors, she feels, are "often out to exploit you for money."

Relationships within the Mexican-American family are characterized by warmth and touching, and there is an expectation that a healer will also provide a personalized relationship. Anglo medical training stresses the development of "professionalism," which often implies a degree of personal distance from the patient and prohibits the use of touching except as is necessary for physical diagnosis. Unrecognized, this differing expectation for conduct during a professional encounter contributes to disaffection with Anglo care.

Mrs. M. cites several examples in which it appears that although the treatment given by doctors was appropriate, she left the encounter unsatisfied. In one instance, her son Johnny sprained his ankle and was taken to the county hospital where ice packs and a bandage were applied, but "the swelling persisted." Mrs. M. then visited the black healer who "massaged the ankle and leg and it quickly got better." Although it is possible that the swelling and pain would have diminished anyway with time, the black healer's treatment was seen to be the one that was efficacious. Many authors have commented on the fact that when a Mexican-American patient seeks simultaneous help from a Western and non-Western healer, cure is frequently attributed to the traditional method and the possible Western contribution to cure is discounted (Saunders, 1954; Rubel, 1960; Clark, 1959). This fact seems to perpetuate beliefs in traditional folk practices.

Mrs. M. also criticizes doctors because "you frequently have to go back and forth without relief." Distinction is not always made by patients between a symptom and an actual disease, and there is an expectation that the symptom will be treated promptly. The physician who takes time to investigate the nature of a disease before instituting treatment may be seen as unhelpful although he or she is acting according to the rules of good medical practice.

In her attitude toward physicians, Mrs. M. does not differ substantially from many other low income people. There are three particular aspects of this case, however, in which Mrs. M. was influenced by ethnic belief. These include the use of herbal remedies, the consideration of folk illness, and the attitude toward Anglo psychotherapy.

Mrs. M. has considerable knowledge about the treatment of minor illnesses because she, like women in many cultures, assumes a major responsibility for the health of her family. In the early days of settlement when little medical help was available, a body of knowledge was handed down by each woman to her daughters. In the Mexican-American culture certain women are thought to have a special gift of healing and are known as *curanderas*. Mrs. M. has considerable knowledge of the correct collection, preparation, and use of herbal remedies. Some of the herbs she uses have been known since ancient times and are common to Spanish-speaking people thoughout the world. Others are locally derived.

Mrs. M. often used herbs concomitantly with antibiotics and other medicines that had been prescribed by physicians, but rarely did she share that information with them. She has also used a number of proprietary medicines sold over the counter that are more typical of Anglo folk medicine. Knowledge of the use of herbal remedies is important to the health care provider. If the herbs are known to have therapeutic properties or to be harmless, the provider can encourage their use and thereby gain trust of the patients by respecting their knowledge. If the herbs are known to be harmful, as has recently been found in Arizona, the provider is in a position to discourage their use and prevent harm to the patient.*

---

*There have been two recent cases in Arizona of cirrhosis of the liver developing from ingestion of *Senecio longilobus*. This hepatotoxic preparation had been mistaken for the widely used, locally marketed product called *gordolobo yerba* prepared from leaves of *anaphalium* species. (Arizona Morbidity. Aug. 1977. Vol. 2, no. 6.)

Mrs. M. first used herbal home remedies including preparations of various teas to help Celia. It is interesting to consider the series of decisions that were made subsequently when these did not provide relief.

When home remedies failed, Mrs. M. then consulted official medicine at the Pima County Clinic. Perceiving no relief, she next considered various folk illnesses and sought the help of a *curandera* who in turn considered *susto* and *empacho*. More detailed descriptions of these can be found elsewhere (Kay, 1972; Clark, 1959).

It is interesting to compare the probable actions of her Anglo counterpart. When children with recurrent abdominal pain are evaluated, it is not uncommon for there to be an exhaustive search for organic pathology before consideration of psychogenic pain despite recommendations that these be considered in parallel (Apley, 1964). Anglo patients, finding no relief, would most likely consider that their child had an "ulcer," "chronic appendicitis," "bad digestion," or "inflammation of the bowel." Since abdominal pain is often found in family members of such patients there may be consideration also of pathology similar to afflicted family members, such as abdominal tumors, gallstones, and so forth. Low income Anglo patients would most likely also resort to proprietary medicines and visit alternative healers, such as chiropractors and naturopaths.

Mrs. M. continued to "doctor shop" and undertook a considerable journey to Mexico to visit a Western-trained Mexican physician. When this treatment also failed, she fell back on witchcraft as an explanation of her daughter's illness. It is hard to know how pervasive the belief in witchcraft is since so many Mexican-Americans are reluctant to discuss it, especially with Anglo physicians. It was only late in the course of this investigation that I discovered Mrs. M.'s belief in this area. After conducting an extensive interview detailing many aspects of the case, I switched off the tape recorder on which I had recorded the interview, and only at that point did Mrs. M. share her belief in the influence of witchcraft and that she truly believed the Yaqui healer was successful because she helped to remove a "hex."

While patient and provider may have differing views on the nature and management of physical ailments, far greater divergence is found in the definition of emotional and psychosomatic illness and in attitudes toward psychotherapy. The underutilization of mental health facilities by Mexican-Americans is well documented, and in this context Mrs. M.'s outright rejection of psychotherapy is quite typical. The conception of "mental health" as opposed to "physical health" does not exist for the Mexican-American who sees "no separation between the psychological and total well being of the individual" (Padilla and Ruiz, 1973). Illness is more likely to be attributed to a physical rather than to a psychological cause. This may explain why, despite the rather full evaluation at La Frontera, Mrs. M. continued to seek help for the physical symptoms and next chose yet another medical doctor (in Mexico).

In instances where *enfermedades mentales* (mental illnesses) are defined and accepted, they are seen as having an external cause. According to Kay (1973:153), the illness is "characterized by its nonvolitional qualities. The patient cannot help getting sick . . . He is a victim of circumstances." It follows, therefore, that for the patient to get well, something must be done to him, and he has little responsibility in the treatment process to get himself well. This is in strict contrast to most Anglo theories in which mental illness is seen to derive from within the person. Many modern therapies place responsibility for the illness solely with the individual.* Indeed, there is a growing body of belief that physical as well as mental illnesses arise as a result of decisions made by the patient and that they are therefore open to conscious control. Cure, according to this view, is possible only if the patient takes full responsibility for his own health and participates very actively in a treatment process (Kay, 1972).

At La Frontera, Mrs. M. failed to understand why so much information was being asked about her family life when she considered this irrelevant to the problem. She objected particularly when Celia was questioned regarding her perceptions of family life; Mrs. M. regarded this as an invasion

of privacy. Celia's discomfort was evident in that she often asked the therapist "not to tell Mother I told you that." Since regular attendance at school was not a primary value for Mrs. M., she was annoyed at the insistence that Celia immediately return to school. In addition, Mrs. M. perceived the doctors as "cold and distant." She could not understand the use of compazine, which she knew to be a tranquilizer, when the main symptom was abdominal pain and nothing was given to relieve that symptom.

In analyzing the underutilization of mental health facilities by Mexican-Americans, Torrey (1968; quoted in Padilla and Ruiz, 1973) offers a number of factors that may be contributory. In addition to geographic inaccessibility and language barriers, which were not operative in this case, he mentions class-bound values, culture-bound values, and the therapist's training and attitude. At La Frontera, Celia was evaluated by a psychiatrist and psychologist who were both from middle class Anglo backgrounds. In their evaluation of the problem they described the diagnosis in terms of traditional psychoanalytic psychodynamics. There was no mention of any cultural data, and it seems unlikely that these were considered relevant or indeed were ever obtained. Evident in their evaluations and their recommendations were values more applicable to the middle class than to the lower socioeconomic status from which Mrs. M. derived. In Mrs. M.'s decision not to return, it is difficult to assess the respective contributions of social distance, ethnic prejudice, and interpersonal differences with the therapist. What is significant is that, for whatever reason, she rejected the help offered and sought treatment elsewhere.

CONCLUSION

In the successful resolution of this problem it is likely that the following factors were important. Detailed information was taken concerning the evolution of the illness and the various methods of therapy from all sources that had been applied. The one exception was the information concerning witchcraft, which is usually the most difficult to obtain and was uncovered late in the treatment of the patient. The perceptions of the problem according to the mother and daughter were requested. Cultural information was specifically sought. The plan of management

*This is true of psychoanalytic theory based on the work of Sigmund Freud, and also of therapeutic models based on the work of Alfred Adler, such as transactional analysis developed by Eric Berne.

included the active participation of the mother and took into consideration her beliefs as to what would be helpful. The influence of the grandmother in decisions by the family was recognized, and she was involved in the management plan. Active participation and cooperation of other healers was sought (although not obtained entirely). The mother's views and knowledge were at all times treated with respect and not scorned, and no attempt was made to try to change her view that the Yaqui healer had effected the major cure. It can be argued that since Mrs. M. had exhausted her list of healers, she was more than willing to accept any help. While this may be a factor, it is perhaps relevant that she continued to visit the hospital on a regular basis for care of her children and in the future rarely missed follow-up appointments. Thus, using an approach that incorporated knowledge of both the cultural and social background of the family, the physician was able to establish a relationship of trust, obtain accurate information, and engage the patient and her family in active cooperation to resolve the problem.

The following recommendations may be useful to health care providers wishing to develop cultural awareness so as to better serve their patients. It is important to become knowledgeable about the health beliefs and practices of the patient groups served. While some generalizations are possible, one should recognize that specific beliefs may vary from region to region among members of a cultural group. Studies of Mexican-Americans, for example, show considerable regional differences between the various groups living in the Southwest and those living in other states such as Colorado and Michigan (Kay, 1972; Clark, 1959).

Each patient should be seen as unique, and all inquiry directed toward his or her specific beliefs in order to make rational therapeutic plans. Once patients recognize that their beliefs will not be scorned they are more likely to be honest. To obtain information about uncommon practices, the manner in which questions are phrased is crucial. In particular the approach should be nonjudgmental. An example might be: "What kinds of treatments have you used to help your child/mother/sister, etc. . . . ?

Some people often use herbs for this kind of problem. Do you know about it and has it helped?" "Some people believe that this illness is caused by _____ ; do you share that belief?"

When there is extensive use of herbal remedies, providers should become knowledgeable about them and incorporate them wherever possible into the treatment plan. Patients are primarily seeking to help themselves and are open to information about herbs that may be dangerous. When there is strong belief in folk medicine, practitioners will be most successful if they accept that belief and work with it. Such belief is supported by generations of "proof" and is unlikely to be abandoned lightly. The most useful way to help the patient is to suggest that he or she use Western medicine "in addition" to the folk remedy.

Providers should make every effort to become familiar with the culture, life-style, values, and aspirations of the people they serve. They are then less likely to make demands on patients that are culturally unacceptable, such as the use of certain foods or medicines. They are also more likely to be viewed as practitioners worthy of trust and respect. Such qualities, experienced by both provider and patient, are the essential prerequisites for any successful encounter.

REFERENCES

Apley, J. 1964. The child with abdominal pains. Oxford, Blackwell Scientific Publications.

Clark, M. 1959. Health in the Mexican-American culture. University of California Press, Berkeley.

Green, M. 1967. Diagnosis and treatment: Psychogenic recurrent abdominal pain. Pediatrics 40:84-89.

Kay, M. 1972. Health and illness in the barrio: Women's point of view. Ph.D. dissertation. University of Arizona, Tucson.

Padilla, A., and Ruiz, R. 1973. Latino mental health: A review of the literature. National Institute of Mental Health, Rockville, Md.

Rubel, A. J. 1960. Concept of disease in Mexican-American culture. American Anthropologist 62(5):795-815.

Saunders, L. 1954. Cultural differences and medical care: The case of the Spanish-speaking people of the Southwest. Russell Sage Foundation, New York.

Torrey, E. 1973. Psychiatric services for Mexican Americans. Quoted in A. Padilla and R. Ruiz, Latino mental health: A review of the literature. National Institutes of Mental Health, Rockville, Md.

CHAPTER 3

Medical anthropology and the health professions: selected literature review

Anita L. Alvarado

This chapter presents an abbreviated over-view of selected literature that is of mutual interest to medical anthropologists and health professionals. The field of medical anthropology has historically been broadly conceived and defined primarily by content (Scotch, 1963). Fabrega (1972) and Colson and Selby (1974) continue this practice in their comprehensive reviews of literature in the field. The statement of definition by the Society for Medical Anthropology, however, specifies that medical anthropology is any area of biological and cultural anthropology that shares its interests with the health professions. This puts a sharper focus on the field. At the same time, it would appear to give impetus to (1) the increasing shift in emphasis away from concern with descriptive ethnomedical studies as ends in themselves, and (2) the increasing shift away from the ancillary role of applied anthropologists as mere facilitators for scientific health care delivery systems. These types of interests will continue, of course, but they are likely to be increasingly oriented toward contributing to what Weidman (1971) calls a "medical behavioral science" that is the result of the integration of medical and anthropological concerns and concepts. Evidence that this proposed integration is already being attempted by medical anthropologists is made clear by some of the literature cited in Fabrega and Colson and Selby.

In addition, physicians and nurses are increasingly aware of the interrelationships between biocultural factors and disease. Medical anthropologists are found with increasing frequency among the speakers at medical symposia and seminars. Professional health practitioners are developing a growing interest not only in cross-cultural concepts of health, illness, and curing as a means for understanding and better serving culturally pluralistic client populations, but are also integrating culturally distinctive points of view from non-Western health care systems into modern medicine. Thus interest in the holistic approach of ethnomedicine is wide-spread among modern medical practitioners. Evidence of this interest is shown in articles such as Miller's (1974) "A New Humanism in Medicine" and in "holistic health" seminars cosponsored by universities, public health departments, and professional organizations, offered both for academic credit and for continuing education credit for relicensing of health professionals. Programs such as those offered by the East-West Academy of Healing Arts, San Francisco, are typical of the content and of the attraction of health professionals from local and national populations.

The movement toward integration of medical and anthropological interests is also clearly evident among health practitioners in the growing numbers of physicians and nurses who are members of the Society for Medical Anthropology, the Committee for Nursing and Anthropology, the Committee for Psychiatric Anthropology, and other committees formed within the Society for Medical Anthropology.

Thus there is a growing population of medical anthropologists and health professionals who are stimulating a new synthesis of biocultural and medical concerns. The publications cited in this chapter are selected, therefore, with the intention of pro-

viding material from a limited range of anthropological and medical fields, which seem
to elicit, in my experience, the greatest
amount of mutual interest. A further intention is to provide a range of recent references
for those who are developing an interest in
these areas but have limited knowledge of
the types of data and resources available.

Already cited as general works of basic
importance in regard to recent trends and
available data are Fabrega (1972), whose
article covers selected literature published
from 1963 to 1970, and Colson and Selby
(1974) who cover 1970 to 1973. This chapter
will deal primarily with publications from
1973 to 1976. However, some publications
not cited in the two previous review articles
will also be considered. There will, therefore, be some supplementation of previous
reviews but no duplication. However, it is
appropriate to emphasize that particular attention should be paid to the glossary in
Fabrega's article which contains concepts
and definitions for use in both fields. Colson
and Selby give an excellent summary of
Clark's (1973) conception of directions in
gerontology, a research field characterized
by increasing interest, funding, and employment opportunities.

In another general work, Barrios (1971)
includes a short annotated bibliography of
health research published on Mexican-Americans, interesting primarily because it presents a Chicano view of academic and health
research. This type of annotated bibliography
is becoming increasingly circulated in mim-
eographed form, and may eventually find its
way into print. Persons interested in black,
Chicano, or Indian perspectives on health
and health programs may find such a bibliography useful. The unpublished forms are
frequently available at local colleges and/or
ethnic organizations.

BIOCULTURAL ECOLOGY AND EVOLUTION

Biological and cultural evolution are so
interrelated that the title of Childe's classic
is succinctly to the point: *Man Makes Himself* (1936). Bennett et al. (1975) have a comprehensive review article with extensive
bibliography dealing with the interrelationships among nutrition, natality, disease,
and adaptation. Alland (1975) considers the

relationships among mind, behavior, and
ecological adaptation. The accelerating interest in developmental relationships among
mind, brain, and environment are also reflected in articles in the next section. Damon
(1975) has edited a collection of high quality
articles dealing with human adaptations to
factors such as heat, cold, nutrition, high
altitude, infectious disease, and stress. Articles dealing with evolution and disease are
by Nye (1966) on cardiovascular disease,
Martin et al. (1973) on factors such as blood
pressure and cholesterol levels in a highly
inbred cultural (religious) isolate, Knudsen
et al. (1967) on the possible selective advantage of cystic fibrosis heterozygotes, Friedlander (1969) on the effects of malaria on the
historial demography of blacks and Indians,
and Vogel and Chakravartti (1966) on the
survival values of different blood group types
with smallpox.

Harrison's article (1975) on the selective
advantage of lactase deficiency and sufficiency in certain environmental areas is important for those interested in nutritional problems of populations. Cairns (1975) considers
relationships between environment and cancer. Dunn (1968) has a classic article on cultural and environmental factors affecting
peoples at the hunter-gatherer phase of technological development. Neel's (1967) "thrifty
genotype" hypothesis deals with the possible
selective advantage of the diabetic predisposition phenotype for hunters and gatherers
who have sporadic meals, high protein and
low refined carbohydrate diets, and high
energy output. Neel proposes that the most
suitable type of metabolism for such populations would be that in which the rapid up-
take and utilization of glucose are permitted.
With modern culture and diet, however, in
which high consumption of refined carbohydrates and sugars occurs in conjunction with
increased sedentariness and generally reduced energy expenditure, the genetically
programmed metabolism, which was "thrifty" for millenia, is rendered deleterious as
glucose pours into the bloodstream. The
body, unable to cope, attempts to reduce the
hyperglycemia through elimination of excess
sugar through the kidneys and through storage in the form of fat, thereby leading to the
eventually fatal sequelae of uncontrolled
diabetes mellitus. Neel's hypothesis is im-

portant in that it presents the feasibility of researching a variety of diseases from the perspective of a once-adaptive characteristic rendered maladaptive under changing cultural conditions.

CULTURAL AND PSYCHOLOGICAL FACTORS

Examination of the interrelationships between culture on the one hand and disease, illness perceptions, health practices, and ethnomedicine on the other continues to be one of the major foci of interest among medical anthropologists and health practitioners. Likewise, the interrelationships among psychological factors in disease, illness, patient response, and ethnomedicine are well studied in medical anthropology and psychiatry. The wealth of resources in Fabrega (1972) and Colson and Selby (1974), coupled with the constraints of limited length permissible here make it feasible to reduce this section to the consideration of a few works of special interest.

Among the most elegant and productive studies ever conducted on the problems of cultural factors and disease, the series of publications on *kuru* among the Fore of New Guinea by Gajdusek and associates (1977) will have a secure place in the history of medicine. Gajdusek summarizes much of the earlier findings, including recognition of the association of the disease with mourning rituals in which cannibalism was the mode of transmission of highly infectious organisms from brain tissue to the mucous membranes and skin of adult women and children of both sexes. The cessation of cannibalism over the last 15 years has led to the disappearance of the disease among children and adolescents of both sexes. Among the most important by-products of the *kuru* research, however, has been the recognition of the role of slow-acting or "unconventional" viruses in a number of human degenerative neurological diseases. In addition, there is now the recognition of the possibility of the transference of some of these viruses between human and nonhuman species (Gajdusek, 1977). Since the nonhuman species may be both pet and pest species, the implications for the control of degenerative neurological disease in relation to other cultural practices are clear. The productivity of this research ensures that the

study of pathological syndromes in small populations will continue to be of primary importance.

In another type of study of cultural and biological factors, Cavalli-Sforza and Feldman (1973) present a theoretical model for the study of biological inheritance and cultural transmission of traits. The problem of distinguishing biologically inherited or influenced traits from environmentally influenced traits remains of continuing interest both within and without medical and anthropological circles.

Demography, historical demography, and cultural practices affecting fertility have high interest value for anthropologists and health practitioners. Newman (1972) has a comprehensive article with an extensive bibliography. Alvarado (1970) discusses cultural factors affecting the fertility of the Havasupai Indians. Nag (1962) takes a broad overview of cultural factors affecting fertility in nonindustrial societies. Kay (1977) discusses important factors in Mexican-American decision-making in regard to culturally acceptable contraceptive methods. McFalls (1973) criticizes arguments that maintain that venereal disease was a dominant factor in black fertility patterns from 1880 to 1950. Mommsen (1973) examines the fertility patterns of highly educated blacks.

Loudon (1976) has edited a collection of papers from a British conference dealing with a wide range of ethnomedical topics, including sexual differences in illness, concepts of health and etiology of pathologies, and the roles of ethnomedical practitioners and patients in non-Western societies. Significantly, one third of the contributors are physicians.

Along the same lines of interest, Maclean (1971) does an excellent service in presenting the alternatives available, in view of the cultural perspectives, to the non-Western patient who has access to both ethnomedicine and Western medicine. It is an interesting case study in the examination of factors responsible for the failure of Western medicine to eradicate ethnomedicine. It is clear, therefore, that there is every reason to expect that ethnomedical systems and scientific medical systems will continue to coexist not only in Africa but around the world. Maclean also points out how ethnomedical systems continue to change through time, incorporating new ideas and methods, at the same time retaining their ability to provide "meaningful answers to questions which are perceived as relevant by practitioner and patient alike" (p. 155). Too often ethnomedicine as well as other cultural subsystems are perceived by Western scholars as "traditional" in the sense of being a form of cultural lag rather than as dynamic systems responsive to present day needs. As Maclean demonstrates, bicultural patients will continue in the foreseeable future to be pragmatic and eclectic, participating in one or both systems simultaneously while fusing selected scientific and Western religious concepts into new orientations and methods in many parts of the world.

Herzlich (1973) has done an interesting study on French middle class and professional perceptions of health and illness. The bibliography includes a number of French language sources and some material on psychological perceptions of illness, which lend themselves to cross-cultural study. The role of personal will in illness, the conception of illness as an enemy against which a fierce struggle must be waged, and the necessity to expend considerable amounts of consciously mobilized energy to "fight" illness are clearly put forth.

Johnson (1976) examines perceptions of health problems of a particular group (migrant workers) by an outside group (the growers). He points out a number of factors that play a significant part in forming such attitudes. The growers, for example, may express highly favorable attitudes toward the proposition that all workers are entitled to good health care, but will not support a system that takes migrants out of the fields. Thus an innovative form of Western health care delivery must be developed that has a highly mobile staff who can serve the migrants at night.

The range of literature dealing with modern problems in ethnomedicine and scientific medicine is extensive. Moody (1974), for example, discusses the phenomenon of modern Anglo-American witchcraft. Stephens and McBride (1976) add to the growing literature on drug addiction by identifying factors associated with first drug usage. They describe the transitional types of social interaction as the individual moves along a continuum from experimental use of addictive drugs to becoming a street addict. Rubin and Comitas (1976) examine the cultural setting in the use of marijuana among working class Jamaicans. The range of appropriate uses of the drug contrasts with the rather limited range of usage in the United States. Studies of this type are also being done on cocaine usage in diverse populations. These studies are instructive in the comparison of the broad cultural contexts of drug usage and lack of a high degree of drug refinement in non-Western settings as compared with Western settings. These factors may be the definitive ones in estimating potential damage resulting from drug usage. Formation of the Committee for the Anthropology of Alcoholism and Drug Abuse within the Society for Medical Anthropology is an indication of the level of concern in these areas.

Interest in psychological and psychiatric problems is also quite high. The establishment of the Committee for Psychiatric Anthropology has already been noted. Willie and coworkers (1973) bring together a broad spectrum of interests in their collection of 15 articles dealing with racism and mental health. Psychiatrists and social scientists present an overview of the area, while other articles deal with the clinical and social contexts of the deleterious effects of racism on the mental health of whites and nonwhites in the United States.

Abel and Metraux (1974), clinical psychologist and anthropologist, respectively, discuss some of the difficulties in dealing with subjects who are members of culturally distinct groups within modern pluralistic societies. They cover a range of subjects including psychopathologies in different cultural contexts, attitudes toward treatment, and problems in communication in therapy. Both authors have worked with Caribbean groups who increasingly, are forming, communities in the United States and with a number of other Western and non-Western groups.

Giordano (1973) and Giordano and Levine (1975) deal with problems involving ethnicity and mental health. Giordano is particularly interested in white ethnic groups of the United States. Because of the widespread interest in American nonwhite ethnic factors in health, illness, disease patterns, and curing, additional references to these groups will be considered in a separate section.

There are a number of interesting, indeed provocative, recent works dealing with linkages between physiological responses and conscious mental control by subjects who can voluntarily manipulate combinations of visceral, neural, and motor responses previously thought to be under the exclusive control of the autonomic nervous system. Schwartz (1975) discusses some of these and presents his recent research into cognitive control of systolic pressure and heart rate, diastolic pressure and heart rate, and alpha wave and heart rate. There is also an excellent bibliography for those interested in pursuing further reading in this rapidly expanding area.

Barber and De Moor (1972) discuss variables in hypnotic induction. Spanos and Barber (1974) detail two different paradigms for conceptualizing the phenomena of hypnosis, their preference being for the "non-state" paradigm. They present extensive discussion of recent studies and literature relating to hypnotic phenomena. Chaves and Barber (1976) examine some of the phenomena associated with the use of hypnosis with surgery as well as an evaluation of the effectiveness of acupuncture. In the latter, the roles of cultural receptivity to the procedure as well as the use of electrically induced distraction are explored.

THE HEALTH PROFESSIONS

Studies of the health professions are increasingly oriented toward the identification of goals, methods, and problems in health care delivery. Part of this intense interest is generated out of United States government statistics, which demonstrate that the United States in the 1970s ranked sixth in international comparisons with other Western nations in terms of life expectancy at birth for females (U.S. Department of Health, Education and Welfare, 1976a). At the same time, the United States ranks highest in the world for expenditures for health services (Anderson, 1972). This apparent paradox has stimulated research into the structure and function of American health care delivery services.

Alford (1975) finds that the crisis-oriented politics of health care systems, mobilized around ideological and interest groups, form effective barriers to provision of adquate delivery of health services. He maintains that "crises" are manufactured to rally public support for funding but that the chronic problems selected for "crisis" publicity are simply exploited, not solved.

Carlson (1975), in a provocative work, attempts to deal with the same problems of high cost and low effectiveness. He sees the solution to be a total change in the medical system, which he feels is reaching its limits of isolation from society through its "self-protective" politics and its focus on parts of the anatomy of the patient while ignoring the environment that produces the disease. He maintains that overspecialization in physiological systems prevents an effective etiological perspective.

Others look at selected aspects of the health care delivery system. Lynch (1972), an economist, sees the vexing problem of physician shortages as a function of affluence: increasing demand and willingness to pay for medical services by individuals coupled with increased demand generated by government programs. The federal government itself sees increasing demand generated by changing cultural values in American life, including the trend toward the view that health care is a basic right (U.S. Department of Health, Education and Welfare, 1976b). Miller (1974) maintains that increased numbers of health professionals alone cannot be effective and that revisions in the physicians' conception of the proper practice of medicine are necessary. Glazier (1973) argues that physicians must change their focus in still different ways: by reorganizing in such a manner as to deal with specific populations within the larger society and by knowing intimately the demographic, social, economic, and behavioral characteristics of that population.

Other areas of interest include the evaluation of quality of health care (Morehead, 1970) in neighborhood health centers. Elinson and Herr (1970) identify what they call the latent functions of neighborhood health centers. Among the so-called latent functions are the improvement of the image of black males, promotion of solidarity among Chicano farm workers, "pacification of hostile communities by colonial powers" (p. 99), circumvention of local elites under the guise of a health center, and radicalization of youth. While not all social scientists would agree with these factors being identified as latent functions, there is no doubt that political activist groups have established health centers in order to improve not only the health of populations that are neglected by local systems of health care delivery but also their groups' image in the local communities. It is unfortunate that there are not more studies of this medical counterculture phenomenon.

Korsch and Negrete (1972) examine some of the causes of mutual dissatisfaction between mothers and pediatricians. Bullough and Bullough (1975) look at the role of sex discrimination in terms of treatment of patients and attitudes toward fellow professionals, maintaining that care suffers directly and indirectly through these factors.

The study of demographic characteristics within the health professions is a growing area of interest. Age, ethnicity or race, and sex of present professionals and students are the characteristics most often investigated. The studies by Johnson (1974), Alvarado (1977), and Knopf (1972; 1975a) are examples of this type of work. Knopf (1975b) and Nash (1974) look at prospects of nurses at graduation. The impact of foreign trained professionals on the American medical system is also of interest. Stevens and Vermeulen (1972) examine various aspects of the foreign trained physician. Minority group perceptions of the nursing profession are becoming available (California Nurses' Association, 1973; Smith, 1975).

Studies of foreign health care delivery systems are appearing with increasing frequency. Field's (1957) study of the Soviet Union remains of interest because of his examination of the difficulties involved in designing a system that takes care of the needs of chronically underserved populations through temporary or permanent relocation of health professionals. While redistribution is still seen as a partial solution to the problem of maldistribution of health personnel in the United States (U.S. Department of Health, Education and Welfare, 1976b), the experience of the Soviet Union seems to indicate that it is much easier for planners to design redistribution systems than to implement them. As is well known, the Soviet Union is characterized by a high degree of centralization of health care delivery planning with seemingly very strong sanctions to compel compliance. Field (1957) reveals that rural districts and culturally distinctive populations are no more attractive to the Soviet physician than to his or her American counterpart. As a result, the Soviet system seems unable to solve the maldistribution problem in large part because of the stubborn refusal of professionals to cooperate. On the other hand, the Soviets appear to have had considerable success with a physician's assistant program in which local peasants are trained as health workers. Theoretically subordinate to a physician, in practice the assistants are often the only health providers in an area. Physicians sometimes feel that these individuals are more effective than doctors from outside the population because they speak the local dialect, understand local cultural variations, and are regarded as community members. Furthermore, they help to provide care for the underserved rural populations because (1) they often prefer to return to their local communities after training and (2) there are no urban employment opportunities for those who might like to work in a city.

Recent attempts in the United States to provide services for underserved urban ghettos and rural populations have been organized primarily around recruiting medical students from these areas in the hope that they will prefer to return to their places of origin to practice (U.S. Department of Health, Education and Welfare, 1976b). These efforts are too recent to permit assessment of their impact on health manpower distribution. The outcome of the Bakke case before the United States Supreme Court may have considerable impact on these programs.

A second type of program is the extension of the roles of professional nurses. These programs are primarily designed to relieve the shortage of physicians (U.S. Department of Health, Education and Welfare, 1976b). There is no doubt that many hoped that nurse practitioners and professionals in other types of extended nurse roles would also provide a significant proportion of services to the underserved. There is growing concern, however, over the number of nurse practitioners who work in physicians' offices, thereby extending the capacities and enlarging the practices of individual physicians. Inasmuch as many of these nurses received their training in underserved urban and rural areas where private practices are available to them, research is needed into the factors that motivate many of them to abandon such practices in favor of association with physicians whose practices consist of the already well-served, relatively affluent, and well-educated urban populations.

PALEOPATHOLOGY AND FORENSICS

Paleopathology and forensic medicine have long been fields of interest to anthropologists and physicians. Medical examiners in many areas of the United States are physical anthropologists. While Fabrega (1971) cites Brothwell and Sandison (1967), it is appropriate to reemphasize the value of this collection for those who are interested in an overview of both fields. It consists of 57 articles, 32 of which were written for the volume. The editors provide some additional help for the inexperienced student by identifying those articles in the collection that are considered classics. The breadth of the volume is impressive. There is an article by Wells on types of agents that change human remains in such a way as to increase the possibility of error in identification of pathologies. There is a section on parasitology. Diseases of the various organs are considered. Arthritis, neoplasm, hernia, and vitamin deficiency in ancient populations are explored. The range of populations studied is equally broad, and includes American Indians, ancient Britons, and early Egyptian and European civilizations. The bibliographies at the end of each chapter, many of which are quite extensive, enhance the utility of the volume.

Armelagos (1969) discusses important factors in methodology and interpretation of findings as well as data. Saul (1973) examines the possible relevance of disease patterns among the ancient Maya as a potential factor in explaining their decline. He also provides additional data for consideration of the problem of whether syphilis existed in pre-Columbian America.

Some of the classic literature in paleopathology and forensic medicine came out of the work of T. Dale Stewart (1931; 1937a; 1940; 1950b; 1951; 1952; 1953; 1956; 1968; 1970; 1972; 1974; 1975b). Stewart, in fact,

has been one of the most productive anthropologists in the field. The works cited above deal primarily with Native American populations and represent only a small portion of his publications. In addition, Stewart's contributions include his studies of pre-Columbian surgical techniques (1937b; 1950a) as well as the identification of a possible source of erroneous attribution to surgical intervention (1975a). Related studies by others include a cross-cultural review and extensive bibliography of the technique of trepanation by modern shamans by Margatts in Brothwell and Sandison (1967) and a classic article on prehistoric and early historic use of the technique by Lisowski in the same volume.

Works by other scholars appear regularly in the *American Journal of Physical Anthropology*. As a matter of interest, this journal has published an issue in honor of Stewart containing 25 articles, the majority of which deal with paleopathology and/or issues of importance to those interested in forensic medicine. The continued integration of paleopathology and forensic interests is evidenced in the 1977 Pan American Conference on the Applications of Anthropology, Dentistry, Medicine, and Paleopathology.

RACE, ETHNICITY, AND HEALTH PROBLEMS

Life expectancies of Americans who are poor and nonwhite are much lower than those of the general population. Two of the primary recent sources for raw health statistics are the U.S. Department of Health, Education and Welfare (1976a; 1976b) and the U.S. Public Health Service (1974). These data reveal that the age-adjusted death rate for nonwhite males is more than one third greater than for white males and that for nonwhite females is one half greater than that for white females. While the infant mortality rate for 1971 for whites was 17.1 per 1,000 live births, the rate for blacks was 30.3 and for American Indians was 20.1. The rates for Japanese-Americans (8.0) and Chinese-Americans (7.8), however, were significantly lower than for all other groups. Nonwhites have higher rates of chronic disease such as heart disease, diabetes, cerebrovascular disease, and asthma. Whites, on the other hand, have higher rates of visual impairments and hemorrhoids. Blacks, American Indians, and

Spanish-surnamed have more nutritional deficiencies than do whites and Asians. Suicide rates are high for young blacks and American Indians but decrease in older age groups; the opposite is true for whites and Asian-Americans. When groups can be matched for income and education, some of the differences tend to even out for some groups and to remain for others. For example, such a study in Los Angeles demonstrated that stillbirths for matched populations of whites, blacks, and Mexican-Americans were 12.9, 13.0, and 15.3 per 1000, respectively. Thus the complex interrelationships among biological, cultural, and environmental factors responsible for health statistics need to be worked out. And, even if these factors come to be understood, there still remain the problems of designing health education and health care systems that are sufficiently acceptable to the client populations to ensure their comprehension and cooperation. To meet these ends, many practitioners in the health professions are becoming increasingly aware of and concerned about issues affecting the health of racial and ethnic minorities. In order to facilitate access to information in these areas, this section has been organized to present resources available in selected aspects of health problems for a small segment of American racial and ethnic groups.

Damon (1969) argues that there are clear associations between race or ethnicity and disease. He also states that similar symptoms across ethnic groups may be indicative of different diseases and hence lead to misdiagnosis and/or needless surgery. He further explores some of the possible determinants of the observed racial/ethnic associations with diseases. These range from errors in the data to genetic differences.

Bucher et al. (1976) examine racial differences in the incidence of ABO hemolytic disease and find it to be significantly higher in blacks than in whites. Their literature review of African populations indicates that the problem may have a genetic basis. Of immediate significance, however, is the fact that physicians and nurses need to be cognizant of the enhanced probability of the disease in black infants with type A or B blood and that the early symptom of jaundice is more likely to be missed in blacks. These factors, coupled with trends toward earlier discharge of neonates in many hospitals, indicate that preventable neurological damage is more likely to occur in black newborns. Diamond (1976) suggests some policies to safeguard the black neonate in light of the findings of Bucher et al.

Kuller and Tonascia (1971) discuss observed racial differences in factors associated with mortality caused by cardio- and cerebrovascular diseases. Shiloh and Selavan (1974) present a collection of studies on black health patterns highlighting genetic and stress factors in relation to morbidity patterns, and consider problems of health care delivery for blacks. Seham (1973) also examines some problems in health services delivery for blacks and includes chapters on the past and present problems of black physicians as well as black medical, nursing, and dental students.

Shiloh and Selavan (1973) also have a volume of studies on morbidity patterns, genetic problems, and behavioral problems of American Jews. One of the genetic disorders, Tay-Sachs syndrome, is also examined in Brady (1971). Generally speaking, however, relatively little seems to be available on American white ethnic groups. Cardinalli and Wurtman, in Damon (1975), discuss briefly the ramifications of exposure to sunlight and skin cancer for Irish populations of a specific phenotype.

Works on American Indian health, on the other hand, are quite numerous. Among the general studies on American Indian health, Hrdlicka (1908) stands as a classic reference on Indians of the southwestern United States and northwestern Mexico. A great deal of basic data on population size and structure, physical characteristics of children (including growth data) and adults, diseases, and concepts of illness and curing are to be found. This volume also has a very complete bibliography of older works on American Indians health and disease patterns, which are often unknown data sources for health professionals. Care must be taken in use of old materials, however. Anthropologists will generally know which sources are the studies of professional anthropologists and which are the writings of journalists or military men, or casual memoirs of frontiersmen. The uninformed should seek assistance in using older works, and Hrdlicka's bibliography can serve as a guide to acceptable older sources. Changes in conditions and improved research techniques must be taken into consideration in utilization of older sources. These are invaluable, however, for certain research problems.

Siever (1966) has a more recent review of disease patterns of southwestern Indians. While he finds duodenal ulcers rare, gallbladder disease is excessive. Hepatic disease is also high and esophageal varices are the major cause of gastrointestinal tract hemorrhage. Other major problems are enteric infections and respiratory diseases, including coccidioidomycosis, a spore-caused disease borne in the dust of the windswept southwestern desert. Blindness is a major problem, but not the open-angle glaucoma, which is probably the major cause of blindness in whites. Blood cholesterol levels are lower than among whites, despite high usage of saturated fat. The health patterns described by Siever are still among the major health problems today.

The incidence of diabetes mellitus is quite high among sedentary tribes in the Southwest (Siever, 1966) and is the best studied disease of American Indians. A study on culture and diabetes among the upland Yumans was done by Smith (1970), a nurse anthropologist. Studies among the Cocopah (Henry, 1969), the Seneca (Doeblin, 1969; Frohman, 1969), the Navajo (Rimoin and Sasaki, 1968), and the Athabascans of Alaska (Mouratoff et al., 1969) represent only a small portion of the resources available. The literature on the Pima alone is voluminous; only a few are cited here (Bennett and Miller, 1970; Bennett et al., 1971; Genuth et al., 1967, Rushforth et al., 1971).

Studies on blood groups and other characteristics have been done by Alfred et al. (1970; 1972a; 1972b). Bowen and associates (1971) have examined serum protein polymorphism in Algonkian, Athabascan, and Siouan linguistic groups.

Recent studies on mental health problems include those by Foulks and Katz (1973) on Alaskan natives, Kaufman (1973) on gasoline sniffing among Pueblo Indian children, and Miller and Schoenfeld (1971) on suicide among the Navajo. Recent studies on alcoholism have been done by Levy and Kunitz (1974), Kunitz et al. (1971), and Westermeyer (1972a; 1972b).

Resources dealing with health care delivery for culturally distinctive populations are growing. Branch and Paxton (1976) provide an overview of cultural traditions of Hispanics, Asian-Americans, American Indians, and blacks. The volume contains the works of contributors from the respective ethnic/racial groups and is innovative in its attempt to provide specific guidelines for safe, effective nursing care and for relevant curricula development for nurses working with members of the selected ethnic/racial groups. The volume also contains an article on the history of the development of ethnic nurses' associations and their perceived relationship with the American Nurses' Association and with the development of the profession as a whole.

Nurge (1975) describes an elective program available for medical students interested in learning how to work effectively with culturally diverse populations. Primeaux (1977) and Kniep-Hardy and Burkhardt (1977) discuss some Indian concepts and examples for those interested in dealing with American Indian health. Schoenfeld et al. (1971), Hackenberg (1970), de Geyndt (1973), and Bain and Goldthorpe (1972) all provide information on developing effective health services for Indians. Velimirovic and Velimirovic (1978) provide overviews of the ways in which traditional medicine and traditional health practitioners have been utilized in the health service systems of several nations. Alvarado (1978) discusses some concerns in attempting to integrate ethnomedical practitioners into Western health care delivery systems.

Other studies have dealt with the problems of the applied medical anthropologist in the field. Bonfil Batalla, reprinted in Weaver (1973), cautions anthropologists on the effects that their own theoretical frameworks may have on their studies. He maintains that the basic problems in public health are frequently not addressed because of a consistent psychological bias (among other biases) in medical anthropological research which tends to address psychological factors that are the manifestations of the particular problem under study, rather than their cause. The misidentification of the cause, he asserts, leads to the failure to recognize the need for changes in structures and conditions that actually determine health status.

Hessler et al. (1975) demonstrate the cultural diversity to be found within a local ethnic group, in this case the Chinese-Americans of Boston. They warn against the assumptions of those who tend to view ethnic groups as relatively homogeneous cultural units. The so-called Spanish-surnamed population is also quite heterogeneous in culture because of different origins as well as different levels of acculturation, class, and length of time in the United States (Penalosa, 1970). Montserrat (1973) notes that Mexican-American concerns and considerations may override Puerto Rican participation in health care planning. Most heterogeneous of all are the American Indians who are actually comprised of a large number of linguistically and culturally distinctive groups. Failure to recognize intraethnic diversity can be a serious problem as so-called cultural awareness by Western health professionals has the potential to create, rather than solve, problems because of stereotyping of ethnic populations. This is not to indicate that the cultural awareness trend in medical education should not be given every opportunity to be tried. But intraethnic diversity must be strongly considered as a factor in planning and service. Attitudes, concepts, and approaches to health care and education that are highly acceptable and successful with one group may not be appropriate for others in the same general ethnic category.

By the same token, intraethnic genetic differentiation must also be recognized (Workman and Niswander, 1970; Workman et al., 1975).

Again, in the area of ethnomedical studies, American Indian concepts of causation and curing of illnesses are among the most widely researched. The works of Basso (1969; 1970) on the Western Apache are among the finest examples. Basso's lucidity makes the highly complex world view of the western Apache comprehensible to the non-Apache and provides data that health professionals can readily use. Navajo ethnomedicine is more complex and more highly specialized than the Apache (Kluckhohn, 1944; Kluckhohn and Leighton, 1946), but Basso's works may be read with profit by health professionals working among the Navajo. Caution is again urged inasmuch as the modern Navajo are quite diverse and the western Apaches are also changing. The Navajo Health Authority, headquartered at Window Rock, Arizona, is quite happy to provide health personnel with data that facilitate their professional activities.

A recent study of Piman shamanism and illness concepts has been published by Bahr et al. (1974). Paul and Paul (1975) examine the role of the Maya midwife, a sacred specialist, indicating the integration of American Indian medicine and religion. Health professionals should realize that the integration of religion and medicine may make the acquisition of ethnomedical information on some tribes impossible to obtain and that persistence in attempts to do so may result in further estrangement. Such knowledge may be restricted even within the tribe, so that only persons of specified status may have access to such privileged information. Ortiz (1969) discusses some aspects of the roles of members of Tewa medicine societies in their total context. Jones' (1972) work on one of the last Comanche medicine women is also of interest.

As a final note, it is well recognized that Western medicine may explain what Hoeppli and Lucasse (1964) call the "how's" of disease causation for non-Western peoples but is unable to satisfactorily explain the "why's". Thus the concepts concerning "why" may continue to be conceived in supernatural terms. It should be pointed out that the same remains true for many modern Anglo-Americans who also seek the "how's" and "why's" in supernatural determinants. Science itself is rejected by a sizable component of Americans (Nelkin, 1976). Thus the answer to the ultimate "why"—"Why do I have a fatal disease" or "Why does my child have this health problem"—may not be meaningfully answered by health professionals, who must continue to recognize the needs of many patients of all cultural backgrounds for religious specialists.

CONCLUSION

This selected literature review is by no means comprehensive, but rather is intended to serve as a guide to the range of resources available. While most of the publications cited are recent, some older works have been included so that students may not misunderstand the depth of the history of research in certain areas. This review should make clear the continuing eclectic nature of the field of medical anthropology. Indeed some of the authors cited would not identify themselves as medical anthropologists but as geneticists, political scientists, ethnologists, and so forth.

The principal purposes of this chapter were (1) to review selected works of mutual interest to medical anthropologists and health professionals, (2) to provide a broad overview of selected areas, regardless of discipline, which have the potential to contribute to the development of Weidman's proposed synthesis of anthropological and medical concerns, and (3) to contribute to the dissemination of types of knowledge that lead to a better understanding of biological and cultural factors affecting health, illness, disease, and curing. In so doing, it is hoped that a contribution is made to the elevation of health levels of all human populations.

REFERENCES

Abel, T., and Metraux, R. 1974. Culture and psychotherapy. College and University Press, New Haven.

Alford, R. R. 1975. Health care politics: Ideological and interest group barriers to reform. University of Chicago Press, Chicago.

Alfred, B. M., Stout, T. D., Lee, M. L., and others. 1970. Blood groups, phosphoglucomutase, and cerumen types of the Anaham (Chilcotin) Indians. American Journal of Physical Anthropology 32:329-338.

Alfred, B. M., Stout, T. D., Lee, M., and others. 1972a. Blood groups and red cell enzymes of the Ross River (Northern Tuchone) and Upper Laird (Slave) Indians. American Journal of Physical Anthropology 36:161-164.

Alfred, R. M., Stout, T. D., Lowry, R. B., and others. 1972b. Blood groups of six Indian bands of northeastern British Columbia. American Journal of Physical Anthropology 36:151-160.

Alland, A. 1975. Adaptation. In B. Siegel, ed. Annual review of anthropology, vol. 4. Annual Reviews, Inc., Palo Alto, Calif.

Alvarado, A. L. 1970. Cultural determinants of population stability in the Havasupai Indians. American Journal of Physical Anthropology 33:9-14.

Alvarado, A. L. 1977. Status and trends in professional nursing of selected ethnic minorities: American Indians, Asian Americans, Blacks, and Hispanics. Paper given at American Anthropological Association meetings.

Alvarado, A. L. 1978. Important factors to consider in the integration of scientific and ethnomedical systems. Modern medicine and medical anthropology in the border population. Pan American Health Organization, Washington. (in press)

Anderson, O. W. 1972. Health care: Can there be equality? John Wiley & Sons, New York.

Armelagos, G. J. 1969. Disease in ancient Nubia. Science 163:255-259.

Bahr, D. M., Gregorio, J., Lopez, D. I., and Alvarez, A. 1974. Piman shamanism and staying sickness. University of Arizona Press, Tucson.

Bain, H. W., and Goldthorpe, G. 1972. The University of Toronto 'Sioux Lookout Project'—a model of health care delivery. Canadian Medical Association Journal 107:523-528.

Barber, T. X., and De Moor, W. 1972. A theory of hypnotic induction procedures. American Journal of Clinical Hypnosis 15:112-135.

Barrios, E. 1971. Bibliografia de Aztlan: An annotated Chicano bibliography. San Diego State College, San Diego.

Basso, K. H. 1969. Western Apache witchcraft. Anthropological Papers of the University of Arizona, No. 15. University of Arizona Press, Tucson.

Basso, K. H. 1970. The Cibecue Apache. Holt, Rinehart and Winston, New York.

Bennett, K. A., Osborne, R. H., and Miller, R. J. 1975. Biocultural ecology. In B. J. Siegel, ed. Annual review of anthropology, vol. 4. Annual Reviews, Inc., Palo Alto, Calif.

Bennett, P. H., and Miller, M. 1970. Diabetes mellitus in Indians of the southwestern United States. Proceedings of the International Diabetes Federation, Buenos Aires.

Bennett, P. H., Burch, T. A., and Miller, M. 1971. Diabetes mellitus in American (Pima) Indians, The Lancet 1716:125-128.

Bowen, P., O'Callaghan, F., and Lee, C. S. N. 1971. Serum protein polymorphisms in Indians of western Canada: Gene frequencies and data on the Gc/albumin linkages. Human Heredity 21:242-253.

Brady, R. O. 1971. Hereditary fat-metabolism diseases. Scientific American 229:88-97.

Branch, M., and Paxton, P., eds. 1976. Providing safe nursing care for ethnic people of color. Appleton-Century-Crofts, New York.

Brothwell, D., and Sandison, A. T., eds. 1967. Diseases in antiquity. Charles C Thomas, Springfield, Ill.

Bucher, K. A., Patterson, A. M., Jr., Elston, R. C., and others. 1976. Racial difference in incidence of ABO hemolytic disease. American Journal of Public Health 66:854-858.

Bullough, B., and Bullough, V. 1975. Sex discrimination in health care. Nursing Outlook 23:40-45.

Cairns, J. 1975. The cancer problem. Scientific American 233:64-78.

California Nurses' Association. 1973. Minorities in nursing. The Association, San Francisco.

Carlson, R. J. 1975. The end of medicine. John Wiley & Sons, New York.

Cavalli-Sforza, L. L., and Feldman, M. W. 1973. Cultural versus biological inheritance: Phenotypic transmission from parents to children (a theory of the effect of parental phenotypes on children's phenotypes). American Journal of Human Genetics 25:618-637.

Chaves, J. F., and Barber, T. X. 1976. Hypnotic procedures and surgery: A critical analysis with applications to acupuncture anesthesia. American Journal of Clinical Hypnosis 18:217-236.

Childe, V. G. 1936. Man makes himself. Mentor Books, New York.

Clark, M. 1973. Contributions of medical anthropology to the study of the aged. In L. Nader and T. A. Maretzki, eds. Culture, Illness and Health: Essay in human adaptation. Anthropological Study no. 9. American Anthropological Association, Washington, D.C.

Colson, A. C., and Selby, K. F. 1974. Medical anthropology. In B. Siegel, ed. Annual Review of Anthropology, vol. 3. Stanford University Press, Stanford.

Damon, A. 1969. Race, ethnic group, and disease. Social Biology 16:69-80.

Damon, A., ed. 1975. Physiological anthropology. Oxford University Press, London.

Diamond, L. K. 1976. Racial inequality and neonatal disease. American Journal of Public Health 66: 835-836.

Doeblin, T. D., Evans, K., Ingall, G., and others. 1969. Diabetes and hyperglycemia in Seneca Indians. Human Heredity 19:613-627.

Dunn, F. L. 1968. Health and disease in hunter-gatherers: epidemiological factors. In R. L. Lee and I. de Vore, eds. Man the hunter. Aldine, Chicago.

Elinson, J., and Herr, C. E. A. 1970. A sociomedical view of neighborhood health centers. Medical Care 8:97-103.

Fabrega, H., Jr. 1972. Medical anthropology. In B. Siegel, ed. Biennial review of anthropology, vol. 7. Stanford University Press, Stanford, Calif.

Field, M. G. 1957. Doctor and patient in Soviet Russia. Harvard University Press, Cambridge.

Foulks, E. F., and Katz, S. 1973. The mental health of Alaskan natives. Acta Psychiatrica Scandinavica 49: 91-96.

Friedlander, J. 1969. Malaria and demography in the lowlands of Mexico: An ethno-historical approach. Proceedings of the American Ethnological Society. University of Washington Press, Seattle.

Frohman, L. A., Doeblin, T. D., and Ememling, F. G. 1969. Diabetes in the Seneca Indians. Diabetes 18: 38-43.

Gajdusek, D. C. 1977. Unconventional viruses and the origin and disappearance of kuru. Science 191: 943-960.

Genuth, S. M., Bennett, P. H., Miller, M., and Burch, T. A. 1967. Hyperinsulinism in obese Pima Indians. Metabolism 16:1010-1015.

de Geyndt, W. 1973. Health behavior and health needs of urban Indians in Minneapolis. Health Services Reports 88:360-366.

Giordano, J. 1973. Ethnicity and mental health research and recommendations. Institute on Pluralism and Group Identity, New York.

Giordano, J., and Levine, M. 1975. Mental health and Middle America. A group identity approach. Institute on Pluralism and Group Identity, New York.

Glazier, W. H. 1973. The task of medicine. Scientific American 228:13-17.

Hackenberg, R. A. 1970. The social observatory: Time series data for health and behavioral research. Social Science and Medicine 4:343-357.

Harrison, G. 1975. Primary adult lactase deficiency: A problem in anthropological genetics. American Anthropologist 77:812-835.

Henry, R. E., Burch, T. A., Bennett, P. H., and Miller, M. 1969. Diabetes in ten Cocopah Indians. Diabetes 18:33-37.

Herzlich, C. 1973. Health and illness. Academy Press, New York.

Hessler, R. M., Nolan, M. F., Ogbru, B., and New, P. K. M. 1975. Intra-ethnic diversity: Health care of the Chinese-Americans. Human Organization 34: 253-262.

Hoeppli, R., and Lucasse, C. 1964. Old ideas regarding cause and treatment of sleeping sickness held in west Africa. Journal of Tropical Medicine 67:60-68.

Hrdlicka, A. 1908. Physiological and medical anthropology among the Indians of southwestern United States and northern Mexico. Bureau of American Ethnology, Bulletin 34. U. S. Government Printing Office, Washington, D.C.

Johnson, T. M. 1976. Sociocultural factors in the intergroup perception of health problems: A case of grower attitudes toward their migrant labor. Human Organization 35:19-83.

Johnson, W. L. 1974. Admission of men and ethnic minorities to schools of nursing. Nursing Outlook 22: 45-49.

Jones, D. E. 1972. Sanapia. Comanche medicine woman. Holt, Rinehart and Winston, New York.

Kaufman, A. 1973. Gasoline sniffing among children in a Pueblo Indian village. Pediatrics 51:1060-1064.

Kay, M. A. 1972. Health and illness in the barrio: Women's point of view. Ph.D. dissertation. University of Arizona, Tucson.

Kay, M. A. 1977. Mexican American fertility regulation, Communicating Nursing Research 10:279-294.

Kluckhohn, C. 1944. Navaho Witchcraft. Papers of the Peabody Museum of American Anthropology and Ethnology, 22, no. 2. Cambridge, Mass.

Kluckhohn, C., and Leighton, D. 1946. The Navaho. Harvard University Press, Cambridge.

Kniep-Hardy, M., and Burkhardt, M. 1977. Nursing the Navajo, American Journal of Nursing 77:95-96.

Knopf, L. 1975a. Graduation and withdrawal from RN programs. A report of the nurse career-pattern study. U.S. Government Printing Office, Washington, D.C.

Knopf, L. 1975b. RNs: One and five years after graduation. National League for Nursing, New York.

Knopf, L., Tate, B., and Patrylow, S. 1970. Practical nurses five years after graduation. Nurse career-pattern study. National League for Nursing, New York.

Knudsen, A. G., Jr., Wayne, L., and Hallett, W. Y. 1967. On the selective advantage of cystic fibrosis heterozygotes, American Journal of Human Genetics 19:388-392.

Korsch, B. M., and Negrete, V. F. 1972. Doctor-patient communication, Scientific American 227:66-74.

Kuller, L., and Tonascia, S. 1971. A follow-up study of the commission on chronic illness morbidity survey in Baltimore. IV. Factors influencing mortality from stroke and arterio-sclerotic heart disease (1954-1967). Journal of Chronic Diseases 24:111-124.

Kunitz, S. J., Levy, J. E., Odoroff, C. L., and Bollinger, J. 1971. The epidemiology of alcohol cirrhosis in two southwestern Indian tribes. Quarterly Journal of Studies on Alcoholism 32:106-720.

Levy, J. E., and Kunitz, S. J. 1974. Indian drinking. Navajo practices and Anglo-American theories. John Wiley & Sons, New York.

Loudon, J. B., ed. 1976. Social anthropology and medicine. Academic Press, New York.

Lynch, M. 1972. The physician 'shortage': The economists' mirror. The Annals of the American Academy of Political and Social Science 399:82-88.

Maclean, U. 1971. Magical medicine. Penguin Books, Baltimore.

Martin, A. O., Kurczynski, T. W., and Steinberg, A. G.

1973. Familial studies of medical and anthropological variables in a human isolate. American Journal of Human Genetics **25**:581-593.

McFalls, J. A. 1973. Impact of VD on the fertility of the U.S. Black population. Social Biology **20**:2-19.

Miller, S. 1974. A new humanism in medicine, Synthesis (Spring).

Miller, S. I., and Schoenfeld, L. S. 1971. Suicide attempt patterns among the Navajo Indians. International Journal of Social Psychiatry **17**:189-193.

Mommsen, K. G. 1973. Differentials in fertility among black doctorates. Social Biology **20**:20-29.

Montserrat, J. 1973. The Boricua perspective. Proceedings of the National Health Manpower Education Conference for the Spanish Surnamed. Inter-America Research Associates, Washington, D.C.

Moody, E. J. 1974. Urban witches. In J. P. Spradley and D. W. McCurdy, eds. Conformity and conflict, 2nd ed. Little Brown, Boston.

Morehead, M. 1970. Evaluating quality of medical care in the neighborhood health center program of the Office of Economic Opportunity, Medical Care **8**: 118-131.

Mouratoff, G. J., Carroll, N. V., and Scott, E. M. 1969. Diabetes mellitus in Athabascan Indians in Alaska. Diabetes **18**:29-32.

Nag, M. 1962. Factors affecting human fertility in nonindustrial societies; a cross-cultural survey. Yale University Publications in Anthropology. No. 66.

Nash, P. 1974. Evaluation of employment opportunities for newly licensed nurses. U.S. Government Printing Office, Washington, D.C.

Neel, J. V. 1967. Current concepts of the genetic basis of diabetes mellitus and the biological significance of the diabetic predisposition. Supplement to the Proceedings of the Sixth Congress of the International Diabetes Federation. Stockholm.

Nelkin, D. 1976. The science-textbook controversies. Scientific American **234**:33-39.

Newman, L. F. 1972. Birth control: An anthropological view. An Addison-Wesley Module in Anthropology. No. 27.

Nurge, E. 1975. Anthropological perspectives for medical students. Human Organization **34**:345-352.

Nye, E. R. 1966. Natural selection and degenerative cardiovascular disease. Eugenics Quarterly **14**:127-131.

Ortiz, A. 1969. The Tewa world. University of Chicago Press, Chicago.

Paul, L., and Paul, B. D. 1975. The Maya midwife as a sacred specialist: A Guatemala case. American ethnologist **2**:707-726.

Penalosa, F. 1970. Toward an operational definition of the Mexican-American. Aztlan **1**:1-12.

Primeaux, M. 1977. Caring for the American Indian patient. American Journal of Nursing **77**:91-94.

Rimoin, D. L., and Saiki, J. H. 1968. Diabetes mellitus among the Navajo. Archives of Internal Medicine **122**: 6-9.

Rubin, V., and Comitas, L. 1976. Ganja in Jamaica. The effects of marijuana use. Anchor Books. Garden City, N.J.

Rushforth, N. B., Bennett, P. H., Steinberg, A. G., and others. 1971. Diabetes in the Pima Indians. Diabetes **20**:756-765.

Saul, F. 1973. Disease in the Maya area; the pre-Columbian evidence. In T. P. Culbemt, ed. The classic Maya collapse. University of New Mexico Press, Albuquerque.

Schoenfeld, L. S., Lyerly, R. J., and Miller, S. I. 1971. We like us: The attitudes of the mental health staff toward other agencies on the Navajo reservation. Mental Hygiene **55**:171-173.

Schwartz, G. S. 1975. Biofeedback, self-regulation, and the patterning of physiological response. American Scientist **63**:314-324.

Scotch, N. A. 1963. Medical anthropology. In B. Siegel, ed. Biennial review of anthropology. Stanford University Press, Stanford, Calif.

Seham, M. 1973. Blacks and American medical care. University of Minnesota Press, Minneapolis.

Shiloh, A., and Selavan, I., eds. 1973. Ethnic groups of America: Their morbidity, mortality and behavior disorders. Vol. I: The Jews. Charles C Thomas, Springfield, Ill.

Shiloh, A., and Selavan, I., eds. 1974. Ethnic groups of America: Their morbidity, mortality and behavior disorders. Vol. II: The blacks. Charles C Thomas, Springfield, Ill.

Siever, M. L. 1966. Disease patterns among southwestern Indians, Public Health Reports **81**:1075-1083.

Smith, C. G. 1970. Culture and diabetes among the upland Yuman Indians. Ph.D. dissertation. University of Utah.

Smith, G. R. 1975. From invisibility to blackness: The story of the National Black Nurses' Association. Nursing Outlook **23**:225-229.

Society for medical anthropology: What is medical anthropology? Washington, D.C.

Spanos, N. P., and Barber, T. X. 1974. Toward a convergence in hypnosis research. American Psychologist **29**:500-511.

Stephens, R. C., and McBride, D. C. 1976. Becoming a street addict. Human Organization **35**:87-93.

Stevens, R., and Vermeulen, J. 1972. Foreign-trained physicians and American medicine. U.S. Government Printing Office, Washington, D.C.

Stewart, T. D. 1931. Dental caries in Peruvian skulls. American Journal of Physical Anthropology **16**:51-62.

Stewart, T. D. 1937a. Different types of cranial deformity in the Pueblo area. American Anthropologist **39**: 169-171.

Stewart, T. D. 1937b. Did the American Indians use the cautery in bone surgery? American Journal of Physical Anthropology **23**:83-89.

Stewart, T. D. 1940. Skeletal remains from the Whitewater district, eastern Arizona. Bureau of American Ethnology. Bulletin 126, U.S. Government Printing Office, Washington, D.C.

Stewart, T. D. 1950a. Deformity, trephining, and mutilation in South American Indian skeletal remains. Bureau of American Ethnology. Bulletin 143. U.S. Government Printing Office, Washington, D.C.

Stewart, T. D. 1950b. Pathological changes in South American skeletal remains. Bureau of American Ethnology. Bulletin 143. U.S. Government Printing Office, Washington, D.C.

Stewart, T. D. 1951. What the bones tell. FBI Law Enforcement Bulletin **20**:2-5.

Stewart, T. D. 1953. The age incidence of neural-arch defects in Alaska natives, considered from the standpoint of etiology. Journal of Bone and Joint Surgery **35-A**:937-950.

Stewart, T. D. 1956. Significance of osteitis in ancient Peruvian trephining. Bulletin of the History of Medicine **3**:293-320.

Stewart, T. D. 1968. The effects of pathology on skeletal populations. American Journal of Physical Anthropology **30:**443-450.

Stewart, T. D. 1970. Skin, hair and eyes (of Middle American Indians). Introduction. In T. D. Stewart, ed. Handbook of Middle American Indians, vol. 9, Austin, Tex.

Stewart, T. D. 1972. What the bones tell today. FBI Law Enforcement Bulletin **41:**16-20.

Stewart, T. D. 1974. Nonunion of fractures in antiquity, with descriptions of five cases from the New World involving the forearm. Bulletin of the New York Academy of Medicine **50:**875-891.

Stewart, T. D. 1975a. Cranial dysraphism mistaken for trephination. American Journal of Physical Anthropology **42:**435-437.

Stewart, T. D. 1975b. Study of human skeletal remains from pueblo ruins in Chaco Canyon, New Mexico, 1935. National Geographic Society Research Reports, 1890-1954 Projects. Washington, D.C.

Stewart, T. D., and Spoehr, A. 1952. Evidence on the paleopathology of yaws. Bulletin of the History of Medicine **26:**538-553.

Symposium in Honor of T. Dale Stewart. American Journal of Physical Anthropology **45**(part II):517-747.

U.S. Department of Health, Education and Welfare. 1976a. Health in the United States, 1975: A chartbook. U.S. Government Printing Office, Washington, D.C.

U.S. Department of Health, Education and Welfare. 1976b. Trends affecting the U.S. health care system. U.S. Government Printing Office, Washington, D.C.

U.S. Public Health Service. 1974. Minority health chartbook. U.S. Government Printing Office, Washington, D.C.

Velimirovic, B., and Velimirovic, H. 1978. Utilization of traditional medicine and its practitioners in health service. Modern medicine and medical anthropology in the border population. Pan American Health Organization, Washington, D.C.

Vogel, F., and Chakravarrti, M. R. 1966. ABO blood groups and smallpox in a rural population of West Bengal and Bihar (India). Humangenetik **3:**166-180.

Weaver, T., ed. 1973. To see ourselves: Anthropology and modern social issues. Scott, Foresman and Company, Glenview, Ill.

Weidman, H. 1971. Trained manpower and medical anthropology: Conceptual organization and educational priorities. Social Science and Medicine **5:**15-36.

Westermeyer, J. 1972a. Chippewa and majority alcoholism in the Twin Cities: A comparison. Journal of Nervous and Mental Disease **155:**322-327.

Westermeyer, J. 1972b. Options regarding alcohol use among the Chippewa. American Journal of Orthopsychiatry **42:**398-403.

Willie, C. V., Kramer, B. M., and Brown, B. S., eds. 1973. Racism and mental health. University of Pittsburgh Press, Pittsburgh.

Workman, P. O., and Niswander, N. D. 1970. Population studies on southwestern Indian tribes. II. Local and genetic differentiation in the Papago. American Journal of Human Genetics **22:**24-49.

Workman, P. O., Lucarelli, P., Agostino, R., and others. 1975. Genetic differentiation among Sardinian villages. American Journal of Physical Anthropology **43:**165-176.

CHAPTER 4

The care component in a health and healing system

Agnes M. Aamodt

A sensation of coolness as soap is rinsed from human skin, a feeling of warmth as heated milk envelopes the interior of the human body, a pleasurable flush following a spirited walk in the early morning, the comforting touch of a cool hand on a face flushed with heat—all of these tell us something of human experience and the ways and means of caring for oneself and others. How human beings care for themselves and others is an essential field of inquiry for serious students of quality health care delivery because of (1) the humanistic dimension the concept of care brings to the health care experience, (2) the practical need for health specialists to understand patterns of care already in use by their patients, and (3) the need to learn how to utilize the cultural dimension to enhance the quality of life for all people. The central focus of this chapter is to examine dimensions of the concept of care as a component in a cultural health and healing system.

All cultures provide a system of rules for care that members of a community use as they confront problems in everyday living. A recurring theme in field work (Aamodt 1976) is ritual behavior associated with taking care of oneself and others in activities of daily living. These life supporting rituals represent a body of knowledge of increasing concern to human beings. Similar patterns of sometimes conscious, sometimes unconscious behavior related to taking-care have probably served as cultural solutions to the vicissitudes of the human condition since the time of early man. Breathing, pain, itching, not breathing, absence of pain, and freedom from itching are experiences that could hardly have escaped the perceptions of human beings when they

became symbolizing, self-identifying creatures.

Patterns of eating, crying, sleep, rest, play, bathing, prayer, sexuality, healing, feasting, birthing, and dying are examples of human experience that vary cross-culturally. These culturally patterned ways for behaving can be explained when linked with other symbolic forms in a culture. For example, in our modern world stomach sensations of an infinite variety are a common focus for taking-care activities. Information about remedies for prevention of a "full" feeling is available in popular self-care literature and on drug store shelves, and is dramatically portrayed in television commercials.

How patterns of caring for oneself fit with other meanings in a cultural system is important information for health specialists. For example, children in a society may decide for themselves when they need care and may report to a community clinic without the knowledge of their parents. However, health workers should know that alternative healers are available in the child's network of health care delivery services. Other patients may believe that ice water predisposes to illness. In this case the health worker should understand the patients' beliefs concerning how ice water fits with the combinations of food that are viewed as antagonistic or complementary. With knowledge of the cultural patterns of caring health workers can make decisions with patients that incorporate a greater understanding of the patients' perspectives and thus increase opportunities for quality health practice.

The purpose of this chapter is to inquire into the nature of the care concept and explore variations in the cultural content of caring behavior. My discussion will follow a framework outlined in an analysis of the care concept previously reported (Aamodt, 1977). In a discussion of the sociocultural dimensions of care in the world of the Papago Indian child and adolescent I identified four themes from ethnographic data: (1) health and healing prescriptions and proscriptions; (2) a multiperson child caring system; (3) belief and unbelief in powerful objects and events; and (4) changes in caring activities during a life cycle. The theoretical positions reflected by these themes represent anthropological tradition and interest in the holistic concept, the interrelatedness of human beings and the environment, culture as a cognitive system of rules, and the change of patterns during the process of enculturation.

The components of care activities often appear illusive, amorphous, and illogical. A clearer understanding of the domain of care in the health and healing system of a community is possible through knowledge of the culture concept.

WHY IS THE CONCEPT OF CARE IMPORTANT?

What is the nature of care? What values are associated with taking care of self and others? How does the concept of care fit in the cultural system of health behavior for members of a community? Answers to these questions will be suggested in the following sections.

Changes in contemporary health practices are emphasizing humanistic values. Consumers of health service are seeking alternative ways for achieving optimal health. Health professionals increasingly recognize that health and illness are largely determined by factors that operate outside of the domain of the formal health care delivery system. Women's health groups, holistic health care, self-care skills, and strategies for relaxation and meditation represent a small part of the movement of consumers to become active agents in their own health care. This trend, which transforms the traditionally passive patient into an active, informed, and effective participant in health care, increases the need for health professionals to become knowledgeable about self-care systems. There is also a need for emphasis on the cultural

variation in strategies for health care, religious and ethical systems of clients, and the caring or humanistic process.

Recently, the concept of care has received increasing attention. Many nursing writers, as well as other health professionals, are studying the content and processes of care as a legitimate subject of inquiry. One may infer from Florence Nightingale's famous goal for nursing, ". . . to put the patient in the best condition for nature to act upon him . . ." (Nightingale, 1859:74), the inevitability of such interest in the concept of care. Ever since Nightingale's time, the concept of nursing has been defined as concerned with principles of healthful living and caring for human beings when they cannot take care of themselves. "Nature" in the quotation from Nightingale can be interpreted as the sociocultural and physical environment of the patient. What exists in this environment that relates to taking care of self and others is discussed in this chapter.

There are different explanations for what nursing is. Experiencing feelings and attending to oneself or others, assisting or protecting, providing for needs, a sense of tenderness and respect as opposed to intolerance, duty, and indifference are emphasized in the work of Krueter (1951). Similarly, relieving discomfort and tension and maintaining and restoring internal and interpersonal equilibrium are utilized by Johnson (1959) who discusses the concept of care as part of the underlying ideology of the nursing profession. The relationship of care to the nursing process is outlined by Titt (1966) who proposes that given a person under stress, a nurse makes a diagnosis, including the individual's perception of the situation, an assessment of how comfort can be achieved, and who and what are needed to help achieve the feeling of comfort. Titt emphasizes that health professionals need information both to avoid counteracting the client's own way of achieving a state of comfort and to facilitate an optimal state of health.

More recently, Leininger (1972, 1977) and Hyde (1975, 1976, 1977) have examined the care phenomenon with the purpose of emphasizing the caring process as the essence of humanistic health practice. Leininger (1977) analyzes the nature and process of caring behaviors using a transcultural perspective. She suggests the dimensions of meaning related to care may be found in concepts such as survival, self-actualization, support activities, humanistically oriented services, and reciprocal behaviors that facilitate interaction.

The emphasis in all of Leininger's work is on the potential contribution of the cross-cultural or transcultural perspective to our understanding of the care concept. She has outlined a model of elements in the idea of care and urges that studying these "blocks" will aid our understanding of health care. Comfort, support, compassion, empathy, helping behavior, coping, specific stress alleviation, touching, nurture, succor, surveillance, protection, restoration, stimulation, health maintenance, health instruction, and health consultation comprise the set of concepts in her model. Although these ideas are neither mutually exclusive nor jointly exhaustive, they suggest dimensions in the caring domain that may serve as a focus for cross-cultural comparisons and the generation of hypotheses, generalizations, and theories. Leininger (1977b) reports that cultures tend to vary in the specific aspects of care that they emphasize.

For example, following an analysis of data collected during extended field work among the Gadsup of the Eastern Highlands of New Guinea, Leininger (1977a) concludes that all cultures rank care concepts according to their importance within the rest of the cultural system. Among the Gadsup, surveillance (that is, monitoring an individual or social group for evidence of danger) is a dominant theme. A second theme is touching. This is an expected pattern of care among women when trouble, anger, or physical illness is present. Nurture of children, adolescents, and adults to grow and develop in healthful ways; health counseling to prevent illness; and the stimulation of ways to maintain health are other themes in caring behaviors among the Gadsup.

Hyde (1976) views care as a characteristic of fully human beings who value and accept themselves and thus are able to reach out to care for others. She sees caring as a perspective toward activities of a balanced life, and calls for research on definition, theoretical formulations, designs, and methodologies for evaluation and measurement. She asks: What is the relationship of caring to curing? What are the expectations of the provider and the user? What problems are there concerning the organizational structure, the setting, the population, reimbursement, and self-renewal of the care givers?

The idea of care is a value-laden construct and, as is reflected in the work of Leininger and Hyde, emphasizes the nature of a sensitive response to the needs of oneself and others. Just as the preservation of life may not be universally valued, so the phenomenon of caring may not be universal. That this humanistically oriented system of behavior may not be valued in all cultures has been suggested in the work of Turnbull (1972), who reports on a society that has few caring behaviors and places a low value on preservation of life.

Four themes related to care serve as a framework for the analysis of care as a cultural domain that follows. These themes are (1) care and a system of health and healing, (2) the multiperson environment and the concept of care, (3) belief and the concept of care, and (4) the developmental process and the concept of care (Aamodt, 1972; 1976; 1977).

CARE AND A SYSTEM OF HEALTH AND HEALING

Every culture provides explanations for the experiences of environment and the inevitable processes of birth, disease, and death. Most ethnographies include information on systems of disease and treatment but often ignore everyday notions about health and the facilitation of a quality of life suggested in the phenomenon of care. Two questions to ask when learning about a cultural system of care that proscribes the behavior of its users are: (1) What activities of care are culturally defined? (2) How does the system of care link with other systems, such as kinship, religion, and the economic system?

The cultural definition of care demands the strategies of the ethnographic interviewer to discover the categories of meaning that organize experience for the user. "Cultures as systems of knowledge" and "everything the individual needs to know in order to behave appropriately in a society" are common generalizations from the work of Goodenough (1957), Spradley and McCurdy (1972), Spradley (1972), and others. Domains of meaning that are culturally relevant are identified in formal and informal interviews with members of a society. Taxonomies are then developed to show relationships among the various domains and to discover the attributes or characteristics of the subset of domains. Briefly, these cognitive systems provide the information that organizes experience for members of a cultural group.

Let me give an example that is relevant to care. Spradley (1972) identified the cultural domain of "making a flop" in a study of skid row tramps. Finding a place to sleep proved culturally revealing in tramp culture because of the variety of places utilized and the wide variety of sociocultural settings that could be related to sleeping behavior. One hundred categories of sleeping places, including paid flop, empty buildings, bathtubs, weed patches, all night laundromats, and used car lots, were named by the informants. Spradley states that tramps emphasize where they sleep whereas most Americans more often refer to how they sleep. For most Americans, "to sleep," does not decode as a place to sleep but rather as a bodily state of rest.

Spradley reports that sleeping behavior, an example of taking-care, has received little attention from social scientists, because there are a relatively small number of places for sleeping in American society. In this way cultural blinders influence what is eligible for investigation. In American society, usually a bed or a place on a bed is the recognized place for sleeping. However, if we choose "napping" behavior as the object of investigation, the cultural domain would enlarge, for among Americans, there are many places to nap, (i.e. chairs, davenports, hammocks, cars, desks, libraries, trains, grass, and so on). This is one example of the kinds of data that are needed in order to understand care as a cultural entity.

In analyzing the components of care in the world of the Papago Indian child I found the phenomenon of "controlling one's thoughts" to be an important subset in the domain of taking-care (Aamodt, 1977). The cultural rule is to avoid angry and envious thoughts. If one does not, sickness or death of oneself or one's relatives may result. Learning this rule is one prerequisite to "becoming Papago," and it is learned in early childhood. For example, a

7-year-old answered, "somebody thoughts me" when he was asked, "What can make you sick?" Thought also controls human experience in other ways. Speaking the name of someone who has died is likely to invoke his or her presence causing illness, misfortune, accident, or fire. If, even before the actual trip, one discusses possible solutions to an accident, these discussions may precipitate the occurrence of such an accident. Also, talking as if something were true may make it true. A 10-year-old cautioned a non-Papago about continuing to talk about not being able to see without glasses: "It might happen . . . it might happen," she urgently warned.

How a system of care links with other cultural subsystems has been reported in the work of Horn (1977), Upreti (1976), and Leininger (1977a). In each study the care system is linked to the social organization of a cultural group. Horn analyzes data from her field experience with the Muckleshoot Indians in the northeastern United States. Caring, according to her informants, is helping, knowing ahead of time what needs to be known, having time to listen, and not refusing a request for help. She identifies rules of taking-care that tell members who to ask for information about health care, who to ask for help, and how to change roles in a kin group when care situations are created. Examples of these rules are:

Relatives who are familiar with what is happening are the ones to ask for help.

Ask your sisters and your family when you need to know something.

When your own mother is not available your aunt is your mother.

Each rule refers, in a different way, to the kinship organization of the community members as well as to the social organization external to the kinship system.

Upreti (1976) analyzes family rituals of child-rearing and their relationship to activities of caring for oneself and others among the Brahmans of Kathmander in Nepal. Pregnancy, for example, prescribes rules of behavior that increase cooperation among family members and shift the center of family activities to the mother and infant. In the first and second trimester, the mother is viewed as polluted and her participation in almost all activities, including religious rituals, is taboo. Thus, in this society, cultural rules legitimate a taking-care role for every mother and facilitate the woman's individual and independent decisions to respond to her need to rest and care for herself in preparation for the birth, growth, and development of her baby. In this example the phenomenon of taking-care is bound with the system of religion, as well as with kinship and role relationships.

The relationship of value and kinship systems to care is reported by Leininger (1977a) in her work among the Gadsup of New Guinea. Female kin provide the majority of caring activities necessary for maintenance of health and prevention of sickness. Male kin assume the curing role of healer when sickness develops. More specifically, women who are closely related to one another are authorities in caring, showing, for example, how to avoid potential sorcerers and sorceresses and how to maintain a "good" Gadsup life. They also provide direct assistance to mothers during pregnancy, monitor female behavior to prevent breakage of cultural rules, and guide the development of appropriate motherly behavior by emphasizing differences between "strong and good mothers" and "weak and bad mothers" when they converse with or counsel young mothers.

Sleeping behavior, controlling thoughts, who to ask for help, what a caregiver should do, ritual activity during pregnancy, and ways of providing health counseling and guidance are patterns for caring behavior in the five cultural systems discussed above. How each of these patterns fits within a cultural system is of critical importance for health care delivery. How each of these activities varies in different cultures, which forms or patterns are universal, and which are unique are questions intriguing to both field worker and theoretician. How a pattern can be changed to fit within another cultural system, thus facilitating quality health care, is a challenge to the promoter of social change.

THE MULTIPERSON ENVIRONMENT AND THE CONCEPT OF CARE

Historically, American health care practice has been characterized by dyads such as mother-infant, physician-patient, nurse-patient, and so on. Emphasis on this two-person interaction is gradually being supplemented with a recognition of the network of individuals that form the personal community of a given member of a society. Documentation of the multiperson environment is evident in many reports of non-Western cultural systems. Knowledge of caring behavior patterns of extended families of Spanish-speaking people, American Indians, and blacks, among others, has increased the sensitivity of social scientists and health professionals to the pervasiveness of the phenomenon of many individuals interacting in situations defined as taking-care.

Papago Indian children interact with many others in an extended family. This pattern has been linked with the multiple health care team available in the Papago health care delivery system (Aamodt 1977). Medicine men, singers, medicine ladies, ladies-who-pray, clinic nurses, and clinic doctors are all part of the health care team. In the same way that there are alternative family members available to a child for counsel, support, and care, so there are also alternative caregivers for child or adult to consult. Taking care of oneself therefore becomes, not a dyadic relationship with one person, but rather an experience of selecting, consciously and unconsciously, from a variety of persons and activities. Choices will vary when rearrangement of culturally constituted stimuli create new situations. Multiple caretaking systems, such as those of the Papago Indian, need to be studied to learn more about possible variations in team membership and the desirable features that will provide optimal health care.

Another form of multiperson environment is the multiple caretaking system utilizing nonparental and parental caretakers that is described by Weisner and Gallimore (1977) in a recent review of child and sibling caretaking. Who assumes responsibility for child care tasks in a household is linked with cultural practices and beliefs. The social structure is one determiner of which individuals are available to assume the role of caretaker. Differential sex status, religious determinants of role performance of community members, and prescriptions for behavior of various age groups are suggested as some of the cultural determiners of who is eligible for caretaking activities. The authors examine the differences between parental caretaking and multiple caretaking, making explicit the caretaking activities of nonparental members in the adult or child community.

In other systems Weisner and Gallimore report that the mother serves as the supervisor of caretakers. This provides a useful strategy for a female worker who has a 5- or 6-year-old child who is able to attend to the activities of a younger brother or sister. The mother monitors from a distance activities such as play, the adherence to rules, and culturally appropriate comforting and cuddling when the smaller child cries because of a fall, hunger, or loneliness. This particular phenomenon has been labeled the concept of the "walking baby carriage." An important objective of Weisner and Gallimore's review is the call for research that could uncover new data on the advantages of multiple caretakers. What nonparental caretaking practice means to quality of life and the optimal experience for both mother and infant is an interesting question. Liberation of the mother and better stimulation for the infant may be contradictory goals. The problem is not only interesting but serious.

A further question concerning multiple caretaking is how active a role the person cared for is given, whether this person is an adult health care client or a child. The phenomenon of the multiperson environment needs to be explored to learn about the optimal variations of caring roles for a given cultural system and which role adaptations should be included in the organization of a health care delivery system.

BELIEF AND THE CONCEPT OF CARE

The cultural domain of care or caring includes beliefs. A belief often depends on what is embued with power. Glick (1967), in describing the cultural systems of illness and responses to illness, suggests we begin with the question, "Where is the power?" Glick further suggests that we look to rules for mobilization of power, forms of resistance to power, and control of power. In other words, we must ask: What is the content of the system of belief about the power of the objects and events in human experience? Rules for behaving in taking-care situations prescribe what holds the power. As we encounter various culturally defined states of well-being, what we believe influences how we interpret our experience.

Experiences such as the blessings of a spiritual leader, the sight of an ancestor "who-has-gone-on," and the presence of a healer invoke various feelings of being cared for in the user of the cultural system. That the objects and events of a healing ritual do not hold the same meaning for different participants does not matter. People are stirred in such ritual situations, and, if only temporarily, reorder their universe in terms that create a whole wherein everything has a new meaning.

Beliefs are learned; processes related to beliefs are beyond the mechanisms related to knowing and understanding. Stomachaches, headaches, itching feet, sore feet, sleepiness, and swollen hands are examples of feeling states that stimulate people to call forth their beliefs. Variation in cultural domains of care that require belief is found in the power of rituals, healers, and certain care activities such as avoidance of cold water, making the sign of the cross when face to face with something holy, combinations of food that predispose to illness, and, in some cultural systems, drinking chicken soup.

How beliefs fit among the elements of a cultural system is important in the implementation of beliefs. Frequently, in the real world of taking care of oneself and others, choices must be made to rank beliefs that are brought into awareness. The reality for all individuals is that implementing a belief may or may not produce the desired result. Mothers, for example, who monitor the status of health and well-being of their children may be called upon to decide which one of two beliefs is most appropriate. One mother reports about a child with difficult respirations: "The breathing is the same and the medicine man made her well then." Another mother said of a child who needed a tracheostomy upon admission to the hospital, "I waited too long!" Yet another mother said to her son of a dangerous lizard who personified a powerful being in their belief system, as she frantically chased the lizard out of the house, ". . . but he's so little." Laughter is another example of appropriate behavior for maintaining well-being (Aamodt 1976). After one hurts one's head, for example, an appropriate response is to look for someone with whom to laugh and thus "take care of oneself."

In each example cited above an alternative cultural rule is available. The mother whose child needed the tracheostomy had a belief system similar to that of the first mother but she interpreted the cause and treatment of the breathing behavior differently. The mother who denied the power of the lizard to her small son knew the difference between the object and the belief. Whereas the son saw the lizard and the Being of Lizard as the same, the mother was aware of the difference and expressed it in terms of the degree of power or potential danger to herself and her family. Caring for oneself with laughter is an alternative to quiet, peace, and rest, or seeking the services of a medicine man, a singer, or a neurologist.

The concept of unbelief provides another dimension to the phenomenon of belief. Children growing up in a multicultural community exhibit various behaviors indicating unbelief. Among Papago Indian boys it is common to throw stones at animals which in the religious system are "beings" embued with power. As they aim the stone they gleefully shout, "If we kill him, he will make us sick." This behavior is followed by laughter that professes their unbelief to whatever audience will listen. In similar fashion, premenstrual young girls suck the juice of lemons as they talk of the dangers to their future health if they persist in this practice. Menstrual blood is believed to back up in their bodies causing their stomachs to become large if they eat lemons or bump hard on their bottoms when they sit down.

The dilemma of the healer in the modern scientific world is that what is "emotional," "feeling," or "esthetic" in a successful regimen is often akin to a magical never-never land where belief prescribes behavior followed by desired results that cannot be explained on any level of analysis. The rationale for such therapy is often legitimized by the principle, *post hoc ergo propter hoc* (since *b* happens after *a*, *b* was therefore caused by *a*). The need for belief, the content of belief, and the processes that are related to belief are important in humanistic health care. Beliefs about taking care of oneself and others will continue to intrigue clients and practitioners alike as long as scientific explanations for human experience in health, illness, and healing are not available.

THE DEVELOPMENTAL PROCESS AND THE PHENOMENON OF CARE

One way of discovering dimensions of care of a particular culture is to examine the processes and content during the enculturation of children. Changes in the content of caring activities and processes are observable during the development of human beings from infancy through aging. Changes during the life cycle of the Papago Indian, for example, relate to food exchange, touching patterns, monitoring the comfort and well-being of others, and controlling one's thoughts (Aamodt, 1977). Throughout the first 18 months of life the child is the care receiver, but soon thereafter begins to take care. A toddler of almost 2 years of age acknowledged the unhappiness of her 4-year-old sister by approaching her with one arm outstretched, standing close, yet not touching her. The mother stood by, immobile and silent, during the dramatic scene. In this situation, the noninterference of the mother was culturally prescribed. Caretaking at other times was observed in the behavior of the 4-year-old holding her 2-year-old sister's hand when she was learning to walk, helping her put on her shoes, offering her pieces of food, and covering the foot of the adult family member because it might be cold.

The child's-eye view provides a source of information on changes in caring behaviors during the life cycle. I reported elsewhere (Aamodt, 1972) that 7-year-old Papago Indian boys view childbirth as a happy, joyful experience, whereas 7-year-old girls seem to view the experience as sickness, identifying elements of going to bed, the doctor, an ambulance, and death.

"What makes you well?" was asked of the same group of youngsters. Deer meat, aspirin, Alka-Seltzer, cough medicine, stomach massage, Band-Aids, and not drinking wine were utilized by the children in stories and drawings of how they got well.

Papago children from two other areas of the reservation served as informants for studies by Kuka (1972) and Clark (1972). This research adds to the list of categories of how children view sickness and taking care of themselves. Kuka interviewed children as they illustrated what was inside of them on an outline of a human body. Her questions related to how the children perceived their bodies, what was in the body, and what it did. Jesus, monsters, the medicine man, valentines, television, cigarettes, catsup, chili, and balloons were some of the referents used to talk about what could be done to and for the human body.

Death, aloneness, and lack of interaction with a caring person were three themes identified by Clark (1972) from drawings and interviews with 7-year-old Papago Indian children in a mission school who were asked about "a time when you were sick." In contrast to the emotionally laden experience of sickness, the question "What made you well?" elicited categories of medicines and medical personnel. Resolving the relationship between the nonpersonal elements that can make someone well with the very personal characteristics of illness as viewed by these children is an interesting focus for further research.

These data represent a small part of the cultural system that prescribes the response of children in this age group in caring situations. The difference between needing and receiving care and the sexual difference in the view toward childbirth are of special interest.

Another developmental change in human beings' perspectives toward the care phenomenon is related to the concept of belief, as mentioned above. Papago children again provide ethnographic data (Aamodt 1977). Eight- and 9-year-old children repeatedly talk about belief. Their questions often relate to beliefs about their cultural system ("It's not true!" "Is it true or not true?") and speculation about whether or not outsiders view their beliefs (what is true in their cultural system) as silly. Discussion of what is true and not true occurs most frequently in early school years until the ages of 11 to 12 years. "They're not going to eat it!" is a comment of small children who pass through the kitchen as food is being prepared for the All Soul's Day Feast for "those-who-had-gone-on."

At yet another time a young boy said, "I don't care if it's true or if it's not true, my father says so and I believe it." This kind of compromise reflects a general response of children to information obtained from the adults in their community.

When children leave the village to attend high school, their perspective on the belief system again changes. At one point the teenager usually becomes a "maybe believer" and asks such questions as: "What do you think is true?" "Do you think our beliefs are silly?" In the middle years of life a return to traditional beliefs is observable in many members of the community. This may be related in part to changes in role expectations as adults assume responsibilities for interpreting cultural beliefs and practices to their own children and, in part, to the children's changing view of the final years of their own life.

How children organize their health care experience is important information for health practitioners. Multicultural children such as these Papago Indian children provide a special source of cultural variation from which generalizations can be developed.

SUMMARY

The concept of care is becoming a central focus of interest for applied anthropologists and health practitioners. A major aim of this chapter has been to illustrate ways in which taking-care-of is a culturally relevant domain that organizes human experience. Four dimensions that relate the care concept to a cultural health and healing system have been briefly explored: the fit in a cultural system of health and healing, the applicability of a multicultural environment for care, the power of belief, and changes in mechanisms of care during the life cycle of human beings.

This brief analysis has barely skimmed the surface of a very complex phenomenon. Formal treatment and elaboration of care phenomena are needed. Ethnographic interviews (the insider's view) and detailed observations (the outsider's view) of activities of taking care of self and others are essential to the task of providing qualitative data from which generalizations can be derived. The contributions to health care and quality human experience will be great.

REFERENCES

Aamodt, A. M. 1972. The child's view of health and healing. In M. V. Batey, ed. Communicating nursing research. Western Council for Higher Education in Nursing 5:38-54.
Aamodt, A. M. 1976. Observations of a health and healing system of a Papago community. In M. Leininger, ed. Transcultural health care issues and conditions. F. A. Davis, Philadelphia.

Aamodt, A. M. 1977. Socio-cultural dimensions of caring in the world of the Papago child and adolescent. In M. Leininger, ed. Transcultural nursing care of infants and children. University of Utah College of Nursing, Salt Lake City.

Clark, M. J. 1972. Cultural patterns of health and healing beliefs in a Papago child's society. Master's thesis. University of Arizona, Tucson.

Glick, L. B. 1967. Medicine as an ethnographic category: The Gioni of the New Guinea Highlands. Ethnology 6:31-55.

Goodenough, W. H. 1957. Cultural anthropology and linguistics. In P. Garvin, ed. Georgetown University round table on language and linguistics, Georgetown University Press, Washington, D.C.

Horn, B. M. 1977. Transcultural nursing and childrearing of the Muckleshoot people. In M. Leininger, ed. Transcultural nursing care of infants and children. University of Utah College of Nursing, Salt Lake City.

Hyde, A. 1975. The phenomenon of caring: Part I. Nursing Research Report 10(1):1-2, 10-11.

Hyde, A. 1976. The phenomenon of caring: Parts II, III. Nursing Research Report 11:2,15.

Hyde, A. 1977. The phenomenon of caring: Part VI. Nursing Research Report 12:2.

Johnson, D. E. 1959. The nature of the science of nursing. Nursing Outlook 1(5):291-294.

Krueter, F. R. 1957. What is good nursing care? Nursing Outlook 7(5):302-304.

Kuka, S. A. 1972. The Papago child's view of body parts. Master's thesis. University of Arizona, Tucson.

Leininger, M. 1972. Leininger's conceptual model for studying transcultural nursing (ethnonursing). Unpublished manuscript.

Leininger, M. 1977a. The Gadsup of New Guinea and early child-caring behaviors with nursing care implications. In M. Leininger, ed. Transcultural nursing care of infants and children. University of Utah College of Nursing, Salt Lake City.

Leininger, M. 1977b. Caring: The essence and central focus of nursing: The phenomenon of caring: Part V. Nursing Research Report 12(1):2, 14.

Nightingale, F. 1859. Notes on nursing. Appleton-Century Crofts, New York.

Spradley, J. P., ed. 1972. Culture and cognition. Chandler and Co., San Francisco.

Spradley, J., and McCurdy, D. W. 1972. The cultural experience. Science Research Associates, Inc., Chicago.

Titt, D. 1966. The case for care. Presented to the Council of Member Agencies. The National League for Nursing, Seattle.

Turnbull, C. 1972. The mountain people. Simon and Schuster, New York.

Upreti, N. S. 1976. Family ritual in child rearing practices: Its implications in nursing practice. Unpublished paper presented to the American Nurses Association, Atlantic City, N.J.

Weisner, T. S., and Gallimore, R. 1977. My brother's keeper: Child and sibling caretaking. Current Anthropology 18(2):169-190.

CHAPTER 5

The profile of some unplanned pregnancies

Shirley M. Johnson
Loudell F. Snow

It has long been known that various combinations of medical and sociodemographic factors contribute to the labeling of a woman as one who is at high risk for pregnancy (Lewis and Patwary 1973; Lesinski 1975; Dott 1976). Medical personnel use such factors to identify those women who need special care and attention throughout their pregnancies if their health and that of their infants is not to be further jeopardized. Medical risks include unfavorable combinations of age and parity, birth interval of less than 2 years, past history of miscarriage or premature birth, and other medical conditions complicating pregnancy.

Social risks include single marital status, membership in a nonwhite ethnic group, less than a high school education for the mother, and living in poverty. It also has been demonstrated that stressful life situations may contribute to pregnancy complications, and this is especially true if the woman lacks a viable support system (Nuckolls et al., 1972; Rabkin and Struening, 1976). Unfortunately, in many cases those women who need the most specialized medical attention often receive no prenatal care, or seek care so late in their pregnancies that little can be done to alter their poor health status.

In 1975 a study was done in a prenatal clinic in mid-Michigan in which the majority of women using the facility were high risk patients for pregnancy. Most of the patients were young, poor, and not well educated; many were single, separated, or divorced. The clinic serves a multiethnic population and ordinary communication problems were compounded by the fact that many women were more comfortable speaking Spanish than English; in some instances patients spoke no English at all. The majority of women also had medical histories placing them at risk, a fact exacerbated by their tendency to arrive for prenatal care when their pregnancies were far advanced. One purpose of the research was to establish if what the women knew and believed about the female reproductive cycle contributed to their ability to plan pregnancies or resulted in undesirable health behaviors.

A questionnaire was developed and administered over a 3 month period to half of all patients arriving at the clinic for their first prenatal visit (N = 31); participating patients were paid a fee of $10.00. Information gathered included demographic details, knowledge and beliefs on menstruation, venereal disease, childbearing, contraception, abortion, pregnancy and birth, and the menopause. A final section dealt with the patient's personal experiences and feelings about health care. All interviews were conducted by women and took approximately 2 hours to complete. Data compiled from the questionnaires were fed into a computer programmed to handle open-ended multiresponse information, and individual and summary data were tabulated from the computer printouts.

RESULTS

Analysis of the data shows that nearly half of the women interviewed (N = 14/31, 45%) had had one or more unplanned pregnancies. It is these women who are the focus of this chapter. Their responses were examined for information about their knowledge of reproduction and for misinformation that might be significant in their ability to prevent pregnancy. Individual responses were also carefully analyzed for their views of why the pregnancy had occurred. On the basis of this information, we made assessments as to whether each of the women would be able to control her fertility in the future.

The ages of the women ranged from 17 to 35 years with a mean age of 23 years. Their educational level varied from 9 years to 13 years, with a mean of 11 years. Two of the women were black, 1 was an American Indian, 3 were Mexican-American, and the remaining 8 were white. Twelve of the 14 were living in poverty as determined by the clinic's own economic guidelines.*

Six women were married, three were separated from their husbands, two were divorced, and three were single. The bare statistics, however, reveal nothing of the variety of living arrangements some of the women had made in response to their marginal socioeconomic status. Only three of them lived in a "normal" nuclear family, that is, husband and children included. Two married women lived in households containing their husband and two unrelated adult males. The other married woman lived in a household consisting of her husband and son, her mother, brother, sister, four members of another family, and one additional unrelated person. Two women lived in extended families; one included the patient, her brother and their grandmother; the other lived with her two children, her sister and brother-in-law, and their two children. One woman shared a home with her employer and employer's four children, where she served as housekeeper/babysitter; because of her own pregnancy, however, she had lost her position and was looking for a place of her own. Finally, five women were living alone with their child or children. Knowing the marital status of a woman gives little information as to the social support system available to her, or much information about the type of household the new infant is entering.

At the time of the interview, the women had had 25 previous pregnancies ($\overline{X} = 1.8$) and had 20 living children ($\overline{X} = 1.4$); 13 of

them were pregnant again, raising the number of pregnancies to 38 ($\overline{X} = 2.1$). One woman proved not to be pregnant, but to have amenorrhea for medical reasons (hyperthyroidism, adrenal imbalance, diabetes mellitus); a few months later, however, she too conceived. Six of the 14 women had histories of miscarriage or premature birth, and another had given birth to a child with severe malformations requiring surgical intervention. All of the other women had either some other medical risk* or presented unfavorable combinations of age, parity, and birth interval, which made them at risk for this pregnancy (Table 1). In short, *all of these women who had been unable to control their fertility were at risk for their pregnancies,* which could only be compounded by future childbearing.

Despite their unfavorable histories, however, only 3 of the 14 women came in for prenatal care during the first trimester of pregnancy. The overall entry into the medical care system ranged from 8 weeks to 35.5 weeks gestation ($\overline{X} \times 22$ weeks). One woman, in fact, gave birth the week after her first and only prenatal appointment and was interviewed in the maternity ward after delivery of her seventh child.

UNDERSTANDING OF THE MENSTRUAL CYCLE

The ability to control fertility is based on understanding the menstrual cycle. Women who are depending upon the rhythm method to prevent conception must know when ovulation is most likely to occur and avoid intercourse at that time. Those methods that are used at the time of intercourse, for example, the condom, spermicides, or the diaphragm, must be used correctly and consistently if they are to be effective. In this study, the women's lack of knowledge about the menstrual cycle and the lack of understanding about contraceptive methods and their proper use made the occurrence of unwanted pregnancies a certainty; there was no way that they could be avoided.

The women did not understand the function and the part that the menstrual cycle plays in fertility (Table 2). In some instances,

---

*The clinic had a sliding fee schedule based on income and number of dependents. A family of three with income of $6,300 or less, for example, would be considered in poverty and pay no fees. In one instance a woman, her husband, and four children had a total income of $2,811 per year; the coming child could not help but be an added economic burden.

---

*Medical risks included hypertension, tuberculosis, venereal disease, severe anemia, diabetes mellitus, drug use (mescaline and LSD), and thyroid disease.

Table 1. Patients having social and medical risks for pregnancy (N = 14)

Patient number	Education < high school	Single, separated, or divorced	Living in poverty	History of miscarriage or premature birth	History of other medical problems contributing to risk	Maternal age a risk factor	Parity a risk factor	Birth interval <2 years	Gravida	Week came in for care
1	X	X	X	XX		X	X	X	3	20
2	X	X	X		X		X	X	3	30
3	X		X	X	X	X	X		7	35.5
4	X		X		X			X	2	20
5	X		X	X		X			3	32
6	X		X				X		3	20
7		X	X		X		X		3	24
8				X	X				1	8
9		X	X				X		3	10
10		X	X		X	X			1	12
11		X	X	X	X		X		5	33.5
12		X	X		X				1	16
13		X			X			X	2	20
14			X	X	X				2	31

Table 2. Patient knowledge of menstruation and menopause (N = 14)

Patient number	Does not understand function of menses	Does not know time of ovulation	Does not know "safe" time for intercourse	Avoids intercourse during menses	Does not know possibility of pregnancy during menopausal years	Does not know special maternal risk in menopausal pregnancy	Does not know special risk to fetus in menopausal pregnancy
1	X	X	X	X	X	X	X
2	X	X	X	X		X	X
3	X		X	X			X
4	X	X	X				X
5	X	X	X	X	X	X	X
6	X	X	X		X	X	X
7	X	X	X	X		X	X
8	X				X	X	X
9	X						
10						X	X
11	X	X	X				
12		X	X	X		X	
13		X	X	X	X	X	X
14						X	X

this doubtlessly contributed to pregnancy. Ten of the 14 women (71%) were unable to correctly answer the questions (1) Where does menstrual blood come from? (2) Why do the menstrual periods begin when they do? and (3) Why do the menstrual periods stop when they do? The women were also questioned as to which times they thought intercourse was most likely to lead to pregnancy. As Table 2 shows, 64% did not know the time of ovulation and 71% could not accurately state the "safe" time for intercourse. Likewise, their ignorance of the menstrual cycle was apparent when they were questioned about its cessation at menopause. Five women, for example, did not realize that it is possible to become pregnant during the menopausal years, and there was little knowledge that such a pregnancy might be unwise. Ten of the 14 women (71%) were unaware that there was additional maternal risk with such a pregnancy. Eleven more (79%) did not know there might be special problems for the child conceived in this life phase. This was particularly disturbing, since these women had already demonstrated their inability to control pregnancy and were found not to have the knowledge needed to do so. Probably, therefore, they were already more likely to continue childbearing into their later years. They already had poor obstetrical histories, which would only compound with each additional pregnancy.

Although the women do not have the correct information about menstruation they do have a variety of folk beliefs which makes the process plausible to them (Snow and Johnson 1977). These beliefs do little to help them prevent conception and, in some instances, probably contribute to pregnancy. For example, many of the women think the purpose of menstruation is to remove collected impurities from the body, and that anything that interrupts this process might endanger their health. A contraceptive method that lessens or even stops menstrual flow (oral contraceptives, for example) may produce anxiety for these patients. They seem to see the uterus as an organ that slowly fills with tainted blood and then opens to let it drain out during menstruation. This view of menstruation as a cleansing process also has been found among lower class women of different ethnic groups and white middle class

teenagers in the United States (Scott, 1975; Whisnant and Zegans, 1975). Unfortunately, this logically leads many women to see impregnation most likely to take place immediately before the menses, when the uterus is beginning to open, during the menses, when it is open completely, and immediately after the menses, before the uterus is entirely closed again. They may then be having unprotected intercourse at a time when they think they are "safe," that is, at mid-cycle, when they believe the uterus to be closed so that sperm cannot enter.

Further, there is a strong feeling on the part of many women that intercourse should be avoided during the menses, making it more likely for it to take place later in the cycle. Seven of 14 patients reported that they did not have intercourse at that time; 2 felt that they were more likely to become pregnant, and the other 5 felt it would be injurious to their health, causing cramps, heavy bleeding and/or infection. Again, contraceptive methods that either produce breakthrough bleeding (oral contraceptives) or increased flow or spotting (intrauterine device) may be problematic for women who feel they must avoid intercourse when vaginal bleeding occurs.

USE AND UNDERSTANDING OF CONTRACEPTION

The women who had had an unplanned pregnancy were aware of available methods of contraception and 12 of the 14 women had attempted to control their fertility by contraceptive use. They had tried on the average three different methods of contraception. The majority of the women (71%) believed the use of contraception to be the woman's responsibility, particularly since she has the baby. Four of the women felt contraception should be shared by both male and female. Despite the fact that 4 unplanned pregnancies were attributed to failure of exclusively male methods (condom and withdrawal) not one of the women at the time of interview felt that contraception was the sole responsibility of the male.

The women were well-informed about the relative effectiveness of contraceptive methods. When asked to name the method of contraception they believed to be most effective, and also to name their own most effective method, the majority of the women identified either "the pill" or the IUD. In spite of their awareness the women were not successful in preventing pregnancy (Table 3); 10 of the 14 indicated that they had failed to prevent a pregnancy while using a method of contraception. Although they knew of the availability of effective methods, their failures mainly resulted from use of less effective methods, for example, douching (2 failures by one woman), withdrawal (3 failures), breastfeeding (1 failure), rhythm (1 failure), and foam (1 failure). Four other unplanned pregnancies occurred while the condom, diaphragm, or oral contraceptives was the method used. When asked why they thought they had become pregnant while practicing contraception, the women's answers revealed a pattern of inconsistent or incorrect use of the methods. In some cases the women forgot to take the pill or did not use the diaphragm each time intercourse occurred. In another instance a woman using the rhythm method "did not watch the calendar carefully." In still others, failure was attributed to the male who did not withdraw in time.

It has been shown that the women lacked correct information regarding the "safe" time for intercourse and did not know the most fertile time during the menstrual cycle. This knowledge deficit was of critical importance when these women attempted to prevent pregnancy with methods that not only required high motivation but also accurate information about the fertility cycle. For example, the motivation necessary to effectively use a coitus-connected method (withdrawal, douche, foam, condom, or diaphragm) must be maintained for every act of intercourse or, at the very least, linked to a reasonable awareness of the most likely fertile period during the cycle. A woman who believes she is most likely to become pregnant during the menses is not necessarily going to be greatly concerned if she fails to use such a method at mid-cycle. Further, a woman who really does not understand the rhythm method, since she states that she does not know how or why it works, may understandably fail to watch her calendar carefully. A new mother who does not know that pregnancy can occur a few weeks after birth or who believes she is safe from another pregnancy as long as the menses has not returned, is certainly not going to consider using other methods of contraception during that time.

Table 3. Unplanned pregnancy with contraceptive use (N = 10)

Patient number	Method used when pregnancy occurred	Method used incorrectly	Did not possess necessary information about method
1	Foam	X	
3	Withdrawal	X	
4	Breastfeeding		X
5	Withdrawal	X	
6	Withdrawal	X	
7			
	Douching (failure 1)	X	X
	Douching (failure 2)	X	X
8	Rhythm	X	X
9			
	Condom (failure 1)	X	X
	Oral contraceptive (failure 2)	X	X
10	Diaphragm	X	
11	Oral contraceptive	X	

Four women in this study had an unplanned pregnancy but were not using any method of contraception at the time of conception. Their experiences exemplify how easily patients can be misled by false assumptions based upon their own experiences, or possible misinterpretation of information presented to them by health practitioners.

Patient 2 was a 21-year-old woman who had not used contraception from the time she became sexually active as a teenager. It took her 2 years of unprotected intercourse to achieve pregnancy (perhaps due to adolescent anovulatory cycles). She assumed her postpartum experiences would be similar and that it would not be necessary to take protective measures for 2 years; she was wrong and became pregnant.

Patient 12 also became pregnant while not using a method to prevent conception. She said that a doctor once told her she was sterile; she was not, and became pregnant.

Patient 13 had used oral contraception for 3 years before discontinuance to achieve a planned pregnancy; it was 6 months before she became pregnant. She then mistakenly assumed that it would take at least that long postpartum for fertility to be restored. She postulated that because she and her husband had refrained from intercourse for 6 weeks after the birth of their child, his sperm had "built up," contributing to this pregnancy.

Patient 14 also became pregnant while not using a method to prevent conception. She too had a history of contraceptive use, but reportedly had had such severe side effects from using the pill and the IUD that she assumed she could not become pregnant. She was wrong, resulting in an unplanned pregnancy.

Anderson and coworkers (1977) reported selection of highly effective contraceptive methods by women who had had unwanted pregnancies, and these investigators expected that use of these methods would prevent recurrence. Since all 14 women in our subsample had had at least one unplanned pregnancy it was of interest to determine if they planned to use contraception in the future. The women reported that they all intended to do so, and most of them indicated that they, too, would use highly effective methods: oral contraceptives (1), sterilization

(3), or IUD (1). Two women intended to use breastfeeding with condom or diaphragm and foam and one woman planned to use breastfeeding only (Table 4).

At first glance the responses to this question are encouraging; the selection of such effective methods by these women who had had an unplanned pregnancy seemed to indicate that they would be able to plan if and when they wanted to produce another child. However, a closer examination of the women's knowledge of how contraceptive methods are used and the mechanisms of action indicate that they did not possess the basic, essential information needed to correctly and consistently use the method they had chosen. Eight of the 11 women who had selected reversible methods of contraception, chose a method that they had either used inconsistently in the past, or one that had produced troublesome side effects which led to its discontinuation. The combination of their knowledge deficits, their history of side effects and/or inconsistent use of the chosen method points to a high potential for yet another failure by 11 of these 14 women (79%) in their future attempts to control their fertility (Table 4).

LACK OF KNOWLEDGE AND MISINFORMATION IN MEDICALLY RELATED AREAS

These women all possessed risk factors that increase the potential for pregnancy complications. In most instances their incomes were low and a child would be an economic burden. Despite this, they had elected to continue the pregnancy and all wished to produce a healthy infant.* As previously noted, however, their first visits for prenatal care were rather late, and they did not seem to see early entry into the health care setting as necessarily contributing to good pregnancy outcome. Part of this may be explained by the fact that they often did not understand the clinical procedures, or believed the procedures to be for purposes that they saw as unrelated to pregnancy.

All, for example, had a pelvic examination

---

*One patient whose amenorrhea was caused by medical conditions was quite disappointed that she was not pregnant at this time and was pleased to achieve a pregnancy some months later.

Table 4. Planned use of contraception and potential for failure (N = 14)

Patient number	Method to be used in future	Does not understand necessary information about method	Has had history of side effects or inconsistent use of proposed method	Potential for failure or discontinuing use
1	Sterilization			X*
2	Oral contraceptive			
3	Oral contraceptive	X	X	X
4	Foam + breastfeeding then oral contraceptive	X		X
5	Oral contraceptive	X	X	X
6	IUD then sterilization	X X	X	X
7	Sterilization	X		
8	Oral contraceptive	X	X	X
9	Oral contraceptive		X	X
10	Oral contraceptive		X	X
11	Sterilization			
12	Breastfeeding	X		X
13	Oral contraceptive		X	X
14	Breastfeeding + condom or diaphragm	X	X	X

*Denied postpartum sterilization because of minor status.

on their first clinical visit. When asked what information such an examination makes available to the doctor, two of the women said that they did not know. The other 12 gave several answers, only three of which directly concerned the pregnancy: to see if the woman is pregnant; to examine the pelvic structure during pregnancy; to check the position of the baby. Some answers were vague: to see if something is wrong; to look for disease; to see if the organs are all right. A number of other responses were more specific: the doctor is looking for infection (2); for cancer (4); for venereal disease (4).

All of the patients had also had a Pap smear made at the time of the pelvic exam, and they were asked if they knew its purpose: again, 2 women said that they did not know, and although 6 of the answers included a check for cancer, 5 had to do again with venereal disease. Since venereal disease is a

risk factor in pregnancy, the women were asked a series of questions designed to determine their knowledge about these infectious diseases. The women were reticent and embarrassed about discussing them.

Although 11 of the 14 women mentioned sexual contact as a possible mode of contracting such diseases, it was by no means the only possibility mentioned. Four of the women also believed that one can acquire venereal disease by simply being dirty, or by sleeping with too many men, none of whom is necessarily infected. One of these young women, in fact, had had gonorrhea the year before, but was still naive about its etiology, and suggested that lack of cleanliness may have been a factor.

The women were particularly unwilling to discuss, or were misinformed about the exact nature of, venereal diseases, the symptomatology, how they are cured, and why reinfection is possible. Their responses to these questions were evaluated for the relative risk that lack of information would present in their ability to prevent or control these diseases; on this basis 9 women (64%) were found to be "at risk" in their knowledge of venereal disease.

All of the women in this group are aware of the fact that venereal disease in the pregnant woman can affect the baby, although their overall knowledge deficit of all other aspects of venereal disease may preclude them from effectively utilizing this knowledge. If a woman does not know exactly what venereal diseases are, does not know the nature of the symptoms, believes that these diseases are contracted from being dirty or promiscuous (and she has not been), the necessity for laboratory examinations early in pregnancy for venereal disease may not be seen as urgent. In this clinic most patients interviewed had arrived for prenatal care after the time that a fetus would already have been infected by syphilis. In one study of venereal disease during pregnancy, not only was it found that more than 7% of the new patients at a prenatal clinic had gonorrhea, but also a 30% rate of reinfection occurred later in pregnancy (*Infectious Diseases*, 1976).

The women were not entirely clear about the necessity for some of the procedures done at the clinic: pelvic examinations, Pap smears, or tests for venereal disease. Their understanding was further jeopardized by the fact that they did not comprehend many of the medical terms used by the clinic staff. At the request of the clinic director, the women were questioned about a number of these terms, first being asked if they had ever heard of them, and, if they had, if they could explain what they meant. Table 5 combines their lack of knowledge of the terms and the amount of misinformation the women had. One young woman could not identify a single term although this was her third pregnancy, and none of the women could properly define them all.

Folk beliefs may also affect health in a negative manner by contributing to anxiety and stress for the individual. In this study these

Table 5. Medical terminology not understood by patients (N = 14)

Patient number	Forceps	Circumcision	Episiotomy	Toxemia	Hysterectomy	Anemia	Hormones	Pap smear
1	X	X	X	X	X	X	X	X
2	X	X	X	X	X		X	X
3			X				X	
4		X	X	X			X	X
5	X		X	X			X	X
6	X		X	X			X	
7	X	X	X	X	X		X	
8	X		X				X	X
9			X	X			X	
10			X	X	X	X	X	X
11			X				X	
12			X					X
13	X		X	X	X			X
14				X				X

beliefs were particularly evident in the folk-lore surrounding pregnancy; it was clearly a time of great unease, and the women's beliefs helped make it so. An overwhelming concern was that their own prenatal behavior might result in miscarriage or fetal death and/or might permanently "mark" the child. Thirteen of the 14 women (93%) stated that lifting or hard work on the part of the mother might result in loss of the child, possibly adding unnecessary feelings of guilt to those who had histories of such pregnancy wastage. Two women also believed that if the mother stretched her arms over her head the cord might wrap around the neck of the fetus and strangle it.

Ten of the women believed their prenatal behavior might mark the child; that an unsatisfied craving for a certain food could result in a birthmark; that a woman who makes fun of a cripple may have her unborn baby crippled as a punishment; that a frightening sight may be imprinted on the unborn child. This belief in maternal behavior directly affecting the child was also examplified by the remarks of two of the women who thought if a pregnant woman smoked tobacco it could affect the unborn baby's breathing: ". . . the baby may inhale some smoke down there." It is small wonder that these women did not see early prenatal care as a factor in producing healthy babies.

SUMMARY

In these 14 women selected from a larger sample of prenatal patients all of the commonly identified medical and sociodemographic pregnancy risk factors were present. These factors may call attention to the woman who is at special risk for delivery; they do not, however, explain why and how she may have failed to prevent a pregnancy which could endanger her health or the health of her infant. We have shown that what women know and believe about the menstrual cycle and its relationship to fertility directly affects their ability to plan pregnancies. We have demonstrated that the potential for contraceptive failure is enhanced when a woman does not truly understand the contraceptive method she has been using or plans to use in the future. We believe that patients' failure to understand commonly used medical terminology contributes to feelings of mystification in medical settings and perhaps to noncompliance with suggested health regimens.

What significance do such findings have for preventing unplanned pregnancies in the future? It seems obvious that the knowledge base of all female patients should be evaluated on an individual basis. Many health professionals do not determine what a woman knows about her own body and how it functions before a method of contraception is recommended or chosen. We believe that such individual assessment must be made and information presented in easily understood language if women are to be able to successfully decide when and if they wish to bear children.

REFERENCES

Anderson, J. E., Morris, L., and Gesche, M. 1977. Contraceptive use at the time of conception for pregnancies resulting in unwanted births. Contraception **15**:705-110.

Dott, A. B., and Fort, A. T. 1976. Medical and social factors affecting early teenage pregnancy. American Journal of Obstetrics and Gynecology **125**:532-536.

Infectious Diseases. 1976. Incidence of gonorrhea in pregnancy alarmingly high in hospital study. **6**:15.

Lesinski, J. 1975. High-risk pregnancy: Unresolved problems of screening, management, and prognosis. Obstetrics and Gynecology **46**:599-603.

Lewis, R., Charles, M., and Patwary, K. M. 1973. Relationships between birth weight and selected social, environmental and medical care factors. American Journal of Public Health **63**:973-981.

Nuckolls, K. B., Cassel, J., and Kaplan, B. H. 1972. Psychosocial assets, life crisis and the prognosis of pregnancy. American Journal of Epidemiology **95**: 431-441.

Rabkin, J. G., and Struening, E. L., 1976. Life events, stress, and illness. Science **194**:1013-1020.

Scott, C. S. 1975. The relationship between beliefs about the menstrual cycle and choice of fertility regulating methods within five ethnic groups. International Journal of Gynaecology and Obstetrics **13**:105-109.

Snow, L. F., and Johnson, S. M. 1977. Modern day menstrual folklore. Some clinical implications. Journal of the American Medical Association **237**:2136-2139.

Whisnant, L., and Zegans, L. 1975. A study of attitudes toward menarche in white middle-class American adolescent girls. American Journal of Psychiatry **82**: 809-814.

CHAPTER 6

Home births: a reaction to hospital environmental stressors

Eleanor Bauwens
Sandra Anderson

Anthropologists talk about culture shock as a reaction that occurs when an individual is placed in an unfamiliar situation. Culture shock results from multiple environmental stressors impinging upon the individual. Environmental stressors may be viewed in the hospital setting as elements that confront the pregnant woman. Perhaps, because of these stressors there is an increasing number of health care consumers who demonstrate dissatisfaction with the present maternity care system by choosing a home birth.

The trend toward home births in recent years has been documented in newspaper articles, professional journals, and lay magazines. Is this trend toward out-of-hospital births an expression of consumer dissatisfaction with hospital maternity care? Why are women again choosing home births? Does the pregnant woman experience dissonance with hospital routines? What environmental stressors in the hospital setting affect the pregnant woman? The purposes of this chapter are to identify the factors associated with the environmental stressors in the hospital subculture, and to discuss the dissonance that occurs with hospital births.

When one looks at the historical perspective, one sees that there is currently a reversal in the well-established custom that the hospital is the only acceptable place to deliver a baby. The proportion of births occurring in hospitals was about 50% in 1950, and has increased to 99% in 1975 (Stewart and Stewart, 1977). However, a change in the commonly accepted setting for childbirth, the hospital, has been documented for the years 1971–1973 when 287 home births took

place in one California county. These home births represent 10% of the 2900 births that occurred in this one California county during these 3 years. Midwives have estimated that three times as many home births had actually occurred in this county during this time (Mehl et al., 1975).

The trend toward home births in a metropolitan Arizona county also has been documented. For example, in 1940, 679 (42.6%) of the births in this county were nonhospital births. Within 10 years (1940–1950), the number of nonhospital births dramatically decreased to 393 (10.0%). Since then, the number has steadily declined to a low of 38 (0.5%) home births in 1971. However, during the years 1972 through 1976, there was an increasing trend toward home births in this county as indicated by 69 (1.1%) registered home births in 1975 and 89 (1.2%) registered home births in 1976 (Pima County Health Department). The choice of a home birth appears to be one method consumers are selecting to meet their own needs during the childbearing event.

THE STUDY SAMPLE

The sample consisted of 69 mothers who had a home birth during 1975 in an Arizona metropolitan county. The mean age for the mothers in the sample was 25.4 years. All mothers were Anglo. Fifty-six mothers (81%) were married. Forty mothers (59%) had attended college with 4 (6%) completing 5 or more years. Twenty-four (35%) of the mothers had experienced a previous delivery. Of the remaining 45 mothers, 36 (80%) previously had experienced a hospital delivery.

Sixty mothers (96%) received prenatal care and 36 mothers (60%) went to a private physician for their care. Thirty-two (46%) began prenatal care during the first trimester of pregnancy, 19 (28%) during the second trimester, and 9 (13%) during the third trimester of pregnancy. Nine mothers (13%) received no prenatal care.

In summary, the demographic profile of the study population indicates that the home birth families were not young, uneducated members of a counterculture group. This finding corresponds with previous home birth studies in other areas of the country (Healy, 1972; Hazell, 1974; Chase, 1976).

CHOICE OF A HOME BIRTH AS AN ADAPTIVE RESPONSE

Why are women again choosing home births? According to Hazell (personal communication, 1978) those who choose out-of-hospital births:

a. Believe that the individual is responsible for her own health.
b. Believe that the choice of place, companions, and method of birth rests with the individual, rather than with the doctor or hospital.
c. Define health or illness in terms different from those of standard American medical practice.
d. Believe that the hospital is not necessarily the safest place to give birth.
e. Assume that the responsibility for the birth outcome is theirs, not the hospital's.
f. View the standard medical practice of the hospital as often causing unnecessary physical and/or psychological trauma and interference.
g. Distrust the conventional health care delivery system.

These items point out that there is a basic dissonance and lack of consensus between the consumer who chooses out-of-hospital birth and the health professions concerning their value system, their individual roles, and those services that are viewed as essential by each.

Bateson (1944:273) has remarked that, "The human individual is endlessly simplifying, organizing, and generalizing his own view of his environment; he constantly imposes his own constructions and meanings; these constructions and meanings [are] characteristic of one culture as over against another."

Specific patterns of behavior are influenced by the individual's value system. All individuals must find some solutions for basic human needs. These solutions are variable and are the result of individuals' attempts at simplifying and coping with their environment. The solutions may be interpreted as adaptive mechanisms. These adaptive responses include cultural behaviors that overturn or disrupt existing societal conditions in order to satisfy needs, and ". . . when the stimuli confronting the person forms a discrepancy with the person's unique perceptions, values, and/or cognitive organization, the mind acts to reduce the dissonance and to make an adaptive response" (Roy, 1976:4).

THEORY OF DISSONANCE APPLIED TO HOSPITAL BIRTHS

Festinger (1957:3) has stated two basic hypotheses dealing with dissonance:

1. The existence of dissonance, being psychologically uncomfortable, will motivate the person to try to reduce the dissonance and achieve consonance.
2. When dissonance is present, in addition to trying to reduce it, the person will actively avoid situations and information which would likely increase the dissonance.

Festinger describes dissonance as the existence of nonfitting relations among any knowledge, opinion, or belief about the environment, about oneself, or about one's behavior; in other words, two elements that do not fit together and which may be contradictory cultural standards. This contradiction or inconsistency is illustrated by childbearing families who desire to have control over the environment but are fearful that they will be powerless in the hospital setting.

Since reduction of dissonance is a basic process in humans, Festinger is not surprised that its manifestation may be observed in such a wide variety of contexts. Activity oriented toward reducing dissonance is experienced by mothers when hospital rules and regulations, medical policies, habits, customs, and rituals are made compulsory for all those seeking obstetrical care in the hospital setting. Anthropologists have studied hospitals as a separate culture or as a subculture of the larger society. The woman in labor must become acquainted with the hospital and its particular sociocultural system at a time when she is preoccupied with the birth of her baby. Therefore, she is a prime candidate for culture shock; that is, she is placed in an unfamiliar situation in which former coping mechanisms are ineffective. Although the pregnant woman may not consider herself ill, entry into the hospital demands an abrupt transition, which includes accepting a state of dependency. This new role in a new setting can be seen as a stressor "that requires not only adjustments in life style, but also in self-perception" (Brink, 1976:134).

ENVIRONMENTAL STRESSORS

Brink (1976) lists five environmental stressors that make the hospital experience conducive to culture shock: (1) communication, (2) mechanical differences, (3) customs, (4) isolation, and (5) attitudes and beliefs. Each of these stressors will be discussed in relation to hospital births.

Communication. The woman will be confronted with obstetrical jargon, which may leave her confused and uninformed. For example, "Speed up the pit. She's not progressing."

Mechanical differences. The woman will be required to cope with routine technological interventions, which may restrict her activity and her choices. For example, she may be attached to a fetal monitor; intravenous feeding may be used; analgesics may be administered. All of these confine the laboring woman to the hospital bed.

Customs. The woman is expected to know both the hospital's customs and appropriate patient role behaviors. A major thrust in childbirth education classes is that of preparing the woman and her family to cope with the foreign environment of a hospital obstetrical unit. Unfortunately, this orientation to the stresses of the hospital setting decreases the time available for the family to learn about labor, birth, and the newborn.

Isolation. In most areas husbands are "allowed" in the labor room if all goes well. Siblings or other friends and family members are usually excluded. However, husbands are still locked out of the delivery room at the whim of the obstetrician or hospital. Following the birth, hospitals usually have rigid visitation policies, which exclude siblings and often even limit husband visitation.

Attitudes and beliefs. The pregnant woman values and would like to expect personalized care. The focus of the hospital staff tends to reduce individualistic considerations. For example, being treated as "the patient in labor room B" limits one's individual image and respect. At this special time the pregnant woman is a low-status subordinate in the hospital hierarchy. In present day hospital obstetrics, the prevalent attitude of control and management leans toward a dependence on the tools of technology, not to open communication and mutual problem-solving. More and more pregnant women want to make decisions about their health care; however, hospital staff often act on the assumption that it is to the patient's advantage to be uninformed or that she does not have the right to know about herself or the birth process (Brink, 1976).

REASONS FOR CHOOSING HOME BIRTH

One way to avoid the environmental stressors in the hospital setting is to choose a home birth. Thus it is important to discover the factors associated with a woman's choice to have a home birth. In order to obtain these data, the question was asked, "What factors played a part in your decision to have this child at home?" Forty-six (67%) mothers responded that they preferred a more personal atmosphere. The individual comments included the following statements:

> "Husband could be with me."
> "Father could deliver and other children could observe delivery."
> "Wanted a very peaceful atmosphere to transfer this feeling to baby."
> "Felt need of family closeness."
> "Child should come into world in its own home."
> "Home atmosphere is more like the womb—very peaceful."
> "Wanted father of baby to be more involved—he felt shut out with previous hospital birth—not allowed to hold child."

The question concerning the choice of having this baby at home prompted 31 (45%) mothers to make negative comments about hospitals. Some of these comments were:

> "Rules in the hospital are too rigid."
> "Hospitals are for the sick and childbirth is not an illness."

"Felt defenseless in position for birth with stirrups."

"Hospitals are too full of germs."

"Not comfortable in a hospital."

"Don't like the bright lights in a hospital."

"Hospitals make you a co-star, at home you are the star."

"Hospitals are more for the doctors' conveniences."

"Everyone talks about a hospital birth as if it were a nightmare."

In order to determine dissonance, questions were asked about satisfaction-dissatisfaction with previous births. The following questions were asked: "Where was your last child delivered? Were you satisfied with that delivery?" Twenty-six (37%) women had previously delivered in a hospital. Of these women, 12 (46%) were dissatisfied. These women were then asked, "Why weren't you satisfied with that delivery?" Statements given as specific reasons for dissatisfaction with the hospital delivery showed difficulty in adjustment to the hospital environment. The statements were categorized according to Brink's (1976) framework. One informant stated that the staff "used words I didn't understand." Other informants mentioned mechanical differences or routine technological interventions as stressors: "Gave me a saddleblock when I said I did not want one." "Tied down because I didn't want medicine." Hospital customs were also cited: "I didn't like the last minute dash to the delivery room." "I didn't like hospital procedures or care given." "I wanted more participation in infant care." Isolation was another stressor mentioned by informants: "My husband was left out." "I was separated from my baby." "I was supposed to have rooming-in, but I did not get it." Stress experienced by confrontation with different attitudes and beliefs was expressed in the following statements: "I was treated like I had a disease." "I didn't like the impersonal atmosphere." "The hospital staff was too pushy." "The nursing staff was prejudiced against the single woman."

These statements reveal that the hospital birthing experience did not maintain the integrity of the individual and also reflect the loss of control in the hospital environment. The dissonance experienced in the hospital environment was absent in the home setting as indicated by 18 (26%) mothers who had

previously delivered at home. All of these mothers expressed satisfaction with that delivery, and would repeat it if they had another child.

In addition to these mothers, those mothers who had their first baby at home also indicated that if they had another baby, they would choose a home birth. These data indicate that the choice of a home birth is appropriate adaptive strategy for these mothers in order to meet their needs during the birth process.

The need to use an adaptive strategy seemed particularly strong in coping with the hospital subculture as a stressor. Was the birth attendant considered as a source of dissonance? In order to determine if this were so, the question was asked: "Who was your attendant for your home birth?" Even though some mothers expressed dissatisfaction with physicians when they had a hospital delivery, 18 (26%) chose to have a physician as an attendant for the home birth. This choice illustrated that an adaptation of the environment alone was a strategy that reduced dissonance for some of the mothers. Perhaps more women would have used this adaptive strategy if more physicians were available and willing to perform home deliveries. Stewart and Mehl in Stewart and Stewart's (1977:28) book, *21st Century Obstetrics Now!* note that:

> Most homebirth couples desire a competent birth attendant, but to most in the U.S. today, no such attendant is available. Such couples often choose an unattended home birth—not by preference—but because their only other alternative is an unsympathetic, technologic hospital whose psychological hazards are a certainty and whose medical "safety" for the low risk is open to question.

SUMMARY

Since dissonance exists in the hospital environment, pregnant women have taken action to reduce this dissonance by avoiding the environmental stressors totally by choosing a home birth. A primary concern for many women has been the lack of control and interferences that are common in the hospital maternity setting. Women want to experience this special event with loved ones, not with strangers who do not share the same value system. When hospital staff are unwilling to give up routines and permit individuals to have some degree of control, and when hospitals insist on separating mothers, infants, siblings, fathers, and friends, feelings of dissonance occur. In order to achieve control and to prevent interference and isolation, some women have chosen to avoid the hospital for childbirth. Lang (1974) notes that: ". . . women are now taking the responsibility of childbirth out of the hospital, into our own hands. It is only with the changing consciousness of our times . . . that we are able to recover the joy and beauty of childbirth."

REFERENCES

Bateson, G. 1944. Cultural determinants of personality." In J. McV. Hunt, ed. Personality and the behavior disorders, vol. II. Ronald Press, New York.

Brink, P. J. 1976. Transcultural nursing. Prentice-Hall, Inc., Englewood Cliffs, N.J.

Chase, E. S. 1976. Home births in Salt Lake County in 1975. Master's thesis. University of Utah, Salt Lake City.

Festinger, L. 1957. A theory of cognitive dissonance. Row, Peterson and Company, Evanston, Ill.

Hazell, L. 1974-1975. A study of 300 elective home births. Birth and the Family Journal 2(1):11-18.

Healy, M. 1972. A descriptive study of the social climate surrounding home deliveries from the viewpoint of public health nurses and hippie type women. Unpublished master's thesis. University of Washington, Seattle.

Lang, R. 1972. Birth book. Genesis Press, Cal.

Mehl, L., et al. 1975. Complications of home birth. Birth and Family Journal 2(4):123-131.

Pima County Health Department. 1976. Division of vital records and health statistics. Tucson, Arizona.

Roy, C. 1976. Introduction to nursing: An adaptation model. Prentice-Hall, Inc., Englewood Cliffs, N.J.

Stewart, D. and Mehl, L. 1977. A rebuttal to negative home birth statistics cited by ACOG. In L. Stewart and D. Stewart eds. 21st century obstetrics now! vol. 1. NAPSAC, Inc., Chapel Hill, N.C.

Stewart, L., and Stewart, D., eds. 1977. 21st century obstetrics now! vol. 1. NAPSAC, Inc., Chapel Hill, N.C.

CHAPTER 7

Health and healing practices among five ethnic groups in Miami, Florida*

Clarissa S. Scott

Ethnic groups from the Bahamas, the West Indies, and Central and South America converge in large numbers in Miami, Fla., and most of these peoples retain their vigorous, indigenous health cultures. The term health culture is used here to refer to "all of the phenomena associated with the maintenance of well-being and problems of sickness with which people cope in traditional ways, in their own social networks."[1] Evaluating the importance of this concept, Weidman and Egeland[1] note that use of this definition sets out the sphere of health belief and behavior as "one of the basic social institutions of a society" and raises it to the same order of classification as the economic or political system.

THE HEALTH ECOLOGY PROJECT

Preliminary findings of the Health Ecology Project, which is conducting comparative research on the health cultures of the five largest ethnic groups in the inner-city area of Miami, reveal that many members of these groups are not moving resolutely away from traditional health beliefs and practices toward scientific (orthodox) medicine. Rather, they are holding fast to numerous prescriptive health beliefs and practices, combining the two systems (orthodox and traditional) in different ways and to different extents. The five groups being studied are Bahamian, Cuban, Haitian, Puerto Rican, and southern U.S. black.

The project is concerned with illness of both physical and psychological origin. It has

two important goals within the context of this paper. The immediate goal is to describe the beliefs and practices relating to health, illness, and healing among the ethnic groups. The second goal is to determine the patterns of use of both the orthodox and traditional healing systems among these populations. Ultimately, the hope is to develop models for more appropriate health care delivery.

The project is using a combined sociological-anthropological methodology. Our six field assistants, who collect the majority of the data, are women who are members of the ethnic communities in which they work. Each community has one full-time fieldworker, except the Puerto Ricans; in this population, two women share one full-time position. The fieldworkers include a Bahamian who uses the services of faith healers and sorcerers, a Haitian whose aunt was a prominent voodoo priestess, and a Cuban who was a practicing attorney in Havana before coming to Miami as a political refugee. Thus, training of these women has been highly individualized, based on both the weaknesses and strengths of each as well as her background.

As part of the research protocol, each field assistant administers a sociological-type questionnaire to 100 families in her ethnic group, and then she selects 30 to 40 families from the 100 to work with on a long-term basis. The families selected are asked to keep a health calendar for 4 consecutive weeks, and the mother (or whoever cares for the family members) records any symptoms of illness or conditions which appear in family members and the precise action taken in response. In

*Reprinted with permission from *Public Health Reports*, 1974, Vol. 89, 6:524-532.

this way, we are obtaining a description of health problems as seen by members of each ethnic group, rather than according to scientific medical terminology. During the long period of contact, the assistants attempt to gain more understanding (from the mother's point of view) of the etiology of the problems and the family's reasons for engaging in certain health behaviors in place of or before others.

Much of the data in this article are based on the techniques that are closely associated with anthropological fieldwork—participant observation and in-depth interviewing over a long period of contact. The bulk of the fieldwork was done by the indigenous assistants and by me in company with them. We are fortunate in also being able to share field data and observations with five behavioral scientists, each of whom acts as a "culture broker" for his or her respective ethnic group and who, in turn, has a team of indigenous workers under her or him. A culture broker, as defined by Weidman[2] in general terms, is a "bridging" person between two health cultural systems confronting each other. More specifically, within the setting of the University of Miami School of Medicine, this person is a medical anthropologist or behavioral scientist with specialized knowledge of a local ethnic group who works to establish linkages between that ethnic community and in-house psychiatric services.

Although the broad overview and statistical data which derive from the questionnaire and other sociological types of field instruments are invaluable in telling us *what* is happening, it is the months and years of daily contact in the communities which provide us with the insight and data to interpret the *whys* and *hows* of the statistical picture.

For further clues and insight into health beliefs and practices, we use behavioral-science literature pertaining to the ethnic groups' country of origin as well as to counterpart ethnic enclaves in other U.S. cities. This must be done with great circumspection because each local ethnic community is unique in some ways while sharing certain commonalities with their opposite ethnic number elsewhere. Unfortunately, virtually no literature describing Miami's ethnic communities has yet appeared in scientific journals.

PATTERNS OF HEALTH CARE

Each of the five populations (Bahamian, Cuban, Haitian, Puerto Rican, and southern U.S. black) tends to use available health systems somewhat differently. The following descriptions of health care patterns were obtained in a pilot study within the overall Health Ecology Project.

Bahamians. Folk remedies and healing techniques thrive among the Bahamians. There is constant traffic between Miami and Nassau (only 30 minutes by plane) and numerous Bahamian herbs and concoctions are brought in by friends and relatives. Many Miami residents retain close relationships with their relatives in the Bahamas by returning for visits, telephoning, and so on. There are several Obeah men in Miami, and at least one commutes between Miami and Nassau to see patients in both countries. Bahamians sometimes "cross the water" (return to Nassau) which automatically removes any effects of Obeah from them. Many use the services of southern black root doctors and spiritual doctors, as well as southern black faith healers.

In anthropology, there is a technical distinction between witchcraft and sorcery. Wittkower and Weidman[3] define witchcraft as involving ". . . innate and extraordinary power which is inherited and is exercised as a psychic act," and sorcery as being "learned" and involving ". . . the use of power which resides in resources outside the individual." Obeah is the term used by Bahamians to indicate sorcery; the southern black term for sorcery is rootwork, and those who practice it are root doctors.

The health calendars of our Bahamian sample indicate chronically poor health. They frequently use the orthodox health system only for crises or in conjunction with folk therapy, for obvious reasons such as language barriers, transportation problems, and "social distance"—the distance between ethnic "consumers" and health "providers" who subscribe to a different set of values. In addition to these manifest reasons there is lack of cultural "fit," which probably also pertains to the four other ethnic groups. This lack occurs when two or more health cultures are dissimilar in crucial ways that make it impossible for a member of one health cultural tradition to accept certain beliefs and behaviors of another. The result is dissatisfaction by both the health care provider and the consumer.

Furthermore, all the ethnic groups in our study attribute certain symptoms and conditions to social and interpersonal conflict and supernatural activity. Their feeling is that "everybody knows" that these are health problems which medical doctors are incapable of curing, therefore it is useless to expect remedial treatment from an orthodox medical practitioner. Among the Bahamians particularly, a person seeks an Obeah man or crosses ethnic lines to use the services of a southern black counterpart, a root doctor. Finally, the intensity with which the Bahamians in the study group practice folk therapy may be related to the closeness of the Bahama Islands to Miami. Visiting and communication can be maintained easily, and there are ample opportunities to replenish home remedies and to reinforce Bahamian health beliefs and practices.

Cubans. Cubans have come to Miami in such numbers that they have been able to duplicate their entire former health care system, including the manufacture of patent medicines previously produced in Cuba. Only a few families in our sample had used a hospital emergency room during the previous 12 months—a significant difference between this group and the others. One possible reason is that a majority of our study families attend 1 of the 23 or more private Cuban clinics, which are operated like a health maintenance organization and are open around-the-clock. Also, according to our data, Cubans seem to be highly motivated toward preventive medicine.

Some Cuban druggists guardedly continue the Latin American practice of selling prescription drugs without prescriptions. Simultaneously, they sell traditional medical plants to their customers. Small churches which include faith healers are found throughout "Little Havana." Large numbers of espiritistas and santeros ply their trade. An espiritista is a practitioner of Espiritismo—a religious cult of European origin based on an ethical code—which is concerned with communication with spirits and the purification of the soul through moral behavior.[4] A santero is a practitioner of Santeria, a syncretic product of African beliefs and Catholic practices.

The santero takes no moral position, as does the espiritista; he works solely in behalf of his client. His activity can be beneficial, of no import, or harmful to others.[4]

The Cuban business district has many botanicas; these religious-article stores sell herbs, lotions, sprays, and other items prescribed by espiritistas and santeros. Home remedies, such as punches, teas, and salves, are used in most of the households in our study.

According to our questionnaire and health calendar data, the Cubans seem to be making full use of the medical resources available to them. Also, at this point in our research, their calendars indicate that they experience less illness than do the other groups. The Cubans who came to Miami on refugee flights are eligible for free care at the Refugee Center, which is staffed by Cuban health personnel; however, the center is being terminated because the Cuban Airlift of refugees has ended. The Refugee Center is not as conveniently located as are other facilities. Families often use it in conjunction with private clinics and physicians, according to their financial status and time available. Cuban health professionals and paraprofessionals have entered the United States orthodox health system in such great numbers that even when a Cuban goes to the public health clinics or to Jackson Memorial Hospital, the university teaching hospital, he is often cared for by Cuban nurses, physicians, technicians, or social workers.

Haitians. The Haitians are relatively recent arrivals to Miami; our pilot study respondents have been here an average of 2.2 years. Medicinal preparations and elements of the traditional Haitian health care system are limited in Miami, possibly because their population is not yet large enough to support more than a handful of indigenous healers.

We know of two priests (Houngan) and one priestess (Mambo) of the Vodun cult in Miami. Herskovits[5] defines Vodun, or voodoo, as "a complex of African belief and ritual governing in large measure the religious life of the Haitian peasantry. . . ." In addition to these, two men represent themselves as spiritual doctors. They use the title "Reverend" and use the power of the holy spirit to cure. Finally, we have knowledge of five "Readers" or "Diviners" (men and

Facsimiles of recent ads that appeared in the *Miami Times.*

women who read cards and hands) who predict and cure. They cure by means of being possessed by a spirit (mystére) which sometimes touches the patient and gives directions for cure.

The Haitian pattern of health care which emerges from our preliminary data is to treat first with herbs and home remedies. When Haitians move into the orthodox system, three characteristics dominate their use of it: (a) frequent use of the emergency room, (b) the names of the same few private physicians and one private clinic appear again and again, and (c) the types of facilities used are more limited in range than those used by the other four groups. These characteristics indicate that the Haitians do not know the territory and thus rely on each other for rec-

ommendations of health facilities. Their economic status is generally low on arrival in the United States. The emergency room at Jackson Memorial Hospital (the only public hospital in Miami) does not demand immediate payment, and therefore it accommodates the needs of the Haitians who lack money.

Catholic Haitians tend to be Catholics in name only and still retain their Vodun beliefs. They are likely to attribute certain illnesses to supernatural causes and, in such cases, many seek out those few native healers who are available in Miami. Baptist Haitians who believe that illness is not responding as it should to either home remedies or the orthodox system are likely to pray (either alone or with their pastors) for God's help in effecting a cure. They have been con-

For legend see opposite page.

verted to a belief in a protective God who is powerful enough to conquer evil with good and to help the doctors cure both natural and supernatural illnesses.

When home remedies and techniques fail, alone or in conjunction with the orthodox system, Haitians sometimes return to Haiti at great expense to use the services of the types of healers who are not yet available in Miami.

Puerto Ricans. Of the five groups, the Puerto Ricans have consistently shown the least use of the orthodox health care system. Compared with the other ethnic groups, a significantly smaller percentage used the services of an emergency room or saw a private physician during the previous 12 months. Checkups were rare. This infrequent use of the orthodox system and the health calendar data indicating extensive poor health lead us to hypothesize that this group may be isolated from its own healing system as well as from the orthodox system and for the following reasons specific to the Puerto Ricans:

• Their lifestyle is such that many wives and mothers remain close to their homes and neighborhoods and rarely feel comfortable venturing outside these boundaries. Submissive and protected, the Puerto Rican woman in Miami takes direction from her husband. The father in one of our study families forbids his wife to leave home during the day, even for a brief time to have a cup of coffee with the next-door neighbor.

• When Puerto Ricans do reach a hospital or clinic, they are usually assigned to Cuban staff because they are Spanish-speaking. There is considerable antagonism between Cubans and Puerto Ricans in Miami, and the Puerto Ricans believe that Cubans treat them in an offensive manner, without respect (respeto). To treat and be treated with respect is a fervently held value. Seda, a Puerto Rican anthropologist, has said that a Puerto Rican possesses "an almost fanatical conviction of his self-value."[6] While Puerto Ricans are especially sensitive to lack of respect by Cubans, this may also be a negative factor in their contact with health care personnel from any ethnic or cultural group.

• Puerto Ricans in Miami do not have as diverse and powerful a folk healing system as they do in New York or Puerto Rico. Although there are several espiritistas in Miami, our information indicates that their following is not large. Puerto Rican and Cuban espiritistas are similar in that they are both practitioners of Espiritismo. However, Garrison[7] characterizes Puerto Rican Espiritismo as a folk-healing cult of the spirit-medium type rather than as a religious cult, as Sandoval[4] describes the Cuban counterpart.

Cuban santeros and espiritistas are thought to be more powerful than the Puerto Rican healers in Miami. When Puerto Ricans believe that "a thing" (hechizo) has been done to them, they often believe that it has been effected by a Cuban santero. They fear that there is little chance of "taking it off" because (a) if they go to a santero, he probably will not work anything against a fellow Cuban and (b) if they go to a Puerto Rican espiritista, he will not have sufficient force for the task. Thus, they often do nothing about this situation.

Puerto Ricans in Miami rely heavily on herbs and folk remedies, which they grow in their yards or purchase from Cuban groceries. Our health calendar data from the pilot study indicate that Puerto Ricans are less likely than any group but the Haitians to take action in response to a symptom. Our preliminary findings concerning Puerto Ricans support those reported by Suchman[8] for New York City: they are the most socially isolated as a group and the most deviant from a standard response to illness.

Southern black. In Miami, the southern blacks show a greater range of variation in their traditional healing system than do either the Haitians or the Puerto Ricans. Home remedies lean more to materials such as vinegar and rubbing alcohol than to herbs. Faith healers appear on radio, television, in revival tents, in churches devoted in large measure to healing, and in "galas" attended by thousands and directed by nationally known figures. There are many spiritualists—those who engage in spiritual healing—who operate out of "temples," "churches," and "candle shops." Root doctors, sometimes known as Hoodoo men or Hoodoo ladies, are numerous. These therapists advertise openly in the local newspaper published by and for blacks; one even focuses attention on his ad with a large drawing of the roots of a plant. If Miami folk therapists are not powerful enough to bring about a cure, southern blacks may travel to Georgia or South Carolina where the reputation of the local root doctors is legendary.

In their use of the Orthodox health care system, southern blacks appear to have numerous, but superficial, contacts. Approximately 50 percent of our sample attended public clinics during the previous 12 months and 23 percent were seen in an emergency room. Nevertheless, the health calendars kept by the families and the accompanying interviews indicate that symptoms and conditions continue week after week, month after

Botanicas are shops where items used in the practice of *santeria* and *espiritismo* are sold. Articles include lotions, amulets, shells, images, and herbs.

month, and are rarely cured. A characteristic of the southern blacks' use of the orthodox system is that private physicians and public clinics are often used within the same family, sometimes at the same time.

USE OF MULTIPLE RESOURCES

Preliminary data suggest that the five ethnic groups have unique patterns for using their own health systems as well as the orthodox system. However, the use of multiple resources—that is the use of different therapies or healers serially or concurrently—is one overall feature that cuts across the five individual patterns. Evident in our study are four types of usage within and among systems. In each of these types, the remedies or healers, or both, are used one after the other or at the same time, as illustrated in the following examples:

Healers and therapies in the orthodox system. A Puerto Rican mother takes her baby who has symptoms of a cold to a public health clinic, and the physician prescribes cough medicine and pills. The mother is not satisfied because she believes that an injection is necessary for a cure. She takes the baby to a succession of private physicians until one

finally gives the child the anticipated injection.

Among the local black populations, many families report seeing a private physician when they can afford to ("because they treat you better") but relying on emergency room treatment when they lack money for private care.

Healers and therapies within a folk system. A 9-year-old Puerto Rican girl had a red and swollen eye, and within 2 days it began to droop. Her mother diagnosed this condition as pasmo, a condition of paralysis linked to the hot-cold theory of disease. (Harwood[9] recently discussed this theory.) She began treating the condition by placing a compress soaked in camphor oil on the eye and giving the girl azufre powder sprinkled on fried eggs. When this treatment failed, she took her daughter to Puerto Rico to find the proper curative plants.

A second example concerns a young southern black woman with general weakness and skin ulcers. She visited a faith healer who gave her home remedies. No change occurred, and she sought the services of a second faith healer. Results were poor after two visits, and she then saw a third faith

Items sold in the *botanicas* for use by *santeros* and *espiritistas*.

healer four times. She now states that she is satisfied with the treatment and is improving.

Healers and therapies in two different folk systems. One way in which an unorthodox healer validates his ability in the eyes of his patients is to tell a patient what is bothering him and what his interpersonal problems and worries are. This presents a problem for sick persons who are members of the still relatively small and tightly clustered Haitian community—they fear that the Haitian healer has heard gossip or rumors about the patient's life and problems rather than having clairvoyant ability. One of our Haitian mothers had just this concern after going to a Haitian reader. She is now seeing a southern black healer in whom she has greater confidence.

In exception to the general pattern, a Puerto Rican espiritista with whom one of our fieldworkers has established a relationship of trust has had Cuban clients come to her to take off spells after they had consulted (unsuccessfully) Cuban espiritistas to do this job. One of the competing Cuban espiritistas even came to her for a reading, masquerading as a client, to find out how she operates.

Healers and therapies in a folk system and in the orthodox system. In addition to the folk and orthodox systems, the following example illustrates the second type of behavior mentioned, the use of healers and therapies within one folk system.

A southern black woman from South Carolina, Mrs. F, drank her Geritol as usual one morning and began to have stomach pains ½ hour later. The pains continued, and 2 days later she suspected that she had been "fixed," probably by a substance added to the Geritol. She took olive oil and a few drops of turpentine on sugar cubes. Later that week she went to see a root woman, who gave her some "bush" to "work it out."

Believing that the poison was "dead," but fearful that it might have rotted away her stomach, Mrs. F went to the emergency room of a local hospital. X-rays showed that although the stomach appeared normal, "something was down there." Mrs. F again went to the root woman who then gave her a new potion to drink, which contained garlic, white onions, and mercury in addition to other ingredients. She next sought the services of a root doctor who operates a candle shop. This healer gave her powder to sprinkle in her house and candles to burn in the corners of the house; he also laid his hands on her and prayed.

After hearing from a neighbor about a sanctified woman in a farming area 20 miles south of Miami, Mrs. F began making two or three trips a week to be treated by her. The woman rubbed Mrs. F's abdomen with a red substance and prayed over her. Mrs. F. subsequently reported that she felt much better. However, she continued to keep candles lighted according to her root doctor's advice, to take the garlic and mercury potion from the root woman, and to be massaged by the sanctified woman. Recently, Mrs. F went to Jackson Memorial Hospital for gastrointestinal tests to "find out what is down there." (Interestingly, Mrs. F's contacts with the orthodox system were not for curative purposes, rather they were to check the effectiveness of the folk therapy.) Our worker first interviewed this woman approximately 8 months after the onset of her symptoms and maintained contact with her until her death a year later.

Another example concerns a Bahamian in our study who complained of abdominal and vaginal pain for months but refused to go for medical care, even if accompanied by the fieldworker and me (to insure prompt, courteous attention). She said it would be useless because her illness was caused by witchcraft, something no medical doctor could cure; the only source of help, she believed, was a root woman who she had seen several times. Ten days before her death—from an organic disease—she did visit the emergency room for treatment of a sore throat, which she defined as amenable to orthodox medical treatment, rather than for treatment of her major illness.

DISCUSSION AND CONCLUSION

Given the wide variety of healers and therapists in Miami, not only practical or obvious factors influence the choice of one over the other. Those factors which motivate an individual to accept or reject the orthodox health system, such as poor transportation or a poor "fit" between specific health beliefs and practices, provide us with only partial answers to the problem of selection. Elements which are specific to each group's health behavior add to but do not complete the picture either. We must search for deeper, more compelling motives which underlie the selection of a particular therapy or healer.

Anthropologists have proposed many hypotheses concerning motivation. Erasmas, quoted by Schwartz,[10] stated that "where medical treatment is quickly effective, dramatic and evident, it will prevail over others." Schwartz suggests that "alternative modes of curing are arranged in hierarchies of resort, with different alternatives being used as the illness progresses without cure, and according to the individual's or group's acculturative process." Another hypothesis, by Bryce-Laporte,[11] is that "when subordinate groups are only partially assimilated within a dominant culture," they tend to be bicultural in their choice of alternative beliefs and behaviors (for example, health beliefs and behaviors). Our data often indicate this simultaneous or serial use of the orthodox and traditional systems.

Still another explanation relates to etiology. Describing his health research among Mestizo communities in Peru and Chile, Simmons[12] proposes that those maladies which are assigned to "the etiological categories of severe emotional upset, ritual uncleanness, and bad air" necessitate treatment with at least one magical therapeutic technique, and a modern therapy with demonstrated value may be used in tandem.

From her study of health beliefs and practices in three Guatemalan cultures, Gonzalez[13] concluded that patients often seek relief from symptoms from a medical doctor while expecting the folk therapist to eliminate the cause of the disease. And, Egeland[14] concluded from her study of the Amish people that in the particularly crucial area of life and death, reliance on only one therapist or therapy or system of health care may be too precarious and more than one are sought.

The findings of our pilot study indicate that the scientific health care system is not sufficiently relevant to multi-ethnic populations in urban U.S. areas. Many persons in the ethnic groups we are studying are completely alienated from the orthodox system, and others use it serially or in tandem with folk health care systems. While we cannot disregard such considerations as language and transportation problems or the lack of cultural fit between health consumers and providers, we must be able to understand the underlying reasons for the selection of therapies and therapists. Only when we have such understanding will we be able to develop models for more appropriate health care delivery for ethnic minorities.

In the meantime, the following are some very practical measures which health personnel might find immediately helpful in providing better health care to ethnic populations:

• Gain knowledge of the health beliefs and practices of local ethnic groups.

• Respect the fact that these beliefs and therapies, although perhaps running counter to the scientific medical systems, have survived in these populations for generations and may indeed be measurably effective. To try to change a deeply rooted health belief either by ridicule or by treating it as unscientific may not only fail but may also alienate the patient.

• Use a treatment plan which shows understanding and respect for the patient's beliefs and which builds on these in a positive way.

Two examples illustrate the preceding points. A physician may assume that a patient from a low-income ethnic group has probably tried home remedies before coming to the orthodox system. "It is important that [he] know what the patient has been using to combat the illness—if it is harmless, it might be left in the treatment plan and the physician's own suggestions added. A harmful practice might be more readily eliminated if the physician simply suggests that since it has *not* seemed to have worked something else might be tried."[15] In developing a new treatment regimen, a physician might well integrate into it the numbers 3 and 9, for example, which are important in the folklore of Puerto Ricans and Mexican-Americans.[15]

The second example concerns the many Puerto Ricans and Haitians who subscribe to the "hot-cold" theory. This is a belief system in which illnesses are classified as hot or cold and food and medicine, also classified this way, are used to restore the natural balance in the body; a "cold" medicine would be used to counteract a "hot" disease. A Puerto

Rican woman who is pregnant (considered to be a "hot" condition) will avoid iron supplements and vitamins because they are also considered to be "hot," and it is believed that they will upset the body's natural balance. The wise physician will advise the patient to take her iron supplements and vitamins with fruit juice which, because it is classified as "cool," helps to maintain the proper balance of hot and cold in the body.[9]

Another practical measure to be considered is to be able to recognize when a patient suspects that he has been hexed. He rarely will volunteer this information, but the physician should be aware that symptoms of "feeling bad," loss of weight, depression, lack of appetite, and abdominal complaints indicate possible rootwork. Often, the patient is relieved to share his fears when a concerned physician or nurse asks, Do you think something has been done to you? or Do you think you've been rooted? It is extremely important that the physician assure the patient that his symptoms are not due to rootwork and are curable with orthodox medicine, if this is true. If the physician determines that the symptoms are psychogenic, he should instigate palliative, supportive therapy and also accept, without ridicule, tandem treatment by rootworkers whose job it is to neutralize or remove the spell.[16]

Many low-income ethnic groups in urban areas do not receive adequate medical care now, nor will they for many years to come. Obviously, there is no "payoff" for them to give up a health culture which has been supportive for generations in order to subscribe to the beliefs and practices of a system to which they have little access. Therefore, we can expect unorthodox health therapies to continue. Those who would try to make the scientific medical system relevant to these urban ethnic groups must first recognize the existence of other health systems and then be willing to respect and work with them. The trust and rapport thus established can form the base for a greater acceptance of the orthodox system in the future.

REFERENCES

1. Weidman, H. H., and Egeland, J.: A behavioral science perspective in the comparative approach to the delivery of health care. Soc Sci Med 7: 845-860 (1973).
2. Weidman, H. H.: Implications of the culture-broker concept for the delivery of health care. Paper presented at annual meeting of the Southern Anthropological Society, Wrightsville Beach, N.C., March 8-11, 1973.
3. Wittkower, E. D., and Weidman, H. H.: Magic, witchcraft and sorcery in relation to mental health and mental disorder. In Social psychiatry, edited by N. Petrilowitsch and H. Flegel. Top Probl Psychiat Neurol 8: 169-184 (1967).
4. Sandoval, M.: Yoruba elements in Afro-Cuban Santeria. Doctoral dissertation, University of Madrid, 1966.
5. Herskovits, M. J.: Life in a Haitian valley. Doubleday & Company, Inc., Garden City, N.Y., 1971.
6. Lauria, A.: Respeto, relajo and interpersonal relations in Puerto Rico. In The Puerto Rican community and its children on the mainland, edited by F. Cordasco and E. Bucchioni. The Scarecrow Press, Inc., Metuchen, N.J., 1972, pp. 36-48.
7. Garrison, V.: Espiritismo: implications for provision of mental health services to Puerto Rican populations. Paper presented in part at annual meeting of the Southern Anthropological Society, Columbia, Mo., Feb. 24-26, 1972.
8. Suchman, E. A.: Sociomedical variation among ethnic groups. Am J Sociol 70: 319-331, November 1964.
9. Harwood, A.: The hot-cold theory of disease. JAMA 216: 1153-1158, May 17, 1971.
10. Schwartz, L. R.: The hierarchy of resort in curative practices: the Admiralty Islands, Melanesia. J Health Soc Behav 10: 201-209, September 1969.
11. Bryce-LaPorte, R. S.: Crisis, contraculture, and religion among West Indians in the Panama Canal Zone. In Afro-American Anthropology, edited by N. Whitten, Jr., and J. Szwed. The Free Press, New York, 1970.
12. Simmons, O. G.: Popular and modern medicine in Mestizo communities of coastal Peru and Chile. J Am Folklore 68: 57-71, January-March 1955.
13. Gonzalez, N. S.: Health behavior in cross-cultural perspective: a Guatemalan example. Hum Organ 25: 122-125, summer 1966.
14. Egeland, J.: Belief and behavior related to illness. Doctoral dissertation, Yale University, 1967.
15. Snow, L. F.: Folk medical beliefs and their implications for care of patients: a review based on studies among black Americans. Ann Intern Med 81: 82-96, July 1974.
16. Wintrob, R. M., Fox, R. A., Jr., and O'Brien, E. G.: Rootwork beliefs and psychiatric disorder among blacks in a northern United States city. Paper presented at Symposium on Traditional and Modern Treatments of Indigenous American People, V World Congress of Psychiatry, Mexico City, December 1971.

PART TWO

STRATEGIES FOR HEALTH CARE

The success or failure of health programs depends to a large extent on the sociocultural context within which the programs take place and how well the programs are planned to take this context into account. Before a health program is established in a community, there needs to be an understanding of the people, their attitudes toward health and illness, and their concept of an acceptable health care system. Chapter 8 discusses some questions that health planners need to ask about a community in order to better understand the attitudes about health, illness, and health services.

Chapter 9 focuses on the area of family planning as a vehicle to explore and propose various possibilities in regard to health action that may be taken as a result of a disrupted sense of well-being. Well-being is dealt with in cultural terms, that is, the meaning of well-being to the individual as a cultural being.

Chapter 10 is concerned with conflicts that arose between two cultures over the use of blood samples to diagnose Chagas' disease. Chapter 11 describes a successful program for the reduction of risk factors for coronary heart disease in a bicultural elementary school. An anthropological view of the program describes several sociocultural considerations, with attention to the interface of the Mexican-American culture, the Western medical system, and the role of the school.

CHAPTER 8

Health attitudes and your health program

Nadine H. Rund
Lynn L. Krause

Health workers who want to establish a program in a community should have an understanding of the people they are working with, their attitudes toward health and illness, and what they think is an acceptable health care system. Health workers in a cross-cultural setting must understand that cultural differences between themselves and their clients are pertinent in providing effective health care. The literature provides examples of the importance of cross-cultural understanding and also covers the methods and techniques available to gather information in a cross-cultural setting. Notably lacking are detailed guidelines describing the specific information needed about the individual, family, and community, or an explanation of how this information can contribute to the smooth and effective functioning of a health service. The literature generally describes cross-cultural health care problems and the value of understanding the culture of those being served, but not enough emphasis is placed upon the need for workers to examine their own attitudes, beliefs, and behavior in health care.

This chapter analyzes two types of health-related information: that related directly to the health care attitudes of an individual or family, and that related to broader sociocultural patterns of the community. In each section, questions are posed that can help provide an understanding of individual and community attitudes toward health, illness, and health care. Workers using these questions should try to obtain as much information as possible in any situation in which they are not native or long-time residents of the community. Even workers who are long-time community residents can benefit from examining their own attitudes about health care. This chapter is not intended to be a compendium of cultural factors relevant to health care. It is intended for health workers who are not students of culture and do not have time to read detailed cultural comparisons, but who would like to provide direct care in a manner appropriate and acceptable to their clients. It is also intended for the health planners who wish to develop and implement acceptable programs that respond to the wants of a community.

GUIDELINES FOR GATHERING INFORMATION ABOUT DIRECT HEALTH CARE

1. **What systems of health care and types of health practitioners are accessible to the community?**

Answering this question gives workers a knowledge of the total health care system of which they are but one resource. This knowledge is important because other practitioners may approach health problems differently but in ways that are highly acceptable to members of the community.

The variety of practitioners available to provide direct physical or mental health care in large urban areas can be extensive. They can include M.D. physicians and surgeons, osteopathic physicians and surgeons, chiropractic physicians, naturopathic physicians, Christian Science practitioners, clinical psychologists, Spanish-American *curanderos*, and American Indian medicine men and women. There are many other individuals who make contributions to health care, such as social workers, child guidance counselors, marriage counselors, educational counselors, and ministers.

Health workers must determine which practitioners are available, what their approaches are to health care, and the degree to which these practitioners are important to their own specific programs. They should also examine their personal attitudes toward these other practitioners, and determine whether the other modes of health care are acceptable or unacceptable to them.

2. What is health and what is illness? How are these concepts defined by the community and by the health workers?

Answers to these questions provide information about how the client and the practitioners conceptualize health and illness. Given this information, workers can better approach their clients.

Several specific questions can clarify the definition of health and illness. Is health defined as the absence of disease, or is it a balance of physical, mental, and spiritual well-being? A health worker functioning with a physiological definition of illness may not be attuned to the spiritual aspects of health and illness, perceiving these to be in the realm of religion. Is health an individual or a family matter? When a family member is ill, is medical attention provided to that person alone or are curing activities provided for the entire family? In many clinical settings, health workers are prepared to talk to, deal with, and treat *only* the individual who seems to be ill.

3. What causes illness?

Answers to this question provide an understanding of the treatment of illness in cross-cultural situations, and of the client-practitioner relationship. The important consideration is the difference between "immediate" and "ultimate" cause of illness. "Immediate" cause refers to the physiological problem—the virus, or bacteria, or other agent that is causing the immediate discomfort or illness. "Ultimate" cause addresses the question of "why me?"—"What has caused this illness to befall me?" The health system followed by most practitioners of Western medicine deals only with immediate cause, and leaves questions of ultimate cause to the realm of religion. Making a distinction between immediate cause and ultimate cause helps workers to appreciate that patients may feel that the ultimate cause of illness is controllable. Therefore, patients may expect their health

practitioners to provide remedies for the ultimate cause, thus preventing a recurrence. It is important to recognize the feeling of security that a belief in ultimate cause and its control can give the patient. Feelings of insecurity or dissatisfaction may result when a practitioner does not deal with the ultimate cause. An American Indian patient may be quite confident of the ability of the Indian Health Service staff to treat the immediate cause of illness but also may seek the services of a traditional Indian healer to deal with the ultimate cause, bringing to bear all of the curing forces possible in the situation. Health workers who are aware of the dual causes of illness will react with more understanding and acceptance when they realize that they and the traditional Indian healers are dealing with different components of health care as perceived by the patient.

4. What is the attitude toward the healthy body? What signs and symptoms does the patient observe?

This knowledge is essential because the Western medical system of health care is based on the expectation that the patient will come to the clinical setting with information that the practitioner needs to make a diagnosis. The information is gained by examining the well body and noting changes in the body which signal illness. A willingness to examine the body is assumed as well as a knowledge of the symptoms of illness and an appreciation of the type of information considered important by the practitioner.

Self-examination is considered an important source of health information by the Western medical practitioner. Therefore, it is important to understand the degree to which clients are comfortable examining their bodies. This understanding will become even more important as preventive health programs and early detection programs increasingly emphasize self-examination. Interest in self-examination is highly variable both from one culture to another and within a society by age and sex, and can never be taken for granted. Before beginning a program based on self-examination, health workers should find out how comfortable their clients are in doing so. Workers may want to devote more time during the initial stages of a program to helping clients become comfortable examining their bodies before addressing the signs and symptoms related to a specific health problem.

A successful encounter with the Western medical practitioner depends upon a knowledge of health and illness and signs and symptoms. Groups differ in the amount of health knowledge they have. Health workers must be aware of the level of health knowledge and the kind of knowledge the people they serve possess.

Health knowledge refers to a wide range of information. It is important to understand the specific context in which patients attempt to collect information about themselves— how they organize information and bring it to the clinic. The patients' own systems of knowledge about the causes of disease define the information they bring to the practitioner. They may come to the clinic prepared to give a sequence of symptoms of illness, but the facts they present may have little bearing on the alternatives the physician is considering. For example, a Mexican-American patient presenting a carefully observed sequence of symptoms indicating an encounter with mal ojo (evil eye) would not be well received by an Anglo physician expecting other types of health information.

5. What modes of treatment and which practitioners are acceptable to clients? How do they relate to the individual patient?

Different medical and religious philosophies encourage different types of health care practices and forbid others. Health workers must be familiar with the belief system of their clients to know whether surgery, transfusion, chemically synthesized medication, prayer or religious counseling, or treatment by a traditional healer would be acceptable to them. Just as important is an understanding of the dietary and daily living patterns of clients, and whether clients would accept suggested changes in these patterns.

If workers can determine what kind of relationship between a client and a local practitioner is the most effective in the delivery of indigenous health care, they can pattern their own approach to the client for the maximum effectiveness. Some practitioners may relate to the client as an equal with different knowledge, as an authority figure, or as a parent figure, whether friendly or punitive. Some may involve the client in the development of the treatment plan and may readily share their knowledge with the client. Knowledge of other styles of patient-practitioner interaction can give health workers insight into the expectations of patients in the clinic setting.

6. What is the responsibility of the patients in the cause, cure, and prevention of illness?

Do patients assume responsibility for their own good health, or is this seen as a responsibility of health care practitioners? The Western medical health care system assumes that all individuals are responsible for their own health. They are responsible for taking preventive measures to remain healthy, for observing the body for signs of illness, for seeking care at the earliest signs of ill health, and for following a treatment plan developed by a health care practitioner. The members of the profession can assume very little *direct* responsibility for keeping people well. If a worker is serving people who believe that it is the responsibility of the health care professionals to *keep* them well, frustration and animosity can develop. This has been observed with the redefinition of alcoholism as a disease. Some alcoholics feel that if alcoholism is a disease then it is not their responsibility but that of the health care providers to restore them to good health. Health care providers with the belief that alcoholism can be cured only by actions taken directly by the alcoholic find this frustrating.

7. Who are the medical decision-makers?

The answer to this question is vital to the acceptance of health care by a client. It may be the patient who will discuss a course of treatment with the practitioner, or there may be others in the family who should be consulted. Many health workers assume that all adults will make decisions for their own care without advice from other family members, and will make decisions for their minor children up to the age of 18. This is not the case in all communities. For example, a young American Indian woman may not wish to make a decision on health care for her children without first consulting her mother or aunt. Furthermore, a health worker asking a mother about care for her child may find the mother responding with "ask the child." It is important to recognize not only the role of family members in the health care encounter, but also that family patterns may differ from community to community. In health care programs serving predominately middle class white populations, the appropriate person in the delivery room with the woman might be the father of the child. In some American Indian communities, the appropriate person in the delivery room might be the woman's mother or aunt. The success of any community-based program depends upon the support of influential leaders. Health workers must know the people who have influence in the community, particularly in matters of health.

The question of medical decision-making can raise certain questions in a health worker's mind for the first time. The expectation that people are responsible for their own health may conflict with the expectation that an individual will follow a treatment plan developed by the health worker. The situation is often one of "you are responsible for your own health, but you must do as I say." Health workers should be aware not only of the views of the community on patient responsibility and the identity of appropriate medical decision-makers, but also their own beliefs and attitudes on these two matters.

8. What are the attitudes and practices related to death and dying?

Death is one of the most sensitive subjects encountered by health workers. Health workers may have different attitudes toward death and dying from those of their patients; therefore, they should become familiar with community attitudes and practices. For instance, death may be accepted as a continuation of the process of life, or it may be seen as the enemy to be fought and held off at all costs. The dead may have power over the living. It may not be appropriate to speak the name of the recently deceased. Health education materials depicting the skull and crossbones or other signs of death may not be acceptable. Family members may be responsible for dealing with the body and preparing for disposal of the final remains. Autopsies may be unacceptable to the community. Discreet inquiry among coworkers will usually provide information on how to behave in situations related to death and dying.

Individual health care workers cannot expect to become students of culture overnight, but if they have an appreciation of the information that can be obtained by asking

the above kinds of questions, they may be able to avoid misunderstandings when providing direct health care to a community.

INFORMATION RELATED TO PLANNING COMPREHENSIVE COMMUNITY HEALTH PROGRAMS

This section concerns the information needed by health planners as they develop comprehensive community programs. A broad knowledge of the community is important in planning such programs, particularly programs that depend upon the cooperation of the community for success. Environmental health projects and community health education efforts are examples of such programs.

Using the method presented in this section, existing information can be organized to identify areas of adequate knowledge and gaps in information. This technique is not intended as a complete data collection method, but rather a method of bringing together and reviewing existing information. Many health planners overlook the fact that much useful information already exists from other programs and from the varied experiences of the health staff. For purposes of planning, the information need not always be detailed. However, planners should ask themselves and their staff members, "Do we have enough information?" and if not, "Where can we find additional information?"

The technique described in this section is basically a checklist examining the historical, environmental, and social aspects of public health planning, adapted from Connor's (1964) "social compass." It is indeed a "compass" in that it is an instrument that can be used to prevent a program from going off in the wrong direction. Ten categories are presented, each with a checklist to assist health planners in evaluating the adequacy of information about a community prior to initiating health programs. The ten categories of information are:

1. History
2. Physical environment
3. Accessibility
4. Technology
5. Human resources
6. Knowledge and belief
7. Values and goals
8. Role and status

9. Norms and sanctions
10. Power and influence

The following outline includes a brief definition of each category and a list of some key points to be reviewed within each of these categories. Health planners may want to add to this list.

1. *History:* an understanding of which health services have already been implemented in the community and how this may affect the success of the current program. The key points are:
   a. The quality of previous relationships between the health agency and the community.
   b. Previous relationships between agency staff and community members.
   c. Relationships between the health agency and other community programs.
   d. Past attempts at similar programs either by this agency or others.
2. *Physical environment:* the environmental conditions and resources affecting the health of the community and the provision of health service.
   a. Climatic conditions affecting the delivery of health services.
   b. The presence or absence of climate-related health problems.
   c. The condition and availability of water.
   d. Types and availability of fuel.
   e. Medicinal herbs and plants available to the community.
   f. Natural barriers that hinder travel.
   g. Health problems related to domestic or wild animals.
   h. Available land for home gardens.
3. *Accessibility:* the physical location and accessibility of services to the entire community.
   a. Location of health services.
   b. Location of private practitioners.
   c. Distance and travel time for most residents to the nearest health care.
   d. Residence patterns—isolated home sites or clusters.
   e. Transportation—bus routes, ambulances, vehicles, and so forth.
   f. Equitable distribution of health services throughout the community.
4. *Technology:* the level of technology available to the community.
   a. Condition of the existing physical plant—hospitals, clinics, community buildings.
   b. The level of medical technology in the community compared to that available in nearby larger population centers.
   c. Location of water lines, power lines, piped or bottled gas.
   d. Degree to which electricity is available to homes.
5. *Human resources:* the people with the skills and training necessary to ensure the success of the program.
   a. Availability of trained health care personnel.
   b. Availability of lay people interested in working with health programs.
   c. Presence of traditional healers.
   d. Ratio of health service personnel residing in the community compared to those who commute from other communities.
6. *Knowledge and belief:* the level of health knowledge related to specific health problems, and the belief system concerning that problem and its treatment.
   a. Degree to which common health-related activities are based upon empirical knowledge or accepted belief.
   b. Willingness to consider other alternatives or new approaches in health care.
   c. Level of health knowledge specific to the problem being addressed by the proposed program.
   d. The degree to which accepted community practices are in accordance or disagreement with Western medical practices.
   e. Significant beliefs in nonhealth-related areas that can affect health behavior, i.e., religious beliefs.
7. *Values and goals:* the basic attitudes of what is considered important in health, and the related objectives toward which community health action is oriented.
   a. The importance of health in relationship to other areas of community life—the place of health in community priorities.
   b. Differences in health-related values by age and sex.
   c. Differences between the health-re-

lated values of the community and the health service staff.

d. Recent changes in health-related values.

e. The relationship between needs and wants in health goals.

f. The reality and feasibility of community health goals.

g. The relationship between the health care priorities of the community and those of the health service.

8. *Role and status:* the expected patterns of individual behavior and the prestige or social rank accorded to individuals and groups.

a. The status of the health service in the community relative to other government or private agencies.

b. The expected roles of males and females in health-related activities.

c. The expected roles of various age groups in health-related activities.

d. Differences in status or prestige accorded a health worker based on age.

e. Ways in which prestige can be gained, enhanced, or diminished in the community.

9. *Norms and sanctions:* accepted standards of behavior and methods for ensuring adherence to standards.

a. Accepted patterns of behavior in health-related activities.

b. Sanctions the community uses to see that accepted standards are followed.

c. Norms of behavior when ill, and variability by age and sex.

d. Recent changes in the definition of accepted behavior.

e. Sanctions that the community can impose on the health service if the health service is not meeting community needs.

f. Sanctions the health service can impose on the community to ensure cooperation, compliance, or assistance in health programs.

g. Sanctions the health service staff impose on patients to ensure compliance with recommended treatment plans.

10. *Power and influence:* Power—the ability to accomplish something through force inherent in the position; the position has the power and whoever holds the position has that power. Influence—the ability to accomplish something through personal persuasion; persuasion may exist whether or not the person has a position of power.

a. The network of power and influence in the community.

b. The relative power or influence of the various governmental and private programs in the community.

c. The attitudes of persons with power or influence toward the health service.

d. The source of power and influence in family medical decision-making.

e. The network of power and influence among the health service personnel.

The above are some key points that can be used to review information about a community. If information is lacking in any category, the health program staff is not prepared to initiate large-scale health programs, especially programs emphasizing disease prevention and community health education. Health planners should realize that to provide complete information within each category would require extensive research efforts. This is not the intent of this chapter, and it will not be to the interest of the health planner. The modified "social compass" is just that—a technique to see if the health program staff is on the right track in understanding the community, identifying community needs, and developing programs that will be consistent with the sociocultural patterns of the community.

REFERENCE

Connor, D. M. 1964. Understanding your community. Antegonish, Nova Scotia.

SUGGESTED READINGS

Brislin, R. W., and Pedersen, P. 1976. Cross-cultural orientation programs, Gardner Press, Inc., New York.

Clark, M. 1959. Health in the Mexican-American culture. The University of California Press, Berkeley.

Foster, G. M. 1962. Traditional cultures and the impact of technological change. Harper and Row, New York.

Knutson, A. L. 1955. The individual, society, and health behavior. Russell Sage Foundation, New York.

Leininger, M. M. 1970. Nursing and anthropology: two worlds to blend. John Wiley & Sons, Inc., New York.

Paul, B. C., ed. 1955. Health, culture, and community. Russell Sage Foundation, New York.

Read, M. 1966. Culture, health, and disease. Tavistock Publications, Ltd., London.

CHAPTER 9

The theoretical significance of a sense of well-being for the delivery of gynecological health care*

Clarissa S. Scott

The term "well-being" is recognized and used widely by lay people, as evidenced by its appearance in numerous Eurasian languages (e.g., *bien-etre*, French; *bien estar*, Spanish; *Wohlfahrt*, German; *Blagopoluchie*, Russian). It is also cited as a component of good health in Africa (Polgar, citing Reed, 1962). It is the purpose of this chapter to focus on this term as it applies to a limited area of health care—gynecology.

The importance of a sense of well-being in taking health action was discovered during field work carried out within the framework of the Health Ecology Project,† a research effort within the Department of Psychiatry, University of Miami School of Medicine. A major goal of the project was to describe the health conditions, beliefs, and behaviors of Bahamians, Cubans, Haitians, Puerto Ricans, and southern United States blacks in an inner city area of Miami. Designed with a be-

havioral science orientation, the project also incorporated geographic and environmental factors as well as demographic, psychological, social, and cultural information into its research strategy. Additional goals were to determine within each of these populations the patterns of utilizing both orthodox (Western) and traditional healing systems and to suggest modifications in certain clinical areas that would make delivery of health care more appropriate to each ethnic group.

Five indigenous female field workers, chosen mainly for their ability to establish a comfortable rapport with mothers in their respective ethnic groups, were trained to gather research data utilizing several field instruments, in-depth interviews, and participant observation.

The training of these assistants, each from the ethnic community in which she worked, had to be flexible and individualized because of (1) their different cultural backgrounds, (2) various educational levels (4 had a 12th grade education or less; 1 held a law degree), and (3) differences in fluency with the English language (the Haitian and Cuban women were not completely bilingual). Staff meetings took place each week during which common problems were discussed and solutions shared; interviewing skills were critiqued; and instruction on the next field work assignment was given. The instruction was always repeated on an individual basis, also weekly, according to the strengths and weaknesses of each field worker; these meetings were conducted in English, Spanish, or French (a language which the Creole-speaking Haitian assistant and the Health Ecology Project field coordinator shared). None of the

*This chapter is a modification of a paper presented at the 73rd Annual Meeting of the American Anthropological Association in Mexico City, November 19–24, 1974. It also incorporates limited portions from "Haitian Blood Beliefs and Practices in Miami, Florida," a paper read at the American Anthropological Association Annual Meeting, New Orleans, November 29–December 2, 1973; "Cart Before the Horse: Birth Control Technology before Knowledge of Body Concepts," presented at the 9th Annual Meeting of the Southern Anthropological Society, Blackburg, Virginia, April 4–6, 1974; and an article published in the *International Journal of Gynaecology and Obstetrics*, 1975.

† The Health Ecology Project was supported by a grant from the Commonwealth Fund of New York. Its principal investigators were James N. Sussex, M.D., professor and chairman of the Department of Psychiatry, and Hazel H. Weidman, Ph.D.; codirector was Janice A. Egeland, Ph.D.

assistants had ever administered open-ended questions or had written the required lengthy field reports before, and developing these techniques involved long hours of shared review of their work. However, these difficulties were minor compared to the advantages of having ethnic field workers from a similar socioeconomic class as their respondents. They were invaluable in many ways: helping with the construction of new interview forms, modifying the language of existing instruments for their respective ethnic groups, and obtaining information that likely would have been withheld had the interviewer been from a higher economic level or from a different ethnic group. (An indication that the experience was as satisfying to the workers as it was to the professional staff is the fact that both the Bahamian and American black assistants are now enrolled in college, working toward a degree in anthropology.)

FIELD INSTRUMENTS

Three basic field research instruments were utilized in the Miami investigation: the Health Ecology Project Questionnaire, the Home Health Calendar, and the Value Orientation Scale. Each will be discussed separately.

Health ecology project questionnaire

This instrument, administered to a minimum of 100 families in each of the five ethnic groups, contained household and demographic information such as characteristics of the respondents' dwelling, and occupation, education, and religion of each family member; standard health survey information, such as the use of orthodox types of facilities and services for a 1 year period; and additional questions, created in Miami, to elicit information regarding the health care priorities, perceptions, and behaviors of the respondents. The questionnaire was designed in such a way that the data generated could be compared with those from the National Health Survey and a community health survey undertaken in Hershey, Pennsylvania.*

An additional unit within this questionnaire was the Symptoms and Conditions List.* The field workers used the standard list of illnesses from the National Health Survey, followed by what we termed the Ethnic Symptoms and Conditions List. This list, comprised of symptoms and syndromes that are culturally rather than medically defined, was different for each group. Two examples of items on each ethnic list are given below.

American black: "falling-out" (as in "I fell-out"); "high blood"
Bahamian: "blacking-out"; "low blood"
Cuban: *empacho; mal de ojo*
Haitian: "*mauvais sang*"; *saisaissement*
Puerto Rican: *pasmo; ataque*

The field workers taped each session in order to preserve the respondents' comments, which were rich in quality and quantity. A minimum of 20 families (within each ethnic sample of 100) had children enrolled in a pediatrics outpatient clinic (within the School of Medicine). This enabled us to obtain clinic records to compare with the family report of health problems for the identical 12-month period.

Home health calendar

This tool was adapted from the Harvard study of Alpert et al. (1967) and refined by Egeland and Wiest against clinical data in the Hershey, Pennsylvania, community health survey. These calendars, maintained daily by the mothers or mother surrogates in each family, depict the symptoms, upsetting events, and action (or nonaction) that was taken in response to the events. In giving the respondents the freedom to define and record illness in their own language (as expressed in their respective ethnic groups), we obtained data on culturally as well as medically defined conditions. In addition, we sought information regarding the degree of "disability" (time lost from normal activities) related to each recorded symptom or condition. A minimum of 35 families in each ethnic population kept calendars for 2 to 4 consecutive weeks.

---

*Janice A. Egeland, Ph.D., one of the codirectors on the Health Ecology Project in Miami, was project director of the Community Health Survey, a study undertaken within the Department of Behavioral Science, The Milton S. Hershey Medical Center, Pennsylvania State University.

*The Health Ecology Project Symptoms and Conditions List was adapted from a list of chronic conditions utilized in the National Health Survey and the symptoms list prepared for the international collaborative study of medical care utilization headed by Kerr White (1967).

Value orientation instrument

This tool, developed by Kluckhohn and Strodtbeck (1961) to provide statistical evidence of the dominant and variant values of a population, had already been applied in a number of cultural settings. The respondent indicates the values by which he lives and is guided by his choice of one of several alternative solutions to a "story" that presents a realistic life situation problem. Inasmuch as health-oriented stories were not included in the original Kluckhohn-Strodtbeck scale, special stories dealing with health behavior were devised for the Hershey Study and subsequently used in Miami. Analysis of the answers to these stories reveals the specific points at which the ethnic groups' health care beliefs and behaviors are a match or mismatch with the orthodox medical system.

During the course of our research in the multiethnic, inner city Miami setting, the importance of beliefs about blood in the three black populations began to emerge in multiple ways: on the Health Calendar, on the Symptoms and Conditions List, and from the assistants' reports of their in-depth interviewing. It evolved further in staff meetings with our field workers as we attempted to gain insight and understanding into the meaning of the field data. The discussion that follows will describe our investigations into: (1) conceptions relating to blood and its functions, a topic which directed our attention to (2) beliefs about menstruation, which led to recognition of (3) the importance of a sense of well-being.

CONCEPTIONS RELATING TO BLOOD AND ITS FUNCTIONS

A file relating to blood beliefs and associated behaviors was opened during the first year of the project as these became an object of interest. Late in the second year we decided to focus on this topic within the Haitian community because it was here that the beliefs appeared to be the most homogeneous.* Our Haitian assistant conducted 11 in-depth interviews structured by two open-ended questions: (1) What precautions do you take

---

*The reason for this probably lies in the fact that the Haitians comprise a new immigrant community in Miami. The vast majority of our sample have been here less than 4 years. Living in predominantly Haitian neighborhoods, most belong to the same social and economic group.

in regard to your blood? (2) What kind of problems might you have with your blood? Responses indicated that along with the prominent place given blood as a basic element in bodily functioning, Haitians see it as having dynamic properties which cause it to vary along numerous dimensions (Scott, 1973). Along some of these dimensions, the normal state is at one end of the scale; in others, the normal state is represented at mid-point, with the abnormal state appearing at either end:

Normal as mid-point on the scale

Too much ⟷ Normal ⟷ Too little
Heavy, strong ⟷ Normal ⟷ Poor, weak, low
Clotted ⟷ Normal ⟷ Thin
Quiet ⟷ Normal ⟷ Rapid, rushing, turbulent

Normal as one extremity of the scale

Unclean, bad ⟷ Clean, good (normal)

High ⟷ Normal
Sweet ⟷ Normal
Bitter (only occurs by ⟷ Normal
  magical means)

Several of these dimensions (too much, normal, too little; clotted, normal; thin; heavy, strong, normal, poor, weak, low; unclean, bad, clean, good, i.e., normal; and high normal) were found to be involved in the beliefs about body functioning as it relates to menstruation. For example, blood that does not flow as much as usual during the period is thought to remain inside the body. This makes a woman more vulnerable to illnesses such as high blood pressure and hypertension. Because the blood does not leave the body, it is seen as collecting and "rising," with high blood pressure the result. It can also become so thick and heavy that it may form clots in the abdomen.

BELIEFS ABOUT MENSTRUATION

At the same time as we were beginning to gain an understanding of concepts of body functioning that relate to blood, Health Ecology Project field assistants were bringing in data that indicated (1) many of the women being interviewed were dissatisfied with oral contraceptives and IUDs (both of which tend to modify the monthly cycle), and (2) many of these women were also IUD and "pill" drop-outs. Having been alerted to the importance of concepts about body functioning in the use and choice of fertility regulating methods (FRMs), we instituted further inquiry with the following hypothesis: a medical product such as an IUD or oral contraceptive, which modifies bodily functioning (i.e., the menses), must fit reasonably well into a woman's conceptions about the workings of her body and what affects her sense of well-being, or its use will be discontinued. The results of this study (Scott, 1974), which elicited information about the functioning and process of menstruation, are summarized below.

A majority of Bahamians, Cubans, Haitians, and Puerto Ricans believed the function of menstruation to be that of ridding the body of "unclean," "waste," or "unnecessary" blood. Many Haitians also expressed the belief that "it means you are a woman" ("woman" here meaning that the "individual has sexual feelings and needs and is not sterile"). A large number of Bahamians stated that menstruation "means you are healthy," underscoring this by the use of the word "health" as a substitute for monthly period; i.e., "my health came down last week" or "I missed my health last month." When questioned about the way in which less bleeding than normal or usual would affect the body/health, the majority believed it would mean "something is wrong." Many worried that there would be too much or unclean blood in the body and, as one Cuban respondent said, "Where is the bad blood going to be stored?"

Response to a question asking how *more* bleeding than normal or usual would affect the body/health, the overwhelming number viewed this in negative terms, such as "you don't have enough blood," and "you know something is wrong."

The responses suggest that:

1. The respondents questioned by our field workers use their menses as a diagnostic measure and as an indication of well-being, in both the physical and social sense (the sex role as it relates to reproduction and heterosexual activity).
2. It is a characteristic of our respondents to perceive the menstrual cycle as vital to the maintenance of one's health by virtue of cleansing the blood of impurities and removing unnecessary blood from the body.
3. The women who were interviewed seemed to feel that experiencing their menses kept them in harmony with nature and the natural rhythm of life.

"A corollary to all of these is that irregularity in the menstrual flow serves as a warning which indicates that 'something is wrong.' The woman feels her sense of health and well-being is threatened" (Scott 1975:108).

Literature pertaining to concepts about blood in other ethnic or cultural groups reflects the same thinking. Singarimbun, quoted in a WHO document (1973:Appendix D, 16), describes Japanese women as believing that:

Menstruation is thought to involve ridding the body of dirty blood, and one, at least, of its functions is to cleanse the blood and thus keep the woman healthy. It is also thought that a regular period is a sign of good health.

Teitlebaum (1973) notes "the relationship between blood beliefs and social relations in Tunisian perceptions of illness," stating that an individual who perceives family members or close associates as harboring ill feelings toward him suffers from worry and anger. This can cause "rotten" or "bad blood," which "must be removed from the body or it will afflict the individual with fever, weakness and pain, and will eventually . . . kill him. Traditionally, rotten blood has been removed by specialists using leeches, the cupping suction method or small incisions in the forehead . . ." (1972:5).

The concept of "bad" or "impure" blood is also present in Kenya (Kiteme, 1973) and East Africa (Gerlach, 1959). The treatment is said to be removal and cleansing of it. The presence of diseases caused by impure blood has also been noted in Ghana (Warren, 1975).

In a brief review of the legend and folklore regarding menstrual blood, McCormick (1973) reports that the menses is considered to have a functional value in that it cleanses the body of impurities and excess blood, thus maintaining the good health of women. Apparently referring to U.S. and Western European cultures, she cites Fluhman and Skultans as saying that the notion is still quite prevalent today. Snow's (1974) research among American blacks in parts of western and northern United States also indicates the prevalent belief in impure blood.

BELIEFS ABOUT WELL-BEING

The findings from the Health Ecology Project studies enhance the conviction (long held in varying degrees of intensity by Baumann, 1961; Schwartz, 1969; and Weidman, 1970) that a sense of well-being is a "key integrating process in any health cultural system" (Weidman et al., 1974).

Schwartz (1969:3-4) includes well-being in her definition of health culture, noting that it "is usually imbedded in more general notions . . . [such as] 'economic' and 'spiritual' well-being." She adds another dimension by hypothesizing that a sense of well-being could be differentiated on a cross-cultural basis. Because a sense of well-being includes dimensions (such as economic and spiritual) that may differ from culture to culture, it follows that the notion of well-being also may vary according to its cultural context.

Until relatively recently, however, it has not been clearly implicated in the behavioral sciences literature as a concept that is central to the individual's health *actions*. Weidman and Egeland (1973:854) were among the first to do this. In addition to incorporating the concept into their definition of health culture, they state that "profoundly held values along various parameters of well-being" may take priority over considerations such as economic factors, lack of understanding, and absence of health education in determining whether or not medical protocol will be properly carried out by the patient.

One of the key points concerning well-being is its multidimensional quality. It can be spoken of in physical, mental, psychological, and emotional dimensions. McCormick (1973:16), for example, refers to the "sense of physical and emotional well-being," while Berkman (1971) measures mental health with an eight-item index of psychological well-being. Other parameters commonly referred to include economic and social well-being.

These are not equal in value among individuals. Unique life experiences may lead one individual to give more weight to the economic than to the physical dimension (as the person who chooses a hazardous but highly paid job), while another might give precedence to the emotional over the eco-nomic dimension (as a teacher or minister). Nor are these dimensions equal in different cultural contexts. A member of an African tribal population would be likely to give more weight to the social dimension of well-being than would a young American seeking emotional and psychological well-being through self-actualization. Not only may the emphasis vary from individual to individual and from population to population, it may also vary in time through an individual's life or through cultural phases. Our Miami data lead us to suggest that cultural values in a particular group influence members of that group to focus on a different dimension of well-being from that which is central to another group; i.e., among Puerto Ricans, the cultural focus might be on the social role aspect and among southern blacks, the biological—both of which might take precedence over the economic dimension.

An example of this setting of priorities within a health care context might be a Puerto Rican woman in Miami who states that, for economic reasons, she would like a small family. However, she does not show interest in any method of family planning, orthodox or indigenous. Knowing that women in this ethnic group have been characterized as viewing the role of the wife and mother as a female's "whole purpose in being" (Owen and Scott, 1974:8), we would say that she has acted in a predictable manner. The economic dimension has been given an inferior position to a sense of well-being in terms of her social role.

Achievement or lack of a sense of well-being (sometimes treated in terms of security feelings) has been an area of interest among psychologists whose investigations provide us with bases for idiosyncratic variation. This chapter, however, deals with the sense of well-being only in cultural terms; i.e., the meaning of well-being to an individual as a cultural being.

Within a cultural context, the concept must be viewed in terms of (1) beliefs and practices that contribute to the maintenance of a sense of well-being, and (2) beliefs and practices that give a sense of mastery in times of stress (i.e., when anxiety undermines a sense of well-being). Both relate to health *action*. Those beliefs and practices that contribute to the maintenance of a sense of well-being can lead us down various paths, according to our cultural or ethnic group. If we are East Indian, we may focus on the maintenance of "order, balance, system, and hierarchy" in terms of our body, soul, senses, mind, and social milieu (Opler, 1963). If we are Puerto Rican, we will be concerned with keeping the proper balance of temperature and moistness in our bodies. We will take care to follow culturally prescribed practices not only in regard to food, but also in respect to contact with air of different temperatures (Harwood, 1971). To be excessively dry, cold, hot, or wet gives rise to anxiety which impinges upon our sense of well-being.

It is the *second* type of beliefs and practices, those which give a sense of mastery in times of anxiety, upon which this chapter focuses. Here, the assumption is that when anxiety is present within an individual, he or she lacks a sense of well-being. Howard and Scott (1965:154) speak of anxiety as:

. . . the response of an organism to a circumstance that threatens its sense of mastery. It may be specific, in response to a particular situation, or generalized . . ., in response to an overall feeling of inadequacy. Such a response is to be expected when an individual is confronted with an unsolvable problem, or set of problems, or when he lacks confidence in the resources available.

Medicine, prayer, and rituals are examples of cultural solutions to an anxiety-producing problem. Taking those steps that are culturally prescribed against that which is producing anxiety, gives us the feeling of mastery over the threat, known or unknown, and hence increases our sense of well-being. Maclean (1969) referring to her study in Nigeria, states that pregnant women, "subject to anxieties, both on their own behalf and on behalf of the unborn child" so fervently desired, look to those traditional healers and magic rituals that give promise that all will go smoothly. They will go on believing in the efficacy of the gods and of the indigenous medical system, because they cannot afford to be without a measure of mastery in time of stress.

Gillin (1951) makes the same point in writing about *The Culture of Security in San Carlos* (Guatemala). All cultures, Gillin states, recognize a certain number of both real and nonempirical threats and provide culturally determined ways for their members to respond to and cope with these anxieties. For example, a "real" culturally recognized threat in San Carlos is physical illness (such as intestinal parasites) for which the culture provides means of handling; i.e., herbal, home and patent medicine remedies, as well as modern medical treatment. ("Germs", a daily, culturally provided worry of North Americans, do not exist as part of San Carlos health concepts and thus do not cause anxiety among San Carlos residents.) A culturally recognized, nonempirical threat would be an attack by witchcraft, for which the culture provides a solution—the victim can seek the help of a *brujo* (witch) who will "take off" the spell. In sum, an individual's culture furnishes him with the kinds of worries he should have concerning his physical and emotional well-being. However, it also supplies "specialists, patterns of procedures, and materialistic remedies to ease his anxieties and, perhaps, to erase his physical pains" (Gillin, 1951:118).

On the basis of our current knowledge from field data and our understanding from the literature, we propose an hypothesis that rests on the following three assumptions:

1. Each individual holds beliefs about the working of the human body that he or she has learned within the cultural group.
2. When body processes that the individual perceives as "normal" and "healthy" change, anxiety results and culturally–prescribed solutions are sought in order to restore a sense of well-being.
3. What a woman perceives as "normal" menstruation may be essential to her sense of well-being in terms of her bodily functioning and social role.

With the proper research design, our initial hunches could be developed into specific hypotheses. Based on our current work in the field, however, our views about behavior include four possibilities. One is that when a woman makes a decision in favor of family planning and the method the doctor chooses disrupts her biologically based sense of well-being, she may discontinue the use of that method and try another in the orthodox repertoire.

American black: I used the coil for only one month because it fell out by itself. Then I started on the pill and I used to get real sick with vomits and dizziness. I decided to stop them without telling the doctor. I became pregnant [with a fourth child] and after that I had a tubal ligation. After I had the tubal ligation, I feel bad. Sometimes I think I should not have [had] that done.

A second possibility is that the woman will discontinue use of that contraceptive method and *not* try another. These fertility regulation methods of the orthodox system have been developed within the Western, scientific medical field. They are the culturally prescribed solutions of the white Anglo health culture to the problem of limiting family size. They are not one of the accepted Cuban solutions within Cuba (inexpensive abortions) nor are they the frequent Puerto Rican response in Puerto Rico (tubal ligation). Neither of these solutions is readily available to these ethnic groups in Miami; nor has exposure to scientific, white Anglo explanations of gynecological functioning been sufficient to change their traditional beliefs about body processes. With her back to the wall, so to speak, the woman in this situation may resolve her conflict by abandoning family planning.

Health Ecology Project field work data revealed many cases in which women who temporarily abandoned all types of fertility regulating methods, but eventually went on to the use of another one in either the orthodox or indigenous system.

A third alternative is that the woman may discontinue use of the orthodox contraceptive methods and fall back on a traditional (indigenous) method. Fertility regulating methods of the orthodox armamentarium may actually precipitate the use of traditional methods in some women by disturbing their sense of biological well-being.

Cuban: Artificial products cause damage to the woman. My uncle who is a doctor showed me a method to use so I do not have to use an "apparatus" [diaphragm] anymore. When I am having sexual intercourse and the man is going to finish, I hold my breath and quickly swallow a glass of cold water which I keep near me. Since my body is warm at this time, swallowing the cold water cools my womb and kills the sperm. Then I go to the bathroom and clean my vagina with water and soap.

Bahamian: I used to use the pills but they made me bleed too much. They made my head hurt and my stomach cramped me. I was so sick the doctor took me off them. He wanted me to take the diaphragm. I said the hell with that. My baby is now two. I use red vinegar and water for douching. It chills the womb and tightens it so the sperm won't go in. It works fine. An old woman told me about this.

A fourth possibility is that the woman will continue to use an orthodox fertility regulation method but *at the expense* of her well-being, and this stress will be expressed in behavioral forms such as "guilt, depression, psychosomatic symptomatology and less frequently, emotional disorder" (Weidman et al., 1974:6). There may be disagreement among medical professionals as to whether certain symptoms are psychosomatic or biologically based. However, we believe that there are sufficient indications from our field data, as well as from medical investigations such as that of Goldzieher et al. (1971), to indicate a need to rule out this possibility. When we see patterned behavior among women who state that a decreased menstrual flow will result in the excess blood rising to the head, and who *also* complain of headaches, the onset of which began in conjunction with the use of oral contraceptives, a sufficient basis for investigation is apparent.

This also has implications for tubal ligations and hysterectomies, which may disturb not only the biological sense of well-being but also the sense of well-being associated with one's social role and sphere of interpersonal relations. Cases have come to our attention in which not only psychosomatic symptoms but even psychosis followed these operations. Anxiety is evident in the following statements. Bahamian: "It can make you lose your nature [fail to enjoy sexual activity] and if you take the pill too long it will kill your female hormones and turn you into a man." American black: "The pill makes me feel drowsy and nervous because I wonder where the flow is going. It might back up . . ." Haitian: "I would like to stop the pill; it makes me feel like crying; I get nervous and my head becomes big and I am tired." Cuban: "The pill stirs your body up in some way." Bahamian: "A pill that can kill egg or a sperm can also kill parts of your body."

Our data indicate a need, as stated by Weidman et al. (1974:6), for basic research into the "relationship between a sense of well-being within the traditional health cultural system and successful implementation of fertility regulating programs by the orthodox health cultural systems."

At this stage of our understanding, a sense of well-being is still only of theoretical significance in the cross-cultural delivery of gynecological health care. There is growing recognition, however, of its importance in applied terms. The World Health Organization Task Force on fertility regulating methods has stated that a method must be "perceived by potential users as being consonant with their well-being" (WHO 1973a). McCormick (1973) has called for systematic research investigations into the relationship of menstruation to concepts of femininity, body image, and a sense of physical and emotional well-being. A cross-cultural model of investigation that utilizes standardized field instruments applicable in populations all over the world could clarify the use/nonuse of fertility regulating methods in terms of biological considerations (conceptions, perceptions, and beliefs about bodily functioning) and primary social roles in sexual, family, and community contexts. It is within these biological and social contexts that those factors that support or disrupt one's sense of well-being are found and that, in turn, influence use/nonuse of fertility regulating methods (Weidman et al., 1974).

REFERENCES

Alpert, J., Kosa, J., and Haggerty, R. J. 1967. A month of illness and health care among low income families. Public Health Reports 82(8):705-713.

Baumann, B. 1961. Diversities in conceptions of health and physical fitness. Journal of Health and Human Behavior 11(1):39-46.

Berkman, P. L. 1971. Life stress and psychological well-being: A replication of Langner's analysis in the Midtown Manhattan Study. Journal of Health and Social Behavior 12(1):35-45.

Gerlach, L. P. 1959. Some basic Digo considerations of health and disease among some East African tribes. East African Institute of Social Research, Makerere College, Kampala, Uganda, pp. 8-35.

Gillin, J. 1951. The culture of security in San Carlos: A study of a Guatemalan community of Indians and Ladino. Publication #16, Middle American Research Institute, The Tulane University of Louisiana, Tulane Press, New Orleans.

Goldzieher, J. W., Moses, L. E., Averkin, E., Scheel,

C. and Taber, B. 1971. Nervousness and depression attributed to oral contraceptives: A double-blind, placebo-controlled study. American Journal of Obstetrics and Gynecology 111(8):1013-1020.

Harwood, A. 1971. The hot-cold theory of disease. JAMA 216(7):1153-1158.

Howard, A., and Scott, R. 1965. A proposed framework for the analysis of stress in the human organism. Behavioral Science 10(2):141-154.

Kiteme, K. 1973. Doctor still makes house calls. Ebony, May, 113.

Kluckhohn, F., and Strodtbeck, F. 1961. Variations in value orientations. Row, Peterson and Company, Evanston, Ill.

Maclean, U. 1969. In defense of their children. New Society 10(July):52.

McCormick, P. 1973. Transcultural perceptions of menstruation. Summary prepared for presentation at the Menstrual Regulation Conference, Honolulu.

Opler, M. E. 1963. The cultural definition of illness in village India. Human Organization 22(1):32-35.

Owen, R. G., and Scott, C. S. 1974. Anthropological considerations in multi-ethnic health care settings. Paper presented at the 102nd Annual Meeting of the American Public Health Association, New Orleans.

Polgar, S. 1962. Health and human behavior: areas of interest common to the social and medical sciences. Current Anthropology 3:159-205.

Schwartz, L. R. 1969. An investigation into the systematics of health care and culture. Research proposal prepared for personal distribution.

Scott, C. S. 1973. Haitian blood beliefs and practices in Miami, Florida. Paper presented at the Annual Meeting of the American Anthropological Association, New Orleans.

Scott, C. S. 1974. Cart before the horse: Birth control technology before knowledge of body concepts. Paper prepared for the 9th Annual Meeting of the Southern Anthropological Society, Blacksburg, Virginia.

Scott, C. S. 1975. The relationship between beliefs about the menstrual cycle and the choice of fertility regulating methods within five ethnic groups. International Journal of Gynaecology and Obstetrics 13:105-109.

Snow, L. 1974. Folk medical beliefs and their implications for care of patients. Annals of Internal Medicine 81(1):82-96.

Teitlebaum, J. M. 1972. Ill humor and bad blood. Paper prepared for the American Association for the Advancement of Sciences, Washington D.C.

Teitlebaum, J. M. 1973. Humoral theory and therapy in Tunisia. Paper presented at the International Congress of Anthropological and Ethnological Sciences, Chicago.

Warren, D. M. 1975. The role of emic analysis in medical anthropology: The case of the Bono of Ghana. Anthropological Linguistics 11(3):117-126.

Weidman, H. H. 1970. Anthropological perspectives on the comparative approach to the delivery of health care. Paper presented for the 2nd International Conference of Social Science and Medicine, Aberdeen, Scotland.

Weidman, H. H., and Egeland, J. A. 1973. A behavioral science perspective in the comparative approach to the delivery of health care. Social Science and Medicine 7:845-860.

Weidman, H. H., Egeland, J. A., and Scott, C. S. 1974. Use or non-use of orthodox (scientific) and traditional (folk) fertility regulating mechanisms (FRMs) by males and females in five inner-city ethnic groups as related to the concept of a sense of well-being, perceptions of bodily-functioning, and definition of social roles. Research proposal to National Institute of Child Health and Human Development.

World Health Organization. 1973a. Terms of reference. Task Force on Acceptability of Fertility Regulating Methods. Doc. ATF-G: 5 (2/73).

World Health Organization. 1973b. Report on a planning meeting of the Task Force on Acceptability of FRMs, Appendix D, 12-14. Geneva (Doc. ATF-G: 6 3/73).

CHAPTER 10

Conflicts in the study of Chagas' disease between a southwestern Indian population and the staff of a southwestern university college of medicine

Thomas G. Betz

DISCOVERY OF CHAGAS' DISEASE

In 1909, Carlos Chagas eloquently described a parasitic disease occurring in the human bloodstream that was transmitted by insects. Although scientifically labeled American trypanosomiasis, this disease is more commonly called Chagas' disease in deference to its discoverer. Chagas' (1909) description of the disease is remarkable in that he not only identified the hemoflagellate responsible, *Trypanosoma cruzi*, but he also correctly identified the insect vectors, species of the family Reduviidae, and the natural mammalian reservoirs, armadillos and similar mammals. His only mistake was that he felt the parasite was transmitted to humans via the bite of the insect, as occurs in transmission of malaria via the salivary glands of mosquitoes. It remained for Brumpt to demonstrate in 1912 that the parasite was located in the hindgut of the insects and transmitted to humans through the insects' feces (James and Harwood, 1969). The insects defecate while feeding and the person is inoculated with the infected feces in the bite site, a skin abrasion, or the conjunctiva.

Chagas initially discovered *Trypanosoma cruzi* in the blood of a young girl. The girl apparently sustained few damaging effects from her disease. She outlived Chagas; she was alive in the late 1960s and she may still be alive today (Wilcocks and Manson-Bahr, 1972). Unfortunately, for many patients Chagas' disease is anything but benign. In South and Central America 35 million people are at risk of developing Chagas' disease. Seven to 8 million persons in these areas actually have the disease. In the United States and most of the civilized world arteriosclerotic heart disease is the major cause of cardiovascular deaths. In South America the major cause of cardiovascular death is Chagas' disease (Hoeprich 1972). Although the disease has been recognized for over half a century it still remains a disease without cure. There are currently no antibiotics considered effective against Chagas' disease. The only effective treatment is prevention—avoidance of contact with infected insects. Experimentation with the development of a vaccine continues, but as of now there are no indications that this will be fruitful.

Charles Darwin formulated his earthshaking ideas on evolution while travelling on *HMS Beagle*. On that voyage, he often ventured into the South American continent. There he was bitten by "kissing bugs," the common name for those insects responsible for the transmission of Chagas' disease. Years later he developed symptoms of congestive heart failure, and many investigators feel that his death was caused by Chagas' disease.

Chagas' disease is an example of man stumbling into a host-vector-parasite situation and becoming himself an indirect host. As a host, man has some faults. In a host-parasite relationship, the object is symbiosis and, ultimately, survival. It does neither the host nor the parasite any good if the parasite causes death of the host, which also results in death for the parasite. Unfortunately, man, as a host for *T. cruzi*, often dies. Whether by direct cytotoxic action or immunological response, *T. cruzi* is capable of causing extensive damage to the human myocardium and cells of the mysenteric or Auerbach's plexuses of the human intestine, along with damage to other tissues such as striated muscle, the reticuloendothelial system, and the central nervous system.

The major results of this tissue destruction are the development of congestive heart failure, usually left-sided with right-sided conduction defects accompanying the left-sided dilatation, or the development of megaesophagus or megacolon in the intestinal tract. Because of some strain differences in *T. cruzi*, the cardiac pathology is more prevalent in Colombia, Venezuela, and northern Brazil, whereas the intestinal pathology is more prevalent in central Brazil.

In the development of Chagas' disease there are three important prerequisites: the presence of the parasite, *T. cruzi;* the presence of a suitable insect vector in which the parasite can survive, mature, and be passed on to suitable hosts; and man.

T. cruzi was first reported in the United States in 1916, after it was found in a kissing bug, *Triatoma protracta*, in California (Kofoid and McCullogh, 1916). In 1936, Triatoma insects infected with *T. cruzi* were discovered in Arizona (Kofoid and Whitaker, 1936); in 1939, infected insects were discovered in Texas (Packchanian, 1939); and in 1961, were reported in New Mexico (Wood and Wood, 1961).

In 1943, Packchanian inoculated a Texas strain of *T. cruzi* into the conjunctival sac of a human "volunteer." Fourteen days later the patient developed a fever lasting 21 days, accompanied by lid edema and axillary adenopathy. The parasite remained in the blood for 84 days. In 1955, Woody and Woody reported on the first naturally occurring case of Chagas' disease in the United States. They discovered *T. cruzi* in the blood of a febrile, 10-month-old girl from Corpus Christi, Texas. The fever persisted for 19 days. Cultures for *T. cruzi* in the blood were negative after 108 days. They identified the insect vector as *Triatoma gerstaeckeri*, a species of kissing bug found in Texas and some other southern states. Woody and Woody (1964) also re-

ported another case of *T. cruzi* in the United States in 1955, which occurred in Houston, Texas. A 5-month-old infant with salmonella meningitis subsequently developed hydrocephalus. *T. cruzi* was identified in the cerebrospinal fluid draining from the left ventricle. This was apparently an incidental finding and did not represent clinical Chagas' disease. This strain was not virulent when tested on laboratory animals.

In 1964, Bice carried out a study on the prevalence of *T. cruzi* among Triatoma insects living in pack rat (Neotomae) nests in the Tucson, Arizona area. He found that 7.5% of *Triatoma rubida* and 19.5% of *Triatoma protracta* were infected with *T. cruzi*. This compares favorably with other studies done in the United States. Most of these studies show rates of infection in Triatoma insects below 50%. Some areas in South American show insect infection rates of 100%.

Woody and Woody (1955) have described the normal evolution of the discovery of Chagas' disease in a country. First, a few initial cases are reported. Then, as more persons become aware of the presence of the disease, there is a rapid and dramatic increase in the number of reported cases. This evolutionary sequence normally occurs within a decade and would certainly be expected to occur as rapidly in the United States. As of May 1978 the two cases of Chagas' disease reported by Woody and Woody in 1975 remained the only reported cases in the United States.

STUDY OF CHAGAS' DISEASE IN THE UNITED STATES

We are now ready to consider the particular case of Chagas' disease in the United States. The following discussion omits any identity of the peoples concerned.

In 1972, blood samples were taken from 452 southwestern Indians for a diabetes mellitus survey. After blood glucose determinations were made, the sera were frozen. In the spring of 1974, some members of a southwestern university college of medicine decided that if Chagas' disease were to be found in the southwestern United States, it would occur in rural areas with fairly open housing. The southwestern Indian life-style fits this description. When it was discovered that the diabetes survey sera existed, a request was made to obtain them for serological studies for Chagas' and some other parasitic diseases. The request was granted and the sera were sent to a competent diagnostic laboratory. The Indians were not consulted in this action since it was felt that their confidentiality was maintained and the studies represented no further risk to them.

The complement fixation tests done for Chagas' disease showed 19 (over 3%) of the sera to be positive. This was a surprising finding since the tests have an accuracy rate of approximately 95%. It appeared that the southwestern Indians were a population within the United States that demonstrated a high rate of contact with *T. cruzi.*

The university staff then approached the Indian tribe and their designated health care agency with the findings. Instead of the expected gratitude, they were met with something between shock and indignation. A scathing letter was sent to the university staff from a member of the designated health care facility for the Indians, and the university staff and the Indian tribe quickly found themselves at odds in this quest for knowledge of Chagas' disease in Arizona.

The first order of business for the Indian tribe was to determine why they had not been consulted before their sera were used in the study. The university staff, on the other hand, was anxious to determine the clinical significance of the positive titers in the patients. The university staff wanted to see patients and blood. The tribe wanted explanations. This continued for 6 months.

During this period occasional contacts were made with the designated health care facility for the tribe in the hope that facility staff would put in a good word for further study of *T. cruzi* among the tribe. The university staff was told that they should deal directly with the tribe. Since no one on the university staff seemed to know what other members of the staff were doing, several individual contacts were made with the Indian health care facility before it finally dawned on the university staff that they should contact the tribe directly. After a hasty initial meeting with some of the members of the tribal health council, which the chairman did not attend because of illness, a formal meeting was arranged in November 1974, between the tribal health council and the university staff involved in the study.

The meeting took on several interesting characteristics. Efforts were made to appease the tribe by apologizing for not consulting them first, although some of the university staff still felt they had done nothing wrong in their failure to consult the tribe. Further efforts were made to point out to the tribe that there were a lot of new faces among the university staff who had nothing to do with the original sera study, apparently in the hope that the tribal council did not subscribe to the concept of original sin. The tribal council accepted the apologies, making brief comments to the effect that this was not to happen again.

The stage was then set for the study proposal. Containing something for everyone, the proposal offered to follow up all those individuals who were positive for Chagas' disease and provide whatever clinical assistance was available from the university staff; to obtain further blood samples from those and other individuals for serological study; to study the insect vectors in the area and suggest ways to exterminate them; to give suggestions for bug-proofing houses; and to train interested Indians in the epidemiology of Chagas' disease. A particularly low point came when someone proposed using insecticides against the kissing bugs. This was tactfully modified by one of the university staff members when he suggested that pyrethrin spray, a *natural* insecticide derived from chrysanthemum plants, could be used against the insects. Following this there was a brief comment by one of the tribal council members that the tribe did not want to be "researched" as guinea pigs. They also demanded that they be consulted in every facet of the study so that no other serological studies would be done without their knowledge.

Then came the question, "What can be done for someone who has Chagas' disease?" Backed into a position of defense, the staff valiantly emphasized the importance of prevention and need for knowledge in a disease for which there is no cure. Somewhat akin to attempting to conceal an elephant under a leaf, it was difficult to hide the fact that little, if anything, can be done for a person with Chagas' disease. The Indians wanted to know why, if Chagas' disease were such a problem, hadn't they seen or heard about it before. The staff members admitted that they didn't know but wanted to find out. Then came a period of silence, sometimes known as an Indian pause.

The pause lasted more than 2 months. During this time the members of the tropical medicine section of the university staff could not believe that the Indians would not eagerly embrace the study. Where was the scientific pride of the Indians? Several secretive and diplomatic phone calls were made to those members of the tribal health council with whom the university staff felt they had the best rapport. At the same time, some of the staff felt that they should submit a grant proposal, based primarily on the study of Chagas' disease among the Indians, prior to tribal consent. However, this was not done after it was pointed out that the tribe might not like this approach.

Also, during this time some interesting points came to light. Although the designated health care facility for the Indians pleaded autonomy from the tribal health council, it was learned that the tribal secretary was close to a staff member of the health care facility. She was not a member of the tribe. Although the chairman of the tribal health council avoided the initial meeting, his sister did attend.

Things did not look good, and hope was beginning to fade. In January 1975, a "feeler" came from the tribe to the effect that they would participate in the study if they were paid for collecting bugs. This came as a shock to one of the staff who felt that the Indians should be delighted to collect bugs in the interest of science.

The person responsible for Indian affairs at the university called to find out what was going on since he had recently heard that the tribe was upset with the university staff. After the past history and the now infamous unauthorized sera study were explained to him, he decided that this was the probable cause of the comments he had received. Then it was learned that blood specimens were going to be drawn from the Indians by one of the physicians at the health care facility. But had the tribe given its approval? Maybe this was the cause of the most recent comments to the director of Indian affairs at

the university. It was not. The tribe had finally agreed to have those individuals with positive titers for Chagas' disease examined at the cardiology clinic of the designated health care facility.

Following the formal meeting in November 1974, the list of patient identification numbers for those individuals with positive titers was sent to the director of the health care facility rather than to the tribal council, so that, if the tribe desired, these individuals could be followed up with maintenance of confidentiality. The director acknowledged receipt of this letter, and the university staff breathed a sigh of relief. However, just as the original list of hospital numbers was about to be sent out, an urgent follow-up letter came stating that the original numbers were incorrect. The correct numbers were included in the letter and another problem had seemingly been averted.

The first cardiology clinic at the health facility devoted to patients with positive titers for Chagas' disease occurred in February 1975. Many hours of planning and effort by the facility staff went into ensuring that this clinic went as smoothly and trouble free as possible. Patients were transported from as far as 80 miles away. Every patient had blood samples drawn, a chest X-ray, and an electrocardiogram. This seemed almost too good to be true. As it turned out, it *was* too good to be true. A comparison of the list of corrected patient identification numbers with the clinic patient numbers showed that none of the patients in the cardiology clinic was one of those with a positive titer for Chagas' disease.

Then the cardiologist walked in. He thought that the idea of Chagas' disease occurring in the southwestern United States was ridiculous, and made no effort to hide these feelings from the staff or the patients. Then he learned that all the wrong patients had been brought to the clinic. It turned out that the corrected list had never been forwarded to the staff of the clinic, and somewhere in the distant past, when everything was confused, the wrong list had found its way into the right hands. Thus the Chagas' study became the object of much hilarity, much to the chagrin of the university clinic staff who had devoted so much of their time to the project. Unfortunately, the tribal council did not think the situation was funny. This seemed to be one mistake too many. Had it not been that the designated health facility had apparently broken the chain of communication concerning the correct numbers, the study most likely would have ended here.

But the study continues.* In March 1975 the cardiologist saw 5 patients with positive titers for Chagas' disease. Fortunately, none has demonstrated evidence of Chagas' disease.

CONCEPTS OF ILLNESS

How does Chagas' disease fit into this southwestern Indian population's concept of illness? Perhaps the more important question is where does Anglo medicine fit into the concept of Chagas' disease? The Indians have assimilated Anglo medicine into their culture where it can exist side by side with their own medicine. They have done this by allocating to Anglo medicine all those problems that cannot be explained by Indian medicine. This distinction hinges on diseases of natural and unnatural causes. If the disease has a natural cuase, it can be diagnosed by an Indian diagnostician who then directs the patient to an Indian curer. A history of symptomatology is not necessary in the elucidation of the illness since the diagnostician can tell what is wrong with the patient merely by examining him.

The Indians believe that animals, plants, crystal rocks, and natural phenomena such as thunder and lightning are "beings" endowed with power which, if disturbed, may cause illness in an individual. This is the result of an imbalance of power between the being (agent causing the illness) and the patient. Once the illness is determined by the diagnostician, the curer can sing appropriate songs directed at appeasing the being, so that it will withdraw its power.

Since many of the plants, animals, and natural elements in the Indians' environment have this potential power, the Indians make efforts to avoid those agents known to be particularly powerful, and to treat others with respect. They are careful not to treat animals with unnecessary cruelty. They feel that the dignity of the animal must be maintained. The beings (agents) themselves are considered harmless. It is the power residing within them that is potentially harmful. Many Indian stories warn against the mistreatment of beings. Thus, in the classical sense, Indian medicine deals directly with those agents within the Indians' natural environment. Anglo medicine is allowed to deal with those problems that do not relate to this natural scheme of things.

It would appear that Chagas' disease has all the elements of an Indian illness. It is an illness, carried by familiar bugs, that causes difficulties with the heart. (It should be noted that the concept of germs or microorganisms does not occur in the classical concepts of illness for this particular tribe.) Emphasis has been placed on the preventive aspects of Chagas' disease by dealing with the insects rather than attempting to cure the disease, as is usually the case in Anglo medicine. The kissing bugs, therefore, appear as a source of power in the scenario of Chagas' disease.

If one subscribes to the classical Indian view of illness, it would be easy to conclude that Chagas' disease fits far better into the Indian system of illness than it fits into the Anglo system. To carry this conclusion one step farther, how, then, can Anglo doctors effectively deal with a "classic" Indian illness? As far as I can determine, the kissing bug is not a powerful being for this Indian population. In fact, I have not been able to find it listed as even a potential source of power. If this is the case, then it might seem to some Indians that the Anglo doctors are out of their element in their efforts to deal with Chagas' disease. If such a disease were important, it would have been noticed by the Indians long before the Anglos mentioned it.

A culture is not a static entity. It changes as the situation demands. Many of the Indians now live within an Anglo system of

---

*By the end of summer, 1975, the study appeared to be in its death throes. Further investigation revealed that perhaps some of the serologies had been incorrectly interpreted as positive. An investigator from the Center for Disease Control decided that the problem with Chagas' disease was probably not very significant and, therefore, did not warrent extensive investigation. Rigor mortis seemed imminent. But, just as the Phoenix rose again out of the desert, so too this study has defied logic, for as recently as the November, 1977, meeting of the American Society of Tropical Medicine and Hygiene, there was an exhibit based on the original positive serologies from the Indians.

medicine. Some may adhere to the classical Indian concepts of illness, but many do not. The preceding paragraphs present a concept of why Anglo medicine might find it difficult to deal with this Indian population in the realm of Chagas' disease. I feel the matter is considerably more complex than that. There is some validity to the idea that, when it comes down to kissing bugs and pack rats, the Indians have more confidence in themselves than in Anglo doctors. After all, these animals are a part of the Indian life-style and environment. On the other hand, the Chagas study has been a fine example of how *not* to carry out an investigation. Many serious mistakes have exacerbated the situation. At times the study has taken on the appearance of a farce. The decision to participate in the study was made by members of the tribe who are in the fringe between Anglo and Indian cultures. They may well be some of the tribal members farthest removed from the classical Indian concepts of illness.

My general impression in dealing with the difficulties involved in the Chagas study is that this Indian population exhibits many characteristics that are common to many minority groups. For many years, when the clinical evaluation of an innovation in medical care or treatment was undertaken, it was often carried out in an area of low income, minority group people. Although this may have benefited the particular community, it did not require much thought on the part of the participants to deduce that they were really involved in an experiment.

Since the 1960s, minority groups have been given, and have accepted, a much greater role in the participation and planning of certain aspects of their lives. Among these has been their participation in medical experiments. In general, people would much rather receive optimal medical treatment than participate in an experiment designed to determine what that optimal treatment is. Unfortunately, in order to determine what the optimal treatment or system is, people who do not receive that treatment must have a significantly poorer outcome.

Thus human experimentation has not been widely embraced by low income, minority groups. Perhaps they would approve of it more if if were carried out on middle and upper class whites. At any rate, this attitude

has been quite evident in the study of Chagas' disease with this Indian population. It is not enough to know that the study will benefit science and mankind; individuals need to know how it will benefit them. Rather than ascribing the difficulties in the Chagas study to differences between the Indian and Anglo concepts of illness, I think it wiser to view the reaction as an expression of a people who have realized that they can have more influence in the control of their destiny. I believe the reaction would be similar if the roles were reversed. As a member of a scientific community, I find the situation frustrating at times. As a more objective viewer, I find it encouraging to see a people begin to feel enough confidence in themselves to demand a major role in a study that involves them directly. They have come to the realization that they can say "no," perhaps not to the benefit of the Chagas study, but certainly to the benefit of themselves.

There still is no good answer as to why Chagas' disease is not more prominent in the southwestern U.S. Certainly, appropriate infectious organisms, insect vectors, and animal reservoirs are present. The insect vectors are coming into contact with man. They are infected. Based on the strain differences of *T. cruzi* seen in South America, it has been postulated that the *T. cruzi* occurring in the United States is not pathogenic for man. However, the *T. cruzi* isolated from the young girl in Corpus Christi, Texas has shown virulence similar to that of a Venezuelan strain of *T. cruzi*. It has produced significant pathology in laboratory animals.

Others have hypothesized that the feeding-defecation habits of the southwestern U.S. Triatomae are different from those of the South and Central American insects. Those Triatomae in South America have a faster feeding-defecation sequence, which is necessary for infection by *T. cruzi*. The southwestern U.S. Triatomae may not defecate until after they have left the host upon which they were feeding. Most of this is speculation. It is fairly obvious that not much is really known about the interactions between *T. cruzi*, the Triatomae, the Neotomae (pack rats), and man in the southwestern U.S.

Many efforts have been made to draw conclusions about Chagas' disease in the southwestern U.S. by using epidemiological data from South and Central America. The situations are simply not the same. It is therefore unwise to make analogies between what is happening in the southwestern U.S. and South America. Chagas' disease may have entirely different manifestations in the Southwest. At present, Chagas' disease in the Southwest presents an epidemiological puzzle that can be solved only by using its own individual pieces.

REFERENCES

Bahr, D. 1974. Piman shamanism and staying sickness. University of Arizona Press, Tucson, Arizona.

Bice, D. E. 1964. The incidence of *Trypanosoma cruzi* in *triatoma* of Tucson, Arizona. Department of Zoology, University of Arizona, Tucson, Arizona.

Chagas, C. 1909. Ueber eine neue Trypanosomiasis des menschen. Mem. Inst. Oswaldo Cruz 1:159-218.

Hoeprich, P. D. 1972. Infectious diseases. Harper & Row, New York.

James, M. T., and Harwood, R. F. 1969. Medical entomology, ed. 6. MacMillan, New York.

Kofoid, C. A., and McCullogh, I. 1916. *Trypanosoma triatomae (cruzi)*, new flagellate from a hemipteran bug from the nests of the wood rat, *Neotoma fuscipes*. University of California, Pub. Zool. 16:113-126.

Kofoid, C. A., and Whitaker, B. G. 1936. Natural infection of American human trypanosomiasis in two species of cone nosed bugs, *Triatoma protracta* and *Triatoma uhleri*, in the Western United States. Journal of Parasitology 22:259-263.

Packchanian, A. 1939. Natural infection of *Triatoma gerstaeckeri* with *Trypanosoma cruzi* in Texas. Public Health Reports 54:1547-1554.

Packchanian, A. 1943. Infectivity of the Texas strain *Trypanosoma cruzi* to man. American Journal of Tropical Medicine 23:309-313.

Shaw, R. D. 1968. Health concepts and attitudes of the Papago Indians. Master's thesis. University of Arizona, Tucson, Arizona.

Wilcocks, C., and Manson-Bahr, P. 1972. Manson's tropical diseases, ed. 17, Williams and Wilkins, Baltimore.

Wood, S. F., and Wood, F. D. 1961. Observations on vectors of Chagas' disease in the United States. III. New Mexico. American Journal of Tropical Medicine and Hygiene 10:155-165.

Woody, N. C., and Woody, H. B. 1955. American trypanosomiasis (Chagas' disease), October J.A.M.A. 159:676-677.

Woody, N. C., and Woody, H. B. 1964. Chagas' disease in the United States of North America. International Congress on Chagas' Disease, 1959, Rio de Janeiro, vol. 5.

CHAPTER 11

The Riverside School Heart Project: a laboratory in applied medical anthropology

Gail G. Harrison
Marie Tymrak
Glenn Friedman

. . . Western models of medical practice or of health theory do not stand alone as cultural fragments but are woven into a larger system of custom and value. Patient-practitioner relations represent peculiarly interesting and complicated conversations across cultures.

R. N. Wilson
The Sociology of Health: an Introduction
(New York: Random House, 1970)

Public health programs usually involve the interaction of two or more distinct cultures or subcultures. Awareness of differences in perception, expectation, and behavior between the innovating subculture and the target group(s) may substantially contribute to the success with which health professionals are able to operate. This chapter will attempt to point out specific sociocultural considerations that have been important to the success of a particular public health program, the Riverside School Family Cardiovascular Risk Factor Screening and Intervention Project. This program is an attempt to lower risk factors for cardiovascular disease among elementary school children and their families in a bicultural (Mexican-American and Anglo) school in Phoenix, Arizona, and is serving as a model for other programs in schools.

ATHEROSCLEROSIS AS A PUBLIC HEALTH PROBLEM

Cardiovascular disease is the leading cause of death in the United States, accounting for 1 million of the 1.9 million deaths recorded in 1970. Ischemic heart disease alone accounted for 666,665 deaths, with stroke run-

ning second as the cause of 207,166 deaths (U.S. Public Health Service, 1974), although there is some evidence that mortality from coronary heart disease has been declining in the last several years (Mann, 1977; Kolata and Marx, 1976). The population most at risk of dying from cardiovascular disease is the middle-aged male population, with overweight, smoking, hypertension, stress, high blood lipid levels, and lack of physical exercise acting as contributory risk factors.

Atherosclerosis is commonly thought of as a disease of middle age, since it results in the death and disability of so many middle-aged and elderly individuals. But the evidence is convincing that the current epidemic of coronary heart disease (CHD) cannot be explained as a normal aging process. Autopsy data on individuals who died of accidents or acute infections during the early 1960s, compared with similar data from 20 years earlier, show that the prevalence of atherosclerosis in people of the same age has been increasing over the last few decades in the United States (Spain, 1966). Further, atherosclerotic lesions have been shown to develop very early in life, making it apparent that the preven-

95

tion of CHD may be more a pediatric problem than a geriatric one. Autopsies of U.S. soldiers killed during the Korean War showed extensive formation of atherosclerotic plaques at the average age of 23 (Enos et al., 1955). Holman et al. (1958) investigated the formation of atheromas in relation to growth, and found in all the children he studied some evidence of fatty streaks in the aorta by the age of 3 years. Moon (1957) studied coronary arteries in individuals ranging in age from fetuses to young adults. Only in fetuses did he find no change in the coronary artieries. By the age of 3 to 4 months, histological changes in the arterial wall were evident, which he interpreted as the forerunner of atherosclerotic disease.

While neither the etiological mechanisms that result in the atheromatous plaque nor the definitions of normal are clearly delineated, it is clear that mortality and morbidity from CHD in adults are consistently associated with a constellation of risk factors that include a family history of heart disease, obesity, cigarette smoking, lack of physical exercise, stress, elevated levels of serum cholesterol and triglycerides, and hypertension. Various studies show that at least some of the above risk factors are present at a high rate among children as well as adults and that many of the risk factors increase in prevalence and severity with age. Further, most of the risk factors are associated with lifelong habits of diet, exercise, and life-style. Therefore, preventive efforts aimed at children seem sensible (Golubjatnikov et al., 1972; Friedman and Goldberg, 1973a).

Most preventive efforts, however, have focused on adult populations. The results of some projects have shown that adherence to a controlled diet can lower serum lipid levels somewhat (Christakis et al., 1966; Dayton et al., 1962; Turpeinen et al., 1968; National Diet-Heart Study Research Group, 1968), and, in some cases, the incidence of new coronary disease (Christakis, 1966; Turpeinen et al., 1968). The difficulty of changing long-established patterns of dietary and other behavior, however, has been evident in all of these trials. It is significant that 6 months after the completion of the feasibility trial for the National Diet-Heart Study, during which serum cholesterol levels in men on experimental diets were lowered an average of 11% in a 2-year period, blood cholesterol levels had returned on the average to prediet levels (National Diet-Heart Study Research Group, 1968).

Coronary heart disease risk factors in U.S. children

Since the Riverside Project is based on the assumption that prevention of coronary heart disease is best accomplished by education of children and their families, it is relevant to review briefly what is known about the prevalence of risk factors for CHD among U.S. children. Since serum cholesterol levels are a fairly reliable predictor of CHD on the population level (Keys, 1970), this parameter is often used for comparison of relative risk of population groups. However, it should be kept in mind that hypercholesterolemia is only one of a number of statistically significant risk factors for CHD, that serum cholesterol levels within populations may not be predictive, and that normal limits for serum cholesterol in children have not been established. Kannel (1971) has recommended that 160 mg/100 ml be considered as the level above which children are at high risk of developing later CHD. This level is not accepted by all investigators, however, and the selection of a cutoff point for the upper limit of normal affects the number of children deemed "at risk" in a study. Hodges (1965) recommends 299 mg/100 ml as the upper limit of normal for teenagers, for instance, and Wilkinson (1950) recommends 220 mg/100 ml. Serum cholesterol levels among children in developing countries are much lower than those in the U.S., as is true for adults. Golubjatnikov et al. (1972) found a mean serum cholesterol level of less than 100 mg/100 ml among 209 Mexican children ages 5 to 14 years in the State of Mexico, for example.

Whatever the level of serum cholesterol at which risk of future CHD may be significantly increased, it is clear that the proportion of U.S. youngsters with hypercholesterolemia is significant. Hodges et al. (1943) report that the mean serum cholesterol level in a sample of 417 normal, nonobese children in New York City ages 6 months to 13 years was 205 mg/100 ml, and that 4% of these children had levels greater than 2 standard deviations above the mean. Golubjatnikov et al. (1972) report that 33% of 328 Wisconsin school children ages 5 to 14 had serum cholesterol levels in excess of 200 mg/100 ml, and the mean level in this group was 186 mg/100 ml. Hodges and Krehl (1965) found 13% to 15% of teenagers in an Iowa sample to have serum cholesterol levels in excess of 200 mg/100 ml, and a similar figure was found among Vermont teenagers by Clarke et al. (1970). Ibrahim et al. (1971) screened 501 eleventh graders in a Buffalo, New York suburb and found that 28% to 46% had serum cholesterol levels over 196 mg/100 ml. And Starr (1971), in a study of more than 2000 children ages 6 to 14 in Seventh-Day Adventist schools in Southern California, found that 6% had hypercholesterolemia defined as over 220 mg/100 ml, with the means for each age group ranging from 161 to 185 mg/100 ml. (Children in this last sample were not, for the most part, from vegetarian families.)

Two recent studies are especially relevant. Friedman and Goldberg (1973b) have published data on the distribution of serum cholesterol levels in 2,033 children from a middle class, predominantly Anglo pediatric practice in Scottsdale, Arizona. These data indicate that serum cholesterol in this population increases with age, with significantly different values for ages 0 to 2 months, 3 to 4 months, 5 to 6 months, 7 months to 8 years, and 9 to 19 years. The distribution of serum cholesterol values was not normal but rather had a pronounced right skew, such that the mean for each age group fell at about the 55th to 65th percentile. The implication of such a distribution is that use of a norm based on the mean plus 2 standard deviations is probably not reasonable; Friedman and Goldberg present a nomogram that can be used instead to assess an individual patient's ranking relative to others of the same age.

Another recent study evaluated a variety of CHD risk factors in 4,829 school children ages 6 to 18 years in Muscatine, Iowa (Lauer et al., 1975). In this study the mean serum cholesterol level was 182 mg/100 ml and there was no significant rise with age. Twenty-four percent had levels greater than 200 mg/100 ml, 9% greater than 220 mg/100 ml, and 3% over 240 mg/100 ml. Casual serum triglyceride levels and blood pressure, however, increased significantly with age in this sample, as did the prevalence and degree of obesity.

Coronary heart disease in Mexican-Americans

Since approximately 40% of the Riverside School population is Mexican-American, it is appropriate to examine what is known about CHD risk among Mexican-Americans. In practice, very little is known about any health characteristic of Mexican-Americans compared to the rest of the population, because very little health information has been gathered that identifies Mexican-Americans separately from the rest of the white population (American Public Health Association, 1974). The 1970 census estimated that there were slightly over 9 million Americans of Spanish origin (4.45% of the population) in the United States and that roughly half of these were of Mexican origin. Other sources, however, estimate that as many as 12 million persons in the U.S. are of Spanish-speaking background (American Public Health Association, 1974).

Moustafa and Weiss (1968) have published a report on health status and practices of Mexican-Americans indicating that in the 1960s there were only two reasonable sources of data on the health status of Mexican-Americans. These were the State of Colorado and the City of San Antonio, Texas, both of which collected health statistics separately for individuals with Spanish surnames. This system of identification has a severe limitation, since a larger number of individuals culturally identified as Mexican-Americans have Anglo surnames (and a much smaller number of Anglos have Spanish surnames), but it does provide some index of differences in health characteristics. The Colorado mortality data from 1960 showed that mortality from cardiovascular diseases (except rheumatic heart disease, which was high among Mexican-Americans) was considerably lower in the Spanish-surnamed population than in the Anglo population. San Antonio data from the period 1960 to 1964 also showed that death rates from heart disease were significantly lower in the Spanish-surnamed population than in the Anglo, and that the difference was greater than could be accounted for by the age structure of the two populations. In 1964, the death rates per 100,000 for heart disease in San Antonio were 136.8 for the Spanish-surnamed populations, 272.4 for other whites, and 311.4 for nonwhites. Even though death rates from heart disease, cancer, and stroke were significantly lower in the Spanish-surnamed than in the Anglo population, these were the three leading causes of death for both groups.

THE RIVERSIDE PROJECT: BACKGROUND AND DESCRIPTION

The Riverside Project grew out of efforts spanning several years by the Arizona Department of Health Services, the University of Arizona College of Medicine, and a pediatrician in private practice in Scottsdale, Arizona. The thrust of these efforts has been a screening and controlled intervention program for children and families contacted through the private practice of the pediatrician, with the goal of reducing the incidence of CHD risk factors. The intervention is accomplished through education utilizing the pediatrician and his staff (a nurse and a nutritionist) and includes attention to 5 modifiable CHD risk factors (hypertension, obesity, serum cholesterol levels, smoking, and exercise). Dietary advice given to patient families is modeled after the American Heart Association's recommendation for a relatively low-cholesterol, low–saturated fat diet.

Of approximately 2000 children exposed to this intervention program from birth to 3 years, 52 were randomly selected for detailed evaluation and compared with age-matched controls from a similar pediatric practice in the same community without the CHD risk factor intervention program. There were no differences between the two groups in height or weight as a percentage of standards, head circumference measurements, skinfold thickness measurements, number of sick visits, hemoglobin or serum protein levels, or scores on the Denver Developmental Screening test (Friedman and Goldberg, 1973a).

Encouraged by the apparent safety of the regime and the acceptance of the program by this relatively affluent, primarily Anglo, and self-selected population (presumably those patient families who do not wish to participate in the program select another physician), the cooperating agencies decided to try to extend the concept to a quite different population—children attending an elementary school located in a low income area and their families.

The Riverside Project was planned for a 3-year period, beginning in the fall of 1974. It was funded through the Elementary and Secondary Education Act (Title III) through the Arizona Department of Education to the Riverside School District. The goal of the project was to develop and implement a pilot cardiovascular risk factor screening and educational model that would be adaptable to other schools. The specific objectives were: (1) to reduce the number of children at risk and the mean values of identified risk factors, and (2) to develop, implement, and evaluate a health education curriculum focused on reducing cardiovascular risk. The five risk factors to be monitored and modified were serum cholesterol levels, hypertension, cigarette smoking, obesity, and sedentary living. The program was to be accomplished through existing school personnel (teachers and school nurse) together with a project coordinator, a nutritionist who worked full time in the school. The project was guided from its earliest planning phases by an advisory committee, which included a number of professionals, the school nurse, and two parents of Riverside students. Consultants in medicine, anthropology, psychology, physical fitness, and curriculum development were employed by the project.

Riverside School includes kindergarten through eighth grade and is located in a semi-rural area on the edge of Phoenix. The school serves a population of about 2000, or about 0.001% of the state's population. Of the 342 children in the school in 1974, 145 were Spanish-surnamed, 167 were Anglo, 11 were black, and 9 were American Indian. These included 61 students classified as educable handicapped and enrolled in special education classes (27 Spanish-surnamed, 28 Anglo, and 6 black). The general economic level of families in the school district is low, as evidenced by the fact that a majority of the children attending the school are eligible for free or reduced-price school lunches. At the time the project began, the school had a well-established school lunch program but no breakfast program and no organized program in physical education.

A control school was utilized for screening without intervention. This school is located only a few miles away and serves an essentially similar population.

Results of the project at the end of 3 years indicate considerable success in terms of gain in cognitive knowledge through the health education program and in terms of increased physical fitness. Other risk factors showed less clear-cut outcomes. The problems of making a valid assessment of smoking behavior rendered the impact of the program on this risk factor not susceptible to analysis. Too few children were deemed initially "at risk" in terms of blood pressure or overweight to document significant impact. Serum cholesterol values were over 160 mg/100 ml for roughly half of the children at both the experimental and the control schools at the start of the project. There was no significant difference between Mexican-American and Anglo children in prevalence of cholesterol levels over 160 mg/100 ml. The 3-year period saw a significant reduction in serum cholesterol levels in both the experimental and the control schools. Thus it was concluded either that some variable outside the project was affecting cholesterol levels at both schools, or that perhaps the screening procedure produced the effect at both schools. Acceptance of the project by the target group(s) is indicated by the fact that Riverside School has decided to continue the screening, education, and evaluation aspects of the project even though outside funding has terminated.

SOCIOCULTURAL CONSIDERATIONS IN IMPLEMENTING THE PROJECT

The Riverside Project involved the interaction over 3 years of several subcultures: the innovating subculture (scientific medicine and public health), the target group (which consists of two major ethnic groups), and the subculture of the school staff (superintendent, teachers, nurse). There were a variety of "culture brokers" whose function it was to mediate and communicate among these groups: the parents on the project's advisory committee, the nutritionist in the school, the teachers, and the school nurse. That there were differences in perception and expectation regarding the project and its role among these subcultures was inevitable. The initial planning and implementation of the early aspects of the program were notably successful in preventing potential conflict based on

diverse expectations. However, the long-term success of the program depended on making use of the unique characteristics of these particular groups to achieve the goal which was, as is often the case in public health programs, a goal originated and stated by the innovating culture rather than by the target population.

Saunders (1954:8) has succinctly stated the nature of the problem in the interaction of disparate subcultures in the context of health programs:

When the practice of medicine involves the application of elements of the institution of medicine in one culture to the people of another, or from one subculture to members of another subculture within the same cultural group, what is done or attempted by those in the healing roles may not be fully understood or correctly evaluated by those in the patient roles. Conversely, the responses of those on the patient side of the interaction may not conform to the expectations of those on the healing side. To the extent that this occurs, the relationship may be unsatisfactory to all concerned.

When persons of widely dissimilar cultural or subcultural orientations are brought together in a therapeutic relationship, the probability of a mutually satisfactory outcome may be increased if those in the healing roles know something of their own culture and that of the patient and are aware of the extent to which behavior on both sides of the relationship is influenced by cultural factors. An even higher probability of satisfaction may result if the professional people are willing and able to modify elements from their medicine so as to make them fit the expectations of the laymen with whom they are working.

The social and cultural factors to be considered in the implementation of a project the scope of this one are complex. In the following pages we shall try to point out some of the more obvious areas for consideration under the following categories: Nature of the behavioral changes required to meet the goal of the project, motivational factors, communication factors, social factors, social distance factors, and cultural compatibility factors as they relate to the major subcultures involved.

Nature of the behavioral changes required

Among the basic assumptions of most practitioners of Western medicine are those of (1) the authority of the health professional and (2) the value of efficiency—maximum effect or benefit from minimum time spent (Clark 1959). Not only may these assumptions not be held by the target group in a public health program, but also, given these assumptions, a slow pace in the acceptance of a program of complex behavioral changes may produce frustration in the health professionals involved. The Riverside Project proposed to reduce the severity and prevalence of five different risk factors through a variety of behavioral changes in the target population. Some of the changes that were proposed are among the most difficult types to achieve. It was important, therefore, that the health professionals involved as well as the teachers and administrators of the school district understood that change could be expected to occur slowly and unevenly with regard to the various behaviors involved.

It was in this context that the role of the anthropologist became important. The particular behavior changes proposed were reviewed in light of the factors facilitating or inhibiting acceptance of innovation presented by Graham (1973). In a review of data on acceptance of various health measures, Graham points out that the following factors seem to be important in influencing the success of a proposed change:

1. *Whether the proposed innovation is incremental or decremental;* that is, whether it involves the addition of a behavior pattern or the elimination of an already established one. There is reason to suspect that incremental behavior changes are usually more successfully accepted than decremental ones.
2. *The degree to which the attributes of the proposed change are overt or covert and how complex those attributes are.* Innovations that are simple and easily communicated are more likely to be rapidly accepted than are those with abstract or subtle advantages or those that are complex and thus more difficult to communicate.
3. *The degree to which trial of the proposed behavior is easy and inexpensive.* Innovations that require a long period of time or substantial resources for trial are less likely to be accepted quickly than those that are easy and cheap to

try since their advantages and disadvantages are not as readily demonstrated.
4. *The degree to which the decision to accept or reject the proposed behavior change is reversible.* For example, birth control pills may be expected to have a greater acceptance rate than tubal ligations or vasectomies in a birth control program, since the decision is readily reversible in the former case and not in the latter.
5. *The number of decisions required to effect the change.* A vote to fluoridate the water supply requires only one decision; stopping smoking, fastening automobile safety belts, and changing dietary patterns require repeated decisions. Innovations requiring repeated decisions for adoption seem to be less attractive as solutions to problems than those requiring only one or a few affirmative decisions.

The behavior changes required to meet the objectives of the Riverside Project involved acceptance of the program into the school by teachers, administrators, and parents; participation in screening processes by both children and families; changes in curriculum structure within the school; participation by teachers in inservice workshops, and by parents in meetings related to the project. Ultimate goals involved changes in families' life-styles to include a reduction in smoking behavior, the seeking of and adherence to medical treatment for hypertension, an increase in exercise, and dietary changes involving a reduction in saturated fat and cholesterol intake and, for those who were obese, weight reduction.

Perhaps the greatest difficulty in "selling" this program arose from the fact that the proposed changes and their advantages are complex and not easily demonstrable. In fact, given the current state of knowledge about the etiology of CHD, it was impossible to *promise* anything as a result of the changes even if they were successful. It is not possible to state unequivocally that an individual will never have a heart attack if he is not obese, never smokes, has a serum cholesterol level below 160 mg/100 ml and a blood pressure reading under 140/90, and exercises regularly. The best that can be stated is that the individual may substantially reduce his risk of a heart attack. When the benefits of preventive health behavior are far into the future, and uncertain at that, the health educator's job is compounded manyfold.

Aside from the problem of complexity and covertness, which is common to all of the changes required by the program, one can look at each of the changes required in light of the combination of attributes mentioned by Graham (1973).

Acceptance of the program into the school required only a single decision on the part of administrator and faculty, and it represented an incremental change; but it was not a readily reversible decision and it required the commitment of substantial resources and time.

Participating in medical screening processes involved several affirmative decisions at intervals, was relatively cheap and easy to do, and is an incremental change; in addition, the immediate rewards were relatively more concrete than with some of the other behaviors required, because results of the screening were made available to participants. For the children a concrete reward (a bag of peanuts, a bookmark or a pencil eraser) was also offered for participation in the screening process.

Participation by teachers in the necessary workshops and restructuring of the curriculum to include the health education required represented a number of consecutive decisions on the part of individual teachers. These changes were incremental, required some investment of time and resources, but were more or less easily reversible on the part of the individual teacher.

Participation by parents in workshops, meetings, etc., also required several decisions, but was relatively easy and inexpensive and was made more so by such practices as providing babysitting services and transportation for parent meetings. Attending such sessions is clearly incremental in terms of the overall behavior pattern, and the decision to attend was easily reversible.

The behavior changes that involve family life-style—eating, exercise, smoking, and health care habits—are more complex. Some are incremental, but some—particularly smoking and dietary changes—may be decremental. All involve many repeated decisions. Most are relatively inexpensive and easy to try and are readily reversible. This last factor, easy reversibility, may operate to enhance initial success but should be kept in mind as a potential difficulty as well. Desirable behavior must be positively reinforced as it occurs, and reinforcement must continue, if the decisions are not to be reversed once the initial enthusiasm wears off. This is especially important since the health benefits involved are long-range and not readily apparent in the short run to the individuals involved.

Motivational factors

There is a fairly large body of literature relative to the problem of who accepts and who does not accept various innovations in health behavior. Three important variables will be discussed here: socioeconomic status, knowledge, and definition of the "at risk" role.

Socioeconomic status. It is commonly accepted that low socioeconomic status is correlated with lack of acceptance of preventive health behavior (Pratt 1971; Coburn and Pope, 1974; Haefner et al., 1967; Bullough, 1972) although there is some conflicting evidence and reason to believe that socioeconomic status per se does not account for all the differences observed.

The notion of socioeconomic status being a single predictor of willingness to engage in preventive health behaviors has been reinforced by the influence of Talcott Parson's (1958) well-known concept of health behavior as a unidimensional phenomenon—i.e., that there is a "health role" in the sense that people who engage in one health-related behavior also tend to engage in others and vice versa. More recent research, however, suggests that health behavior is a multidimensional concept and that factors other than socioeconomic status are important in influencing acceptance of preventive health services. Steel et al. (1972), in a study of incidence of physical checkups, dental visits, visits to the eye doctor, and possession of health insurance, found that these four health-related behaviors were not highly correlated. Dental visits seemed to be more or less directly related to income; all behaviors were influenced by distance from medical care and recency of illness episodes. Bullough (1972) in a study of low income mothers of three ethnic groups in Los Angeles found that the more well-known barriers to utilization of preventive health services (cost, transportation) were reinforced by alienation, including feelings of powerlessness, hopelessness, and social isolation. Family planning was the type of preventive care most influenced by alienation. In this study the black mothers felt more powerless and alienated than did the Mexican-American mothers, and in spite of little difference in income utilized preventive health services less.

Knowledge. The role of knowledge and/or education in the association between poverty and health behavior has been investigated only sporadically. What research there is suggests that specific knowledge may be less important than commitment to and reinforcement of concrete behavior patterns. For example, Pratt (1971) found in a study of low income New Jersey city residents that general health knowledge was not related to level of health, and recommended that health programs should focus on highly specific health practices—concrete behavior patterns—rather than focusing efforts on provision of large amounts of complex information.

Stromberg et al. (1974) studied 601 middle-aged Yugoslav men who were invited to participate in a complete medical screening. Those who accepted and participated scored higher than nonparticipants on previous involvement with a local medical system, utilization of health services, availability, willingness to participate in other voluntary activities, education, and occupational status. There was no association of health beliefs or attitudes with participation. The best single predictor of participation was an affirmative response to the question, "Would you be willing to have a thorough physical examination so that your actual health status could be determined?" Thus commitment to a decision ahead of time seemed to be more important than beliefs about the value of the examination per se.

The apparent value of prior commitment is also illustrated by the findings of Lewin (1958) on acceptance of change in food practices. During World War II, programs were undertaken to convince homemakers to use variety meats, which were generally unpopu-

lar. One group of women was exposed to a lecture on the benefits of using the meats. The second group was given the same information but in the form of discussion and then was asked to decide by a show of hands whether they were willing to try one of the meats during the following week. Follow-up questioning indicated that 32% of the women who had made a public commitment had served one of the meats while only 3% of the lecture group had done so. Subsequent investigations of a similar nature concerned gaining acceptance for giving cod liver oil and orange juice to babies, and similar results were obtained.

Knowledge of particular diseases and their effects, however, has been shown in a number of studies to be positively related to acceptance of preventive health behavior. Particularly important seems to be involvement of a relative or friend with the disease, or a recent high incidence of the disease among persons known to the individual. Deasy (1956) found a greater acceptance of poliomyelitis vaccination among individuals who had a previous high incidence of the disease in their neighborhoods; Merrill et al. (1958) also found a correlation between adults obtaining polio immunization and their knowledge of the disease. Naguib et al. (1968) in a study of response to a cervical cancer screening program found that more acceptors than nonacceptors had relatives or friends who had had the disease. It would seem that this phenomenon could be used to advantage in programs such as the Riverside Project, since coronary heart disease strikes approximately 1 out of 2 Americans at some time in their lives, and it is a rare family that has had no exposure to a friend or relative who has had a heart attack or a stroke. Acknowledgement of such close acquaintance with the disease may help to make the advantages of a long-term preventive regimen more real.

Definition of the "at risk" role. A clear motivational task for the Riverside Project was to induce families to accept a definition of themselves and their children as "at risk" for the development of CHD. This task is complicated by the fact that health, illness, and risk of illness are culturally defined states, and the attributes of these states vary cross-culturally. Saunders (1954:142-143) states the situation with regard to health and illness:

Illness and disease, it must be remembered, are social as well as biological phenomena. On the biological level they consist of adaptations of the organism to environmental influences; on the social level they include meanings, roles, relationships, attitudes, and techniques that enable members of a cultural group to identify various types of illness and disease, to behave appropriately, and to call upon a body of knowledge for coping with the condition defined as an illness. What is recognized as disease or illness is a matter of cultural prescription, and a given biological condition may or may not be considered an illness depending on the particular cultural group in which it occurs . . . What should be done about a given condition defined culturally as illness, and the proper relationships of a sick person to other people are also culturally prescribed. An individual thus has cultural guides that enable him to know when he or others may be regarded as sick, something about the cause and nature of the sickness, what may be done to alleviate or remedy the situation, and the behavior expected of him and others in the situation.

The notion of being in a state of risk for development of a disease is a much more loosely defined concept. Baric (1969) calls upon the physician, as the traditional legitimizer of the "sick" role in this culture, to take a more active part in legitimizing the "at risk" role, for unless the patient defines himself or herself as at risk, there is no reason to undertake any change in behavior with the goal of remaining healthy.

The idea of being ill or at risk while exhibiting no symptoms and feeling well is a notion much more readily accepted by upper and middle class Anglo society than by less future-oriented subcultures. It may be a difficult idea for Mexican-Americans to accept (Martinez and Martin, 1966), for in this subculture one is not usually considered ill unless he is not able to carry out his normal activities. Clark (1959:227-228) discusses the implications of this difference for health care:

In Sal si Puedes [the neighborhood in San Jose, California, in which Clark did her study] illness is generally defined as a state of bodily discomfort. A person who has no debilitating symptoms is usually held to be well and healthy even though the diagnostic tests of scientific practitioners may reveal such serious pathological processes as carcinoma, tuberculosis, or heart disease. It is difficult for the people to understand how a sick person can feel well and go about his normal tasks without discomfort. To say to a patient without symptoms "You are sick," is to invite confusion and disbelief.

The 'preclinical' stage of disease is a concept which is familiar in folk belief; for example, a person may not develop the symptoms of *susto* [a folk disease caused by a frightening or traumatic experience] for some time after the frightening episode which produces the illness. If prophylactic measures are taken during this time, the disease may be avoided. It is not clear just why the preclinical stages of scientific syndromes are not recognized. Perhaps it is simply because the situation has not been presented to the people in familiar terms.*

Communication factors

Perceptions of heart disease. It seems obvious that educational efforts will be successful only insofar as communication of concepts is successful. But implementation of this basic concept is not simple, since it requires finding out just what the target group already knows about the subject and what their perceptions are. This is especially important when cultural differences exist, since the definition of disease is a cultural process. Within the school classroom, teachers may be expected to be able to find out with reasonable accuracy how much students know about a given subject. When dealing with parents, however, it is not possible to assume *a priori* a given level of knowledge or content of that knowledge. Thus it is important to take the time to find out just what concepts the people already have about, in this case, heart disease—its definition, etiology, and treatment as well as prevention.

Unfortunately, studies of perceptions of disease in cultural groups similar to the ones involved in the Riverside Project are scarce. Probably the most useful one is the study by Kay (1972) on concepts of health and illness among Mexican-Americans in a barrio in Tucson. Kay's informants recognized *mal de corazón* (heart disease), *ataque de corazón* (heart attack), and *estrok* (stroke) as *enfemedades graves* (serious and perhaps incurable diseases). In all of these diseases, fatigue, weakness, and incapacity were seen as characteristic, although

In the case of *mal de corazón* ('heart disease'), defining features are not known. "That's why one

---

*Copyright 1970 by The Regents of the University of California; reprinted by permission of the University of California Press.

goes to the doctor; he knows," I was told. If someone is reported as dying suddenly, the first assumption . . . is that death was caused by *ataque
de corazón*. Death may be preceded by pain in the
chest.

These perceptions would seem to be compatible with those of Western medicine, and
not very well defined, thus providing a potentially fertile ground for education. However, Kay's informants also recognized several other kinds of heart disease: *corazón grande* or *crecimiento de corazón* (enlarged heart)
and *corazón debil* (weak heart). Both of the
above are thought to be chronic, inherited
diseases. "Enlarged heart" is gradually inca-
pacitating and ultimately fatal; "weak heart"
is characterized by a heart that "beats too
much" (Kay, 1972:149). Still another syndrome was recognized as *aire en el corazón*
(air in the heart), characterized by weakness, incapacitation, nausea, and stabbing
pains in the heart, and caused by breathing
cold air (Kay, 1972:137).

Thus among Mexican-Americans in a Tucson neighborhood a few years ago, concepts
of heart disease were neither simple nor
completely the same as those of Western
medicine. There is no basis for assuming that
other Mexican-American groups perceive
heart disease in the same ways as Kay's informants in Tucson did, but the very complexity of the notions she was able to uncover
among her informants makes it clear that
careful investigation is essential in order to
learn how people perceive the disease, its
etiology, and its consequence.

Language. The fact that the target group
for the Riverside Project was partly Spanish-
speaking raised further communication considerations. All of the teachers in the school
are Anglo and instruction is in English. However, it could not be assumed that all parents
(and grandparents) were comfortable with
English. On the other hand, as Kay (1972)
points out, few American-born Mexican-
Americans can read Spanish. Again, the best
remedy is to gather as much information as
possible about the local situation and the
preference of the local group. Mexican-
American parents of children in the school
felt that bilingual materials were important,
and it was determined that a significant number of parents preferred Spanish-language

materials. Thus all materials developed for
parents, such as a project newsletter, were
bilingual.

Channels of communication. The project
made great efforts to directly involve the
parents of the school children. Before the
project was accepted by the school, a small
screening project was carried out on one class
with permission of the parents. Parents were
given the results and were invited to an
evening talk and slide presentation. Further efforts involved parents directly whenever possible. Such a strategy was facilitated
by the fact that the school nurse was a former resident of the area, had been the school
nurse for many years, and had well-established personal ties with many of the families.
Direct contact with parents is desirable, as
pointed out by Clark (1959) in her report on
health behavior in a Mexican-American community in Northern California:

> School children are sometimes used as couriers
> to carry information back to their parents. Al-
> though this procedure is satisfactory for factual
> reports, it is not very effective for the introduc-
> tion of new ideas designed to change attitudes or
> behavior patterns because the young have rela-
> tively low status . . . It is recommended that adults
> be contacted directly whenever possible.*

A similar recommendation was made clearly
by one of the Riverside parents at a meeting
of the advisory committee when she said,
"You educate me; I'll educate my children."

Social distance factors

The role of the health professional is perceived differently in different subcultures,
and these differences may be the source of
vast amounts of misunderstanding. Clark
(1959:230-231) points out the problem with
regard to Anglo medical practitioners in
Mexican-American groups:

> The Anglo medical practitioner is taught that
> an impersonal objectivity is a vital part of his role
> as an applied scientist. He places a premium on
> "efficiency"—he tries to "come directly to the
> point," dispense with "unnecessary" formalities,
> and achieve maximum output in minimum time.
> He assumes also that his status as a trained special-

---

*Copyright 1970 by The Regents of the University of
California; reprinted by permission of the University of
California Press.

ist gives prestige and authority to his opinions and his recommendations.

The people of Sal si Puedes, however, expect quite different behavior from therapists. Their expectations are based largely on the usual behavior patterns of Mexican folk curers. People who expect a curer to be warm, friendly, and interested in all aspects of the patient's life find it difficult to trust a doctor who is impersonal and "clinical" in his manner. Nor do they accept his authority to "give orders." He may suggest or counsel, but an authoritarian or dictatorial approach on his part is resented and rejected. His behavior, culturally sanctioned in his own society, is often interpreted by Spanish-speaking patients as discourtesy if not outright boorishness.*

Thus health workers should not hesitate to take time to make friends with patients, to observe formalities and social amenities. Surely, personalization of any program of health care is important, but it is even more vital when the rewards of the program to the patient are not immediate or dramatic. In such a case social rewards become important as motivational and reinforcing factors.

In the Riverside Project, the position of the school nurse as friend, health professional (and often provider of primary health care), and former neighbor of many of the families was a unique advantage. The fact that the project extended over several years and that the nutritionist had a full-time position in the school enabled her to establish warm and continuing relationships with local families. Professionals who had more indirect contact with the project (such as consultants), were sensitized to the implications of their manner during brief visits to the school and to families; since they lacked the opportunity to establish extended relationships, they took care to work always through the nurse and nutritionist, who had gained social acceptance.

Related to the issue of social distance and personalization is the utilization of appropriate "culture brokers." The unique position of the school nurse has already been mentioned. The nutritionist was also in an advantageous position as a culture broker between the innovating culture and the subculture of the school, since she is a certified

teacher and therefore has had greater credibility with teachers than would an individual with no teaching experience. The parents who served on the advisory committee also served as culture brokers; this role for parents was expanded by utilizing parents whenever possible in various aspects of the project —as occasional classroom aides and advisors on plans for meetings and materials.

Cultural compatibility factors

The notion of cultural compatibility underlies much of the social science research on innovation. As early as 1927, Sumner and Keller stated that "even if a culture is conceived as formed by contagion from without . . . its reception [of innovations] must follow along the lines of adjustment already laid down in the societal organization which is to take it over." Linton (1936), Malinowski (1945), Kroeber (1948), Barnett (1953), Gillin (1945), Stern (1927), and Graham (1973) all point out that whether an innovation can be considered an opportunity for betterment depends upon the content of the culture prior to its introduction. If the behavior, ideas, and material apparatus that accompany an innovation are compatible with those existing in a culture, the chances for its acceptance are greatly enhanced. Examples of this phenomenon are legion. People who were avid movie-goers were the quickest to accept television (Graham, 1956). Residents of a village who could not accept the practice of boiling drinking water, because this was previously done only for sick people, were easily persuaded to use tea (previously consumed in small quantities) instead of water—a culturally congruent change that accomplished the same health objective. Similarly, the Navajo at one time retained their traditional medicine for the diseases that had been indigenous in aboriginal times, but accepted white medicine as not being incompatible with their own culture for diseases introduced by whites (Graham, 1973).

The selection of culturally congruent methods of achieving the desired results in a given situation depends on knowing rather a lot about the existing culture. In the case of health education projects, it is essential to find out not only how heart disease, its etiology, and treatment are perceived, but also some details about existing patterns of

---

*Copyright 1970 by The Regents of the University of California; reprinted by permission of the University of California Press.

health care behavior and existing food habits. Clark (1959:227) recommends that health professionals ". . . should not try to encourage sudden and marked changes in diet. Better results can be obtained by recommending the use of different proportions of foods already in the local diet." Thus it is essential to know what people are already eating before trying to initiate change, and it is well to have some notion of the beliefs and values that condition existing practices. The project nutritionist conducted in-depth interviews with some families regarding food habits, shopping practices, and health care. The results were helpful in designing proposed changes that were culturally compatible. Similarly, investigation of usual and acceptable exercise patterns for various age and sex groups helped to determine whether jogging, competitive sports, or noncompetitive sports were the most acceptable to suggest for increasing exercise levels. For example, the local park was not considered a safe place for young women, but a chaperoned evening stroll *(pasear)* was acceptable.

Related to the notion of cultural compatibility is a concern for whether the proposed ideas and behaviors run counter to any accepted ideas of health maintenance or medical care. A great deal has been written about folk illnesses, their etiology, and treatment among Mexican-Americans in the United States (see Rubel, 1960; Foster, 1953; Martinez and Martin, 1966; Samora, 1961; Clark, 1959; Kay, 1972; Holland, 1963; Baca, 1969; Grebler, 1970). These studies all indicate the survival of varying degrees of belief and practice of traditional Mexican folk medicine, including diagnosis and treatment of diseases that are not known to Western medicine as such (such as *susto, empacho, mollera caida, mal ojo,* and others), the use of folk healers, and culturally prescribed behavior for the avoidance of illness and the maintenance of health. Even where traditional folk medicine is not practiced to a great extent, certain underlying themes are relevant to preventive health behavior in Mexican-American populations. The pervasive strength of religious conviction should not be underestimated. Illness may be seen as an act of God, and healing as a gift of God, an attitude that is common to fundamentalist religious groups regardless of ethnicity. The fatalism that ac-

companies such a belief, however, is often overrated by health professionals. As Saunders (1961) points out, the typical Mexican-American family will undertake any activity that seems to offer hope in order to effect the cure of a sick family member, even while professing that the ultimate outcome is the will of God (see also Rubel, 1966). Nevertheless, the notion that the future is in God's hands may not be as conducive to engaging in preventive health behavior—especially if the behavior is uncomfortable or inconvenient—as is the belief that today's actions may directly affect one's health far into the future.

The idea of balance is pervasive in Mexican-American folk medicine and underlies much of the culturally prescribed preventive health behavior, such as avoidance of certain foods and sudden changes in body temperature. As Kay (1972) points out, the idea of balance is widely held cross-culturally with regard to health, and indeed is the basis for the concept of homeostasis in Western medicine. This underlying theme of both target cultures was capitalized upon in the development of curriculum materials for the Riverside Project.

CONCLUSIONS

The Riverside Project serves as a model for the concrete application of cultural anthropology in a public health program. The long-term health and other effects of the project, if any, cannot be assessed at this time. In the short-term, however, there is little doubt that the project was well accepted by the target population. Early and continuous attention to the cultural contexts of the project was crucial to its success.

REFERENCES

American Public Health Association. 1974. Minority health chart book, APHA, Washington, D.C.

Baca, J. 1969. Some health beliefs of the Spanish speaking. American Journal of Nursing 69:2172-2176.

Baric, L. 1969. Recognition of the 'at-risk' role—a means to influence health behavior. Int. J. Health Educa. 12:24-34.

Barnett, H. G. 1953. Innovation: The basis of cultural change. McGraw-Hill, New York.

Bullough, B. 1972. Poverty, ethnic identity and preventive health care. Journal of Health and Social Behavior 13:347-359.

Christakis, G., et al. 1966. The anti-coronary club: a dietary approach to the prevention of coronary heart disease—a seven year report. American Journal of Public Health **56**:299-314.

Clark, M. 1959. Health in the Mexican-American culture: a community study. University of California Press, Berkeley (reprinted 1970).

Clarke, R. P., et al. 1970. Interrelationship between plasma lipids, physical measurements and body fatness of adolescents in Burlington, Vt. American Journal of Clinical Nutrition **23**:754-163.

Coburn, D., and Pope, C. R. 1974. Socioeconomic status and preventive health behavior. Journal of Health and Social Behavior **15**:67-78.

Dayton, S., et al. 1962. A controlled clinical trial of a diet high in unsaturated fat. Preliminary observations. New England Journal of Medicine **266**:1017-1023.

Deasy, L. C. 1956. Socioeconomic status and participants in the poliomyelitis vaccine trial. American Sociology Review **21**:185-191.

Enos, W. F., Jr., Beyer, J. C., and Holmes, R. H. 1955. Pathogenesis of coronary disease in American soldiers killed in Korea. Journal of the American Medical Association **158**:912-914.

Foster, G. 1953. Relationships between Spanish and Spanish-American folk medicine. Journal of American Folklore **66**:201-217.

Friedman, G., and Goldberg, S. 1973a. Is a low saturated fat, low cholesterol diet safe for infants and children? Circulation XVII, supplement No. IV, Abstract No. 27, p. 8.

Friedman, G., and Goldberg, S. 1973b. Normal serum cholesterol value—percentile ranking in a middle-class pediatric population. Journal of the American Medical Association **225**:610-612.

Gillin, J. L., and Gillin, J. P. 1945. An introduction to sociology. Macmillan, New York.

Golubjatnikov, R., Paskey, T., and Inhorn, S. L. 1972. Serum cholesterol levels of Mexican and Wisconsin school children. American Journal of Epidemiology **96**:36-39.

Graham, S. 1956. Class and conservatism in the adoption of innovations. Human Relations **9**:91-100.

Graham, S. 1973. Studies of behavior change to enhance public health. American Journal of Public Health **63**:327-334.

Grebler, L., et al. 1970. The Mexican-American people. Free Press, New York.

Haefner, D. P., et al. 1967. Preventive actions in dental disease, tuberculosis and cancer. Public Health Reports **82**:451-459.

Hodges, T. C., Chen, C. P., and Wilver, J. 1943. Serum cholesterol values for infants and children. American Journal of Diseases of Children **65**:858-867.

Hodges, R. E., and Krehl, W. A. 1965. Nutritional status of teenagers in Iowa. American Journal of Clinical Nutrition **17**:200-210.

Holland, W. R. 1963. Mexican-American medical beliefs: science or magic? Arizona Medicine, May pp. 89-102.

Holman, R. L., et al. 1958. The natural history of atherosclerosis: early aortic lesions as seen in New Orleans in the middle of the 20th century. American Journal of Pathology **34**:209-235.

Ibrahim, M. A., et al. 1971. Screening of the coronary prone by study of offspring. HSMHA Health Report **86**:517-582.

Kannel, W. V., et al. 1971. Serum cholesterols, lipoproteins, and the risk of coronary heart disease. Annals of Internal Medicine **14**:1-10.

Kay, M. A. 1972. Health and illness in the barrio: women's point of view. Ph.D. dissertation, University of Arizona, Tucson.

Keys, A. (ed). 1970. Coronary heart disease in seven countries. Circulation **41**, Supplement 1.

Kolata, G. B., and Marx, J. L. 1976. Epidemiology of heart disease: searches for causes. Science **194**:509-512.

Kroeber, A. L. 1948. Anthropology. Harcourt Brace, New York.

Lauer, R. M., et al. 1975. Coronary heart disease risk factors in school children: the Muscatine study. Journal of Pediatrics **86**:697-706.

Lewin, K. 1958. Group decision and social change. In Maccoby, E., Newcomb, T. M., and Hartley, E. L. (eds.). Readings in social psychology. Holt, Rinehart and Winston, New York.

Linton, R. 1936. The study of man. Appleton-Century, New York.

Malinowski, B. 1945. Dynamics of culture change. Yale University Press, New Haven, Conn.

Mann, G. V. 1977. Diet-heart: end of an era, New England Journal of Medicine **297**:644-649.

Martinez, C., and Martin, H. W. 1966. Folk diseases among urban Mexican-Americans. Journal of the American Medical Association **196**:161-164.

Merrill, M. H., et al. 1958. Attitudes of Californians toward poliomyelitis vaccination. American Journal of Public Health **48**:146-152.

Moon, H. D. 1957. Coronary arteries in fetuses, infants and juveniles. Circulation **16**:263-267.

Moustafa, A. T., and Weiss, G. 1968. Health status and practices of Mexican Americans, Mexican American Study Project Advance Report # 11. UCLA School of Public Health, Los Angeles.

Naguib, S., Geiser, P., and Comstock, G. 1968. Responses to a program of screening for cervical cancer. Public Health Reports **83**:990-998.

National Diet-Heart Study Research Group. 1968. The National Diet-Heart Study final report. Circulation **37**, Supplement 1.

Parsons, T. 1958. Definitions of health and illness in the light of American values and social structure. In Jaco, E. G. (ed.). Patients, physicians and illness. Free Press, New York.

Pratt, L. 1971. The relationship of socio-economic status to health. American Journal of Public Health **61**:281-291.

Rubel, A. J. 1960. Concepts of disease in Mexican-American culture. American Anthropology **62**:795-814.

Rubel, A. J. 1966. Across the tracks: Mexican-Americans in a Texas city. University of Texas Press, Austin, Texas.

Samora, J. 1961. Conceptions of health and disease among Spanish-Americans. American Catholic Sociology Review **22**:314-323.

Saunders, L. 1954. Cultural differences and medical care. Russell Sage Foundation, New York.

Saunders, L. 1961. Healing ways in the Spanish Southwest. In Report of the Southwestern conference on cultural influences on health services and home economics programs. University of Arizona, Tucson, Arizona.

Spain, D. M. 1966. Atherosclerosis. Scientific American **215:**48.

Starr, P. Hypercholesterolemia in school children. American Journal of Clinical Pathology **56:**515-522.

Steel, J. S., and McBroom, W. H. 1972. Conceptual and empirical dimensions of health behavior. Journal of Health and Social Behavior **13:**382-392.

Stern, B. J. 1927. Social factors in medical progress. Columbia University Press, New York.

Stromberg, J., et al. 1974. Predicting participation in a screening examination for ischaemic heart disease risk factors—experience from the Zagreb preliminary study. Journal of Health and Social Behavior.

Sumner, W. G., and Keller, A. G. 1927. The science of society. Yale University Press, New Haven, Conn.

Turpeinen, O. 1968. Dietary prevention of coronary heart disease: long-term experiment I. Observations on male subjects. American Journal of Clinical Nutrition **21:**255-276.

U. S. Public Health Service. 1974. Facts of life and death, PHS publication (HRA) 74-1222. National Center for Health Statistics, Ročkville, Md.

Wilkinson, C. F., Jr. 1950. Essential familial hypercholesterolemia: cutaneous, metabolic and hereditary aspects. Bulletin of the New York Academy of Medicine **26:**670-685.

Wilson, R. N. 1970. The sociology of health: an introduction, Random House, New York.

PART THREE

NUTRITIONAL ANTHROPOLOGY

Chapter 12 examines the relationship of a population's established foodways to the environment and the nutritional requirements of that population. Examples are given to illustrate an evolutionary process that has been important in the history of our genus, the interaction of biological and cultural changes. An evolutionary viewpoint is of considerable utility to those who are involved in planning or promoting changes in dietary patterns. For those who are planning change for a population, it provides a framework for understanding the relationships within that system and, therefore, anticipates the effects of various possible changes. For those involved in promoting change, it provides a framework for understanding and coping with the attitudes, beliefs, and habits of those who are being encouraged to accept the change.

Chapter 13 focuses on pica, the practice of ingesting unusual substances. Both nutritionists and anthropologists have questioned whether pica is a cultural phenomenon or a disease state. Nutritionists most often have been concerned with possible relationships of pica to anemia, toxemia, and psychological or behavioral problems. Anthropologists have been instrumental in documenting pica and offering sociocultural explanations of the practices. The integration of these two approaches to further explain pica would benefit both fields of study.

Chapter 14 compares the food behavior and health status of persons living in Poland and Poles who emigrated to the United States. The impact of maintaining "old world" food behaviors rather than adopting an American diet is discussed in terms of nutritional status and risk for disease.

Chapter 15 offers various approaches for studying both food and diet ethnographically. These methods may assist nutritional anthropologists as well as health professionals.

CHAPTER 12

Human foodways: a window on evolution

Cheryl Ritenbaugh

All around the world people need to eat. Human populations must obtain enough food to meet their nutritional requirements, including adequate energy, protein, fat, vitamins, and minerals, if they are to survive. The dietary protein must be of acceptable quality, providing the proper proportions of essential amino acids. Given this problem, the variety of solutions is staggering.

I will use the term foodways to refer to the behaviors that affect what people eat. The foodways of a culture thus include its definitions of what is food and what is not, the methods of preparation and acceptable combinations of foods, and the rules for distributing particular foods within the culture. For example, in many cultures dogs are perfectly acceptable food, but in the United States it would be virtually unthinkable to consume a *real* "hot dog."

Cultural anthropologists have been enormously impressed with the variety of foodways possible within the limits of survival, and have focused their attention on the cultural meaning of the foodways. Foodways have long been recognized as playing an important role in cultural identity; this is one of the reasons why a change in foodways is one of the more significant changes made by individuals who are acculturating.

The view that other people's foodways are irrational and that one's own is natural and sensible is common and has led to some cavalier attempts to change the food behavior of Third World countries by the U.S. and other Western countries. An example of this is the distribution and promotion of the use of powdered milk, which will be discussed in more detail below.

Recently, anthropologists have begun to view foodways in a wider context, attempting to understand how the particular foods utilized fit into the ecological context of a culture. Harris (1974) has used this approach in his attempts to explain why the Hindus do not kill their cattle and why Jews do not eat pigs. In Harris' view, the ecological considerations are central, with the religious prohibitions developing to reinforce essential behavior patterns, although others (e.g., Simoons, 1973) argue that such behavior is primarily religious in origin. However, even such culturally oriented ecological approaches often do not squarely address the biological reality of how the foodways of a population fulfill the nutritional requisites for survival.

This chapter examines some details of the diets of various cultures in an attempt to understand how these diets meet the nutritional requirements of the populations. From this vantage point it may be possible to understand some additional sources of resistance to foodway change. This look at foodways will take an evolutionary viewpoint, in which human evolution is seen not just as a process of biological change, but also as a process of cultural and technological change that allows the biological requirements of the species to be met in new environmental contexts without genetic change.

EVOLUTIONARY THEORY AND HUMAN FOODWAYS

In order to discuss foodways in an evolutionary context, it is necessary to review briefly some basic principles of evolution. Since the time of Darwin, it has been known that one of the major mechanisms for evolutionary change in the biology of populations is the process of natural selection. Natural selection means that, overall, the individuals with a particularly useful trait in the given environment will bear slightly more offspring (who will become successful breeders themselves) than individuals without that trait. Thus, if the trait is genetically determined, there should be a slightly higher proportion of individuals in the subsequent generation with the trait than in the previous generation. A trait that allows individuals to successfully reproduce and raise more offspring is called an adaptive trait. Often such a trait allows individuals to be more efficient in their utilization of resources. By looking at the population (as opposed to the individual) and its relationship to the environment, one sees that often, when a new adaptive trait spreads through that population, a greater total number of individuals of that population can survive in that environment than could previously. In ecological terms, the new trait has caused an increase in the carrying capacity of that environment for that population.

As a result of natural selection species become more specialized to environmental situations. As species develop biological traits that allow them to be more efficient in a particular environment, those traits simultaneously may make them less efficient in other environments. For example, the ancestors of modern humans probably developed bipedalism because of its advantages in the savannah for seeing and carrying; simultaneously, however, bipedalism made them less efficient in arboreal locomotion. In contrast, humans have evolved to be quite generalized with regard to many of their other characteristics. For example, the human hand is very generalized and is quite similar to that of prosimians (very simple primates). The human digestive apparatus, including teeth and intestines, is not highly specialized for eating any particular kind of food. Humans are not adapted for rapid locomotion, nor would they be able to survive in a wide range of climates without cultural innovations. Our species survives across a broad range of environments because of cultural specializations that act as buffers against the environment.

Many models of cultural evolution have been developed that focus primarily on the stages of evolution, rather than the process of change. The stages are generally either based on the technology available or on the social structure, with some common categories being big-game hunting, hunting-gathering, horticulture, agriculture, and industrialization. These stages are seen as having distinct forms of social organization as well as different technologies. An obvious point generally overlooked is that all of these frames of reference in some way refer to food procurement. Several of the critical changes in human cultural evolution have been in food procurement and processing. Sharing and distribution are central characteristics of the feeding behaviors of humans; thus it makes sense that the ways in which food is procured, processed, and utilized are central to many other aspects of human social organization.

In the remainder of this chapter, I will be discussing foodways in terms of adaptation. I will define a foodway as functionally adaptive if it allows a population to be better nourished, or if it allows the same level of nurture to be achieved with reduced utilization of critical environmental resources. Thus an adaptive foodway would permit the survival of more individuals on the same amount of land. Agriculture, by this definition, would be an adaptive innovation in many environments. This approach necessarily implies a considerable time depth. Changes occurring within a relatively short time on an evolutionary scale (5 to 10 generations or 100 to 200 years) may only have begun to show their positive or negative impact.

When one looks at foodways and nutritional requirements, one can examine biological and cultural aspects of their interaction. There are important questions to be raised about human biological variability, such as whether all humans have the same nutritional requirements and digestive capabilities. Regarding human behavior, one needs to know if the foodways of a particular population result in meeting the nutritional requirements of the individual members. Success in meeting those requirements might be achieved through technological innovations, food combinations, or both. Not all foodways are necessarily adaptive. Some may be neutral; others that seem harmful may represent recent changes, the nutritional impact of which has not yet been felt. For ostensibly harmful practices of greater duration, it may be useful and possible to determine the forces that serve to maintain the behavior in the culture, or that can compensate for the negative impact.

BIOLOGICAL ADAPTATION AND NUTRITION

Relatively little is known about the range of human biological variability both among and within human populations with regard to such common parameters as nutritional requirements, physiological response to malnutrition, and digestive capabilities. The evolution of human milk is the most obvious example of natural selection relating to nutrition. The wide variety of ways in which the biochemistry of human milk fulfills the unique nutritional needs of the human infant and provides protection against the most common infections is *only beginning* to be understood (Jelliffe and Jelliffe, 1975).

Similarly, information is now increasing regarding the complex behavioral interactions that are associated with the establishment and maintenance of the nursing dyad; these interactions appear to be quite important in maternal-infant bonding, and may have broader ramifications for social organization (Jelliffe and Jelliffe, 1976; Newton, 1971; Kennel et al., 1975).

An example of variability in digestion among human populations involves the ability to digest lactose (milk sugar). It was assumed by the scientific community until the middle 1960s that most human adults could digest milk. This belief was characterized by ads such as "every body needs milk." In the middle 1960s physicians began to be concerned with lactose intolerance, a condition in which people who consumed lactose, either through drinking fresh milk or eating foods that had been prepared with it, would get such symptoms as intestinal cramps, bloating, and diarrhea. These were found to be caused by an absence of the intestinal enzyme, lactase. Its absence was thought to be either the result of an earlier intestinal infection (viral, bacterial, or parasitic) that was known to be capable of temporarily halting production of the necessary intestinal enzyme or a normal physiological response to the absence of a lactose challenge. It was known at that time that the presence of lactase in the adult intestine was a uniquely human trait, with other mammals losing their

ability to digest lactose some time after weaning. Studies were begun (see Harrison, 1975, for a summary of relevant articles) to investigate the frequency of adult lactose intolerance in a variety of human populations.

Simoons (1969, 1970) and McCracken (1970, 1971) each have demonstrated a high correlation between the historical absence of dairying in a population and high rates of lactose intolerance. However, not all dairying populations are lactose tolerant; those that are intolerant generally utilize the milk in a fermented or curdled form (yogurt, kefir, buttermilk, cheese). When milk ferments, the bacteria digest the lactose; in curdled milk, the residual lactose is lost with the whey. Thus these milk products do not require lactase for digestion.

The consensus today is that the continued presence of intestinal lactase in the adult is a trait under genetic control, with lactase sufficiency as the lower frequency ("abnormal") trait for the entire species. Several authors have sought to explain the biological variability observed. McCracken (1971) and Simoons (1970) initially hypothesized the advantage to be the capability of extracting more of the energy from the milk, since a failure to digest the lactose results in the loss of the food energy of the sugar. However, human populations generally have not been so deficient in available food sources as to make this advantage critical. Flatz and Rotthauwe (1973) present a more plausible explanation based on the observation that most adults with intestinal lactase are of northern European ancestry. A major environmental stress in that geographical area has been the relative lack of sunlight and the consequent difficulty in producing the vitamin D essential for intestinal absorption of calcium. The absorption of calcium is also facilitated when lactose is present and is being digested; this is especially useful to all mammalian infants during their rapid growth. Flatz and Rotthauwe (1973) propose that the major advantage of the continued ability to digest lactose is that it promotes calcium absorption and thus maximizes the efficiency of the available vitamin D. This would further help to prevent rickets and osteomalacia, each of which can decrease fertility and survival.

Thus we have a situation in which the appearance of a biological trait (the presence of lactase in the adults of a population) is related to a foodway (the form of milk products consumed) and possibly to an environmental stress (low amounts of solar radiation). Conversely, biological adaptation appears to have occurred in response to a cultural trait: without the practice of dairying and the potential for continued milk consumption after childhood, there could be no advantage to or selection for adult lactase production. The probable interaction of biological and cultural evolution is clear.

From this example, however, we can also find evidence of the dietary ethnocentrism mentioned previously. Powdered milk has been a major source of protein distributed world-wide as food aid. It has been assumed until recently by the sending countries (with populations of northern European ancestry) that powdered milk is close to an ideal food; any resistance to its use has been seen as primarily the result of its lack of compatibility with traditional food habits—a problem of ignorance that could be overcome with adequate education. Today, however, it is recognized that milk powder may, for intolerant individuals, promote diarrhea and thus interfere with absorption of other nutrients. Since even intolerant individuals can generally consume small to moderate amounts of milk without symptoms, it may not be necessary to stop distribution entirely. However, it is clear that all programs for distribution of powdered skim milk to individuals over 3 years of age will have to be reexamined, and, in many cases, modified.

Another set of biological adaptations among human populations includes the developmental responses to a shortage of food energy. When humans are faced with a shortage of calories during childhood, the rates of bone and muscle growth decrease, conserving the available nutrients to protect organ development. Thus with slightly limited energy intakes, fully normal adults are produced who are only slightly smaller in overall stature than would otherwise be the case (Stini, 1975). The particular growth pattern that results from food shortage may be under genetic control and may vary among populations. Results from the 7-year Tucson Growth Study (Taylor, personal communication) indicate that growth patterns between ages 6 and 15 for local American Indians (pre-

dominantly Papago), whites, and blacks are quite different, with the patterns of local Mexican-Americans intermediate between whites and Papagos, a distribution that fits our understanding of genetic distance between these populations. When the distribution of children from the poorest areas of the city is compared with that for children from middle class areas, it is found that the ethnic groups are more dissimilar to the groups from the poorer environment. While some might argue that this contrast is the result of a greater admixture of genes from the white population in the other middle class ethnic groups, a careful analysis of these data suggests instead that the pattern of increase in similarity seems to fit best with the hypothesis that growth patterns become more similar in a favorable environment.

A second developmental response to limited availability of food energy is the delayed onset of puberty in both sexes, and of menarche (onset of menstruation) in females, a delay of up to several years in comparison with the U.S. average. Thus the energy-demanding adolescent growth spurt is delayed and sometimes eliminated, and the first pregnancy is postponed for females until adequate body reserves are available to successfully complete it. Finally, it appears that the duration of lactation amenorrhea may be extended when the nutritional status of the mother is poor as well as when the intensity of suckling continues to be high, as would generally be the case when adequate weaning food is in short supply (Frisch, 1975).

Each of these responses has favorable consequences for the individual and the population. A smaller achieved stature and total lean body mass will mean lower energy requirements for the adult, although clearly a limiting factor for smallness is the size and strength necessary to do the work of the society. Small pelvic size may increase the difficulties associated with childbearing. Interestingly, in many societies women recognize the hazards inherent in attempting to birth too large a child, and consciously limit food intake during the third trimester. The consequences of such a limitation to both mother and child have not been thoroughly investigated. Factors that tend to limit the duration of the childbearing years and increase the spacing between children reduce both the population growth rate and the nutritional stress on women and children.

Very little is known about intra- or inter-population variations in requirements for micronutrients. Vitamin C may be an example of such variation in requirements. Recent studies of human requirements for vitamin C have been conducted predominantly in the United States, with subjects who have been consuming moderate levels of vitamin C throughout their lives. There is enormous variation around the world in vitamin C consumption. Documented intakes of vitamin C in people who are (apparently) healthy range from 10 mg to several grams per day in the U.S. (Haas and Harrison, 1977).

The deficiency disease associated with a lack of vitamin C is scurvy. While in some locales or situations this may become a widespread illness, it is rarely, if ever, observed either in pregnant women or infants. This absence of scurvy frequently occurs even though there are strong food taboos against vitamin C–containing foods for both women and infants. The reported levels of vitamin C present in breast milk are generally quite low; this is especially true when the lactating mother is consuming no vitamin C–rich foods. A study done in India by Rajalakshmi et al. (1961) has demonstrated synthesis of vitamin C in 27 of 40 human placentas. This finding has not been replicated to my knowledge, but suggests that there may be some heretofore unknown ability in humans to synthesize vitamin C. The distribution of this ability, if it does exist, is completely unknown at this time. In most animals vitamin C is synthesized in the liver; although the adult guinea pig lacks the necessary enzyme, the fetal guinea pig produces vitamin C in the liver. Studies on higher primates are lacking; a German study of human fetal livers did not show evidence of vitamin C synthesis (Hornig, 1975). This should be an exciting area for future research, and may lead to the examination of variability in requirements for other micronutrients.

The preceding examples indicate broad areas of human variation about which we still know relatively little. Each of these characteristics is adaptive under certain circumstances and can be seen as an example of human biological adaptation in terms of nutritional requirements and utilization. Each

also may have ramifications in terms of food planning and policy.

EVIDENCE OF SELECTION ON FOODWAYS

If one looks at the broad sweep of human evolution, one finds that a major shift in foodways occurred at the time of the agricultural revolution (from 10,000 to 12,000 B.C. in the Middle East, 8,000 to 10,000 B.C. in the Far East, and 3000 to 5000 B.C. in the New World). Prior to these events, the human populations in each area utilized some form of a hunting and gathering subsistence, becoming increasingly efficient through time in extracting food from the environment. With the increasing efficiency came a slow increase in population density, although it is not clear whether the population increase was the cause or result of improved technology. During this preagricultural period, populations continued to depend on a wide variety of edible species for survival, and this variety generally ensured an adequate supply of micronutrients whenever energy needs were met. The continued reliance on hunting provided adequate protein of high quality.

The agricultural revolution led ultimately (although probably not immediately) to a significant change in this situation. Instead of a wide variety of edible species being collected, most energy was invested in the production of a few staple crops with a high yield of food energy. Along with this new technology came increasing population density, and ultimately the abandonment of local hunting as a dietary supplement because of local extinctions ("collecting" of small animals continues in many areas). Herding was developed in some areas to provide a high quality protein source as well as to serve other functions, but today the staple crop can provide over 70% of the food energy for some portions of populations. Any deficiencies that these crops might have in providing micronutrients or in protein composition would clearly become a problem for such a population; behavioral ameliorations of these limitations would be highly adaptive.

One of the most widely used staple crops in the world is maize *(Zea mays)*, a plant with quite a high energy yield per acre that is adapted to a range of climates with wide variation in altitude, rainfall, and temperature.

However, maize is especially deficient in available niacin, an important vitamin. The small amount of niacin present is insoluble and therefore essentially unavailable. In the human body niacin can be made from the amino acid tryptophan so that foods that are niacin deficient but have adequate tryptophan do not lead to niacin deficiency (pellagra). However, maize is also deficient in tryptophan so that populations dependent on maize as a staple crop are considered to be at risk for pellagra.

If one looks at the distribution of maize consumption in the world, one finds that many areas with high maize consumption have (or have had until recently) a high prevalence of pellagra (e.g., Italy, the southern U.S.). This is not the case in much of the Americas where maize is an indigenous crop. Katz (1974) has shown that the indigenous techniques for processing maize in much of the pellagra-free New World alter the maize in such a way as to free the bound niacin and increase the proportion of tryptophan in the protein. Apparently, the processing technique that accomplishes this includes soaking the maize in lime water or other alkali before grinding, a practice found throughout Mexico and in parts of the U.S., Central America, and South America. When maize is soaked in an alkali the main protein of maize (zein) is made partially insoluble. This is the protein component that is very low in tryptophan. Maize contains another protein but in smaller quantity; this protein is usually relatively unavailable, but it becomes available after alkali treatment. This second protein is relatively high in tryptophan compared to zein and the additional tryptophan can be converted in the body to niacin. Further, when maize is soaked in alkali the bound niacin is released. The food (masa) prepared in this way from maize has a relatively adequate supply of available niacin and tryptophan; therefore, people who consume this food are at minimal risk for pellagra. This technology compensates for a major deficiency in the staple food crop. Given the widespread use of some kind of alkali soak (wood ash in much of maize-producing Africa) with maize consumption, the question arises as to the origin and mode of dispersal of the food processing pattern, since it seems to have appeared independently in at least two locales. Apparently, the treatment makes it easier to grind maize into a finer flour. Clearly, this development left its users able to satisfy their nutritional requirements with lower resource utilization, since they did not need to produce and consume as much animal protein or beans to complement the maize.

Many of the other food crops that are used around the world also require complex processing to be edible. One of these is cassava or manioc. Cassava contains a compound called prussic acid, which is highly toxic and has an extremely bitter taste. In order for the cassava to be edible, the prussic acid must be leached out by pounding and then soaking the root for a considerable period of time. However, after this process, when most of the acid has been removed (probably along with water-soluble vitamins), cassava provides a very high yield of almost pure carbohydrates. The growth of cassava and manioc depletes few minerals from the soil. These vegetables are grown easily in tropical areas when other cultivation is either harmful to the environment or impossible. The yield of food energy per acre is quite high, even though the protein content is low; in areas where a high energy production is important cassava is a very good crop.

Leaching techniques are not limited to root crops; California Indians used them on acorns, which have a high natural level of tannic acid. In areas with large stands of wild oak, adequately processed acorns have provided a good staple crop yielding high quality protein, as well as energy, without any need for cultivation.

Another important food preparation innovation that has received relatively little attention is fermentation. It is a widespread practice with substantial benefits, particularly in the tropics (van Veen and Steinkraus, 1970). First, fermented foods can be safely stored more easily than unfermented foods; the low pH of fermented foods makes them resistant to further bacterial or fungal action. Second, fermentation often makes otherwise inedible portions of crops edible. For example, bongkrek and ontjom, the fermented products of coconut and peanut press cakes respectively, are widely consumed in Java. If not fermented, the press cakes (which result from the extraction of oil from the plant) would be unfit for human consumption because of their high levels of fiber and insoluble materials;

they would either be discarded or used less efficiently as animal fodder. Similarly, fermentation permits the conversion of small, freshwater fish, which might otherwise be unusable, into fish pastes and sauces that are important sources of protein and calcium in Southeast Asia. Third, fermentation frequently improves the vitamin content of foods, particularly increasing thiamine, riboflavin, niacin, and B_{12}. These are vitamins that typically are in short supply in predominantly vegetarian diets. Finally, fermentation generally improves the desirability of the food by improving the flavor and decreasing the necessary cooking time (for example, from 6 hours for soybeans to 10 minutes for the fermented soybean product tempeh). Inadequate cooking of the unfermented product often results in decreased availability of nutrients: fermentation helps to ensure complete utilization. Clearly, fermentation can be considered an adaptive foodway.

A major problem of staple crops that human populations must cope with is the quality of the available protein. The human body utilizes amino acids in a particular ratio. Thus the complete absence of one or more essential amino acids (those that the body cannot produce) in a food protein means that little or none of the ingested protein is available to the body for making other protein, but rather serves only as an energy source. This type of protein is referred to as low quality, or incomplete. In fact, most low quality proteins are found in plants. The example of maize given above illustrates one type of cultural device used to overcome this problem. Another is to combine two or more protein sources in a single meal in such a way that the deficiencies in each protein source are compensated for by the other. For example, maize is low in lysine, isoleucine, and tryptophan, all essential amino acids. In many areas of Mexico, maize is still commonly consumed in the same meal with black beans, which are high in all three essential amino acids, but low in the sulfur-containing amino acids found in masa. In this way, the deficiencies of one protein are complemented by the strengths of the other, and the resulting combined protein is of higher quality and can be more thoroughly utilized.

Clearly, not all possible pairs of plant proteins will have this effect. However, a survey of the plant combinations eaten in areas of high population density, where the diet is based predominantly on a few staple crops, provides a list of such complementary combinations. Maize and beans in the New World, rice and pulses (lentils, mung beans, soybeans) in the Far East, and wheat and dairy products in Europe, the Middle East, and North India are but a few examples. Often foods eaten as condiments, such as fish or some vegetable sauces served on rice in Southeast Asia, serve the same purpose. The development of these food combinations as dietary staples may be considered to be a case of selection operating on foodways. Protein deficiencies are rarely found among adults with adequate access to the standard local diet.

OTHER FORCES THAT MAINTAIN FOODWAYS

In the preceding sections I have discussed biological and foodway adaptations that serve to protect the nutritional status of populations. Not all foodways, however, are in this category. Many foodways that are essentially neutral or even deleterious are maintained through their cultural role.

Some of the oldest known foodways intimately tied to cultural systems are those that regulate available food to individuals on the basis of sex and life stage. In many cultures, meats and the products of hunting are associated with males while plant foods are the domain of females. This distinction relates to consumption as well as production. The most valued parts of an animal generally go to males; female access is often restricted to what remains after all males (adults and children) have had their fill. When exceptions in this pattern occur, the usual recipients of animal products are women who are pregnant or in the early postpartum period. Among the Chagga of Tanzania (Zalla, personal communication), traditional food for a woman during her confinement (approximately 3 months surrounding childbirth) is a mixture of animal blood, milk, and fat. This practice provides additional nutrients to the female at the time of her most critical need with blood and milk supplying iron and calcium, two of the elements most likely to be inadequate on a limited vegetarian diet.

However, not all dietary practices related to pregnancy and lactation are so clearly beneficial; in many parts of the world severe restrictions are placed on women at these times. The mechanisms for maintaining these restrictions probably center on the inherent danger and uncertainty associated with childbirth. Food restrictions are attempts at minimizing the risk through avoidance of "dangerous" foods. A bad result confirms the danger of a restricted food inadvertently consumed, or, if all restrictions were followed, it calls into question foods formerly thought to be safe. In this manner, many fruits and vegetables (and, in some areas, virtually anything but maize and white rice) have become restricted to Indian woman of Mexico in the 40 days postpartum (Werner, 1970). Women in South India are severely limited in their access to a variety of foods containing iron, calcium, and vitamins A and C during menstruation, pregnancy, and the early portion of lactation (Ferro-Luzzi, 1973a, 1973b, 1974). In fact, if one considers the time spent in one of these categories by an average Hindu woman, it appears likely that dietary restrictions are in effect for one-third to one-half of her life from age 13 or 14 years to menopause.

The most difficult period of food restriction for the child is the weaning period. Most cultures have firm notions of "appropriate" weaning foods for children, many of which provide marginal nutrients. Bananas are considered the best weaning food in many parts of the world, particularly Africa, in spite of their low caloric density and low protein content in comparison with cereal products. For example, some Liberian groups prefer bananas or cassava to rice as a weaning food because the more rapid body growth associated with the rice diet is thought to occur at the expense of intellectual development (Harrison, personal communication). Thus recognition of what Americans would consider evidence of good nutritional status, i.e., growth, in this case leads away from nutritious food.

All over the world, foods are differentiated on the basis of their desirability, with those that are more desirable generally being associated with higher status. The level of desirability, however, is often unrelated to the nutritional content. In India, polished rice is considered to be a higher status food than brown or unpolished rice, even though polished rice (unless enriched or parboiled) is nearly devoid of thiamine, a B vitamin. If an individual has access to other major sources of thiamine, polished rice represents no threat. But many individuals who consume polished rice for status reasons do not have access to such foods and as a result develop beriberi. This form of malnutrition is, in some parts of the Far East, a status symbol for it indicates reliance on the preferred form of rice. In much of the West, high status foods are often those considered to be "rich," an interesting expression that generally indicates a high butterfat content. In the U.S., prime beef is the best (i.e., most expensive) and its rating is based on the high fat content of the muscle. If, in fact, a high animal fat and cholesterol diet does turn out to be a major causal factor in various forms of cancer or heart disease, the Western pattern would be consistent with that of the Far East; in today's environment, the high status diet would itself be responsible for considerable morbidity and mortality.

Many dietary changes are taking place in the world today that represent a shift from the traditional pattern to one that is associated with Western culture, and that comes to be seen as higher status through advertising and promotion. The prime example of this is the change from breast- to bottle-feeding of infants that is occurring in the urban areas of the Third World with disastrous consequences for infant health. Another is the widespread consumption of Coca-Cola and other carbonated beverages in spite of their high cost in Third World countries compared to dietary staples. While the spread of these changes is the direct result of efforts by manufacturers looking for new markets and more profits, their rapid success results in part from the willingness of people to alter food consumption patterns to gain status.

Social and cultural change is leading to changes in the foodways in many areas. The promotion of Western foods is only one aspect of this change. For example, among the Chagga, many aspects of the traditional family structure and division of labor have changed so that few women today experience an extended confinement during the perinatal period. With the shortening of confinement has come a decrease in the consumption of the traditional perinatal foods (blood and milk); this virtually eliminates female access to animal products, since the traditional vegetarian diet has not expanded in other ways. Also, migrant laborers have aided in the introduction of maize as a new cash crop in this traditionally banana-based economy. Maize is consumed as a thick porridge (ugali) of cornmeal and water, which replaces a soup made of bananas, meat, and milk. Beans are available, but viewed as low status, so that a maize and bean combination is rarely consumed. The substitution of ugali for soup is clearly a step in the direction of poorer nutrition. The problem is compounded for the young children by the standard ways in which these foods are served. The traditional soup is served in individual bowls, with a special bowl generally prepared for the weanling child to ensure a reasonable meal. Ugali (and the accompanying relish of vegetables or meat) is eaten with the fingers from a communal pot on a competitive basis. The smallest children are least able to secure an adequate meal because of their small size and lack of manual dexterity. The tradition of preparing a special bowl for children has not been carried over to the new food. The change is one of the factors contributing to an increased prevalence of kwashiorkor in weanling children (Zalla, personal communication).

CONCLUSIONS

It has become clear in reviewing a wide range of foodways that one of the most significant indicators of the probability of a particular behavior being adaptive is its time depth. Practices that are central to the culture and that have been in existence over hundreds of generations are far more likely to be nutritionally beneficial, or at worst neutral, than are practices that have been introduced as recently as this century. In attempting to evaluate the sources of malnutrition in a society, a first step should be to assess the nutrient content of the available foods. Information should be collected on food as it is actually prepared and consumed. An analysis of maize from a field will not provide accurate information on the nutritional content of masa; separate calculations of the available protein from maize and beans will significantly underestimate the usable protein in a common meal.* Information such as this also sug-

gests that the food value of some crops may be as readily improved through changes in processing techniques or in combinations consumed as through genetic changes developed in agricultural experiment stations. Information on the nutrient alterations accompanying traditional food preparation techniques is a necessary data base for future work.

Before recommending foodway changes it is necessary and feasible to assess the cultural context. For example, it would be important to know the traditional role of the food to be discouraged, replaced, or supplemented, as well as the probable position of the product being introduced. These factors have not usually been considered. It is not surprising that in this society weight loss diets with heavy dependence on salads and vegetables are less popular than those based on beef and high fat foods to the exclusion of vegetables; the former foods are low status and feminine while the latter are high status and masculine. One might anticipate greater resistance to the new Dietary Goals for the U.S. (Select Committee, 1977), which emphasize nonbeef protein sources, than can be explained by industry opposition. Another important aspect of the cultural context would be the setting in which food is served; the replacement of the traditional soup by ugali among the Chagga led to nutritional changes related to mode of eating as well as nutrient content.

An anthropological and evolutionary viewpoint should allow us to avoid one of the pitfalls mentioned in the beginning of the chapter: the attitude that our own foodways are natural and sensible while those of others are unnatural and irrational. The same processes of natural selection are taking place today as in the past, although it is difficult for us to view them in our own lifetimes. Without additional intervention, the widespread infant malnutrition in the Third World associated with bottle-feeding is unlikely to continue for many generations. But without intervention, the toll in morbidity and mortality will be great before a more efficient system—whether a return to breastfeeding or further technological change—becomes widespread. Culture change is leading to the rapid disruption and disappearance of many established and adaptive foodways. Attempts to alleviate some of the resulting malnutrition, which are based on inadequate understanding of the

---

*These are not isolated examples; many others can be found in the journal *Ecology of Food and Nutrition*, 1971 to the present.

complex relationships between populations and their diets, are unlikely to succeed, and may compound the current problems.

REFERENCES

Ferro-Luzzi, G. E. 1973a. Food avoidances at puberty and menstruation in Tamilnad. Ecology of Food and Nutrition 2:165-172.

Ferro-Luzzi, G. E. 1973b. Food avoidances of pregnant women in Tamilnad. Ecology of Food and Nutrition 2:259-266.

Ferro-Luzzi, G. E. 1974. Food avoidances during the puerperium and lactation in Tamilnad. Ecology of Food and Nutrition 3:7-16.

Flatz, G., and Rotthauwe, H. W. 1973. Lactose nutrition and natural selection. Lancet ii:16-17.

Frisch, R. E. 1975. Critical weights, a critical body composition, menarche, and the maintenance of menstrual cycles. In E. S. Watts, F. E. Johnson, and G. W. Lasker (eds.). Biosocial interrelations in population adaptation. Mouton, The Hague.

Haas, J. D., and Harrison, G. G. 1977. Nutritional anthropology and biological adaptation. Annual Review of Anthropology 6:69-101.

Harrison, G. G. 1975. Primary adult lactase deficiency: A problem in anthropological genetics. American Anthropologist 77:812-835.

Hornig, D. 1975. Metabolism of ascorbic acid, World Review of Nutrition and Diet 23:225-258.

Jelliffe, D. B., and Jelliffe, E. F. P. 1975. Human milk, nutrition, and the world resource crisis. Science 188:551-561.

Jelliffe, D. B., and Jelliffe, E. F. P. 1976. Adaptive suckling. Ecology of Food and Nutrition 5:249-253.

Katz, S. H., Hediger, M. L., and Valleroy, L. S. 1974. The anthropological and nutritional significance of traditional maize processing techniques in the New World. Science 184:765-773.

Kennell, J. H., Trause, M. A., and Klaus, M. H. 1975. Evidence for a sensitive period in the human mother. In Parent-Infant Interaction, Ciba Foundation Symposium 33 (new series), Mouton, The Hague.

McCracken, R. 1970. Adult lactose intolerance. Journal of the American Medical Association 213:2257-2260.

McCracken, R. D. 1971. Lactase deficiency: An example of dietary evolution. Current Anthropology 12:479-517.

Newton, N. 1971. The psychological differences between breast and bottle feeding. American Journal of Clinical Nutrition 24:993-1004.

Rajalakshmi, R., Subbolakshmi, G., Ramakrishnan, C. V., and others. 1961. Biosynthesis of ascorbic acid in human placentas. Current Science 36:45-46.

Select Committee on Nutrition and Human Needs. 1977. Dietary goals for the United States, U.S. Senate, U.S. Government Printing Office.

Simoons, F. J. 1969. Primary adult lactose intolerance and the milking habit: A problem in biological and cultural interrelations. I. Review of the medical research. American Journal of Digestive Diseases 15:819-836.

Simoons, F. J. 1970. Primary adult lactose intolerance and the milking habit: A problem in biological and cultural interrelations. II. A culture historical hypothesis. American Journal of Digestive Diseases 15:695-710.

Stini, W. A. 1975. Adaptive strategies of populations under nutritional stress. In E. S. Watts, F. E. Johnson, and G. W. Lasker (eds.). Biosocial interrelations in population adaptation. Mouton, The Hague.

van Veen, A. G., and Steinkraus, K. H. 1970. Nutritive value and wholesomeness of fermented foods. Agricultural and Food Chemistry 18:516-578.

Werner, D. 1970. Healing in the Sierra Madre. Natural History, Nov., pp. 61-66.

Wilson, C. S. 1973. Food taboos of childbirth: The Malay example. Ecology of Food and Nutrition 2:267-274.

CHAPTER 13

Pica—a nutritional anthropology concern

Carolyn J. Lackey

Pickles, watermelon, ice cream, strawberries craved in the middle of the night—there must be a pregnant woman near. When one delves into food cravings during pregnancy, a "magpie" may appear. A magpie is a bird noted for eating and carrying away a variety of extraneous objects—thus a bird with an unusual array of dietary and behavioral habits.

The Latin word for magpie is *pica*. The term pica evokes a variety of connotations to nutritionists, anthropologists, and those in the medical professions. While Webster defines pica as "a craving for and eating of unnatural substances (as chalk, ashes, or bone) that occurs in nutritional deficiency states (as aphosphorosis) in man or animals or in hysteric or insane conditions in man," Cooper (1957) in a review of early pica research defines pica as "the habit of eating clay, plastic, ashes, charcoal, etc." Others have defined pica as "persistent ingestion of substances commonly considered unfit for food" (Gutellius et al., 1962); "a perversion of appetite with persistent and purposeful ingestion of unsuitable substances seemingly of nonnutritional value" (Lanzkowsky, 1959); and "a longing for substances not fit for food" (Posner et al., 1951).

The approach to classifying food behavior as pica in this chapter will be more consistent with the broad definitions of Halsted (1968), "the eating of any foreign substance," and Crosby (1976), "the compulsive eating of anything."

Pica is the general term given to those food cravings, whether they are considered perverted behavior or less than a perversion but still compulsive. Several terms have been coined for the more commonly noted forms of pica. Geophagia is the eating of dirt or clay. Pagophagia refers to the compulsive eating of unusual quantities of ice. Amylophagia is specific for starch eating. Since these three types of pica are the most prevalent, they have warranted names for themselves. Geophagia, pagophagia, and amylophagia are often used in pica literature. Classifying every different type of craving could lead to an absurd array of names, which might include the "cautopyreiophagia" coined by Perry (1977) for burnt-match ingestion.

Pica cannot be relegated to the historical interest files. Geophagia and amylophagia were once thought to be practiced only by low income southern blacks. And these practices were believed to belong to a bygone era in southern history. Pica is not dead nor is the practice restricted to any racial, geographic, or historical area.

HISTORICAL REVIEW

Cooper (1957) made a careful study of literature that contained references to pica from medieval times to the mid 1950s. His literature search revealed that prior to the 1800s pica was considered a complication of pregnancy. In the literature of this past era, pica incidences were reported for all ages and both sexes; however, the practice was more attributable to pregnant women.

Even in these early reports pica substances were not restricted to unusual or nonfood items. Other cravings such as lettuce, clabbered milk, or river oysters were listed. Cravings were categorized based upon the types of substances craved. The more serious category, pica, was a craving for absurd things, whereas the term "malacia" was used when the craving included usual food items in addition to absurd things.

Various therapies suggested in these early writings included whipping of boys, medication, venesection, diversion, good nutrition (which was specified as fresh fruits and vegetables and fresh cooked meat), restoration of a healthy mind, special tea infusion, and iron therapy.

Early explanations for pica included the body's response to an unnatural state (for example, pregnancy), which was translated by the mind into desires for unusual substances.

Cooper followed up this report of early references to pica with a discussion of explorers' and anthropologists' observations beginning in the 1800s. As in earlier literature, all ages and both sexes were pica practicers. Reports included the eating of clay, lime, and a "clay butter" made for bread. Clay was given to babies to quiet them. During the 1800s, speculation of an association between clay eating and anemia was made.

One of the most complete surveys from an anthropological point of view is that conducted by Laufer (1930). He discusses the distributions of geophagia in North and South America, Asia, Africa, and Europe. He concludes that pica occurs sporadically and is not associated with any geographic region, race, creed, culture, or status within a culture.

Cooper's historical discussion of pica in North America centered on the colonial days and black plantation slaves. Consistent with the literature already reported, all ages and both sexes were included as pica practicers. The most common form of pica was manifested in clay and dirt eating. Pica was thought to be a result of emotional and physiological factors, which for the black slave included hunger, peer imitation, mental homesickness, disease, and the combination of poor living conditions and diet.

As in early reports, pica was associated with anemia and inadequate diets. Suggested treatment included iron therapy and improved diet and living conditions. The same observations and conclusions were made for the practice, etiology, and treatment from Cooper's review of early colonial literature; however, the reports were limited to discussions of black slaves.

In a following chapter, Cooper presents reports of pica in Europe and the New World, nonspecific to race. The same generalizations can be made for this group of pica practicers. All ages and both sexes were found to practice pica; however, women, especially pregnant women, and children were the most common practicers. Items listed as pica included not only unusual substances but also food items. Etiology was associated with anemia, malnutrition, and parasitic infestations. However, pica's association with lead poisoning, especially in children, was a new speculation from this group of authors. Reference to pica being caused by psychological or nutritionally physiological factors was consistent with previous attempts to explain pica behavior.

Throughout Cooper's discussion several factors are stressed that not only are of historical relevance but indicate how early conjectures about the etiology of pica have not yet been solved by advanced medical technology. Dietary inadequacy and physiological stress are often suggested as causative agents. However, why this is manifested in the form of pica is still a researchable topic.

Since Cooper's extensive review was published, research has been conducted to determine the relationship of pica to many medical conditions and cultural and psychological states. Researchers have sought association of pica with hemoglobin levels, prematurity, perinatal mortality, parotid enlargement as a result of starch ingestion, lead poisoning in children, heavy metal binding that leads to malabsorption of minerals (iron in particular), anemia, hookworm, hunger, cultural traits, sideropenia, oral needs, and behavioral disorders. Few research findings have been conclusive or consistent among researchers.

From this nonexhaustive list of researched topics, anemia and malnutrition bear closer review by both nutritionists and anthropologists. Research data on these two topics will be presented with special emphasis on the pregnant woman and pica behavior in the following section.

ASSOCIATION WITH ANEMIA AND MALNUTRITION

Several researchers have reported higher incidences of anemia in pica practicers than in nonpica practicers, whereas other researchers found no difference in anemia frequency in pica versus nonpica populations. Edwards et al. (1964) studied complications experienced during pregnancy by clay and cornstarch eaters versus a pregnant nonpica control group. Approximately twice as many cases of hypertension and edema occurred in the clay eaters as in the cornstarch eaters or controls. Moderate to severe anemia was found in 27% of the clay eaters and 17% of the cornstarch eaters compared with 7% of the pregnant women in the control group.

Keith and coworkers (1968) sampled approximately 1000 pregnant women and collected hemoglobin, hematocrit, and red blood cell count data. Approximately 35% of the total group sampled were starch eaters. The incidence of amylophagia was significantly higher in the Negro population than in the Caucasian. These researchers reported twice as many cases of severe anemia in starch eaters as in nonstarch eaters. Adequate hemoglobin levels were 2½ times more frequent in nonstarch eaters than in the amylophagia group. The amount of starch eaten correlated with hemoglobin levels, thus leading these researchers to suggest that anemia was caused by pica. The suggested etiology was that the starch eaten displaced foodstuffs that contain iron, thus lowering dietary sources of iron.

Sage (1962) found significantly lower hemoglobin levels for amylophagic pregnant Negro females compared with a control group who did not eat starch.

Other researchers have not found an association between pica and anemia. O'Rourke et al. (1967) studied clay and laundry starch eaters in Georgia. Of the 200 patients interviewed, 55% ingested clay or starch, mostly when pregnant. Although the average hemoglobin level of the pica group was 1 Gm/100 ml below the nonpica group, this was not a significant difference. In addition to clay and starch, other substances ingested included dry milk of magnesia, coffee grounds, and paraffin.

Rogers (1972) sampled iron deficient pregnant women in Alabama for incidence of pica. Forty-five percent of the women practiced pica. She found no significant difference in hematocrit, hemoglobin, serum iron, total iron binding capacity, or red blood cell count between the pica group and the nonpica group.

The question of an association between pica and iron deficiency anemia is still unsettled. If there is a relationship, is the iron deficiency a cause or the effect of pica? That question, too, has puzzled researchers. In their review article, Ansell and Wheby (1972) present data that support both theories, cause or effect, and other data that can be used to show no relationship between iron deficiency anemia and pica. Research in support of the hypothesis that iron deficiency anemia is a cause of pica was presented in reviews of six research reports. Three of the literature citations concerned the disappearance of pica in children following iron therapy. Two other reports contained data that were probably the most conclusive in demonstrating iron deficiency as a cause of the pica. These two studies were of pagophagia, the one type of pica whose cure responded best to iron therapy and whose manifestion, ice eating, was usually significantly associated with iron deficiency.

The sixth article supporting anemia as the cause of pica was a rat study in which iron deficient rats chose a significantly greater amount of their daily water consumption in the form of ice rather than water. In pagophagia the correction of anemia in most cases causes a cessation of ice eating.

Ansell and Wheby do not include studies of pregnant females in their selection of recent research to support anemia as a cause of pica. These authors also discuss iron deficiency anemia as a possible result of pica. In support of this theory are two reports of the iron binding properties of clay. The reasons for the initial eating of clay were not documented; as will be discussed later in this chapter, these reasons are the most difficult to ascertain. The other two articles cited in support of pica causing anemia both pertain to starch ingestion. Starch unlike clay does not possess iron binding properties and thus would not affect iron absorption from the gut. Starch was implicated as a causative agent since it might be used as a dietary displacement of foodstuffs from which iron could be made available to the body. By supplying calories, starch would satisfy hunger, precluding the ingestion of foods of greater nutrient density.

Two principal studies cited by Ansell and Wheby show no relationship between pica and iron deficiency anemia. One study involved children who practiced pica. One-half of the group received iron therapy, whereas the other group received a placebo. There was no significant change in hemoglobin levels between the two groups. The other study (O'Rourke et al., 1967) has already been discussed. Gutelius and coworkers (1962) in a double-blind study also could not establish that iron was significantly better in curing pica in children than the saline-administered placebo.

Other researchers also have sought to distinguish the cause or effect relationship of pica and iron deficiency anemia. Roselle's (1970) research was with nonpregnant New Yorkers who ingested either clay or starch. All subjects had iron-deficiency anemia. After iron therapy hemoglobin values returned to normal, however, the patients continued to eat starch or clay. He therefore suggested that the iron deficiency was an effect of pica, not a cause. This was a different conclusion from that presented by Lanzkowsky (1959) who reviewed the literature and concluded that iron deficiency is the major cause of pica and that iron therapy is curative.

McDonald and Marshall's (1964) work supports Lanzkowsky's hypothesis. These researchers divided pica practicing children residing in Cape Town, South Africa, into two groups. One group received iron therapy and the other group a saline solution. Treatment with iron resulted in the cessation of pica after 3 to 4 months in all cases. In the saline treated group only 3 children stopped practicing pica. After 5 to 6 months the difference between cure rates for the two groups was not impressive since some children's hemoglobin levels had dropped and pica was resumed. The authors conclude that permanent cure is dependent upon maintenance of the higher hemoglobin levels. Crosby (1976) has reviewed several research reports of the 1960s and 1970s and developed the "unquestionable" conclusion that pagophagia and food picas are common symptoms of iron deficiency. He lends credibility to his conclusion based on his association with iron deficient patients. He reports that more than 50% of patients with iron deficiency had some type of pica. He suggests a therapeutic trial of iron when a patient's medical history reveals a pica practice. Crosby relies heavily on the cure of pagophagia through iron therapy for an extrapolation to all types of food pica.

From the above literature selections, it seems possible to conclude that iron deficiency and pica are associated in some manner. Whether the pica is the result or the cause appears to be related to the specific type of pica, the pica practicer's physiological status other than iron deficiency, and sociocultural variables. A blanket statement of cause or effect does not emerge from my review of the presented research. Pagophagia is the only type of pica for which the research evidence supports the theory that iron deficient individuals are more susceptible than individuals who are not iron deficient. Certainly, not all iron deficient individuals practice pagophagia, which would suggest some physiological difference in those individuals who do or do not indulge in ice eating.

Sayers et al. (1974) present a review of pica literature that leads to the same conclusion. The association between pica and iron deficiency has long been noted; however, the reason for the association is still controversial. How can iron deficiency pervert the appetite? The pathogenesis is not known. The craving does not appear to be compensatory since substances eaten are not foods rich in iron (Crosby, 1971). Crosby concludes that pica is not psychologically induced because the cravings disappear with treatment in iron deficient patients.

The conclusion of this section is only the beginning of still more "which came first, the chicken or the egg" theorizing and researching. Iron deficiency is one result of malnutrition, although conclusive evidence of etiology is not available. Another important form of malnutrition associated with pica is caloric replacement as is suggested in starch ingestion. If the pica substance is consumed in sufficient quantities so that it becomes a replacement for foodstuffs comprising an adequate diet, other nutrient deficiencies may occur. For example, a 1 pound box of laundry starch supplies the amylophagiac with approximately 1800 calories (almost pure complex carbohydrate), while supplying no other vital nutrients such as protein, fat, vitamins, or minerals. Laundry starch is an inexpensive source of energy, and research evidence supports prevalence of use among adults when the socioeconomic circumstances are poor. Halsted (1968) has reviewed geophagia in man and includes a discussion of clinical implications. Hunter (1973) has proposed that pica is abnormal behavior caused by a subconscious response to physiological needs of the body under stress. He contends that pica is a cultural phenomenon only because it has been culturally institutionized through a period of time as a behavioral response to physiological needs.

PICA DURING PREGNANCY

As can be seen from the preceding discussion of pica, various topics could be singled out for further discussion, such as pagophagia and iron deficiency, children and lead paint poisoning, male pica practices, and cation binding capacity of pica materials. The following discussion will include a discussion of my research and observations of pica in low income pregnant women.

What the pregnant female craves and eats is of real concern to the dietitian, nutritionist, medical professional, and nutritional anthropologist, since any behavior that might keep her from obtaining appropriate amounts of needed nutrients must be recognized.

Is pica during pregnancy a cultural phenomenon, a disease state, or a psychological or physiological response? This question has been approached by both nutritionists and anthropologists. Nutritionists most often have been concerned with possible relationships of pica during pregnancy with anemia, toxemia, other complications during pregnancy; psychological or behavioral problems of the mother; and the health status of the fetus. Anthropologists have been instrumental in pica documentation and offering sociocultural explanations for its occurrence. Both approaches have proved unsuccessful in explaining *why* pica is practiced.

Pica behavior during pregnancy was investigated by me in 1972 and 1973 in an outpatient clinic in east Tennessee. In the course of conducting a general survey of the food knowledge and practices of outpatients at the University of Tennessee Memorial Research Center and Hospital (UTMRCH) women were asked the question: "Did you or

a friend eat cornstarch, clay, chalk, paper, or ashes when you were pregnant?" Forty-eight percent of the predominantly white clinic population practiced pica, knew someone who did, or had heard of the practice. A variety of substances were named including: clay, dirt, cornstarch, laundry starch, cake magnesia, soot, charcoal, slate rock, flour, coffee (both raw and grounds), cigarette ashes, chalk, coal oil, and coal.

Edwards (1964) reports that pica practice during pregnancy is the result of powerful influences of superstition and custom. The UTMRCH interviewees said time and again, "I've never told my doctor that I'd eaten those things." Finding little conclusive evidence in the literature about the motivation and attitudes of women who practice pica, I designed a 36 item, open-ended questionnaire to obtain selected demographic data, knowledge and attitudes of pica, and reasons for practicing and terminating pica behavior. One hundred complete interviews were obtained from women ranging in age from 16 to 77 years in the outpatient clinics of the same hospital. All of the women had experienced at least one pregnancy. Twenty-six of the randomly selected interviewees were black and 74 were white. Data were analyzed to describe the group of pica practicers and then explore motivations and attitudes surrounding the practice of pica in pregnancy.

What is the reaction of most women when asked if they craved any substances while pregnant? First, usually came a nervous laugh, then a listing of foods such as watermelon, pickles, ice-cream—those foods we have come to expect pregnant women to crave. In all, 69 different foods were named (Table 6). None of the foods were craved in unusual amounts, which then would be considered a form of pica.

While this information was interesting and contributed information about the pregnant female's diet, the clients were asked more specifically: "Do you know anyone who eats clay, cornstarch, ashes, dirt, block magnesia, or anything else that is not usually served at mealtime?" Sixty-nine of the 100 interviewees said yes. Eventually 34 of them stated that they had eaten an unusual substance or substances themselves. Approximately one fourth of those 34 women, how-

Table 6. Foods most frequently craved during pregnancy by 100 UTMRCH* outpatients

Food	Number of times cited
Watermelon	12
Pickles	10
Ice cream	9
Strawberries	6
Apples	6
Peaches	5
Chocolate	5
Candy	4
61 other foods	1-3 each

*University of Tennessee Memorial Research Center and Hospital, 1973.

Table 7. Pica behavior of UTMRCH* outpatient women according to race (N = 100)

	Race			
	Black		White	
Category	Number	Percent	Number	Percent
Practiced pica during pregnancy	14	54	20	27
Never practiced pica during pregnancy	12	46	54	73
Totals	26	100	74	100

*University of Tennessee Memorial Research Center and Hospital.

ever, readily volunteered a pica practice. Once the investigator talked with the women for a little while, sometimes relating the pica practices of other women, the interviewees were more at ease to describe their own pica practice.

Chi square analyses showed the number of pica practicers (in the outpatient sample) to be significantly different from chance at the 1% level. An attempt to further characterize this group of 34 women pica practicers was made.

Race often is associated with pica behavior (Table 7). Twenty of the pica practicers were white and 14 black. This difference was significant at the 5% level. Fifty-four percent of the black women interviewed and 27% of the white women interviewed practiced pica. Testing the association between race and pica behavior resulted in only a moderate association in this population. For this sample, the chance of error in predicting pica behavior by race computed as lambda is reduced 52%. Although in this sample race is only moderately associated with pica behavior, it is important to recognize that 27% of the sample who practiced pica were white. Other researchers usually have studied pica behavior in black populations and have concluded that there is a racial distinction in pica behavior among pregnant women. Several articles are included in the selected readings at the end of this chapter that state specifically that pregnant pica practicers are blacks whose practice is linked to their southern heritage.

The 34 pica practicers cited 16 different substances (Table 8). These substances were examined in relation to race. Some form of starch was eaten by 10 (29%) of the pica practicers. Nine of those 10 were black women. Some form of dirt, clay, or mud was eaten by 10 (29%) of the pica practicers. Seven were black women and 3 were white. In general, the white pica practicers ate such items as ice, coffee grounds, apple and orange seeds, and potato peelings.

Pica behavior also was examined in terms of the age of interviewees and the educational level attained. Seventy-one women were 54 years of age or younger; 20 of these had practiced pica. Twenty-nine women were 55 years or older and 14 had practiced pica. Chi square analysis indicated no significant difference in pica behavior defined by these age groups among the interviewees.

The women were grouped into three educational classes: those completing 0-6 grades; 7-9 grades; and 10 or more grades in school. Chi square analysis did not indicate statistical significance for pica behavior and educational attainment. The pica practicers in this sample, therefore, could not be definitely characterized by race, age, or educational attainment.

Attitudes toward pica practiced were then explored with the 100 interviewees. They were asked why women might crave unusual substances during pregnancy. Nonpica practicers expressed about the same opinions as pica practicers. For the most part, the opinions were speculative and not firm beliefs.

Table 8. Substances eaten during pregnancy by the 34 pica practicers interviewed at UTMRCH* outpatient clinic

Substance (N = 16)	Number of times cited (N = 49)
Starch	10
Mud, clay, dirt	10
Ice	5
Coffee grounds (dry or wet)	4
Block magnesia	3
Baking soda	2
Cornmeal	2
Flour	2
Whiskey	2
Charcoal, coal	2
Burnt matches	2
Cocoa (dry)	1
Oatmeal (dry)	1
Apple and orange seeds	1
Potato peelings	1
Tire inner tubes	1

*University of Tennessee Memorial Research Center and Hospital.

Comments ranged from "don't know" to "it's a lack of vitamins" or "it's something born into a person" to "it's just an unexplainable craving." Some associated the craving with a habit—a psychological response since everybody says a pregnant woman is supposed to have cravings. One respondent's interesting theory was that when a woman is pregnant she needs more food and something like fresh strawberries, cold ice cream, or juicy peaches is more likely to catch her attention when she looks through magazines or goes shopping. Others felt that the pica substance served a medicinal value, either relieving constipation, helping digestion, or quieting nausea. The nausea explanation is interesting since most of the substances craved were of a dry consistency. Eating soda crackers is a common suggestion for pregnant women who experience nausea.

The pica practicers were asked how they felt if they were unable to obtain the pica substance. Some expressed an urgent need for the substance: "Maybe I felt like someone on dope." "I had to have it." "I felt terrible (cranky, awful, or nervous)." "I felt like when you run out of cigarettes." "I'd walk the floor or walk to town to buy it." Others

denied giving in to a craving: "I could control myself." "It was not a habit with me."

Pica practicers were queried regarding why the substances should not be consumed. The majority answering this question felt that the pica substance might harm the child or mother. One respondent was sure that pica had caused her cancer. A starch eater said that starch had made her gain too much weight while pregnant. Another respondent linked starch with the formation of lumps in the stomach which turn to sugar causing you to drink lots of water—the results being harmful when you are pregnant. A clay eater felt that her form of pica was "bad for the bowels." It is interesting to note, however, that all of the pica practicers who said their practice might have been harmful did not discontinue the practice until their pregnancy was terminated.

The theories of harm would be incomplete without relating one last case. One pica practicer stated that she "had eaten large quantities of Argo starch followed by a chunk of block magnesia." She fully expected her babies to be born covered with a nasty white coating because of the starch she had eaten. But she said, "You know that magnesia must have cleaned them right off because they was the cleanest, 'pertiest' little things you ever saw."

Although there was only one incidence of pica associated with tire inner tubes, this case does bear further discussion. When approached about her cravings during pregnancy, one respondent named potatoes, cornbread, pickles, and ice cream. I related stories other interviewees had given me and she did not volunteer any unusual cravings. Her husband was at the clinic with her and said, "Well, if you won't tell her, then I will." After a few minutes of "oh no's" and "go ahead's," the woman related her craving for tire inner tubes. She would cut the inner tubes into strips, scald them in hot water, and then chew on a strip until it was thin and then get another.

She had had ten pregnancies and craved inner tubes during each pregnancy. Her husband volunteered that they did not need a pregnancy test for her because at about 3 months pregnant she started looking for inner tubes. As their children grew older they would hunt for inner tubes on the roadside for her since many of her pregnancies were during World War II days and inner tubes were scarce. Her description of taste was that "inner tubes tasted better than any food." She was nervous when she could not get inner tubes but her children usually kept her supplied. She was advised by her mother-in-law not to chew the inner tubes because the children might be marked, but all the children were fine. She said she thought it was a foolish thing to do but she had to have the inner tubes to chew.

Why then did these women stop eating their substances? Their answer was, "I just didn't crave it anymore" and, curiously enough, that generally happened when the pregnancy came to full term.

Cultural transmission did not account for many incidences of pica. Only four pica respondents had mothers who had practiced pica. Five other pica practicers had been advised by or seen a friend practice pica. Two of the respondents who said pica practice was "picked up by" themselves indicated they had eaten dirt as children.

No matter how long the interviewer spent with the interviewees, the women were not able to express firm beliefs or offer much explanation for their cravings; where they learned about the craved substance; how they decided to consume the substance; or what effect the substance had upon their emotional feelings, appetite, health, or health of the unborn child. The interviewees rarely exhibited an ill-at-ease behavior when discussing pica, once they knew of the interviewer's knowledge of the practice, and they were engaged in an easy, flowing conversation with the interviewer.

Hochstein (1968) presents six hypotheses related to the etiology of pica, which cover both theories of disease states and custom. A very brief discussion of these hypotheses follows. (1) Pica may be a psychological response of someone seeking attention. (2) An anthropological hypothesis contends that the practice of pica is associated with the cultural climate of the group. (3) Pica is a response to hunger. (4) Pica may be the body's response to needed nutrients. (5) The microbiological hypothesis is one rarely suggested but pertains to the intestinal pH created when clay is ingested. (6) Pica is of a physiological origin. An example of this is that dry substances (starch, clay, or flour) have the ability to absorb the sometimes excessive amounts of saliva produced during pregnancy.

Some of the responses from the UTMRCH sample could be categorized into one or more of these six hypotheses. However, further documentation and explanation from an interdisciplinary approach are needed to remove pica from the "black box."

In summary, black and white women of all ages and educational levels in this UTMRCH sample were found to practice pica during pregnancy. The attitudes and motivations of pica practicers could not be classified into neat categories that would explain the majority of reasons given by the interviewees for craving unusual substances during pregnancy.

With this and other current research that indicates pica is still being practiced by pregnant women, it is interesting to note the coverage this subject has in Goodhart and Shils' 1973 edition of *Modern Nutrition in Health and Disease*. Pica is mentioned in the chapter on iron as being practiced by some patients with iron deficiency. Pregnancy cravings are not mentioned in the brief, three sentence discussion. Pica is once again discussed in this noted diet therapy text in reference to eating problems of older children and the association with lead poisoning.

As stated earlier, most of the pregnant women's cravings ceased when the child was born. One interviewee, aged 77 years in 1973, ate Argo starch and red clay, whether she was pregnant or not, until the last baby was born. Her eyes glistened as she told of the red clay that would crack into pieces in a favorite mud puddle when sunbaked after a rain. When asked why she stopped eating the clay she said "it didn't look good anymore." Her husband had warned her that it might have germs in it but that did not stop her. As I was ready to leave, she leaned over and quietly said that she really stopped eating clay because her husband got so mad at her eating it that one day he went down to her favorite clay collecting spot "and he wee-wee'd right in the middle of . . . *my mud puddle!*"

REFERENCES

Ansell, J. E., and Wheby, M. S. 1972. Pica: Its relation to iron deficiency, a review of recent literature. Virginia Medical Monthly 99:951-954.

Cooper, M. 1957. Pica. Charles C Thomas, Springfield, Ill.

Crosby, W. H. 1971. Food pica and iron deficiency. Archives of Internal Medicine 127:960-961.

Crosby, W. H. 1976. Pica. Journal of the American Medical Association 235:2765.

Edwards, C. H., and others. 1964. Effect of clay and cornstarch intake on women and their infants. Journal of the American Dietetic Association 44:109-115.

Goodhart, R. S., and Shils, M. E. (eds.). 1973. Modern nutrition in health and disease. Lea & Febiger, Philadelphia.

Gutelius, M. F., and others. 1962. Nutritional studies of children with pica. II. Treatment of pica with iron given intramuscularly. Pediatrics 29:1018-1023.

Halsted, J. A. 1968. Geophagia in man: Its natural and nutritional effects. American Journal of Clinical Nutrition 21:1384-1393.

Hochstein, G. 1968. Pica: A study in medical and anthropological explanation. In T. Weaver (ed.). Essays on medical anthropology. Southern Anthropological Society Proceedings 1:88-96.

Hunter, J. M. 1973. Geophagy in Africa and in the United States—a culture-nutrition hypothesis. The Geographical Review 63:110-195.

Keith, L., and others. 1968. Amylophagia during pregnancy. Obstetrics and Gynecology 32:415-418.

Lanzkowsky, P. 1959. Investigation into the aetiology and treatment of pica. Archives of Disease in Childhood 34:140-148.

Laufer, B. 1930. Geophagy. Field Museum of Natural History Publication 280. Anthropological Series XVIII:2.

McDonald, R., and Marshall, S. R. 1964. The value of iron therapy in pica. Pediatrics 34:558-562.

O'Rourke, D. E., and others. 1967. Geophagia during pregnancy. Obstetrics and Gynecology 29:581-584.

Perry, M. C. 1977. Cautopyreiophagia. New England Journal of Medicine 296:824.

Posner, L. B., and others. 1951. Pregnancy craving and pica. Obstetrics and Gynecology 9:270-272.

Rogers, M. E. 1972. Practice of pica among iron deficient pregnant women. Master's thesis. Auburn University.

Roselle, H. A. 1970. Association of laundry starch and clay ingestion with anemia in New York City. Archives of Internal Medicine 125:51-59.

Sage, J. D. 1962. The practice, incidence and effect of starch eating on Negro women at Temple University Medical Center. Master's thesis. Temple University.

Sayers, G., and others. 1974. Relationship between pica and iron nutrition in Johannesburg black adults. South African Medical Journal 48:1655-1660.

SUGGESTED READINGS

Abbey, L. M., and Lombard, J. A. 1973. The etiological factors and clinical implications of pica: Report of case. Journal of the American Dental Association 87:885-887.

Chandra, P., and Rosner, F. 1973. Olives—craving in iron deficiency anemia. Annals of Internal Medicine 78:973-974.

Coltman, C. A. 1969. Pagophagia and iron lack. Journal of the American Medical Association 207:513-516.

Dickens, D., and Ford, R. N. 1942. Geophagy (dirt-eating) among Mississippi Negro school children. American Sociology Review 7:59-65.

Edwards, C. H., and others. 1954. Odd dietary practices of women. Journal of the American Dietetic Association 30:976-981.

Edwards, C. H., and others. 1959. Clay and cornstarch eating women. Journal of the American Dietetic Association 35:810-815.

Gelfand, M. D., and others. 1975. Geophagia—a cause of life-threatening hyperkalemia in patients with chronic renal failure. Journal of the American Medical Association 234:738-740.

Gutelius, M. F., and others. 1963. Treatment of pica with vitamin and mineral supplement. American Journal of Clinical Nutrition 12:388-393.

Hertz, H. 1947. Notes on clay and starch eating among Negroes in a southern urban community. Social Forces 25:343-344.

Jacobs, S. (ed.). 1972. Medical grand rounds from Tourno Infirmary—the starch eater. Journal of the Louisiana State Medical Society 124:19-83.

Mengel, C. E., and others. 1964. Geophagia with iron deficiency and hypokalemia. Archives of Internal Medicine 114:470-474.

Moss, J., and others. 1974. Successive picas. Annals of Internal Medicine 80:425.

Mustacchi, P. 1971. Cesare Bressa (1785-1836) on dirt eating in Louisiana—a critical analysis of his unpublished manuscript "De la Dissolution scorbretique." Journal of the American Medical Association 218:229-232.

Payton, E., and others. 1960. Growth and development. VII. Dietary habits of 511 pregnant southern Negro women. Journal of the American Dietetic Association 37:129-136.

Whiting, A. N. 1947. Clay, starch and soot eating among Southern rural negroes in North Carolina. Journal of Negro Education 16:610-612.

CHAPTER 14

I won't cook turnip greens if you won't cook kielbasa: food behavior of Polonia and its health implications

Kathyrn Kolasa

AMERICANS COMING TOGETHER

"Do you like kielbasa?" Wanda asked her new Southern housemate. "Do I like kab— what?" was the reply. "You know," said Wanda, "fresh Polish sausage." "Never had it," said Annie Mae, "but I'm willing to try anything once. Where did you get it?" "Babcia made it for Easter," said Wanda. "What's a babcia?" queried Annie Mae. "Grandmother, silly. Don't you WASPs know anything!" exclaimed Wanda. "OK. Let's have the ka—, the sausage for dinner tomorrow. It's your turn to cook."

So the next afternoon Wanda took the two 8-inch long links of pink sausage, immersed the 2-inch diameter links into cold water and put them on to boil, then simmer for an hour. She licked her lips in anticipation. After all, she couldn't get good, fresh kielbasa in this town—and of course, no one makes kielbasa like Babcia.

About 45 minutes later Annie Mae walked toward the house taking a deep breath in the evening air and suddenly wrinkled her nose in distress. What was that strong, garlicky smell? Slowly it dawned as she opened the door and heard the pot on the stove gurgling—it's the kielbasa.

Wanda greeted Annie Mae saying, "Doesn't it smell great. I can't wait to eat!" Annie Mae, trying to hide the fact that her tummy is doing backward somersaults ignored the question. They sat down to eat, Wanda dove into the sausage with gusto and ate almost noisily. Annie Mae stared at the sausage, now gray in color, thick skinned and filled with visible chunks of fat. She forced herself to cut a tiny piece and lifted it to her mouth. Nope. No way to eat that food!

Wanda looked up from her black bread, sausage, beets, and potatoes. She noticed Annie Mae's look of despair. "Don't you like it?" asked Wanda incredulously. "Not exactly," replied Annie Mae, reserving her true sentiments.

There was silence. Then Wanda said, "Maybe it will grow on you—eat some more. This is the best kielbasa." Annie Mae, now gagging, said nothing.

"Tell you what," said Annie Mae. "Remember you didn't like those turnip greens I fixed last week—delicious turnip greens boiled and seasoned with salt pork."

"You mean those dead gray turnip greens you boiled and boiled and poured grease all over," asked Wanda.

"I beg your pardon, that was salt pork from home I seasoned those greens with," retorted Annie Mae. "Anyway, I'll make a deal—if you won't cook kielbasa, I won't cook turnip greens."

"Well, OK," hesitated Wanda. "I guess I can eat kielbasa when I visit my folks in Detroit."

"Great!" exclaimed Annie Mae with relief. "Now I'm starved, let's order a pizza."

And so it goes. As long as American Poles and other ethnic groups live together in ethnic communities, traditional folkways, in particular foodways, are preserved. But as second and third generation American ethnics leave their ethnic communities, marry outside their ethnic groups—as they assimilate into the larger American culture—food as an external attribute of their culture loses its importance as a carrier of ethnicity. In short, food habits change.

It has been said that food habits are stable and change little, and yet it seems that food habits are continually changing. Some food habits bring added health benefits to the individual, some changes are neutral, and some may increase risks to health. This chapter will explore the food behavior of Polish-Americans, one ethnic group that has

130

brought its culture to the U.S. The purposes are to explore the food behavior of Polish-Americans, how food behaviors change with generations, and some health implications of changing to the dietary pattern of the larger American population.

DO YOU EAT LIKE YOUR GRANDPARENTS?

Sandberg (1974) suggests that ethnicity declines generationally. He further proposes that the salience of ethnicity is inversely related to social class and that the rising affluence in the U.S. also affects ethnicity.

This might suggest that the majority of ethnics adopt the American way of life, including food habits, by the second generation, relegating ethnic customs to holidays and ceremonies. However, others have observed that the last part of the "old life" that immigrants give up is their food behavior. It is said that immigrants may be pressured to conform with language, dress, and other customs, but in the privacy of their home, foods can be selected, prepared, and enjoyed to meet old or new cultural expectations as long as foods or ingredients or reasonable substitutes are available.

This process of adapting to the forces at work in an alien environment is a learning process and can be termed acculturation. Prior to the 1960s black revolution in the U.S. the American acculturation process was governed by the melting pot theory. Immigrants and other subgroups were encouraged by the American culture to lose all distinctive characteristics—to be, in a sense, "boiled down" to form a "new American." For some immigrant groups the alterations of food behavior required to maintain health and well-being were major, such as the adoption of completely new foods or loss of core foods from their diets. For others, acculturation may have required subtle changes in preparation methods of familiar foods.

What is the situation? First, is it necessary for Polish-Americans to change their food habits so that they appear American? And if so, have they modified or lost their characteristic food habits?

It is difficult to describe food behavior of one ethnic group such as Polish-Americans since food behavior varies from region to region. Also, the methods for studying food consumption patterns are imprecise. Despite the lack of information a brief look at the food habits of Poland is appropriate.

The pattern of the Polish before coming to America has been described anecdotally (Strybel, 1975; *Michigan Challenge*, 1972). The Poles ate a hearty breakfast. At rising they took milk soup or white coffee with sausage, ham, cheese, cottage cheese and chives, eggs, bread, and butter. A break was taken in the later morning for sandwiches, apple, cake, and hot tea. The main meal of the day was eaten between 2 and 4 P.M. and consisted of soup, meat, potatoes, salad or hot vegetable, and dessert. The evening meal was served around 8 P.M. and consisted of cold cuts, eggs, sour milk, and grain or blintzes.

Historical research on food consumption in Poland is discussed by Dembinska (1971). Data for food consumption patterns in Poland before the 20th century do exist. The core of the Polish diet was comprised of foods that grow well there, including rye, millet, barley, buckwheat, maize, potatoes, onion, radishes, turnips, kohlrabi, beets, beans, cabbage, and cucumbers.

The meal pattern and the crops listed above include items that are familiar and available in the U.S. mainland. It might be expected, then, that the Polish migrants could bring their food preferences and maintain them in the new environment.

The data available seem to support this supposition. An attempt to document the food behavior of various ethnic groups, including Polish-Americans, in the U.S. was completed by the Committee on Food Habits in the 1940s (Joffe, 1943; and Benet and Joffe, undated). The Polish-Americans were thought to be a fairly homogeneous group, generally of peasant background (Thomas and Znaniecki, 1918). The core diet was described as comprised of grains (rye, wheat, buckwheat, barley), potatoes, cabbage, legumes, and green vegetables supplemented with milk, cheese, sour cream, eggs, home raised pork, fruits, berries, wild mushrooms, and fish. Salt, sugar, tea, and coffee were not core food items for the Polish people since they were imported items to Poland and generally expensive.

Acculturation for the Polish immigrants who settled in urban areas meant adoption of white sugar (Time, 1976) and flour and abandonment of rich vegetable soups, bean soups, and cottage cheese dishes. Some disruption of a meal pattern that provided adequate nutrition occurred as well as disruption of a society based on the family living on the land. Change in environment caused some changes in food habits. As we will see later, the relationship of environment and dietary habits may be important in the health of any group.

The effect of differences in national backgrounds on consumption of dairy products, meat, and certain fruits and vegetables was studied by Fliegel (1961). First and second generation Polish-Americans residing in Pennsylvania recorded their food consumption for 1 week. These families consumed whole milk, other milk, ice cream, and cheese, 12.8, 1.2, 0.9, and 1.6 times per week, respectively. When compared with Americans, Germans, and Italians the Polish-Americans' consumption of cheese and ice cream was low.

The role of meat consumption in promotion of health will be discussed later. It is important to recognize that these Polish-Americans ate weekly beef (3.3 times), pork (3.9 times), veal (0.4 times), poultry (1.0 times), luncheon meats (2.9 times), and meat soups (1.6 times). In comparison with the same groups noted above, the Polish-Americans reported the highest consumption of pork, luncheon meats, and meat soups. A shift to a more typical American pattern would have required increased consumption of beef and less of pork veal, and poultry. Many Polish-Americans made this adaptation.

Citrus fruits were consumed 1.2 times each week while other fruits, citrus juice, and other juices were consumed 2.8, 1.8 and 0.2 times, respectively. The consumption of vegetables also was low: leafy green, 2.0 times; other green, 3.9 times; and yellow including tomatoes, 6.0 times.

It is not too surprising that consumption of vegetables (other than white potatoes) by Polish-Americans was low. Green vegetables (considered by many Poles to be weeds) were introduced in Poland by an Italian Princess, Bona, wife of the Polish king Sigismund II, in the 1500s. Many plants brought from Italy were not hardy enough to survive the Polish climate. Vegetables, then as now, were considered luxury items. It took time for the vegetables to be accepted.

Fliegel also asked Polish-Americans about hypothetical meals to gain some inferences about attitudes toward food. Table 9 lists the average frequency of mention of food in special situations.

The data on milk do not agree with the frequency of consumption data reported earlier. It might be assumed that the respondents took milk for granted. It is interesting to note, also, that pork was not viewed as a food that promotes health, but it does have a special role in holidays.

In view of the role of fat in the diet in relationship to health (discussed later), it is unfortunate that butter consumption was not included in this study. It has been reported that Polish-Americans consume a wide variety of fats and oils, and frequently consume cream, sour cream, and butter (American Dietetic Association, 1976; Ujda, 1975). Some Polish women would say that butter would be the last item to eliminate in a restricted food budget.

Table 9. Average frequency of the mention of food in special situations

Food	Health	Guest	Liked	Restaurant	Holiday
Milk	0.4	—	0.2	0.1	0.2
Ice cream	0.1	0.1	—	0.2	—
Beef	0.6	0.4	0.5	0.5	0.1
Pork	—	0.3	0.2	0.1	0.9
Poultry	0.1	0.4	0.2	0.2	0.5
Noncitrus fruit	0.4	0.3	0.2	0.1	0.5
Green vegetables	1.5	1.6	1.4	1.6	1.3
Yellow vegetables	0.8	1.1	1.1	1.1	0.9

The American Dietetic Association (1976) has prepared a guide to food habits of American ethnic groups. In general, the description of Polish food habits agrees with Fliegel's work about milk consumption, indicating sweet milk and buttermilk are well liked. The guide indicates that meat is commonly consumed, beef and pork being popular. Pig's knuckles, meat soups, sausages, smoked and cured pork, chicken, goose, duck, and variety meats including liver, tripe, tongue, and brains are listed as meats eaten. Fish that is fresh, smoked, dried, or pickled is used.

Potatoes are an important part of the Polish diet. Other vegetables include carrots, beets, turnips, cauliflower, kohlrabi, broccoli, green pepper, peas, spinach, and green beans. Fruits, with the exception of dried fruits, were not typically consumed.

As the guide continues through the basic four food groups, it indicates that bread, especially pumpernickel, sour rye, or white, is consumed at each meal. According to the guide, candies, sweet cakes, honey, and coffee with cream and sugar are favorites. Polish cooking also is highly seasoned and salted.

The Polish-American group, also called Polonia, is neither Polish nor American, but a mixture of both cultures. Polish-Americans, like other ethnic groups of European ancestry, can be found in all states. Concentrations of Polish-Americans in the 1970s are found, in order, in New York, Pennsylvania, Illinois, Michigan, Massachusetts, New Jersey, Connecticut, and Ohio. Smaller numbers are in Wisconsin, Rhode Island, Indiana, Minnesota, New Hampshire, Maryland, West Virginia, Washington, D.C., Vermont, Delaware, California, Florida, Colorado, Montana, Texas, Virginia, and Washington (Polzin, 1973). The largest concentrations of Polish-Americans in 1971 were in the Northeast and North Central states and in neighborhoods within metropolitan areas of 250,000 or more.

It does not appear that Polish-Americans had to drastically change their food habits because of food availability except during World War II, when all Americans modified their food habits to meet the availability and rationing situations. But it can be assumed that changes in food habits did occur.

For example, a girl named Helena tells the story of coming home from school every day crying and hating her mother for sending her to school with a sandwich made from "un-American rye bread" rather than "American white bread." As soon as she had control, Helena made sandwiches from white bread.

Children of Polish descent, when asked to describe what they eat, might list hamburgers, french fries, steak, and pizza; when asked what Polish people eat they name Polish foods including kapusta (sauerkraut), golabki (stuffed cabbage), babka (holiday bread or coffee cake), czarnia (duck blood soup sometimes called chocolate soup by children), paczki (donuts), chrusciki (bow tie pastries also known as angel wings), and pierogi (dumplings filled with ground meat or cheese or sauerkraut and potatoes or plums or berries). If asked why Polish people sautee bread crumbs in butter and pour them over vegetables, they might reply "I guess it tastes good," rather than recount the belief that bread is the holiest of all edibles, and that Polish people have never wasted bread. The people of Poland have lived and fought fearlessly through famine and wars and have used every bread crumb for food. Bread crumbs have been collected and used to thicken gravy, line baking pans, or season foods.

Zand (1961b) suggests that Polish-American patterns were manifested in traditional foods in the home in the past but most folkways have been modified or dropped because of the influence of assimilationist tendencies.

The question remains, "Do Polish-Americans regularly eat Polish foods?"

Sanders and Morawski (1975) refer to a 1964 study by Jurczak that measured the regularity with which Polish-Americans in five communities ate Polish food. As expected, the regularity varied with communities. Among Polish-Americans, 55% to 77% of first generation, 38% to 57% of second generation, and 13% to 58% of third generation Polish-Americans reported eating Polish foods. Overall, that was a drop of about 30% from the first to the third generation. Fewer than 6% of those interviewed said they never ate Polish food.

Gould (reported in Sanders and Morawski, 1975) also notes a significant decline in the use of Polish foods generationally. Two thirds of first generation but only one third of the second generation Polish-Americans reported regularly eating Polish foods.

The Polish-Americans did not have to drastically modify their food behavior. Many Polish immigrants came to the U.S. with a core diet consisting of foods readily available in the U.S. but changed some aspect of the preparation of those foods. The next generations who moved from ethnic centers such as Polish neighborhoods in Hamtramck, Michigan; Buffalo, New York; or Chicago (Roucek, 1937) into the larger American culture were required to further modify their food behavior to fit the generalized food consumption pattern in the U.S. Changes in environment affect the food attitudes, beliefs, health, and habits of people living in the United States. Since changes in food habits have occurred and the changes may be beneficial, neutral, or detrimental to health, the process of the transmission of food habits should be understood.

DO YOU EAT LIKE YOUR MOTHER?

The transmission of food behavior from parent to child often has been alluded to in the food behavior literature. Many researchers suggest that food behavior and food habits are stable and resistant to change, in part because of their establishment in early life. However, by observation, this statement cannot be applied to children of immigrants to the United States or to second and third generation Polish-Americans.

Sociocultural experiences dominate the learning of food behavior, because all societies attempt to pass on traditional foodways and all children tend to imitate or model their behavior on that of others. Food behavior may be transmitted to each new generation and become entangled in the culture, but it is still susceptible to change. The transmission of food behavior and the factors effecting changes are of interest in relation to the preservation of food behavior that promotes good health and modification of poor food behavior that increases risk of disease.

While the total family, the society, and the mass media play roles in transmission of foodways, both formally and informally, the mother has been traditionally seen as the primary transmitter. In many cultures, including the Polish culture, the mother has been a pivot of the family life (Bloch, 1976). It has been the mother who teaches the child what foods are desirable, satisfying, delightful, good for you, not to be eaten with other foods, and so on. The mother has been viewed in American culture as the repository for foodlore. Sims et al. (1972) view the American mother as a central figure in the nuclear family; as the major link between the outside environment and other family members; she is typically responsible for the preparation and distribution of food to the rest of the family. Again, the importance of the relationship of environment, including food, to health is intriguing.

How universal and enduring is this maternal effect on the food behavior of children as they mature? The role of the mother in relation to food behavior can be viewed as continuing throughout life. The mother might transmit cultural food heritage in two ways. The mother can be the (1) source of nutrition information for the child and (2) the daughter's cooking teacher. Later the mother can give advice to the grown daughter in matters of food; and as a grandmother she might advise in the feeding of a newborn. The immigrating process, however, breaks continuity with the past. Perhaps, the role of the woman has changed in the upheaval of changing environments. For example, Bloch (1976) has compared women living in a rural village of Poland with similar women who moved to the United States. She has found that the domestic roles changed immensely and affected the entire family life. The mother, once the pivot of family life, in America has become just another member of the family intent on earning a living wage.

It can be suggested that several generations of immigrants to the United States, including the Polish-Americans, did not transmit their cultural attitudes, beliefs, and food knowledge to their children. Chrobot (1976b) suggests that most American children and grandchildren of ethnic Americans have little or no knowledge of their heritage.

The following conversation was overheard last spring and supports Chrobot's contention: "Sorry, I can't go to the basketball game Saturday afternoon. I have to go to Detroit to get the food blessed," said Mary to her boyfriend. "I don't know why," she continued, "it's something Polish we've always done the day before Easter." Mary does not always understand her family's customs, but she still participates. However, how long can traditions endure if the meaning is lost?

Sanders and Morawski (1975) suggest that perhaps folk religiosity is better preserved than folk food habits of Polish-Americans. Several religious holidays and festivities, such as Christmas Eve dinner *(Wigilia)*, sharing of the Christmas wafer *(Oplatek)*, caroling *(Koledowanie)*, Lent *(Wielki Post)*, blessing of food *(Swieconka)*, and the wedding *(Wesele)*, include the use of special foods (Zand, 1960; Janasik, 1963; Zieleniewicz, 1971; Polanie Club, 1972; Ziemba, 1972; Chrobot, 1976a; Marshall, 1976; Strybel, 1976; Kozlowski, 1977; and Laskey, 1977).

Sanders and Morawski also report that 88% and 76% of the second and third generation Polish-Americans, respectively, in one community shared the Christmas wafer; 76% and 48%, respectively, blessed Easter food, and 57% of each generation observed the traditional Christmas Eve celebration.

There is talk of the revival of ethnic pride and identity in the U.S. today. There are those who argue for "new ethnicity": a growing awareness in our country that we are a nation of groups culturally distinct but mutually interdependent; each striving to preserve the best of its heritage in a culturally pluralistic society (Chrobot, 1976a).

If one chooses to be a cultural pluralist, what does that mean in terms of food and diet. Chrobot (1976b) says the cultural pluralists can easily balance their folk and urban cultures; that is, the person sees no reason why he or she cannot be a part of the larger society while remaining loyal to traditions. Does that mean adopting an old Polish dietary pattern? It could if that diet provided not only special meaning, but health benefits. It might mean including cultural foods only for special holidays or festivities.

For example, cultural foods were served at a banquet sponsored by the Black-Polish Conference of Detroit to foster better understanding. The entrees listed as soul food were chitlins, boiled then fried hog intestines (familiar to the black culture) and flaczki (a dish from the Polish culture). These dishes were a part of the slave and peasant cultures of the blacks and Poles because of lack of available meat (Chrobot, 1976b).

While frequent consumption of these two items might have an effect on the nutrition and health of an individual, infrequent consumption of soul food—foods that have deep significance or emotional meanings to a person or group—only affect satisfaction.

The impact on the health of an individual of maintaining special foods for holidays would be negligible. However, a shift in food habits may increase or lower an individual's risk to the development of a disease. Concern for the relationship of cancer, food habits, and environment has surfaced in recent years. Since data are available comparing Polish immigrants and Americans, the role of food habits in this health problem is presented.

DID YOU SAY WHAT I EAT MAY CAUSE CANCER?

No! However, the relationship between dietary patterns and incidence of specific cancers is of interest to cancer researchers today. Let us take a cursory look at some of the facts known and some of the guesses about the relationship between diet and cancer.

Three types of dietary factors have been noted in the etiology of cancer (Peter, 1975): (1) the presence of a carcinogen (any substance that produces cancer) in the food, (2) the introduction of a carcinogen in the food preservation or preparation stage, and (3) the absence of factors in the food protective against cancer. The availability of foods varies throughout the world as do food preparation techniques. The presence and use of pesticides, mycotoxins, hormones, and food additives also vary with environments. Cancer, too, has been shown to vary with population and ethnic groups and geographic distributions. Barrett (1975) has suggested that sufficient laboratory and epidemiological data are available to say diet and nutrition are environmental factors in the etiology of various forms of cancer.

A variety of immigrant populations, including Polish-Americans has been studied. In many cases, the immigrants' cancer risks are changed as they change environments and modify food habits.

For example, Staszewski and Haenszel

(1965) compared the cancer risks found in Poland, those for Polish-Americans, and the greater American population. For stomach cancer, the risk was high in all three groups. For breast, colon, and rectum cancer, however, the risk was low in Poland but high in both the Polish-American and American groups. The persons leaving areas of high stomach cancer risk continued to display high risk in their new environment. Could the persistence of characteristic dietary habits in a new environment be a consideration here?

Stomach cancer has shown marked variation in geographic distribution. Barrett (1975) indicates several dietary factors have been implicated. Generally, in the U.S. a high incidence of stomach cancer has been associated with a high intake of cooked fish and canned fruits and low intakes of lettuce and tomatoes (Peter, 1975). Yet, no single food has shown a one-to-one correspondence with the geographic distribution of stomach cancer.

The risk of *colon cancer* for Polish immigrants is increased in the new environment. It appears that the colon is the cancer site most responsive to new surroundings (Peter, 1975). Some have suggested that the fat content of the diet is the most important dietary factor involved; others argue that it is the lack of dietary bulk (fiber). Barrett cites one study that suggests populations on high meat, high fat diets are more likely to get colon cancer than groups on vegetarian or low meat diets.

Since most Polish migrants were from a low socioeconomic group, generally associated with a low consumption of meat, it is interesting to speculate if the move to the U.S., which increased their socioeconomic status enabling them to buy and consume more meat, might not be involved in the increased risk of colon cancer.

Of course, it is not as simple as that. As already stated, one particular food item cannot be identified as the *cause* of cancer. The increased consumption of a food (for example, meat) may alter the intake of other foods or perhaps alter the absorption of nutrients into the body.

Reddy et al. (1974) believe that the consumption of animal protein and fat may be important causal factors in colon cancer. They define the daily Western diet as 454

gm of beef, pork, or chicken; 2 servings of vegetables; some potato or rice; 4 servings of cereal grain; 1 citrus and 2 other fruits; 2 cups of skim milk, and butter as needed. They suggest that this diet enables stomach microflora to release carcinogens or other toxic substances.

Wynder and Reddy (1973) agree that populations with a high incidence of colon cancer also consume large amounts of fat and protein. It has also been reported that consumption of beef fat is associated with a high incidence of tumors (Peter, 1975).

Others have suggested the Western style diet means more food ingested, more fat, more meat, more cholesterol, more eggs, more sugar, more additives and processed foods, and less carbohydrate foods, especially crude cereals; this in turn enhances the risk of cancer (Peter, 1975). These are also the consumption patterns attacked by the U.S. Select Committee on Nutrition and Human Needs (1977), which will be discussed later.

Breast cancer, too, appears to be affected by the environment and dietary behaviors. It has been suggested (Peter, 1975) that hormone-dependent cancers, such as breast cancer, are cancers of affluence, which implies environmental factors. It is again no surprise to see the risk of breast cancer increased when Polish women migrate to the U.S. Immigrant populations adapt, at least somewhat, to the habits of the host country. The risk of breast cancer might be expected to rise for the Polish immigrant as she assumes the dietary practices of the high risk American population.

Barrett (1975) indicates an increase in the incidence of breast cancer is associated with an increase in socioeconomic status. Further, the increased incidence is seen in populations that are adequately or overnourished. Peter indicates that the role of fat in the conversion of androstenedione to estrone is associated with an increased risk of breast cancer in women over age 50. This conversion has been associated with obesity. A high correlation between breast cancer mortality, total fat intake, animal protein intake, and total calorie intake has been demonstrated (Peter).

Barrett also suggests that a high fat diet may play a role in the etiology of breast cancer. He suggests that a greater synthesis of estrogen and/or altered hormonal storage in adipose tissue occurs in high fat consumers.

Buell (1973) has compared the incidence of breast cancer in Japanese and Polish immigrants. He indicates that the largest migration of both Polish and Japanese women occurred between 1890 and 1920. Both groups were mainly of rural origin; however, most of the Polish women settled in urban areas in the U.S. while the Japanese attempted to establish rural residences.

The Polish women demonstrated a substantial increase in the risk of breast cancer by 1950. The Japanese women did not experience an increased risk until many years later. Buell suggests that perhaps the Japanese women retained a greater proportion of their traditional culture longer. When the Japanese women shifted to the new culture and environment at a preadult or adult stage, then the risk to breast cancer increased.

It appears the Polish immigrants have had opportunities to learn about American foodways. For example, Renkiewicz (1973) reports that social workers in Philadelphia in the early 1900s visited immigrants' homes to teach women how to buy and cook with American foods. The social workers taught Polish women which American foods were "wholesome."

What is the relationship of *breastfeeding* to risk of breast cancer might be asked also. Staszewski and Haenszel (1965) note that in Poland the incidence of breast cancer among urban residents is higher than among rural residents (who tend to breastfeed infants more frequently and for longer period of time). Since most Polish migrants to the U.S. reside in the urban areas, it may be important to further explore the relationship between breastfeeding and protection from breast cancer.

In summary, it appears reasonable to assume that nutrition and some cancers are related. The dietary factors may not cause but may enhance the risk of cancer. It is interesting to note that the same dietary factors associated with heart disease—fat, animal protein, cholesterol—also appear to be associated with cancer. It is important to remember that *association* does not mean *causation.*

The Polish migrants who came to the U.S. were predominantly landless peasants and members of the lower urban class. While these people were of rural origin they did not settle in rural areas in the U.S. By 1950 fewer than 5% of the Polish-American population lived in rural areas. Most were settled in the urban areas of the Northeastern and North Central states. It is certainly easy to question the relationship between changes in environmental factors and increased risk of cancer.

Staszewski and Haenszel (1965) indicate that a review of cancer mortality among Polish immigrants reveals distinctive site-specific patterns of displacement in risk; the same occurs for other ethnic groups in the U.S. They suggest a need for additional data to identify and classify regularities in the behavior of persons subject to change in environment that might increase cancer risk.

It appears that some diseases, including cancer, may occur as a result of reactions to various conditions, such as food habits, over time. Again, at this time, no food can be identified as common to all high risk groups. It is important, therefore, to look at the dietary pattern of the past, the adaptations made to the larger American culture, and the resultant effects on health. Since particular foods may not be important in the etiology of disease, it may be important to look at food classes and food preparation methods.

For example, Marie, a second generation Polish-American, was interviewed about her food habits. She said, no, she never prepared ethnic foods such as kielbasa, or bigos* or kiszka.† Rather she fixed prime cuts of beef. Although the food items are not the same, it was clear from discussion with Marie that she liked fatty meats.

ABANDON THE POLISH DIET FOR THE AMERICAN DIETARY OF AFFLUENCE? OF COURSE!

As stated earlier, there are limited data to describe the American and the Polish-American dietary patterns. It can be assumed, how-

---

* Hunter's stew made from roast beef, roast lamb, roast pork, venison or hare, chicken or duck, ham, sausage, roast veal, sauerkraut, dried mushrooms, salt pork, onions, flour, salt, pepper, sugar, and wine.
† Sausage made from pig's feet, pig's snout, pork steak, pepper, salt, pork liver, coarse buckwheat grits, onions, allspice, marjoram, salt, pepper, pig's blood.

ever, that Polish-Americans adopt, at least in some measure, the diet of affluence practiced in the U.S. The Senate Select Committee on Nutrition and Human Needs (1977) pictures this diet as:

Fat, 42%
    Saturated, 16%
    Poly- and monounsaturated, 26%
Protein, 12%
Carbohydrate, 46%
    Complex carbohydrate, 22%
    Sugar, 24%

The Committee suggests that the U.S. adopt dietary goals to alter the diet so it would be:

Fat, 30%
    Saturated, 10%
    Poly- and monounsaturated, 20%
Protein, 12%
Carbohydrate, 58%
    Complex carbohydrates and naturally occurring sugars, 48%
    Refined and processed sugars, 10%

Senator George McGovern indicates that dietary changes over the last 50 years represent a threat to public health. He suggests that too much fat and too much sugar or salt can be linked to heart disease, cancer, obesity, stroke, and other killer diseases.

However, the American Medical Association stated in April 1977, that "insufficient evidence at this time is available to assume benefits will be derived from the adoption of such universal dietary goals." The American Dietetic Association in September 1977, could not recommend outright adoption or rejection of the goals, also indicating sufficient evidence to support the Committee's health claims was not available.

What do the dietary goals mean in terms of foods Americans and Polish-Americans eat? To meet the goals an increased consumption of fruits, vegetables, and whole grains would be necessary. Polish-Americans have not been fruit and vegetable consumers, past or present. However, Polish-Americans were large consumers of whole grains in the past and more recently are adopting American refined grains in their diets.

A decreased consumption of meat, especially beef, and an increased consumption of fish and chicken would be necessary. The Polish-Americans have been meat consum-

ers. They have modified their preferences, consuming more beef (because of its availability) in the U.S. Traditional preferences, however, would indicate that fish and poultry are acceptable foods.

A decreased consumption of food high in fat and partial substitution of polyunsaturated for saturated fat would be necessary. Poles have always had a high fat and high saturated fat consumption. The links between fat in the diet and risks of disease are too clear for those concerned about health to ignore. Changing the fat content of the Polish-American diet would require a drastic change in the dietary pattern. Perhaps, here, it would be well for Polish-Americans to adopt the food patterns of the larger society.

Substitution of nonfat milk for whole milk also would be recommended. This is another dietary pattern that would be difficult to adopt for the Polish-Americans who generally like whole milk.

Decreased consumption of sugar and foods high in sugar content is suggested. The use of sugar is a pattern that Polish people adopted in the U.S. Although noted for their "ethnic sweet tooth," refined sugar was not readily available in Poland. Wiegelmann (1974) indicates that sugar was an innovation from the luxury class and descended down the social class ladder since the 19th century. The increased availability of cane and beet sugar has made it a prevalent taste, largely determining the character of food.

Finally, to meet the dietary goals, the consumption of salt and foods high in salt content would need to be decreased. Again, the traditional Polish-American food pattern includes salted meats, salted fish, pickled vegetables and fish, and salt as a seasoning. Retention of traditional dietary patterns here may not be beneficial to health.

SHOULD I STOP EATING POLISH FOODS? SHOULD I EAT MORE POLISH FOODS?

Americans excited about the "new ethnicity" might argue that the U.S. needs diversity and pluralism and that ethnicity brings it to the culture. They suggest that vitality is brought by counteracting the movement to sameness throughout the U.S.

It appears that the question of retaining or modifying traditional food patterns moves beyond the realm of ethnic pride and into the health arena. Rising affluence in the U.S. has affected ethnicity—few third generation Americans regularly eat Polish food. The rising affluence in the U.S. seems to have affected health status based on diet, too. In light of medical evidence available, some modifications from a traditional Polish dietary to an American one (i.e., increased use of sugar) may have had a negative effect on the health status of an individual while other adaptations (i.e., increased fruit and vegetable consumption) might promote health. As stated earlier, one food cannot be directly implicated in health risks. Therefore, it is important for groups to examine their total dietary pattern in relation to current medical knowledge. The Polish-American group, like other ethnics, have experienced changes in environment and in dietary practices. The interrelationships among environment, diet, and health need continuing study for all Americans.

REFERENCES

American Dietetic Association. 1976. Food patterns in U.S. A.D.A., Chicago.

Barrett, V. K. 1975. Dietary factors in the etiology of cancer. Report No. 18. National Cancer Institute, Rockville, Md.

Benet, S. M., and Joffe, N. 1943. Polish food patterns. The Committee on Food Habits. National Research Council, Washington, D.C.

Bloch, H. 1976. Changing domestic roles among Polish immigrant women. Anthropology Quarterly 49(1):3.

Buell, P. 1973. Changing incidence of breast cancer in Japanese-American women. Journal of the National Cancer Institute 51(5):1479-1483.

Chrobot, L. 1976a. Polish-American customs and traditions. Monograph 16. St. Mary's College, Orchard Lake, Mi.

Chrobot, L. F. 1976b. Toward a definition of the integrated pluralist or why we should not all be just "American," Monograph 18. St. Mary's College, Orchard Lake, Mi.

Dembinska, M. 1971. Historical research on food consumption in Poland. Ethnologia Europaea 5:130.

Fliegel, F. C. 1961. Food habits and national background. Bulletin 684. Pennsylvania State University, Agricultural Experimental Station, University Park, Pa.

Gordon, M. M. 1964. Assimilation in American Life. Oxford University Press, New York.

Janasik, B. 1963. Polish-American Lenten customs. Journal of Polish American Studies 20(2):97.

Joffe, N. F. 1943. Food habits of selected subcultures in the United States. In The Problem of Changing Food Habits. Bulletin No. 108. National Research Council, National Academy of Science., Washington, D.C., pp. 99-102.

Kozlowski, L. G. 1977. Easter eggs, Polish style. Alliance College, Cambridge Springs, Pa.

Laskey, D. 1977. Paczki, they are "smaczne"—delicious. The Mamistee News Advocate. Mamistee, Mi. Feb. 19, p. 8.

Marshall, K. K. 1976. A taste of Poland, Sokol Polski, Pittsburgh, Pa., October 15, p. 8.

Michigan Challenge. 1972. That famous Polish food. 12(5):26.

Peter, S. J. (chairman). 1975. Symposium: Nutrition in the causation of cancer. Cancer Research 35(11, pt. 2):3231-3550.

Polanie Club, Inc. 1972. Treasured Polish Christmas customs and traditions. Polanie Publishing Co., Minneapolis, Mn.

Polzin, T. 1973. The Polish-American—whence and whither. Franciscan Publications, Pulaski, Wi.

Reddy, B. S., Weisburger, J. H., and Wynder, E. L. 1974. Fecal bacteria B–glucuronidase: Control by diet. Science 183:417-417.

Renkiewicz, F. 1973. The view from the outside: As a people they have been much abused. In The Poles in America, 1608-1972. Oceana Publishing, New York.

Roucek, J. S. 1937. Poles in the United States of America. Baltic Institute, Gydnia, Poland.

Sandberg, N. C. 1974. Ethnic identity and assimilation: The Polish-American community. Praeger Publishing, New York.

Sanders, I. T., and Morawski, E. T. 1975. Polish-American community life: A survey of research, The Community Sociology Monograph Series, Vol. II, Community Sociology Training Program, Boston University and Polish Institute of Arts and Sciences in America, Inc.

Select Committee on Nutrition and Human Needs. 1977. Dietary goals for the United States, ed. 2. United States Senate, U.S. Government Printing Office, Washington, D.C.

Sims, L. S., Paolucci, B., and Morris, P. 1972. A theoretical model for the study of nutritional status: An ecosystem approach. Ecology of Food and Nutrition 1:197.

Staszewski, J., and Haenzel, W. 1965. Cancer mortality among Polish born in the United States. Journal of the National Cancer Institute 35:291-297.

Strybel, R. 1975. Nazdrowie—or health of our heritage. Dziennik Polski, Detroit, Mi. April 26, p. 2.

Strybel, R. 1976. Treat your family to wigilia. Polish Daily News, Dec. 18.

Time Magazine. 1976. Poland—no sugar daddy. August 30, pg. 49.

Thomas, W. I., and Znaniecki, F. 1918. The Polish peasant in Europe and America. University of Chicago Press.

Ujda, H. 1975. Polish food behavior. Personal communication. Birmingham, Mi.

Warner, W., and Srole, L. 1945. The social systems of American ethnic groups. Yale University Press, New Haven, Conn.

Wiegelmann, G. 1974. Innovations in food and meals. Folk Life 12:20-29.

Wynder, E. L., and Reddy, B. 1973. Studies of large bowel cancer: Human leads to experimental applications. Journal of the National Cancer Institute 50(5): 1099-1106.

Zand, H. S. 1960a. Polish-American folkways. Journal of Polish American Studies 17(3-4):100.

Zand, H. S. 1961b. Polish American profile. Journal of Polish American Studies 18(2):94.

Zieleniewicz, A. 1971. Poland. Center for Polish Studies and Culture. The Orchard Lake Schools, Orchard Lake, Mi.

Ziemba, W. 1972. The Polish-American—his customs, traditions and characteristics. Michigan Challenge 12 (5):15.

SUGGESTED READINGS

Bakanowski, C. R. A. 1968. My memoirs—Texas sojourn. Journal of Polish American Studies 25(2):106.

Barclay, M. J. 1972. Changing images of Toledo's Polish community, 1870-1920. Northwest Ohio Quarterly 44(3):64.

Carpenter, N., and Katz, D. 1929. A study of acculturation in the Polish group of Buffalo. University of Buffalo Studies 7(4):103-133.

Gowaskie, J. M. 1976. Polish community in America: An annotated and classified bibliographic guide. Burt Publishing, Franklin, New York.

Graff, G. P. 1970. Michigan's Polish and Lithuanian immigrants—settlers of city and countryside. In The People of Michigan. Michigan Department of Education, Lansing, Mi.

Hall, D. E. 1938. Discussion at section meeting on culture and personality. American Journal of Orthopsychiatry 8:618.

Keefe, E., Bernier, D., Brenneman, L., and others. 1973. Area handbook of Poland. U. S. Government Printing Office, Washington, D.C.

Krolikowski, Z. 1976. More Indian corn. Poland 6(262): 11.

Kusielewicz, E. 1969. Reflections on the cultural condition of the Polish American community. Czas Publishing Co., New York.

Lopata, H. Z. 1976. Polish-Americans—status competition in an ethnic community. Prentice Hall, Englewood Cliffs, N.J.

Ludanyi, A. 1976. Polish jokes and American destinies. Phi Kappa Phi J. LVI(3):44.

Mackun, S. 1964. The changing patterns of Polish settlements in the greater Detroit area: Geographic study of the assimilation of an ethnic group. Unpublished Ph.D. thesis. University of Michigan, Ann Arbor, Mi.

Miller, F. H. 1896. The Polanders in Wisconsin. Parkman Club Papers. No. 10. Milwaukee, Wi.

Williams, C. 1968. Life History of a Polish immigrant. Journal of Polish American Studies 25(2):86.

Zand, H. S. 1961a. Polish-American leisure ways. Journal of Polish American Studies 18(1):34.

CHAPTER 15

Developing methods for studying diet ethnographically

Christine S. Wilson

Study of food and diet offers anthropologists a variety of potential approaches. As examples, there are those of the historian, such as Salaman's (1949) *History and Social Influence of the Potato* and the more recent *Food in Chinese Culture* (Chang, 1977) and *Food: The Gift of Osiris* (Darby, 1977). One can make folkloric studies of food, of the utensils used to obtain, prepare and eat it, and of the settings in which it is stored and cooked. Research on food and its markets is one interest of the economic anthropologists. For those concerned with anthropological aspects of health, however, techniques more directly applicable are those of dietitian-nutritionists and field ethnographers. Adaptations of methods from both these fields have been used by nutritional anthropologists to study human nutrition from the sociocultural point of view.

A number of techniques from each discipline, as well as combinations of techniques, are suited to examination of how food use influences nutrient intake and status in a population. A review of several techniques that have been utilized has been published (Wilson, 1977). Thus far the methods have been quite individualized. Since there have been far fewer research efforts in social nutrition than in biochemical or clinical nutrition, no attempts have been made thus far to standardize the techniques used so that results of different workers studying different populations might be compared.

Not only should guidelines be formulated for methods already in use so that they may be reproduced by others, but there is also need for development of new, replicable ways to cope with new topics of study that

nutritional and other medical anthropologists are turning to in increasing numbers.

EXAMPLES OF METHODS USED
"Early" studies

Since this field has been pursued only in the current century, the term "early" is relative. Serious study of diet from a social science viewpoint seems to have begun spontaneously about the time that Raymond Firth called for such work in 1934 (see also Wilson, 1973; Freedman, 1977; Montgomery and Bennett, 1978; Montgomery, 1978).

Although ethnographers from Malinowski to Mead included observations on food getting and food use in their field work, the outstanding examples of pioneer anthropological studies that emphasized food were done by Richards (1932; 1939), DuBois (1944), and Rosemary Firth (1966). Richards, who researched published sources to elucidate the fundamental significance of food in the lives of the Bantu peoples of South Eastern Africa (1932), later made an ethnographic field study among the Bemba of Northern Rhodesia, in what is now Zambia (1939). While her approach in both studies were sociocultural and ethnographic, she collected and weighed typical diets of these people, which the nutritional biochemist, Elsie Widdowson, calculated and analyzed for nutrient content (Richards and Widdowson, 1936).

DuBois (1944), whose purpose in studying the people of Alor, an island in the Indonesian Archipelago, was to observe the psychological development of the child in a culture other than her own, also learned the importance of food and hunger in the psychological makeup of these people. Her study

141

utilized techniques of the psychologist combined with participant observation and other anthropological methods. This research showed that anxiety about availability of food can lead to distinct, lifelong patterns of attitudes toward the use of food.

Firth (1966) made a study of housekeeping and household management among selected families of Malay sea-fishing peoples in 1939, which included collecting detailed budgets of daily expenditures for food and other items for nearly 5 months. Thus she was able to learn daily and seasonal fluctuations in availability to each family of rice, fish, fruits and vegetables, and other meal accompaniments, as well as the amount of income allotted to food and the relative importance of different food items. Although she did not publish nutrient intakes represented by these foods, she was able to assess the nutritive value of the diets so elicited.

More recent methods

Following the end of World War II, few reports appeared of ethnographic research that centered on food or was concerned with nutrients. In a study of the foodways of the Attawapiskat Indians of Northern Ontario made in 1947–1948, Honigmann (1961) as a participant observer elicited social and economic determinants of the food habits of these people. In 1958–1959 McArthur, a nutritionist-biochemist-anthropologist, performed a study for the World Health Organization of interrelationships among culture, social customs, nutrition, and health in two villages in Malaya. In this work, published as a World Health Organization (WHO) Assignment Report (1962), she combined participant observation and detailed budgetary studies of several households during one period with "dropping in" at meal preparation times to see what was to be served and on occasion share a meal with that family.

Although, like Firth (1966), McArthur did not calculate nutrients provided by the food intakes as determined from the household consumption, she was able to assess the qualitative adequacy of these diets. She also observed what foods and how much of each one were eaten by each member of the household with which she partook, data particularly pertinent to the nutritional status of reproducing women and young children.

Shortly before McArthur made this study, Scudder and Colson examined social, political, and ecological aspects of the life of the Valley Tonga in the Kariba Lake Basin in what is now Zambia (Scudder, 1962). Interested in why the Gwembe Valley had long been an area of intermittent famine, Scudder arranged for interpreter assistants to obtain food consumption data for midday and evening meals of several households over an 11-month period. He used published analyses to calculate nutrient contributions of the leaves used as the chief relishes of the diet.

More widely known, perhaps, is the research carried out by Rappaport between 1962 and 1963 among Maring speakers in the Bismarck Mountains of Papua, New Guinea (Rappaport, 1968). As part of his study of ritual in the ecology of these people, Rappaport weighed all the vegetable foods brought home to four hearths for about 240 days between March and November. From this information he calculated average per person potential caloric, protein, and calcium intakes represented by this food. This work has been criticized on a number of grounds, both anthropological and nutritional (McArthur, 1974), not the least of which is that it is unclear how the amount of food reserved for the pigs was determined. This study, nevertheless, represents one of the first recent efforts by an anthropologist to quantitate food and nutrient intakes for the people whom he observed.

Methods currently in use

Methods used by clinical nutritionists and dietitians to assess nutrient status are outlined below so that the potential nutritional anthropologist may learn what techniques these scientists have developed, and recognize their limitations and potential. Nutritional status may be determined by (1) clinical examinations performed by physicians trained to recognize physical signs of deficiency (or superficiency); (2) biochemists measuring blood or urine levels of given nutrients or their metabolites; or (3) dietitians weighing foods in the home before and after preparation and eating, or administering standardized questionnaires. Standard food composition tables are then used to calculate nutrients represented by each food item weighed or reported (Interdepartmental Committee on Nutrition for National Defense, 1963).

Because the effect on the body of food consumed is cumulative and not necessarily swift, depending upon the body's needs, the nutrient under scrutiny, the individual's current and recent activity, and other experiences (stress, for instance), nutrition surveys properly combine these three approaches (clinical, biochemical, and dietary) for a better assessment of what people are eating at present and what they may have been eating in the recent past (Wilson, 1964).

Biochemical and clinical examinations permit evaluation of nutritional status of an individual at a given time. The dietitian's approach, on the other hand, has hitherto been a study of household food consumption rather than that of the individual (with some exceptions to be suggested below). These studies are usually made on one household at a time, and calculations of nutrient intakes are made either on a per caput basis (total food divided by number of consumers), or with use of weighted numbers (arbitrarily designating a child of a given age to be one half an adult, for example). None of the standard methods of dietary assessment takes into account seasonal, or even daily, fluctuations in food available, save for such household observations that are extended to one week for a given family.

The dietitian needs to use a questionnaire recall of the previous day's foods to determine the consumptions of individuals, and repeat this process at intervals for a fairer picture. The amounts and kinds of foods consumed by the small child can usually only be learned by questioning the mother, who may not see all that her offspring consumes if he wanders from her side. Household weighings usually need to be arranged for ahead of time; the food in the house at the time of the survey visit may, therefore, have been obtained to impress the investigator. Similarly, administration of questionnaires may result in answers the interviewee thinks the questioner wishes to hear. Food diaries kept by a family member may be modified to maintain appearances, or the recorder may make inaccurate estimates of amounts served.

Because of the drawbacks cited above, nutritional as well as social scientists have been concerned with developing better means to learn nutrient intake and status of individuals, especially those most vulnerable to interruptions or other disturbances in a normal food supply: the child just past weaning, the reproducing woman, the elderly. (Some nutrition scientists have also been concerned with another facet of nutritional anthropology, the reasons behind particular food choices. This type of research is, however, outside the scope of this chapter.)

Van Veen (Chassy et al., 1967) has developed a method for determining food habit changes in societies that come into contact with different cuisines or foodstuffs. The technique utilizes a Guttman scale of increasingly less inclusive steps to categorize foods available that are commonly consumed. The technique has been used to study infant feeding practices in a Mexican village (Sanjur et al, 1970); it has been modified to determine nutritional adequacy indirectly by measuring degree of complexity—variety—of diet in another part of rural Mexico (Dewalt and Pelto, 1977).

Some of the methods used by anthropologists in the earlier studies discussed above have had the potential to provide information on food intakes of given individuals and on seasonal variation and other desired data. Recent efforts of nutritional anthropologists have helped point the way to new techniques, both anthropological and nutritional, and modifications of older ones. Only a few examples are cited (for further information see Wilson, 1977; Montgomery, 1978).

Rathje and Harrison (1978), as well as others, have modified archeological techniques to apply them, along with systematic sampling procedures, to a study of household waste that makes no direct contact with individuals of the population studied. The waste is sorted and weighed at a community collection area. A "batch" can be identified as from a particular location where average household size is known, and thus can be related to economic status of the consumers (or nonconsumers). The method is impersonal and unobtrusive, and could be used to examine other consumer practices.

Montgomery and Johnson (1977) have studied behavioral, ecological, and technological factors that influence food energy production, consumption, and expenditure. These workers documented randomly sampled, time-allocated activities of the members of a population for an annual cycle. Using indirect calorimetry to determine the energy expended in activities for which published data were not available, they were able, by computerization of the time studies, to report energy and time use by age, sex, time of day, and season. This method points a way to better assess the energy needs of populations whose activities are not dictated by office or factory hours.

Williams (1973) and Wilson (1974) have developed a method that may be considered a modification of participant observation. The method, called "person following," allows the investigator to learn 1 day's food intake for an individual. The observer remains near enough the subject under study for the course of the day, from rising until bedtime, to record in a small notebook everything the subject eats. Quantity of each food eaten is estimated by eye, a method learned by prior practice (and refreshed on later consideration of the resulting data by comparison with measures of standard sizes, such as cups or tablespoons), and verified by weighing similar example foods on a small portable scale. The drawbacks to this technique are that only one individual can be studied at a time, and it may result in self-conscious alterations in food practices if attempted with adults in a technologically sophisticated setting. It is most useful for studying preschool children in a rural or village setting where a bus or auto is less likely to whisk the selected child off to visit elsewhere, to the dismay of the observer. (Such observations may be prearranged with a parent, but this enhances possibilities for bias or distortion in usual, day-to-day practices.)

RESEARCH TOPICS IN NUTRITIONAL ANTHROPOLOGY FOR WHICH METHODS NEED TO BE DEVELOPED

There are dozens of topics needing to be examined by persons with nutritional anthropological skills or training. Methods are not yet devised for many. Some may not be amenable to any techniques that have been or could be envisaged. The following are samples of problems I feel colleagues should consider addressing in the future. Approaches for the study of some are also suggested. There may, however, be better ways. Nutrition scientists as well as nutritional anthropologists would welcome any breakthroughs that would help solve some of the methodological problems these examples present.

Food distribution among family members

How can individual food intake be determined in societies such as those of Gypsies and some African tribes, where separate food receptacles are not used, and every partaker dips into one central pot for food? Conceivably, one could obtain permission to observe what was put in the pot, and practice weighing handfuls (using one's own hand and those of willing local volunteers) of similar foods at another time, noting range, means, or deviations in weight of each. Some form of participant observation of meals would be necessary, and the investigator would need a predetermined code for various sizes of handfuls and a small data book previously marked with separate columns for each person dipping into the cauldron. The observations would, of course, need to be repeated at different times for several families in order to approximate usual eating practices of the group under study.

Food distribution within families is a similar dietary question, and it might be similarly studied. McArthur's (1962) method of "dropping in" about meal time is a useful means of making qualitative judgments regarding how evenly or appropriately foods are apportioned. One needs care in doing both these kinds of home visits, but especially this one; some societies cannot allow a visitor to remain unfed while family members eat. Others will accept excuses, such as, "I have just eaten. I am satisfied."

In order to obtain quantitative data one needs to calibrate, using a small scale (gram or ounce), quantities of the main food items represented by usual eating utensils (spoons, bowls, or fists). This should be done before beginning visits. A data book prepared with columns for each individual as described for the previous research is required for recording, and some method of coding foods, by spoons or handfuls, for example, is advisable. If more than 8 to 10 people are eating at once, keeping up with the amounts of various dishes eaten by each one is probably not feasible. If plates are used, one should also estimate waste at meal's end, if it is desired to know how much of the prepared food is not consumed.

Patterns of energy expenditure

Where indirect calorimetry is not feasible a variation on the person-following technique can be used to learn activity patterns and arrive at an estimate of energy expenditures. A motion picture camera could be used to film one individual at set, repeated intervals (5 minutes out of every 15, for example) all one day. (To my knowledge, this method has not been attempted.) Time-motion studies using a stopwatch and recording all activities as well as their duration should also be attempted.

Twenty-four hour questionnaire

There is need for a substitute for or improvement in the dietitian's long-standing method, the 24-hour recall questionnaire. This tool requests the interviewee to remember all that he or she ate the previous day. Even among literate people accustomed to filling out forms, both over- and under-estimation occur (Nutrition Reviews, 1976). For less technologically sophisticated populations the question will likely elicit the response, "the same as today!" A further drawback to its use is that, at best, it produces information on one day's food intakes, which for any number of reasons (illness, holiday, family or financial problems) may not be typical for that person. (Twenty-four-hour recalls have most often been used in one-time surveys of persons who were not reinterviewed at a later date.)

To get around the first objection, I have modified the approach to make the time-span no longer than the previous 12 hours. In a study (unpublished) in which families were visited daily for 2 weeks at about the time of the evening meal, recall was asked for the time starting with that morning. After a day or two, respondents became "trained" to make complete recollections.

Determination of waste

Methods need to be devised to determine food waste in non-Western societies and to relate it to nutrients lost. How much of it is recycled via food animals or "green manure" might be estimated by techniques used by ecological anthropologists. A closely related problem in such populations is the study of food loss to pests, predators, too much heat or cold, and the like. These data would be valuable for agricultural economists and other nutrition planners.

Taste preferences

A problem needing input from workers in different disciplines, including physiology and psychology, is the time and manner of implantation of taste preferences. This question may require controlled laboratory experiments in animals, since it is possible for the child to acquire them transplacentally. Cross-cultural observations of child feeding practices are of course, also necessary.

Other questions

Some other questions await methods not yet brought to light. What are good ways to learn client-perceived reasons for success or failure of food introductions? Is observation best for determining actual (versus reported) methods of weaning? How can one collect data on food beliefs without interference of bias on the part of the interviewer and interviewee? How can food-related disasters such as famine or starvation be studied ethically without interfering by trying to help or by other direct involvement on the part of the investigator? How can we learn of potential protein resources hitherto not used by man? Perhaps we should seek collaboration with primatologists and biologists familiar with nonhuman food-seeking patterns.

Paleodietetics is providing some information on prehistoric diets. Can other methods, including historical and ethnobotanical techniques, be used to reconstruct man's past diets to determine their nutrient content and balance, and to learn of since-rejected or otherwise vanished good nutrient sources?

What would be the least obtrusive way to determine what percentage of a woman's time is devoted to food getting and preparation in relation to nutrients provided for the family? Probably some form of person-following, plus early structuring of schedules so observed, amenable to computer data processing, would give the information needed regarding activities. Foods provided by this work would then need to be weighed, directly or in replicate, and nutrient content calculated.

INVENTORIES

A number of inventories of foods and activities related to foods would be of value and interest to nutritionists and anthropologists alike. Methods for determining some are probably self-evident. Others require more ingenuity, or collaboration with botanists and other scientists, such as chemists or biochemists, who have laboratory facilities. The following inventories are worthy of examination.

Inventories of oral activities

Recently, Whiting (personal communication) has pointed to the need to observe and record ingestion and inhalation of nonnutrient substances that affect health through interference with good nutritional status. A well-known example is the appetite-depressant, cocaine-containing physiological stimulant, the coca leaf, *Erythroxylon coca*, which has been chewed in the Andes since the time of the Incas (Mazess and Baker, 1963). Ethiopians use the leaf of the shrub, *Catha edulis*, *ch'at*, for its similar effect (Simoons, 1960; Interdepartmental Committee on Nutrition for National Defense, 1959). Studies made in Thailand have shown that betel nut chewing interferes with thiamine status (Vimokesant et al., 1975). Betel nut *(Areca catechu)* is chewed in South and Southeast Asia as well as throughout the South Pacific. In most cases this "chew" includes calcium carbonate (lime, from seashells) and the leaf of the pepper, *Piper betel* (for which the whole chew has been named). The betel pepper leaf contains provitamin A (beta carotene), some of which may be swallowed, as well as calcium; it is probable that the other leaves cited here may provide small amounts of these nutrients to those who use them.

Such oral activities should be systematically recorded, with potential beneficial as well as adverse effects in mind. Others include consumption of kava, fermented beverages and foods, use of various drugs (especially those known to affect nutrient status), and pica, the ingestion of substances not defined as food, such as clay, dirt, laundry starch, and ice cubes (Halsted, 1968; Bogert et al., 1973). Pica is seen particularly during preg-

nancy, but it is also practiced by children (Chapter 13).

Appropriate methods for obtaining these inventories appear to be modifications of participant observation, systematized to include suitable population sampling methods, or use of simple questionnaires, or both. Literate persons might be induced to keep records of how many cigarettes they smoke per day or how many beers they drink, for example.

Use of commercially available inhalants and ingestants can be determined indirectly through examination of market channels (including querying shop owners on their sale) and individual and family purchases as reported in homes.

The study of pica presents some peculiarities in needed approach. To determine the effect of the practice on the individual one needs to observe what and how much of the substance is taken, how often and for how long, and relate this activity to food intake during the same time span to determine the degree, if any, to which the ingestion of the nonfood interferes with normal food and nutrient consumption. The substance eaten should be subjected to chemical analysis, if this has not been done, or if its consumption is not well known (ice being one exception, but even this practice should be quantitated, since resulting hemodilution depends upon the amount chewed). Because some workers have postulated that eating of dirt, clay, and similar substances is a physiological response to a need for some mineral in short supply (Bogert et al., 1973), laboratory analyses of the items used should be made for trace elements known to be required by human beings.

Use of the person-following technique for each subject for several days or for a randomly selected sample of days in a week or month would appear to be the best method to determine the extent of the pica practice for that individual. Learning who are the practicers will require a combination of observation and questioning (bearing in mind people will not always admit to the practice). Depending upon the social sanctions given this oral activity or craving, the investigator can determine whether direct query will give reliable answers regarding the duration and extent of the habit. Locally perceived reasons for the practice should be elicited by direct questioning of those who practice pica and of others in the community.

The nonnutrient or pharmacological effects of any of these orally enjoyed nonfoods can best be ascertained through laboratory analyses of substances that have not yet been so examined.

Nutrient contributions of stimulants

Closely related to the above should be an inventory of alcoholic and other stimulant beverages and foods that contribute rather than inhibit nutrients. Such study involves collecting samples as imbibed, preservation of the samples, preferably chilled, and shipment to a collaborating laboratory for chemical analysis. Measurement of alcoholic content should be part of this. Locally made yeasts or other ferments should be included in this inventory, along with how they are made and utilized. Methods of preparation of foodstuffs made from them should be recorded. Such preparation should be observed, if possible, as well as queried. Pertinent local conditions, such as temperature, that influence the product should also be noted. (It is strongly suggested that ethnographers wishing to study food should include in their equipment a simple ambient air thermometer as well as a gram or ounce scale. Standard measures such as a cook's measuring cup and spoons are also useful for determining relative amounts of ingredients. For more sophisticated study of a food preparation technique, a candy thermometer, which can be inserted into liquid or semisolid cooking material, can give approximations of the temperature at which a food is prepared.)

Other inventories

Further information on the following is much to be desired, even though in some cases data have already been collected. For each item or class of items, one would like to know how it is obtained by the individual or family and how it is prepared; frequency and amount of use; and, where pertinent, the situation or setting in which it is used.

1. Wild foods gathered or collected for consumption, and their nutrient value
2. Pharmacologically active foods, such as yams
3. Foods that are consumed even though they contain naturally occurring or environmentally caused toxins (e.g., the poisonous fish eaten under public health control by the Japanese; certain species of mushrooms, deadly except in small doses)
4. Fermented and sprouted foods (Does the process enhance nutritive quality?)

Most of these inventories can be obtained and categorized by combinations of observation, querying, collecting, and laboratory analyses.

SUMMARY

Some methods developed and used in the last several decades for studying diet ethnographically have been described, in order to provide concerned readers with information that can be used as a base on which to build their own approaches to research of this nature. Some unsolved problems of nutritional anthropology have been set forth, with suggestions for ways to try to answer them that seem to be amenable to trial, and to have the potential of practicality and of providing reasonable, reproducible results. Should further methods be developed, they would be welcomed for trial by others.

The next efforts in this field of developing methods in nutritional anthropology should then most appropriately be attempts to standardize some or all of the methods with which we will find ourselves armed.

REFERENCES

Bogert, L. J., Briggs, G. M., and Calloway, D. H. 1973. Nutrition and physical fitness, ed. 9. W. B. Saunders, Philadelphia.

Chang, K. C. (ed.). 1977. Food in Chinese culture. Anthropological and historical perspectives. Yale University Press, New Haven, Conn.

Chassy, J. P., van Veen, A. G., and Young, F. W. 1967. The application of social science research methods to the study of food habits and food consumption in an industrializing area. American Journal of Clinical Nutrition 20:56-64.

Darby, W. J., Ghalioungui, P., and Grivetti, L. 1977. Food: The gift of Osiris. Academic Press, New York.

Dewalt, K. M., and Pelto, G. H. 1977. Food use and household ecology in a Mexican community. In T. K. Fitzgerald (ed.). Nutrition and anthropology in action. van Gorcum, Assen, The Netherlands.

DuBois, C. 1944. The people of Alor. A social-psychological study of an East Indian island. University of Minnesota Press, Minneapolis.

Firth, Raymond. 1934. The sociological study of native diet. Africa 7:401-414.

Firth, Rosemary. 1966. Housekeeping among Malay peasants, ed. 2. Athlone Press, London.

Freedman, R. L. 1977. Nutritional anthropology: An overview. In T. K. Fitzgerald (ed.). Nutrition and anthropology in action. van Gorcum, Assen, The Netherlands.

Halsted, J. A. 1968. Geophagia in man: Its nature and nutritional effects. American Journal of Clinical Nutrition 21:1384.

Honigmann, J. J. 1961. Foodways in a Muskey community: An anthropological report on the Attawapiskat Indians. Department of Northern Affairs and National Resources, Ottawa, Canada.

Interdepartmental Committee on Nutrition for National Defense. 1959. Ethiopia: Nutrition survey, Government Printing Office, Washington, D.C.

Interdepartmental Committee on Nutrition for National Defense. 1963. Manual for nutrition surveys, ed. 2. Government Printing Office, Washington, D.C.

Mazess, R. B., and Baker, P. T. 1963. Calcium: Unusual sources in the highland Peruvian diet. Science 142:1466.

McArthur, A. M. 1962. Malaya 12. Assignment report, June 1958–November 1959. World Health Organization, Regional Office for the Western Pacific, Manila, The Philippines.

McArthur, M. 1974. Pigs for the ancestors: A review article. Oceania XLV(2):87-123.

Montgomery, E. 1978. Anthropological contributions to the study of food-related cultural variability. In Margen, S. (ed.). Progress in human nutrition, vol. 2. Avi Publishing Co., Westport, Conn.

Montgomery, E., and Bennett, J. W. 1978. Anthropological studies of food and nutrition: The 1940s and the 1970s. In W. Goldschmidt (ed.). The uses of anthropology, American Anthropological Association, Washington, D.C.

Montgomery, E., and Johnson, A. 1977. Machiguenga energy expenditure. Ecology of Food and Nutrition 6:97-105.

Nutrition Reviews. 1976. The validity of 24-hour recalls. 34:310-311.

Rappaport, R. A. 1968. Pigs for the ancestors. Ritual in the ecology of a New Guinea people. Yale University Press, New Haven, Conn.

Rathje, W. L., and Harrison, G. G. 1978. Monitoring trends in food utilization: Application of an archeological method. Federation Proceedings 37(1):49-54.

Richards, A. I. 1932. Hunger and work in a savage tribe. A functional study of nutrition among the southern Bantu. G. Routledge and Sons, London.

Richards, A. I. 1939. Land, labour and diet in northern Rhodesia: An economic study of the Bemba tribe. Oxford University Press, London.

Richards, A. I., and Widdowson, E. M. 1936. A dietary study in North-Eastern Rhodesia. Africa 9:166-196.

Salaman, R. N. 1949. The history and social influence of the potato. Cambridge University Press, Cambridge.

Sanjur, D., Cravioto, J., and van Veen, A. G. 1970. Infant nutrition and socio-cultural influences in a village in central Mexico. Tropical and Geographical Medicine 20:443-451.

Scudder, T. 1962. The ecology of the Gwembe Tonga. Kariba studies, Vol. II. Manchester University Press, Manchester.

Simoons, F. J. 1960. Northwest Ethiopia. Peoples and economy. University of Wisconsin Press, Madison, Wisc.

Vimokesant, S. L., Hilker, D. M., Nakornchai, S., and others. 1975. Effects of betel nut and fermented fish on the thiamin status of northeastern Thais. American Journal of Clinical Nutrition 28:1458-1463.

Whiting, M. Personal communication.

Williams, A. W. 1973. Dietary patterns in three Mexican villages. In C. E. Smith, Jr. (ed.). Man and his foods: Studies in the ethnobotany of nutrition—contemporary, primitive and prehistoric non-European diets, University of Alabama Press, Birmingham, Ala.

Wilson, C. S. 1964. A review of methods used in nutrition surveys conducted by the Interdepartmental Committee on Nutrition for National Defense (ICNND). American Journal of Clinical Nutrition 15:29-44.

Wilson, C. S. 1973. Food habits: A selected annotated bibliography. Journal of Nutrition Education Jan.-Mar. 5 (1, Suppl. 1):38-72.

Wilson, C. S. 1974. Child following: A technic for learning food and nutrient intakes. Journal of Tropical Pediatrics and Environmental Child Health 20:9-14.

Wilson, C. S. 1977. Research methods in nutritional anthropology: Approaches and technics. In T. K. Fitzgerald (ed.). Nutrition and anthropology in action, van Gorcum, Assen, The Netherlands.

PART FOUR

ANTHROPOLOGICAL PERSPECTIVES ON AGING AND DYING

Chapter 16 explores the cultural dimensions of aging and the aged. One of the major tasks of an anthropological perspective on aging is the examination of the ways other societies have conceptualized and treated their old people. There have been few studies on aging done by anthropologists. The few cross-cultural studies that have been done make clear the great variety of styles and forms of aging in different cultural settings.

Chapter 17 illustrates one study on aging that has been done by a nurse-anthropologist. The cultural and physiological aspects of aging in women are analyzed from an anthropological perspective. Areas of concern are historical and contemporary trends in the care and treatment of women with disorders relating to the reproductive system, physiological changes in the middle years, and cultural influences on aging in cross-cultural perspective.

Older persons are described as family persons in Chapter 18. The necessity of coping with the reality of present family or the reality of the family in memory is emphasized. Difficulties inherent in the role-reversal phenomenon from supported-child by supporting-parent to supported-parent by supporting-child are explored with examples given of the successful achievement of this process. Problems and challenges in areas of home care with family and nonfamily, long-term care also are explored. Attitudes of older persons toward professional helpers (nurses, physicians, social workers) are examined. The chapter includes suggestions for improving the performance of health professionals by becoming aware of attitudes about aging.

Chapter 19 moves to a discussion of the dying. The chapter delineates a model, that of selected neglect, and discusses indications for its use for perimortality (terminal) care in community settings. Some families of chronically and acutely ill patients with poor prognoses agonize over the eventualities of their loved ones' terminal care. Families tend to make role choices for themselves and for health care personnel. However, when the health caregivers do not meet the families' expectations, selective neglect occurs. The selective neglect model can be used predictively by community health personnel to prevent some of the trauma associated with perimortality care for the patient and the family.

CHAPTER 16

Aging and the aged in other cultures: an anthropological perspective*

Barbara Myerhoff

It is unfortunate that the stereotype of anthropology as "the study of the exotic by eccentrics" is not entirely unfair, for while a very strong case can be made supporting the relevance of an anthropological approach to the subject of aging, the fact is that very few anthropologists have considered the matter systematically. Some possible reasons for this have been suggested by Margaret Clark: she wonders if negative attitudes toward the aged disincline American anthropologists to consider a subject that is vaguely repellent to them (Clark 1967:56):

My own experience with Americans (including some anthropologists) is that there is among them a common view that old age, or even late maturity, is a horrible state; one shouldn't really think about it or look at it too closely—as though it were the head of Medusa. To contemplate later life is often seen as a morbid preoccupation—an unhealthy concern, somewhat akin to necrophilia. Since anthropologists are indeed creatures of their own culture, it may be that prevailing American attitudes toward aging are manifesting themselves in unconscious decisions by ethnographers to ignore this aspect of the life cycle.

This possibility is rather appalling since one of the professional goals of the anthropologist is to rid oneself of cultural blinders in studying one's own as well as other ways of life. The neglect of the role of the aged and the nature of aging is particularly surprising since anthropologists have given close attention to the life cycle as a general topic of inter-

*Originally prepared for and presented to the Summer Institute, Andrus Gerontology Center, University of Southern California, 1968.

est up to but excluding old age. Clark suggests that this may be in part attributable to the Freudian bias that characterized so much early work in culture and personality studies and that provided that early life experiences were the most significant explanatory forces in understanding adult behavior. Many anthropologists recently have given lip service to the proposition that personality changes over time, and that the adult cannot be understood fully in terms of infancy and childhood; however, this recognition has not been accompanied by greater attention to adulthood and old age in actual field studies.

There are important exceptions to this charge: Simmons (1960) has concentrated on the aged in primitive and preindustrial societies, using the Human Relations Area Files to identify relationships between cultural traits and the status of the aged. Specific studies of the age-principle and age-grading in social organization exist; especially notable here are the works of Eisenstadt (1956) and LeVine (1963). Considerable attention has been devoted to the relationship between the aged and political organization in studies of gerontocratic societies. Kleemeler (1961) has also gathered descriptions of aging and leisure in many diverse cultures. But in all, there is no great or systematic body of work such as one might expect despite the fact that ethnographers have traditionally relied heavily upon reports from the aged in collecting their field data. The old people are the repositories of experience, memories, authority, and wisdom, and many an anthropologist gives few thoughts to the accumulated information to be gathered from his or her own grandmother while devoting the utmost attention and solemn respect to the garbled mutterings of the feeble, gnarled "ancient ones" in some exotic place.

The state of affairs is especially unfortunate since those cross-cultural studies of aging that do exist make abundantly clear the cultural determinants of aging; if any generalizations can be made, they point to the great variety of styles and forms of aging in different cultural settings. Here one is struck by diversity rather than uniformity, by variation rather than universality. The studies that are available suggest that social scientists must be as diligent in including the role of cultural factors in aging as they are in including them in studies of childrearing and childhood. Not all anthropologists may agree, but in the opinion of many the data point toward the malleability of the human organism and the significant role of nonbiological factors; in other words, culture appears to explain more of the peculiarities and idiosyncrasies of aging than do factors that are attributable to a "common humanity." In comparison with old age, infancy and childhood display striking patterning and regularity in part because of predictable and inevitable physiological events. Ethological studies of primates are impressive for their suggestions that the socialization process has certain fixed determinants and sequences that result from the interaction of chemical, biological, and endocrinological factors (Roe and Simpson, 1958; Washburn, 1961; Washburn and Jay, 1968). The primate mother (including human) lactates when she hears an infant crying. A primate adult becomes agitated by the sight and sound of a helpless child in distress and must offer assistance to maintain his own well-being. These are the physiological givens whereby the dependence of the child and the nurturant response by the adult are articulated, thus assuring the immature members of the group a heightened chance for continued existence. One of the most significant characteristics of the very old is also helplessness, yet one does not encounter similar built-in protective devices to assure the aged assistance. As Simmons (1960) has pointed out, concern and care for the aged are strictly human. Such concern

is entirely the result of cultural as opposed to biological considerations.

Aging and the aged, then, are not "givens" in any sense. Because of the striking variability concerning them, nearly every statement made about attitudes toward the elderly, treatment of them, and conceptualizations and expectations concerning them in any one culture can be contradicted by equally valid but differing evidence drawn from another culture. No easy generalizations are presently justified by the literature.

Why, this being the case, should a person in one culture be concerned with the aged elsewhere? Why are cross-cultural studies of the aged relevant? Can't one suppose in the face of this variability that the study of aging in other cultures will be gratuitous—perhaps interesting and, like history, part of the human record, but basically unessential to the principal concerns of understanding aging in our own culture? In other words, why should we take the trouble to employ an anthropological perspective in considering aging at all?

The answer to this question occurs on two levels: First, theoretically, social scientists continue to seek generalizations, regularities, and even lawful relationships among the phenomena they study. In lieu of a true laboratory in which isolated variables can be manipulated the social scientist turns to varying social situations that occur naturally in the world in hopes of understanding the relationships among the issues they are concerned with. Differing social conditions, for the most part, are their only "experiments." These differences must be sought across as well as within societies in order to make "culture-free" generalizations about aging wherever it occurs. The specific task of anthropology has been to consider its subject matter cross-culturally. Second, on the practical level, a cross-cultural perspective can help investigators recognize and possibly suspend their own cultural biases. The necessity for doing so is underlined by Clark's previously mentioned observation that perhaps it is the American's negative attitude toward old age itself that has prevented anthropologists in this country from examining this period of life with the specificity and care it merits.

But there is another reason, perhaps most

significant of all, why anthropology makes a unique contribution to this subject. Mention has been made of the fact that old age, unlike earlier phases in the life cycle, appears less governed by well-known biological determinants and therefore may be more responsive to cultural conditioning than other periods of life. There is abundant evidence that aging follows a variable course psychologically as well as physically.* Reliable predictions are available about the behavior and capacity of 3-year-olds or even 21-year-olds in all cultures, but predictions about the interests, skills, and developmental sequences of 50-year-olds cannot be made with equal confidence. If one can generalize about this part of life at all, perhaps the safest statement would be that it is more variable than regular, within as well as across cultures. This irregularity is greatly compounded by the societal variables that we see operating in our own culture. Old age in this country is a time of life with very little structure and support. Some expectations exist for people at this time of life but these are not uniformly imposed and often not even clearly recognized. Old people in rural areas often can expect greater social participation than urban people of comparable age. Some age-homogeneous organizations are available for social support but membership is far from universal and in some places not even widespread. This means that investigation of aging must be quite comprehensive in its inclusion of explanatory variables—the biological, psychological, societal, and cultural dimensions must be taken into account since so far as we know none can be cited as exclusively or even primarily responsible for the course and form of aging. Anthropologists are properly responsible for sorting out some of the societal and most of the cultural influences in this process.

The cultural dimension of aging and the aged is of special concern here. First, something must be said regarding the way the term "culture" is being used in the context of this chapter. Even anthropologists, who regard the culture concept as perhaps the

single unifying concern that ties together the various specializations within the field of anthropology, do not agree on its definition. Most would agree, however, that the concentration on culture—its nature and consequences—is one of the features that sets anthropology apart from the other social sciences (Kroeber and Kluckhohn, 1963).

Perhaps the simplest and most general view of culture considers it the conglomerate of customs, traditions, and habits of a particular group sharing a way of life at the same time and place. Some anthropologists stress the material manifestations of this way of life; others trace its historical development. Some focus on patterned social relationships between groups and individuals while others concentrate on institutions, their functions and interrelationships. Equally valid is the orientation that regards culture as an adaptation to a given environment and duly considers technological and ecological factors as of primary interest.

There is yet another orientation toward culture that seems especially useful for those interested in aging, and that is the view of culture as primarily an ideological phenomenon—a set of shared understandings that characterize a particular group; this orientation can be called a *Weltanschauung*, or a group's "collective representations." In this view, humankind is fundamentally a symbol maker. A person can bear almost anything but a sense of meaninglessness and chaos. Culture provides the individual with a means for interpreting the world, one's fellows, and one's life. An anthropologist of this persuasion, Clifford Geertz (1963:13), has defined culture as a set of symbols that establish basic and powerful moods and motivations that formulate a conception of the order of existence. These shared symbols constitute what a group of people agree to be "reality." Mankind is able to tolerate anything, Geertz suggests, except the failure of our symbols, for this amounts to a threat to our very powers of conception. When such a failure occurs we are more helpless than the beavers. He puts it this way:

> The extreme generality, diffuseness, and variability of man's innate (i.e.: genetically programmed) response capacities means that without the assistance of cultural patterns he would be functionally incomplete, not merely a talented ape

---

*Although some biologists would argue that aging is the playing out of a "programmed" series of events, others see it as a more idiosyncratic, biologically variable event, particularly in comparison with the growth cycle.

who had, like some under-privileged child, unfortunately been prevented from realizing his full potentialities, but a kind of formless monster with neither sense of direction nor power of self-control, a chaos of spasmodic impulses and vague emotions.

Even the most remote suggestion that one's symbols may fail arouses the most severe anxiety, so great is one's dependence on them. In this approach, culture provides humanity with meanings, and the greatest and most definitive feature of humanness itself is the need as well as the ability for conceptualization. Langer has said (1960:187), "Man can adapt himself somehow to anything his imagination can cope with; but he cannot deal with Chaos." Culture in the form of shared symbols provides mankind's most important assets—the ability to "grasp" the world, to agree on what is "really real." These are ultimate concepts, which endow one with the sense that the world is orderly and is what it is supposed to be. It is the human quest for lucidity and meaning that enables mankind to deal with great pain. Evil, loss, suffering, misfortune, and disappointments can be accepted as long as life is an explicable experience.

One of the most dramatic examples of this quest for lucidity is described by Lévi-Strauss (1963) in his analysis of a cure by a South American medicine man. The medicine man in this analysis gives the suffering person a vocabulary, a set of labels for comprehending illness. In this case the mere naming of the ailment proclaims that the sick person's previously unique, confused experience has been known before, felt by others, and has a term that makes sense of the symptoms. Thus the term serves as a codified response to the individual's suffering by the culture. The application of the label makes a previously idiosyncratic event, which isolated and terrified the patient, into a social experience, predictable and treatable. In other words, the sickness is symbolized, hence incorporated as part of social and shared experience that can be understood. Being understandable, it now can be endured. It might be said that the mere provision of a name for the illness—that is, the application of a collective symbol—constitutes the greatest part of the cure.

This is a useful and dramatic illustration of the power of symbols that conveys some of our justification for regarding culture as a set of shared meanings or symbols, and, as has been mentioned, this approach to culture is especially helpful concerning the matters of aging and the aged.

One of the most significant features concerning aging in contemporary American society is the very absence of shared meanings and collective representations for this period of life. There are in this culture many rather vague feelings, attitudes, habits, and expectations about aging, but these are not truly symbols for they are not widely shared with clear connotations, nor do they provide us with meanings. It is important to distinguish between our diffuse and usually negative stereotypes and preconceptions regarding the aged and a collective, specific interpretation of the meaning of being aged in American culture. The ambiguity and confusion surrounding the last phases of life for most Americans is tantamount to an absence of meanings by which to comprehend its significance. This very lack is a cultural phenomenon, for when other societies are considered, especially preliterate and preindustrial ones, the greater clarity of conceptualizations regarding old age is impressive. That is not to say that "they" have "solved" it and "we" have not; let us not fall prey to that occupational hazard common among anthropologists of romanticizing "the natives" and pointing out with lightly disguised delight how much better they are doing than we civilized folk. It does seem fair to say, however, that industrial, Western civilizations have dealt with aging less directly and satisfactorily than many simpler societies. The reasons for this are manifold; perhaps most important is the fact that the aged are genuinely less necessary as well as far more numerous here and now than in other times and places.

One of the major tasks of an anthropological view of aging is the examination of some of the ways other societies have conceptualized and treated their old people, some of the social and cultural variables that seem to contribute to these alternatives, and some of the conclusions that may be drawn from these examples that are of potential use to our own society in solving what is considered, appropriately, a social problem. In considering other cultures the reader must bear in mind that definitive answers or even recommendations for our own problems cannot be anticipated; however, we can hope to locate some of the important questions and some useful clues. No attempt can be made here to survey other cultures systematically. The following cases and issues have been selected on two grounds: First, for their potential relevance for understanding our own culture's problems and circumstances concerning the aged. (Throughout this discussion the implications of phenomena in other cultures for our own will be brought out wherever possible.) Second, material is used that illuminates three dimensions pertinent to aging and the aged in any society: (1) the ideological dimension, that is some of the collective representations and value orientations relevant to aging; (2) some social organizational features that appear closely related to differing modes and styles of aging; and, (3) some of the implications of social complexity for aging and the aged.

THE IDEOLOGICAL DIMENSION

To begin with conceptions of the stages of life, of which aging is one part, and their corresponding roles, expectations, and attitudes, it must be noted that no fixed cross-cultural definition of old age is valid. In our own society we have precise chronological and legal as well as psychological and biological cut-off points for each stage of life. Some psychological and biological definitions of age with varying degrees of precision can be found in all cultures, but exact chronological and legal definitions are unique to Western literate society, with its written records and preoccupation with quantified units. In all societies "perceived age" and "attributed age" exist and are relevant; what varies is the precision of the definitions and the amount of discrepancy between the two.

One of the most useful lessons of anthropology concerning life stages is this: that there are no universal criteria for life stages, nor are there even universal divisions of a crude sort. Some societies have no conception of a period of old age per se. This is demonstrated in some of those groups that stress the continuity of membership in corporate

kin groups where, for example, the clan is considered to include all living members, all the forebears who have ever existed, and all children yet unborn within a given descent line. This is not to say that roles are not distributed according to chronological age, but rather that a distinct, well-formulated set of experiences and attributes for particular age spans is not provided.

Such a state of affairs may seem surprising at first glance, for one might expect that no society can fail to recognize the potentialities of different ages, just as no society can fail to take account of sex differences in its division of labor. But at one time our own society did not recognize the period that it is presently most preoccupied with—childhood. Before the Renaissance the child was viewed as a miniature adult having no distinctive characteristics or needs associated with his age (Aries, 1962). This means that even such matters as childhood and old age, which we are inclined to think of as "givens" in nature that all societies must acknowledge —even these life phases prove to be cultural conceptions that may or may not be present in various societies at different times. Thus while every society differentiates between some life stages defined by age, there is no fixed correspondence across societies as to what these ages are, how many there are, and what features characterize them.

It is useful, therefore, to distinguish between age span and age grade. The latter is usually thought of as a general "human type," a broad cultural definition of human potentialities and behaviors appropriate to an individual at a time of life. As such, *age grading* provides a basis for self-identification and societal role allocation. One of the essential functions served by age grades is the maintenance of continuity achieved by the interaction of different age grades or generations. While some societies lack conceptions of childhood and old age, it seems that all have an age grade of "adult," a full-fledged member of the society who has received the social heritage from the previous age grade and transmits it to the younger one.

In contrast, we may think of *age span* as a chronological rather than sociological time period; in other words, it is a period of time rather than a set of expectations. Another useful category is that of *age set*, a social category for which expectations are quite precise. An age set is actually a corporate body with a definite and limited membership defined on the basis of the age principle. Age-homogeneous groups may be coterminous with the entire social organization in some cultures, so that the age principle is the fundamental basis for allocation of all rights and responsibilities; more will be said about such arrangements later.

The ethnographic record is quite explicit in showing that age, like sex and descent, is a biological building block that is very freely used by culture. Each society, therefore, must be examined empirically, for there are no absolute, universally valid definitions of the meanings or even the existence of a given set of life stages. The "clo" Bushman is the individual who has three living children. An Eskimo male who can no longer hunt, and the female whose teeth are too worn to chew the frost off frozen furs, are old. The Irish peasant whose father still lives and controls the family farm is called "boy," and although he is 30 or 40 years old, he is not permitted to marry, and thus cannot become an adult member of his group. In the United States, regardless of chronological age, a Negro male may be called "boy," signifying that part of the American value system that equates economic impotence with immaturity. Very few cultures define age in formal, chronological terms as we do when we retire people at age 65, permit them to marry and smoke at age 18, drink and vote at age 18 or 21, and so forth. Most definitions of age are more functional and flexible than this, but then the American approach to time, a quantifiable and objective entity, plays a large part in explaining our attitude toward age as chronological. More will be said concerning this shortly.

Part of a culture's conceptualization of a stage of "old age" involves its notions of "over-age" or senescence and death. Senescence is widely recognized culturally as the time of maximum dependence and minimum social utility, a universally pathetic and hopeless period of the life cycle. It is a time remarkable in our own culture because our technological competence has transformed it into a social problem by preserving substantial numbers of such people. At no other time and place has this been true. In simpler so-

cieties these dying members may be regarded as anomalies who are too few to require special institutions or elaborate conceptualizations. They may be treated more or less well. Our brethren in preliterate societies cannot be heaped with praise on this matter. The dying are charity cases everywhere, and their fate is subject to hazards. They may be exposed, abandoned, suffered, cherished, succored, ignored, or eliminated. This may be done with honor, indifference, or callousness.

The reasons for these different treatments are not always clear. The terribly poor and primitive Yahgan of Tierra del Fuego have been known to carry their ancient members on their backs despite one of the most extreme climates, a desperately impoverished and nomadic life, and a miserable technology. Their neighbors, the Ona, who share a very similar way of life, subject their old people to exposure. Elderly Eskimos who can no longer contribute to their society may walk off alone never to be seen again or they may be given a departure ceremony at which they are honored, then ritually killed. Here, for example, is a description of such a ceremony and its meaning among the Greenland Eskimo (Freuchen; 1961:194-195):

In some tribes, an old man wants his oldest son or favorite daughter to be the one to put the string around his neck and hoist him to his death. This was always done at the height of a party where good things were being eaten, where everyone— including the one who was about to die—felt happy and gay, and which would end with the angakok conjuring and dancing to chase out the evil spirits. At the end of his performance, he would give a special rope made of seal and walrus skin to the "executioner" who then placed it over the beam of the roof of the house and fastened it around the neck of the old man. Then the two rubbed noses, and the young man pulled the rope. Everybody in the house either helped or sat on the end of the rope so as to have the honor of bringing the old suffering one to the Happy Hunting Grounds where there would always be light and plenty of game of all kinds.

In general, only immediate necessity has caused simple people to abandon their aged parents. The abandonment is often lightened by the cultural provision for their honorable death and the hope of an attractive afterlife. Inherent in a society's conceptions concerning the aged are its handling and understanding of death. Death, like aging, is striking because of the variety of emotions it arouses in the hearts of men. It may be regarded as a final state or a transition; it may be glorified or denied; it may arouse fear, envy, or indifference in those remaining behind. The dead may be incorporated as part of the ongoing society, vigilantly watching and influencing continuing human life; they may be supplicated, shunned, or deified. Lévi-Strauss (1964:219) has an interesting approach to the question of social attitudes toward death. He sees a fundamental opposition between nature and culture, and considers death as the arch-enemy of man's humanity.

In fact and law alike, death is both *natural* and *anticultural*. That is to say that, whenever a native dies, an injury is done not only to those near to him, but to Society as a whole; and Nature, in consequence, is held to be in debt to Society.

When a man dies among the Bororo of South America that debt is extracted from Nature in the form of a collective hunt to kill a large and important animal in retribution for the human loss.

Where the dead are deeply involved in the lives of the living, one may encounter many forms of death and/or ancestor cults. Interpretations of the reasons for death cults and ancestor worship have been numerous and often contradictory: Freud (1913) regarded ancestor worship as expressing the omnipresent ambivalence between the living and the dead and the resentment toward authority. Frazer (1890) considered it the oldest and most primitive form of religion, based on an "innate" fear of corpses. Malinowski (1916) stressed hostility toward death in general, which is then extended to the dead. Hertz (1907) saw death cults as serving to maintain continuity of succession between the generations. He felt that death cults serve to deny the mortality of the human body by stressing the immortality of the social group. This is achieved through worship of the group's dead. And Fortes (1961) has suggested that ancestor worship is the social projection of filial ties, which are extrapolated and extended to the spiritual level.

Ethnographic evidence exists that can contradict any one of these interpretations. That death does not necessarily arouse emotions of fear, dread, and resentment is attested, for example, by this excerpt describing the attitudes of the Eskimos (Freuchen, 1961: 194):

Fear of death is unknown to them, they know only love of life. The Eskimos are themselves unaware of the difficulty of their existence, they always enjoy life with an enviable intensity and they believe themselves to be the happiest people on earth living in the most beautiful country there is. When an old man sees the young men go out hunting and cannot himself go along, he is sorry. When he has to ask other people for skins for his clothing, when he cannot ever again be the one to invite the neighbors to eat his game, life is of no value to him. Rheumatism and other ills may plague him, and he wants to die. This has been done in different ways in different tribes, but everywhere it is held that if a man feels himself to be a nuisance, his love for his kin, coupled with the sorrow of not being able to take part in the things which are worthwhile impels him to die.

Regardless of cultural variations of feelings about death and treatment of the dead, death is never overlooked by the living. Lévi-Strauss (1964:216) may be quoted again here:

There is probably no such thing as a society which does not treat its dead with consideration. At a time when mankind as we know it had hardly come into being, Neanderthal Man already buried his dead in tombs made up of a few rough stones.

Some societies have a concept of retirement, as they do about old age, and others do not. Simmons (1960) noted that the aged find most valuable occupation in societies of sedentary cultivators. Here they are gradually phased out of the work force as they assume progressively less demanding tasks. In simpler societies sustained by collecting, hunting, and fishing, fewer opportunities for productive work exist for the aged. Here the old people may retire to the campfire and take on a specific status of "no longer able to work." The meaning of such a period varies from culture to culture: it may be a time of deserved rest and honor or it may be a period of sadness and loss of social esteem. Simmons (1960:74) wisely suggests:

Opportunities to keep on working at essential but light tasks are obvious psychological and social assets in old age; but such labors which continue far into senescence may insure little more than bare subsistence, if that, and quite often become very burdensome. Complete release from enforced labor may sometimes prove more rewarding than repeated demotions into lower levels of drudgery. Compromise tasks, while lighter than previous work, often involve threats to prestige, as in the case of the dignified old warrior confined to "woman's work" in the house. The physical efforts in the late stages of one's dotage prove to be little more than toeholds on security.*

No discussion of the ideological components of age and aging can afford to overlook the closely associated collective representations concerning time, change, and progress. The Western view of time is linear—it has a beginning, middle, and end. It does not flow in a subjective continuum but marches jerkily along in quantifiable units. It is objectified, as Whorf (1956) has pointed out, and conceived of as a series of things, like apples sitting on a shelf. As such it can be added, subtracted, divided, multiplied, gained, lost, saved, earned, squandered, garnered, and allocated. Western notions of the nature of time are illuminated and revealed by our Calvinistic ethic where, as Tawney (1926) and Weber (1930) have demonstrated so convincingly, these notions may be seen as inextricably involved with our habits and values concerning money, growth, and power. Indeed, our conception of time can be regarded as pivotal to the Puritan dogma, which provided the substratum for so much of the American value system. If time is understood as finite, then the close of life is an irredeemable tragedy, an irreversible loss.

Without the sense of the continuous nature of time provided by some cultures, humans face the end of life as an extermination that severs them from everything meaningful. For some, the Christian after life cushions the shock, but it may not carry enough appeal to compete with the more entrenched and deeper value on the future of *this* life. In her writings on American value orientations, Florence Kluckhohn (Kluckhohn and Strodtbeck, 1961) points out that as a culture we cherish the future over the present, the capacity to alter our environment over the acceptance of it, the importance of *be-*

*From Simmons, L. W. 1960. Aging in primitive societies. In C. Tibbitts (ed.). Handbook of social gerontology: Social aspects of aging. University of Chicago Press, Chicago.

coming rather than of *being*, and achieving over accommodating. Old people are devalued as belonging to the past, and they are slipped into parenthetical slots in the social structure. If they are accorded any importance other than that of being tolerated or ignored, it is because of their remarkable accomplishments as individuals. As a group they are esteemed by the culture. Ironically, it is often the individual's refusal to demonstrate or accept old age, the very demonstration that *flaunts* his status, which wins him respect and attention.

Just how ironic this is has been shown by Clark (1961) who illustrated some of the ways our dominant value orientations work against the aged in this society. She has compared two groups of elderly people; one defined as adaptive in value orientations and the other as maladaptive to the point of mental illness. The members of the adaptive group are concerned with consideration for others, are congenial and interested in preserving their physical and financial resources. They try to coexist with the inevitable, are oriented toward relaxation, and have been freed from desire to compete. In direct contrast, the mentally ill aged people are interested in status and achievement, are acquisitive rather than conservative of their resources, are aggressive, try to control their lives, are ambitious, competitive, and more oriented toward progress than continuity and toward the maintenance of a high level of aspiration. A set of values that emphasizes achievement, success, change, progress, individualism, and the future is a source of disappointment for the aged, for these are categorically unattainable to them. Time is their enemy. They are defeated from the beginning. The mentally ill aged, of course, are demonstrating a type of behavior and orientation that may make a younger person successful. In other words, they are victims of a sharp cultural dichotomy that defines one type of behavior as a requisite for success at one time of life and quite a different, almost opposite type of orientation as a requisite for success at a later phase of life. It is difficult to comprehend how old people manage to make this reversal at all. Some people are simply more flexible than others and can accommodate to the role reversals. Despite the sharp discontinuities between adolescence and adulthood, many of those who are successful as adolescents also become successful as adults. Many adults make the successful shift in values to become well-adjusted old people.

Transitions from one period of life to the next are not managed with equal smoothness in any society. In our own society, relatively speaking, childhood is handled well, adolescence badly, adulthood well, and aging badly —all in terms of social support, consistent roles and expectations, appropriate training, and provision for esteeming those who achieve status and skills.

Industrial, rapidly changing societies favor the young while the aged fare better in more static, sedentary environments. More will be said later concerning the kinds of societies in which the aged are most likely to feel secure and valued. As a final consideration of the relationship between aging, change, and conceptions of time, Simmons (1960:88) has offered a general principle that is quite useful:

In the long and steady strides of the social order, the aging get themselves fixed and favored in positions, power and performance. They have what we call seniority rights. But, when social conditions become unstable and the rate of change reaches a galloping pace, the aged are riding for an early fall, and the more youthful associates take their seats in the saddles. Change is the crux of the problem of aging as well as its challenge.*

Where change is equated with "the good" and where time is a commodity, the aged have little opportunity. Their life situation categorically denies them what is most valued, what gave the life they knew its significance. It is poignant and paradoxical that the virtues characterizing the well-adjusted old people in Clark's (1967b) study amounted to "not getting in anyone's way." These virtues lead to invisibility, anonymity, and all too often, insignificance. The value syndrome can be indicated by an adage for the achievement of "good" adjustment by all dependent populations—children, hospitalized people, inmates of all kinds: "Don't make waves."

Clark (1967b) points out that one should examine cultures whose values for those in

the prime of life correspond to the values manifested by her well-adjusted group. Peasant societies, for example, typically regard all the virtues of life as in short supply; this is Foster's (1965) "image of the limited good." Peasants characteristically regard the good things of life as finite, of limited quantities, and beyond their power to increase. Such a value system is diametrically opposed to the American value system that dictates competition, acquisition, and the exploitation of the environment.

Aged people are faced with limitations on time that they cannot alter; hence, Clark reasons, the old should find themselves more comfortable in societies such as that of peasant groups, which esteem acquiescence. Similarly, the values of some Mexican-Americans may incline that group to the meeting of difficulties by adjusting to them and accepting them as "fate." Perhaps the aged feel less stress in societies that have such values, but they are not necessarily more secure or more greatly esteemed there. They may not be required to make a drastic shift in values as they pass out of adulthood, but their problems are only partly psychological to begin with. Their social position may be just as precarious as it is in our society. These are actually empirical questions: Do Mexican-Americans adjust more readily to old age than their fellow Americans who share dominant core value orientations? Is the concept of "fatality" and is acquiescence an aid in making the transition to the end of life?

We might go on to examine the adjustment of people with other conceptualizations of time, most particularly Orientals, who stress continuity with the past and who esteem those who have existed for a long while. People whose culture provides ancestor cults, in which the aged are regarded as founders of the group and are accorded the reverance usually reserved for the deities should also be examined for the treatment of the aged. So should those cultures that have a circular conception of time usually associated with a religious scheme that stresses reincarnation.

In all these different cultures one may assume that the aged have a better environment than that of our own society. Our prognosis for solving our ideological problems concerning the aged is poor, for our evalua-

---

*From Simmons, L. W. 1960. Aging in primitive societies. In C. Tibbitts (ed.). Handbook of social gerontology: Social aspects of aging. University of Chicago Press, Chicago.

tion of the old is a product of our most cherished symbols—as Langer would say, part of our very *Weltanschauung*. Basic values change very slowly and even if our society successfully solves the mechanical, bureaucratic, maintenance, administrative, and economic aspects of the problems of the aged, it will still face the biggest task: that of finding a reason for them to exist, and of according them the esteem they need to feel wanted and secure. So much else would have to change before our society values the aged, regardless of how well they are treated that little optimism on this point seems justified.

SOCIAL ORGANIZATIONAL DIMENSIONS

The ways in which the aged, the dying, and the dead are placed in the social organizations of different cultures are no less variable than the ideas and conceptions concerning them. Nor are they truly separable, for ideas both reflect and shape the institutions provided for handling these categories. Perhaps one of the social characteristics most relevant to the explaining of different placement of and expectations for the aged is a society's system of reckoning kinship. It is useful to reduce the great variations in kinship systems to two major types: those organized on the basis of the lineal and those on the collateral principles. The former stresses social relations in a single line of descent over time. The latter emphasizes both lines of descent so as to include as relatives all those living at a given time.

Two kinds of kinship groupings arise as a result of emphasizing one of these principles over the other: the kindred is one grouping, and the lineage or clan is the other. The kindred, characteristic of our own society, includes all those people defined as relatives traced from a single individual's point of view—its point of reference is, by definition, egocentric. Thus no two individuals except full siblings have the same kindreds. For this reason kindreds are not discrete membership groups, balanced and equal as are clans and lineages, but are more like networks of overlapping ties.

The lineal principle, by contrast, usually traces descent through one parent and includes as members all those descendants

from a given ancestor (male or female) for a given number of generations. In its most complete form of expression, the lineage members regard their oldest common ancestor as the founder of the group.*

The implications of these two different arrangements are far reaching, and it is not accidental that kindreds are more often found in the rapidly changing, industrial, and Western societies that stress individuality, achievement, and mobility. (No causal relationship is suggested here, for as Tawney [1926] has pointed out, the familial and the economic characteristics of our society developed simultaneously and reciprocally.) Where the lineal principle is used to generate the most important societal groups, the older members of the society accumulate great authority and status. The authority automatically accruing to age in this arrangement is nicely illustrated by the existence of the ancestor cults already mentioned. Such cults are a conspicuous feature of African religious systems. Fortes (1965:122) states that, "Among the Tallensi of Ghana . . . [ancestor cult] so pervades their social life as to put them on a par with the Chinese and Romans in this respect."

Ancestor worship among some peoples is interlocked with the political system, so that the social, religious, and political organizations are fused and undifferentiated. Societies that have elaborate ancestor cults are found on many different levels of complexity, from the very simple to those comprising entire kingdoms and nations. The King of the Swazi kingdom of South Africa appeals to his own ancestors on behalf of the entire nation. On the local level, the head of the compound appeals to his ancestors on behalf of the residents of the compound (Kuper, 1947). Among the East African Tallensi, sacrifices to the ancestor can be offered by a son only through his older living male relatives in the same line: his father, uncle, or older brothers. The son has no individual right of ritual access to his ancestors while his elders are still alive (Fortes, 1945). Thus ancestor worship becomes an extension of the authority of

---

*Following British usage, a clan is regarded as a group of lineages, including as members the living, dead, and yet unborn; a lineage is all those living members, usually covering a three generation span.

the older generation. This is the case regardless of the ancestor's personal attributes. Fortes (1965:133) puts the matter like this:

This was repeatedly brought home to me by Tallensi elders. A man may be a liar, or a wastrel, or an adulterer, or a quarrelsome neighbor, or a negligent kinsman; he may be a mean and bad-tempered parent who has made his son's life miserable; he may have been abroad for years and have contributed nothing to their upbringing. If he dies leaving a son he becomes an ancestor of equal standing with any other ancestor. To put it in the believer's words, he acquires the power to intervene in the life and affairs of his descendants in exactly the same way as any other ancestor.

The ancestors are the source of all misfortune and of all prosperity. Just as a son cannot directly approach his ancestors except through his father, neither can these ancestors intervene in the life of the son except through his father. Such an arrangement encourages the greatest filial respect and responsibility, since the man who neglects his duties to his forebears incurs the wrath of a large population, both those living and those dead. A good relationship with his father is the means by which a son may ensure the intercession of supernaturals who affect his well-being. Of course, the observance of filial duty, which is assured by this arrangement, has no necessary emotional correlates; individuals may detest their fathers. Indeed, ambivalence between the generations is often most pronounced in societies with ancestor cults. Nevertheless, the official status of senior citizens is guaranteed regardless of private emotions that may be expressed toward them.

Among the Swazi, who are patrilineal and patrilocal, the social structure is dramatized by the actual physical arrangement of the compound or household, one of the most important features of which is the "Great Hut." This hut is presided over by the headman's mother and contains the skulls of cattle sacrificed to his ancestors. It is specifically dedicated to the headman's senior paternal relatives, a category of kinsman to whom only the old man has direct access, and whose supernatural hegemony contributes greatly to his control over the members of the entire compound. Daughters-in-law, living in their husbands' compounds, have no access to the Great Hut. In addition, they must detour to

avoid passing the front of the doorway, avert their eyes, and drop their voices when they approach it. These in-marrying women must return to their own parental homes to participate in religious observances. Their participation is through their brothers and fathers who sacrifice on their behalf. Thus age and sex interact to delegate authority to a single group, the older men. Lineally based societies, in addition to solving the problems of distribution of authority by invoking the age principle, have also solved the problem of intergenerational continuity. Among these societies we can expect to find the transitions between age spans most neatly provided for and clearly structured.*

But once more it must be emphasized that smoothness in handling these matters does not imply any particular psychological state. Tensions between the generations may be just as acute and acrimonious as those encountered in our own society where treatment of the aged is less structured. This will be illustrated by the use of the age principle to which I now turn: age-graded societies, or, more precisely, societies where age spans are formed into corporate groups and used as primary social and political units.

These units, sometimes called "age sets," may take the form of ritual groups, military regiments, age-homogeneous villages, corps of occupational specialists, and so forth. One of the most striking features associated with the use of the age principle as a basis of social organization is the flexibility of groups so formed. The resultant units easily fill a great variety of different functions. In general, all the men born within a certain number of consecutive years are admitted to one age set and the number of years varies from place to place. At the end of a given period, the set is closed and recruitment for a new one begins.

---

* Eisenstadt (1956:53) has developed a very complex theory concerning the relationship between the generations, which suggests that in societies where social maturity and status are withheld by the older generation from the younger, age homogeneous units are likely to be very important. "These [age-homogeneous] units have their origin in the tension between generations, and as their function is to find outlets for these tensions, they may function . . . as starting points for deviant groups." In these situations the group's specific functions may be rebellion against the older generation rather than the complementary interaction that might otherwise occur between them.

The sets are usually named and a man goes all through life with the same age mates with whom he may have the closest ties and the most serious obligations.

A typical series of age sets is found among the Galla of Southwest Ethiopia, where there are 6 sets, each composed of 8-year spans, rotating in a 40-year cycle. The first set is comprised of children, not yet counted as full citizens, who fill the tasks of messengers and junior and senior warriors, while the second set is made up of adolescent boys who function as shepherds. The third and fourth sets are junior and senior warriors, while the fifth set is made up of public officials with responsibilities for the administration of the government. The last set is the leaders who regulate and provide for the ritual life of the people. The head of the most senior set functions as "president" of the entire group; the head of the senior military set is chief military commander, and so forth. Thus the age sets function as tribal police, parliament, warriors, administrative staff, and religious leaders. Socialization and intergenerational continuity are handled automatically by the age set system.

Another advantage of the system is that among dispersed people, age sets may function to achieve cross-tribal unity, since age set members are frequently recruited by stressing age and disregarding local residence. Thus a man from a given age set has age mates in the surrounding tribes, to whom he can turn for aid and hospitality when he is out of his own territory, and who provide him with support. Age mate solidarity may also function as a bulwark against entrenched authority in strongly age-oriented societies. An Australian aborigine who believes he is being wronged by the seniors of his horde may turn to his age mates for support against the elders and wrest his rights from the old man with the assistance of his peers, who are organized into cohesive and enduring groups. Among the Tiv, in fact, there are regular rebellions against the entrenched authorities, which are launched by groups of age mates who seize power and hold it until younger men wrest the leadership from them.

One of the most distinctive characteristics of societies that use the age principle to form age sets is that transitions through the life cycle take place, not gradually and imperceptibly as is the case for many of the transitions in our society, but in a series of jumps. Each of these jumps is characterized by (1) status change of the entire group rather than of individuals, and (2) ceremonies and rituals that accompany the passage into each new stage. The formal transfer from one grade to another is always an occasion of public significance to the entire community.

The major features of these age set systems in general can be summarized as follows: (1) the age principle is used as a means of establishing corporate groups; (2) formal transitions of these groups from one social status defined by age to another occurs; (3) they result in the exercise of authority by a senior group of council of elders whose authority is backed by the influence and sanctions of ancestors on whose good will the well-being of the entire group ultimately depends; and (4) where age sets are not used as the basis for forming local or residential groups the grades may be used to provide unity and cohesion over a wide range that cross-cuts locale and is synchronized with age groups among neighboring people. Age grades thus serve multiple and quite diverse functions: they may provide for quick mustering of armed warriors among peoples who are not highly centralized politically; they handle socialization and continuity between generations; they buttress traditional values and provide authority; they are occupational specialists and they serve as public welfare organizations by requiring support (financial and emotional) among age mates. Describing conservative Swazi households, Kuper (1964:51) shows how age grades sustain the status quo and may serve as a bulwark against change:

When conflict breaks out in conservative homesteads between parent and child generations or between older and younger siblings, it is not a conflict of ideologies but of personality. Sons may covet the power of the father but when he dies they hope to exercise over their own sons the authority they themselves once resented. Young people are anxious to possess the privileges of their seniors, not to abolish the privileges of seniority; young brides may rebel against the way particular inlaws abuse the rights of age, but they agree to the principle that age and sex are entitled to those rights. At the present time, the social structure which gives power to the older generation is challenged by the money economy, a new legal system, and schooling for a literate society.*

Examples may be found in societies with age set systems in which relations between generations involve more stress than in our culture, and in which hostility toward the aged is as acute. Examples of societies may also be found where old people are accorded the greatest esteem and security. Smooth transitions from one stage of life to another and effective structuring of cross-generational continuity assured by age set systems have no necessary correlation with emotion or attitude. This state of affairs may be interpreted optimistically for our own society. Although we have not yet solved the problem of the place of the aged in the social structure, because the ethnographic evidence suggests that emotion and social status may vary independently, we hope eventually to untangle our mixed emotions toward our aged members and to accord them esteem and value, if not power, influence, and structural relevance.

SOCIAL COMPLEXITY, TECHNOLOGY, AND DIVISION OF LABOR

It is frequently remarked, and indeed has been a recurrent theme throughout this discussion, that literate, complex, Western, industrial societies penalize old age most heavily. It is the rapid change endemic to such societies, rather than the fact of complexity itself, that is probably responsible for this condition. Ethnographic data suggest that the simplest societies are not the best for the aged, since these societies are often (but certainly not always) found in harsh environments with very rude technological development. These foraging and hunting or fishing societies are often marginal in terms of subsistence and simply cannot afford to support any sizable body of people that can no longer support itself. Infanticide and something for which the term "geronticide" might be used occur in these cultures, although attitudes toward children and the aged may be those of the greatest affection and esteem. Accounts of Eskimo and Bushmen young people leaving their beloved parents behind to die are

*From Kuper, H. 1964. The Swazi: A South African Kingdom. Holt, Rinehart & Winston, New York.

heart-wrenching precisely because of the absence of justifying values or rationalizations. Such behavior is a matter of stark necessity but is no less sharply lamented. Such a situation is the inverse of that in our society; we sustain our old people physically but abandon them psychologically and emotionally. Thus it may be said that for quite different reasons the situation of the aged in the simplest and the most complex societies, the richest and the poorest, is equally unsure.

Simmons (1960) has offered a very interesting hypothesis indicating that it is in the middle-range societies—rural, agrarian, peasant communities—that the aged are most useful and sometimes (again, not always) because of this, more secure. There are opportunities in these settings for the aged to perform many tasks requiring manipulative skill rather than heavy manual labor, and thus they are more able to hold their own. One might further speculate on the reasons for the security of the aged in agricultural societies: that is, the common value accorded to the ownership of land and the association of the land with time. Here, too, one finds the lineage-based social organizations such as ancestor cults and clans in which land is often owned by the group (which is to say, by the ancestors and administered by the elders). Just such a configuration is found in Vietnam but is given little recognition by the intervening nonpeasant powers. There the attempt to relocate a family jeopardizes its affiliation, contact with, and protection by its ancestors.

But regardless of societal complexity, the division of labor awarded to the elderly has many similarities across cultures. Midwifery, entertainment, story-telling, beauty treatment, scarification, socialization, and ritual and religious specialization are often the business of the old men and women of the group. In preliterate societies, the acquisition and retention of knowledge and experience are directly related to living. Thus the old are the repositories of the wisdom accumulated and transmitted orally. This is one reason why anthropologists, in their work, must rely so heavily on aged informants. Age is often directly related to the amount of cultural knowledge accumulated. The point is illustrated by Thomas (1958) in her ethnography on the Bushmen. In this passage the author describes how the Bushmen have just caught a springbok and the anthropologists ask one of the men to dissect it in an effort to ascertain the extent of the group's knowledge of anatomy and systems of the body.

Gai agreed to tell what he knew, so the springbok was dragged to a sandy spot and a small fire was built. All the people sat around to watch as Bill opened the belly of the springbok and rolled it onto its back. He pointed to the diaphragm and asked what it was. Gai told him the name.
"What is it for?" Bill asked.
"We eat it."
"Is it for anything else?"
"We don't know. We just eat it."
. . . Gai became embarrassed . . . and Ukwane then said that he would explain instead, because he was an old man. . . . Gai could not speak of sex in front of women because it was both improper and dangerous and would weaken his power to hunt, but Ukwane was too old for hunting and besides was past the age when many of the tabus concerning sex applied to him. Old Bushmen understand everything better anyways, young Bushmen say.
Ukwane knew a great deal. He named every major part, inside and out, of the animal, even naming the major veins and arteries that lead to and from the heart. . . . "I am an old man," he would say, "and I know that the diaphragm separates the heart and lungs from the stomach," or, "I am an old Ukwane and so I know that, when the heart is gone the animal cannot live . . ." (pp. 71-72).*

In many gerontocratic societies, such as the Arunta of Australia, the old men jealously guard their knowledge instead of sharing it. They often form secret societies that they use to increase their influence by withholding knowledge. The power they wield over younger members by keeping this knowledge from all but those of whom they approve gives them the assurance of group stability. The old are deeply entrenched in the status quo and use all their authority to inhibit change of any kind through the closely regulated transmission of the accumulated tribal wisdom and ideology. Naturally, literacy and with it the provision of equal access to knowledge by younger men rapidly undermine the authority of the elders.
It is not merely elderliness and the accumulation of knowledge that seem to explain

*Thomas, E. M. 1958. The harmless people. Copyright 1958. Alfred A. Knopf, Inc.

the frequency with which one finds the aged (and the dead) in special ritual positions. Individuals who have passed a certain age often take on mystical attributes in the eyes of their group; they are the magicians and religious specialists—the shamans, witches, priests, medicine men, and sorcerers. Seemingly, they have withstood the attrition of life itself and are regarded as beyond and therefore immune to the spiritual hazards of mortality. They are almost spirits themselves and they begin to command the knowledge and influence of the dead over the living. Fear of the extremely old and the attributing to them of evil will are quite common; witches, even in Western lore, are usually old people.
The affinity of the aged for the dead and the spirit world is analyzed brilliantly by Eliade (1964). She suggests that these are the people viewed as most likely to be able to transcend time itself by returning magically to a lost paradise, a dream time that existed before men became mortals and lost touch with the gods, the dead, animals, the underworld, and the heavens. Old people bring back special knowledge of this primordial timeless condition and may share it with their people by relating and interpreting their dreams and visions. Special treatment accorded the dead is often extended to the aged who have almost reached this sacred state. Interestingly, the sacred state is shared by children as well as old people. Both categories of people are often viewed as mystical and are felt privy to the special powers of the innocent. The bond between grandparents and grandchildren among the Huichol Indians illustrates this concept of continuity between the recently born and the about-to-die. On their Sacred Peyote Hunt when these Indians symbolically and actually return to the land of their origins where the gods live (which the Ancient Ones left in becoming mortal) and when they arrive at this home of their ancestors, the old men are called and treated as little children.

CONCLUDING REMARKS

In looking over these observations for any generalizations of value to us in this culture, two points emerge as particularly relevant: First, there is no fixed or given manner of aging, or viewing or treating the aged and the dead. Our own society represents one alternative among a great variety. It is unique only in representing the extreme along a continuum, since this society is changing more rapidly than many. More important, it is unique in that there are more old people to understand and place in the social structure as usefully as possible. In actuality there are more old people among us to assimilate and accommodate, for at present it seems fair to say that the aged constitute a dislocated group—societal refugees—structurally alienated and unabsorbed. In dealing with the "problem of the aged" we are concerned with a number of equally urgent, closely related problems. Enhancing the meaning of leisure in an acquisitive society is one of these problems. It is a problem that must be solved for great numbers of people in our automated society, not merely for the aged. We must attempt to utilize the talents and experiences of the aged that are presently wasted. This situation also exists among other dispriviledged populations—women, blacks, Chicanos, rural folk, and the unskilled. When the numbers of all these groups are tallied, it may appear that our country is distributing its privileges to and accepting the services of a group so small as to constitute an elite. Broadening this base is a challenge indeed and will carry us far toward our self-conception as a culture that values humanity for its own sake in all its many forms. For idealistic as well as practical reasons, it behooves us to turn our closest attention toward these populations, and solutions achieved for the aged should be able to be generalized far beyond this particular group. The anthropological survey conducted here suggests that if there is no single desirable solution, neither is failure foreordained; it is both frightening and reassuring to conclude that anything is possible.

REFERENCES

Anderson, B. 1964. Stress and psychopathology among aged Americans. Southwestern Journal of Anthropology **20**:190-217.

Arensberg, C. M. 1937. The Irish countryman: An anthropological study. MacMillan, New York.

Aries, P. 1962. Centuries of childhood: A social history of family life. Knopf, New York.

Arnhoff, F. N., Leon, H. V., and Lorge, I. 1964. Cross-cultural acceptance of stereotypes toward aging. Journal of Social Psychology **63**:41-58.

Beattie, J. 1964. Other cultures. Free Press, New York.

Benedict, R. 1953. Continuities and discontinuities in cultural conditioning. In C. Kluckhohn and H. A. Murray (eds.). Personality in nature, society and culture. Knopf, New York, pp. 522-531.

Benedict, R. 1948. Anthropology and the abnormal. In D. G. Haring (ed.). Personal character and cultural milieu. Syracuse University Press, Syracuse, pp. 176-194.

Bengtson, V. 1967. Occupational and national differences in patterns of role activity and life-satisfaction: A cross-national pilot study. Paper presented at the 20th annual meeting of the Gerontological Society. November. St. Petersburg, Fla. (Mimeograph.)

Bohannan, P. 1951. Justice and judgment among the Tiv. Oxford University Press, London.

Bradbury, R. E. 1963. Fathers, elders and ghosts in Edo Religion. In M. Banton (ed.). Anthropological approaches to the study of religion. Praeger, New York.

Buettner-Janusch, J. 1966. Origins of man. Wiley, New York.

Campbell, J. K. 1964. Honour, family and patronage. Clarendon, Oxford.

Clark, M. 1967. The anthropology of aging, a new area for studies of culture and personality. Gerontologist **7**:55-64.

Clark, M., and Anderson, B. 1961. Culture and aging: An anthropological study of older Americans. Charles C Thomas, Springfield, Ill.

Eisenstadt, S. N. 1956. From generation to generation. Free Press, New York.

Eliade, M. 1964. Shamanism. Bollingen, New York.

Feifel, H. 1959. The meaning of death. McGraw-Hill, New York.

Forde, D. 1961. Death and succession: an analysis of Yoko Mortuary Ritual. In M. Gluckman (ed.), Essays on the ritual of social relations. Manchester University Press, Manchester, pp. 124-174.

Fortes, M. 1945. The dynamics of clanship among the Tallensi. Oxford University Press, New York.

Fortes, M. 1965. Some reflections on ancestor worship in Africa. In M. Fortes and G. Dieterien (eds.). African systems of thought. Oxford University Press, London, pp. 122-142.

Fortes, M. 1961. Pietas in ancestor worship. Journal of the Royal Anthropological Institute. p. 2.

Foster, G. 1965. Peasant society and the image of limited good. American Anthropologist **61**:293-315.

Frazer, J. G. 1922. The golden bough. MacMillan Co., New York.

Freuchen, P. 1961. Book of the Eskimos. World Press, Cleveland.

Freud, S. 1921. Totem and taboo. New Republic, New York.

Garn, S. M. 1963. Culture and the direction of human evolution. Human Biology **35**:221.

Geertz, C. 1963. Religion as a cultural system. In M. Banton (ed.). Anthropological approaches to the study of religion. Praeger, New York.

Gluckman, M. 1965. Politics, law and ritual in tribal society. Aldine Press, Chicago.

Hertz, R. 1960. Death and the right hand. The Free Press, Glencoe, Ill.

Kaplan, B. (ed.). 1961. Studying personality cross-culturally. Peterson-Row, Evanston, Ill.

Kleemeler, R. W. (ed.). 1961. Aging and leisure. Oxford University Press, New York.

Kluckhohn, F., and Strodbeck, F. 1961. Variations in value orientations. Peterson-Row, Evanston, Ill.

Kroeber, A. 1952. The nature of culture. University of Chicago Press, Chicago.

Kroeber, A. L. and Kluckhorn, C. 1963. Culture: A critical review of concepts and definitions. Vintage, New York.

Kuper, H. 1964. The Swazi: A South African kingdom. Holt, Rinehart and Winston, New York.

Langer, S. 1960. Philosophy in a new key. Harvard University Press, Cambridge.

Levi-Strauss, C. 1963. Structural anthropology. Translated by C. Jacobson and B. Schoepf. Basic Books, New York.

Lévi-Strauss, C. 1964. Tristes tropiques: An anthropological study of primitive societies in Brazil. Translated by J. Russel. Atheneum Press, New York.

Malinowski, B. 1925. Magic, science and religion and other essays. (Reissued in 1948.) Glencoe Press, Beverly Hills, California.

Roe, A. and G. Simpson (eds.). 1958. Behavior and evolution. Yale University Press, New Haven.

Simmons, L. 1960. Aging in pre-industrial societies. In Handbook of social gerontology, C. Tibbitts (ed.). University of Chicago Press, Chicago.

Tawney, R. 1926. Religion and the rise of capitalism, A historical study. Harcourt, Brace, New York.

Thomas, E. M. 1958. The harmless people. Alfred A. Knopf, Inc., New York.

Washburn, S. L., and Jay, P. C. (eds.). 1968. Perspectives in human evolution. Holt, Rinehart and Winston, New York.

Washburn, S. L. (ed.). 1961. Social life of early man. Aldine Press, Chicago.

Weber, L. 1965. Retrospect and progress. American Anthropologist **67:**623-637.

Whorf, B. L. 1964. Language, thought and reality. M.I.T. Press, Cambridge, Mass.

Wilson, M. 1951. Good company: A study of Myakyusa age-villages. Oxford University Press, London.

CHAPTER 17

An anthropological perspective on aging and women in the middle years

Molly C. Dougherty

Anthropology is noted for a holistic orientation to the study of humankind. The holistic approach, encompassing all aspects of humanness, is comprised of various domains of interest and inquiry. Here, women and aging are viewed in terms of psychosocial, cultural, and physiological (biochemical) changes. Although research requires categorization of ideas and materials, any device that separates a totality into component parts risks losing an understanding of their interrelatedness.

The importance of studying the totality of human behavior to gain a predictive science of humankind has been long recognized. When this goal is viewed in light of available research one realizes how idealistic it remains. Factors that limit research on the totality of human behavior and function include ways to:

1. Assess the influence of culture on women's lives in cross-cultural perspective
2. Separate the effect of age-related changes from the effects of generational time (culture change)
3. Identify variables that are relevant to research on women cross-culturally
4. Acquire the breadth and depth of knowledge required to undertake comprehensive and intensive inquiry
5. Develop interdisciplinary research that can address a holistic study of women.

These factors, and others discussed later, limit understanding of aging in women cross-culturally and in this culture. The credibility that research findings acquire in the scientific community and contemporary culture is important, not only to researchers and professionals, but also to all women who receive

health advice from clinicians who are influenced by research results.

The plan for this presentation is to discuss the heritage of inquiry concerning women and aging in the first section; contemporary materials on psychosocial, biomedical, and cross-cultural aspects of women and aging in the second section; and, in the final section, to examine issues in the study of women and aging.

THE HERITAGE OF INQUIRY ON WOMEN AND AGING

Cultural beliefs about women persist through generations of time. Although change occurs it is an imprecise process and beliefs of earlier historical periods continue to influence the behavior of people and the constructs on which research is based. Beliefs about women in Western cultures of earlier years affect the study of aging women. The dichotomy between men and women found in the literature on women is powerful; the roles filled by women have been reinforced by biomedical explanations credible in various periods of history. The emphasis on the childbearing and nurturing role of women reveals how women's roles are defined and reinforced by physiological regularities associated with menstruation, childbirth, and, to a limited extent, the post-childbearing years. Beliefs and behavioral patterns prevalent in the past century are useful in understanding the present status of aging and women.

Although the cultural context of the Victorian era is beyond the scope of this presentation, it should be remembered that it was a period of rapid social change kindled by the industrial revolution. Middle class Victorian women have been analyzed frequently; working class women, it appears, were not subjects of inquiry and do not appear to be victims of hysteria or other maladies that intrigue physicians and authors. Population increases are welcome during periods of expansion such as industrialization and colonialization. In the West this period initiated a redefinition of sex roles, family, and social class consciousness. Such changes provided status elevation for women based on reproduction, and fostered beliefs about distinctions between men and women.

Reproductive capacity, along with menstruation, was central to the beliefs about women and appropriate behaviors for them. It was widely believed that menstruation caused weakness and that educational pursuits caused nervousness in women. The idea that women are ill during menstruation (which constitutes one fourth of their adult lives) and that they were particularly susceptible to shocks during menstruation was widely reported in the medical literature and served to reinforce a secluded and private existence for women. In the late 19th century spokesmen for American universities agreed that higher education was destroying the reproductive capabilities of women by stressing them at a critical point in their physical development. Such beliefs are a reflection of the way scientific knowledge reinforces rather than defines the biases of an era (English and Showalter, 1970) and suggests that we have only begun to understand the effects of changes initiated by industrialization (Morantz, 1974). Physicians treated hysterics and other maladies of women that may have had their origins in social change and the roles middle class women filled.

Consistent with an emphasis on reproduction, menopause, signaling the termination of childbearing, also was seen as a major loss, and accompanying behavioral and emotional changes in middle aged women were validated by the belief system. Puberty, sexual activity, childbirth, and menopause became important in medicine. Physicians were accepted as authorities on normalcy (although they treated the sick) as well as cultural expectations concerning not only medicine, but women's place in the family and society.

It was during this period that Freud generated a theory of personality based, in large part, on his experiences with women seeking relief from stress originating in their assigned roles. Viewed historically, Freud articulated in a highly organized way cultural beliefs about normal women and men and those in acute emotional distress. The use of case studies to develop theory, and unique formulations regarding unconscious thought and motivations, secured for him a prominent place in medicine and Western thought.

If Freudian theory had become fashionable only in medicine its impact would not have been so great, but it diffused into all institutions in slightly revised and highly credible forms. Psychoanalytic theory was (and, some would hold, still is) of great importance in childrearing and education where it was employed as the rationalization for seeming differences in competencies and role paths of young men and women. The long-range impact of Freudian theory is testimony to its excellent fit to prevailing thought concerning differences between men and women. Twentieth century physicians embraced psychoanalytic theory as an explanation for the poorly understood features of women's reproductive regularities. The tendency in medicine has been to use women with physical and/or emotional symptoms as a sample for study. Studying a small, convenient sample of women and making inferences about women in general are marked in the study of menopause and menstruation where symptoms are often transitory and documentation of physiological and hormonal regularities has progressed slowly. Medical literature prior to 1970 reflects the continuities in thought and theory from the 19th century and the difficulty researchers have encountered in addressing physiologically and emotionally or socially based changes associated with aging and the menopause.

The 1930s are remembered for the introduction of hormone replacement therapy (ERT) and an interest in explaining mental illness arising in middle-aged women. The "menopausal syndrome" and "involutional melancholia" were labels associated with emotional changes surrounding the menopause. Psychiatric clinicians who treated women in the middle years drew heavily on reproductive losses to explain symptoms. Saunders (1932:267) states:

Adjustment on a frank reality basis, even in the most normal, at this period of life is that of loss, reproductive, possibly economic. . . . Neglect arising from too implicit acceptance of invalidism at the menopause may result in discouragement and lack of constructive physical or mental intervention. The involution is a period of accommodation to loss, to a waning capacity which requires revaluation of assets for the healthy as well as for the neurotic.

Failing ovarian function was seen as creating social as well as physical symptoms, but social losses were seen as more significant.

Later, organized efforts to survey the symptomatology of the menopause were undertaken. Greenhill (1946) and Stern and Prados (1946) interviewed 50 women with the "menopausal syndrome" who were referred for treatment. The frequency and intensity of symptoms were documented. Greenhill (1946:793) concludes that there is no justification for the term "menopausal syndrome" if it includes the presence of a psychiatric disorder, and suggests that it may be defined as, "a clinical state in which a combination of symptoms including amenorrhea, hot flashes, masculinization, obesity, arthritis, hypertension, and mild autonomic lability may occur in the presence of physiologic hypoovarianism." Stern and Prados (1946) report that in over half the cases emotional disturbance was not the chief complaint of the women; in cases of "menopausal depression" the causes were almost exclusively associated with marriage and reproduction. Findings based on patients reflect continuities from earlier years, but also include a consideration of ovarian changes. Into the 1960s research focused on symptoms reported by women and simultaneous life changes; relatively little was known of the hormonal and biochemical alterations surrounding the menopause. Interviews with 80 middle-aged patients (Newton and Odom, 1964) revealed menstrual irregularities, hot flashes, and depression. In the 1960s ERT, popularized by Wilson (1966), was thought to prevent hypertension, osteoporosis, skin changes, endocrine disorders, and other alterations associated with the menopause.

ERT was depicted as halting the aging process; estrogen deficits were called a "cruel trick" of nature (Wilson and Wilson, 1963), and replacement therapy was seen as a preventive treatment for conditions found in older women patients.

It is discouraging to those who pursue the study of women's health that nearly all research deals with women who are patients. An exception is Neugarten and Kraines (1965) who report on a survey of over 400 women, 13 to 64 years of age, contacted through community associations. Women's responses to questions about menstruation and menopause show that the frequency of symptoms is highest during adolescence and menopause, which are periods of psychosocial transitions and physiological changes. Interest in middle life aging and women has shifted from the conjectural psychosocial emphases of the 19th century to a focus on the relationship between psychosocial and physiological processes. In the next section, contemporary research on women and aging is addressed.

RESEARCH ON WOMEN AND MIDDLE LIFE AGING

Universal in women in normal health are alterations in hormonal production during the middle years. Role and behavioral changes are frequent during this period among Western women; cross-cultural evidence suggests that the menopause has differing effects on women's emotions and behavior in non-Western cultures. This section addresses current clinical management of the climacteric, hormonal changes and mental health, and psychosocial and cross-cultural research.

The climacteric—a medical view

There is considerable historical evidence that the age at menopause has remained relatively constant over the past 100 years; the most frequently cited age at menopause is 50 years (Diers, 1974). Menopause is customarily defined as the physiological cessation of menstruation. Age at menopause, according to Diers (1974) and Hammond (1976), is not correlated with age at menarche, parity (number of births), or prolonged anovulation (associated with use of oral contraceptives).

Married women typically reach menopause later than do single women (Diers, 1974). The climacteric, the gradual decline of gonadal function, is the focus of medical research (Hammond, 1976). The climacteric encompasses several years during which the menopause occurs and is associated with a gradual decline in ovarian function and decrease in estrogen production. Hormonal changes characteristic of the menopause begin at about 40 years of age. According to Hammond about half of all women experience menopause between 45 and 50 years of age, one fourth before age 45, and one fourth after 50 years of age. There are about 27 million women over 50 years of age in the United States with an average life expectancy of 28 years beyond the menopause (Ryan and Gibson, 1972). Age-related changes in women are becoming more important as the population of older persons and the life expectancy of women increase.

Certain physiological changes that accompany the climacteric and postmenopause are of interest to health professionals and women. These include symptoms usually associated with the climacteric (hot flashes, depression, emotional instability, lethargy, and fatigue), and others associated with the postmenopausal years (changes in vagina, urinary tract, breasts, skin, and bone). Changes in the postmenopausal years are beyond the scope of this presentation, but symptoms associated with the climacteric are discussed after a presentation of the biochemical changes occurring in the climacteric.

Biochemical changes. Basically, the categories of hormones that regulate the menstrual cycle and undergo change in the climacteric are estrogen, androgens, and gonadotropins. There is more than one form of each of these hormonal categories but for simplicity only three are discussed. In premenopausal women, estrogen levels fluctuate in relation to the development of the ovarian follicle and the corpus luteum. There is a marked decrease in circulating estrogen in postmenopausal women. The major source of estrogen in menstruating women is direct ovarian secretion, but limited amounts are converted from other hormones (androgens). In postmenopausal women most estrogens are produced by peripheral conversion of androgens (and other hormones) in the skin. A limited amount of estrogen is produced by the adrenals, but in postmenopausal women direct ovarian secretion of estrogen is minimal.

Androgens are produced by menstruating women with small fluctuations throughout the menstrual cycle. There is marked decrease in androgen production in the postmenopausal years, although some of one form of androgen continues to be secreted by the ovary.

Gonadotropins from the hypothalamus and pituitary regulate ovarian hormone production and menstruation; they are elevated in the climacteric. In menstruating women gonadotropins demonstrate a cyclic rise and fall triggering ovarian activity. The elevation of gonadotropins in the climacteric is thought to be a reaction to lessened secretion of estrogens by the ovary and an attempt to force the ovary into normal activity.

The climacteric is highly variable among women; measurable biochemical changes of the same order result in different feelings and experiences among individual women. The process by which menstruation ceases is highly variable. Occasionally, menstruation abruptly ceases; more often the menstrual flow gradually becomes more scanty and the interval between periods is increased. As ovarian activity decreases, the cycle often becomes irregular but may continue for years. Intermittent absence of ovulation may cause missed or brief periods reflecting low estrogen production while in some women uterine bleeding is prolonged and profuse and the cycles are highly irregular (intervals between menstrual periods may be 2 to 6 weeks or more); this pattern is indicative of high estrogen production (Hammond, 1976).

These changes seem to occur in all women with intact ovaries regardless of cultural or psychosocial circumstances during the middle years. Cessation of menstruation has been associated with significant psychological and social alterations, which have a negative valuation in American society. Yet, it is difficult to separate alterations caused by physiological changes and culturally imposed shifts in women's roles and their feelings about themselves. There is great variability among women in the physical experiences they report during the climacteric; likewise, the clinical management of the climacteric varies in the United States and Europe. Management is strongly influenced by the orientation of individual physicians and the request for treatment made by women in different countries.

Estrogen replacement therapy (ERT) continues to be important in the clinical management of the climacteric. Research and sophisticated biochemical analyses have modified the position supported by Wilson and Wilson (1963) in the management of the menopause and postmenopause. ERT remains popular among physicians in the United States and in Europe. When physicians prescribe ERT, the dosage of estrogen and the duration of treatment depend on their orientation to the management of the menopause. Polar positions are: the menopause is a normal physiological process and little intervention should be initiated; it is a deficiency disease with deleterious consequences that should be circumvented by therapy.

Hammond, an American physician, states that treatment of the climacteric involves education, the consideration of replacement of systemic estrogen or topical estrogen, and the use of tranquilizers. When estrogen is replaced it is usually prescribed to be taken on 21 day cycles (1.25 mg conjugated estrogen). If the uterus is intact, progestin is added during the last 5 to 7 days of therapy; it is thought to avoid hyperplasia (overgrowth) of the endometrium (the lining of the uterus). Endometrial hyperplasia is problematical for women because it requires diagnostic curettage of the uterus to rule out cancer. Hammond (1976), Goldman (1976), and others recommend that estrogen replacement be individually regulated; the smallest effective dosage should be prescribed to alleviate menopausal symptoms (hot flashes, sweating, and so forth).

The literature on ERT is replete with possible side effects of estrogen. There are several potential side effects of concern to both women and physicians. Prolonged estrogen therapy may restore endometrial growth and cause estrogen withdrawal bleeding and endometrial hyperplasia. Although further work is clearly needed, the relationship be-

tween estrogen and cancer is of concern. Certain strains of rats develop breast cancer when given large doses of estrogen, but the data have not been confirmed in women. There are higher rates of endometrial cancer among patients who have prolonged, high levels of estrogen (unopposed by progesterone). Some patients, according to the literature, with preexisting endometrial and breast cancers have increased growth rates if estrogens are administered, and these patients are improved by estrogen deprivation. Both synthetic and naturally occurring estrogens have been incriminated in the development of thromboembolic disease (Hammond, 1976: 419).

In Europe where clinical experience treating the climacteric is more widespread, differing views hold favor. Lauritzen (1976), a German physician, suggests that the physician should correct nature where it is thought to fail, but that long-term estrogen treatment can be recommended only it it bears no appreciable risk and if the benefit is much greater than any possible risk. He states (1976:394),

> The practice and experience of more than 30 years post menopausal estrogen therapy on a large scale involving about two million women years published in the literature has shown, in my opinion, that even long term cyclical therapy with natural estrogen in the usual doses causes virtually no significant increase in unwanted severe side effects and has not produced a noticeable increase of carcinoma and thromboembolism so far.*

In the Federal Republic of Germany between 10% and 20% of all climacteric women receive estrogen replacement.

In England, menopause clinics have been established primarily in academic settings. They are partly financed by the National Health Service and are partly supported by drug companies. Beard (1976) reports that a woman whose menopausal symptoms are successfully treated by estrogens should be continued on ERT if she wishes; a woman over 40 years of age who is taking oral contraceptives successfully should continue on oral contraceptives until the age of 55 years

---

*From Lauritzen, C. 1976. A European viewpoint. In S. Campbell (ed.).

and then change to natural estrogens providing there are no medical contraindications. Beard states that improving the general health and welfare of aging women may be more beneficial than long-term ERT. Others hold that the menopausal syndrome has a limted course of 2 or 3 years and that ERT need not be long term (Yen, 1977).

The administration of long-term ERT is controversial in the United States and Europe. Many investigators and clinicians question whether the benefits (alleviation of menopausal symptoms and possible protection against osteoporosis) are outweighed by the risk (not yet quantified) of coronary artery disease, thromboembolism, and malignant disease. Women and health professionals are aware of the controversy surrounding ERT. Well-informed women weigh the discomfort physical symptoms cause them, and discuss the effectiveness of therapy with their physicians.

The use of tranquilizers in the climacteric is as complex as ERT. The long-range consequences of such therapy is open to question, and the long-range effect of mood-altering drugs on the coping ability of women is unknown. Informed women approach the pharmacological regulation of the climacteric with caution and maintain sensitivity to the alterations occurring within their bodies. Consumers of health care are increasingly aware of the influence of drug companies on the therapy that is available, and of the influence that tradition and medical practice has on their health.

Symptoms. Research on the menopause focuses on the symptoms reported by women in the middle years. These include insomnia, nervousness, depression, dizziness, weakness, joint pain, headaches, and palpitations (Coope, 1976). Vasomotor symptoms (hot flashes or flushes and sweating) are directly related to decreased estrogen levels (Yen, 1977; Ryan and Gibson, 1972), and along with vaginal dryness are the only symptoms that are clearly alleviated with estrogen replacement (Beard, 1976). The others are less definite and show no clear relationship to hormonal changes characteristic of the climacteric. Population surveys reveal the symptoms women report (Jaszmann, et al., 1969; McKinlay and Jeffreys, 1974), but no clear relationship to the hormonal changes of the climacteric is demonstrated in studies of women in normal health. The incidence of depression and other emotional shifts in middle-aged women has prompted several investigations on psychiatric status and hormonal changes. Caution is indicated in the interpretation of the results because of the sampling methods and questionable validity of inferences to women generally.

Many clinicians agree that it is difficult to separate symptoms of the menopause from symptoms of mental illness. Abe et al. (1975) have attempted to separate these by assessing symptomatology, then administering estrogen and reassessing to ascertain whether symptoms are emotional or hormonal in origin. While some physicians report that emotional states associated with the menopause occur and may be successfully treated with tranquilizers (Bodner and Catterill, 1972), others report no significant increase in affective disorders surrounding the menopause (Winokur, 1973). Research by Altman et al. (1975) suggests that depression in the post menopause is a result of reduced hormonal levels (luteinizing hormone).

The frequency and intensity of emotional disequilibria and menopause symptomatology in normal populations are addressed in survey research. Ballinger (1975; 1976) reports on a postal survey of over 500 women in which psychiatric morbidity and menopause experiences are elicited. She reports psychiatric morbidity in 40% of the menopausal women while other age categories in the middle years have less than 30% psychiatric morbidity as measured by a paper-and-pencil instrument designed for psychiatric cases. Vasomotor symptoms are more frequently cited as significantly increased in the menopause among women who do not have psychiatric disorders, but those with psychiatric disturbance more often report vasomotor symptoms before, during, and after the menopause. It is suggested that women with evidence of emotional disturbance are less tolerant of vasomotor symptoms and more likely to seek treatment than those who do not have psychiatric disorders. Kerr (1976) reports that women with mood changes in middle age undergoing psychiatric therapy respond well to high doses of estrogen and progestin. The difficulty in separating psychosocial and physiological aspects of women's experiences has led to estrogen replacement therapy trials in double blind* cross-over† studies. Campbell (1976) and Coope (1976) report that the placebo effect of estrogen replacement is high. In addition, estrogen, which is known to control hot flushes, has a domino effect and tends to alleviate other symptoms when the vasomotor symptoms are controlled.

Osofsky and Seidenberg (1970), in reviewing the medical literature on menopausal depression, state that psychological and physiological components of the menopause have been confused; estrogen is prescribed to treat depression, and psychotherapy is employed to suppress symptoms having a physiological base. They suggest that the etiology of problems is to be found in the social expectation of submissiveness and urge that reproduction and childrearing be choices that do not exclude other avenues of fulfillment for women. Although medicine has demonstrated a longer interest in aging in the middle years than other disciplines, behavioral scientists' contributions are important to a holistic understanding of aging.

PSYCHOSOCIAL AND CULTURAL ASPECTS

In many disciplines research on women is a relatively recent development. The emphasis is shifting away from women as childbearers and nurturing figures and toward women as they live, work, and relate to others. The growing body of literature from the behavioral sciences offers revised assessments of the aging process.

Traditionally, it has been assumed that personality development occurs primarily during the years of physical development and that adult personality is relatively unchanging. Popular literature (Sheehy, 1974) addresses changes in the adult life cycle; the

*Double blind: Neither the subjects nor their physician knows during which treatment period the drug or placebo is administered (an uninvolved third party provides the medication).
†Cross-over: The subjects are divided into two groups. One half receives one treatment for the first half of the study and the other half receives a second treatment. In the second half of the study the treatments are reversed.

professional literature also suggests a reorientation.

Neugarten (1975) in discussing personality in aging adults states that the characteristics usually associated with maleness and femaleness undergo change in middle and later years. Women become more responsive toward, and less guilty about, their aggressiveness and egocentric impulses, while men become more receptive to their affiliative, nurturant, and sensual components. These findings provide an interesting comparison with the finding that postmenopausal women in non-Western cultures fill roles not permitted women of childbearing age (healer, midwife) and often behave in ways usually reserved for men. Flint (1975), who has studied nearly 500 women in India, found that very few women had any problems with the menopause other than changes in menstruation. She has found no depression, dizziness, or incapacitations. Flint proposes that the explanation may be that women who reach the menopause are permitted significant role change. They may be unveiled, unsecluded, and partake of men's talking and drinking home brew. Women are no longer considered contaminative, a significant change from their menstruating and childbearing years. Many non-Western cultures clearly define the distinctions between male and female by taboos and social sanctions; postmenopausal women are often relieved of obligations to observe them. In the West, where the distinctions are more implicit, the postmenopausal role is widely associated with a lower status and considerable emotional and physical distress. Additionally, menopause is defined medically and is often a medically managed process. Women often take the opinion of their physicians, or their interpretation of physicians' opinions, to be a behavioral prescription for them. A long tradition of respect for physicians encourages an integration of medical and popular belief about aging in women and it is difficult to separate the two.

A study of Caucasian and Japanese women in Hawaii (Goodman et al., 1977) suggests that the tradition of medical treatment among Caucasian women is related to differences in menopausal experiences of women from the two cultural backgrounds. Caucasian women exceed Japanese women in frequency of surgery for female disorders and medication before and after menopause. These authors doubt that the variation represents a physiological difference. Cross-cultural differences in menopausal experiences have yet to be fully explored, but it appears that social class is a significant variable in beliefs and experiences in the middle years among American women. Neugarten (1973) in a study with 100 American middle class women reports that the women show relatively little concern with the menopause as a major life event. Only 4 of 100 mentioned the menopause, but more than half considered their major concern to be widowhood, getting older, fear of cancer, or children leaving home. Middle class women may be influenced by the orientation that menopause is a natural event, one best left alone unless it is especially bothersome.

The incidence and frequency of menopausal symptoms in the general population are reported in several studies. A national health survey (1960–1962) reports that 10% of women have severe menopausal symptoms, 16% are completely free of any symptomatology, and about 75% experience some disturbance or discomfort, but few seek medical treatment (MacMahon and Worcester, 1966). A study conducted in Hawaii indicates that 28% of Caucasian women and 24% of Japanese women report menopausal symptoms such as hot flashes and sweats (Goodman et al., 1977); about 15% of menopausal women report no symptoms. Crawford and Hooper (1973) discuss a sample of women in England; 25% report no menopausal symptoms, 38% only physiological conditions, and 13% report both types of symptoms. Hammond (1976) states that 25% of women will consult physicians because of menopausal symptoms, and that 5% to 10% will have symptoms that are improved with estrogen replacement therapy. Surveys of women in normal health consistently indicate that the menopausal experience is highly variable, and that most women, even in the West, are relatively unaffected by the experience.

It is well known that women have a longer life expectancy than men. Studies of aging demonstrate that women have greater social adaptability in the aging process than men (Palmore, 1974). Adaptability may result from the transitions necessitated by women's roles as childbearers, spouses, and employees and the psychological support for children with changing developmental needs. Descriptions of personality development in adulthood for men and women offer the intriguing possibility that personality changes, such as introspection, have survival value, and have different meanings for individuals of various ages.

Contemporary research on middle life aging is influenced by cultural expectations of women and their response to such expectations. Researchers are also influenced by cultural norms and design projects that reinforce traditional views of women. Problems in and the potential for research on women and aging are discussed in the next section.

ISSUES IN RESEARCH ON WOMEN AND AGING

A review of the research literature on women and aging leaves the reader with the overwhelming impression that a holistic understanding of the aging process is lacking. Although materials on the subject are plentiful, there are few studies in which the cautious reader can place confidence. When the heritage of inquiry about women is examined, it is clear that women have been considered to be more heavily influenced by emotion than have men. The literature on conditions experienced only by women is examined by Lennane and Lennane (1973), who state that belief in psychogenesis is remarkably persistent even after physiological causation for a condition is established. They suggest that conditions affecting only women are influenced by illogical beliefs that persist, in part, because specialists and authors are predominantly men. Although they hesitate to postulate sexual prejudice, they do indicate that there is a need for the application of objective scientific methods to the study of exclusively female conditions.

The persistence of psychogenesis as an explanation is partly explained by the shared belief system of scientific communities. Specialists in scientific fields share a common orientation, which is resistant to change. Usually change occurs when more powerful and attractive alternatives are proved to be of equal or greater value. The study of aging and women may be at such a juncture. Traditional models that assume that women are excessively influenced by emotion and are primarily nurturant are losing appeal among social and medical scientists. Future research will encompass greater breadth in conceptualizations about women and their roles. Whether revised major shifts in research strategies emerge remains to be seen.

There is a call for a reexamination of assumptions about women. Beeson (1975) points out that research on aging has been far more sensitive to the transitions of men than to any aspect of aging in women, and that there is little basis for the parity assumed between retirement for men and widowhood for women. The lack of studies on women in retirement, when a significant portion of women do retire from the work force, is questionable, especially because the rationale for equating retirement and widowhood is sex biased. Research that addresses successful aging in women often interprets women's successes as being the result of the pervasive domestic role women fill during adulthood, and how this role is suited to retirement and the restricted environment of advanced years. It is becoming more clear that the economic limitations experienced by widowed and aged women affect changes in social behavior, i.e., restricted social contact and health status. There is a need for research methods that assess age-related changes and that do not interpret changes away from adjustment in the early and middle adult years as dysfunctional.

Much research, while producing valuable information, is not designed to distinguish results arising from the influence of culture on the subjects from those reflecting a universal aging process. It is difficult to separate such influences by studying only one culture. Socialization and social control may be the most powerful influences on what happens to women at all ages, but these factors and others cannot be evaluated until theoretical models based in the reality of women's experiences cross-culturally form the basis of research.

Methodologies to delineate the aging process and hold constant the influence of culture are needed. Just as the 19th century hysterical woman has disappeared, so may symptoms associated with the menopause. McKinley and McKinley (1973) suggest that menopausal symptomatology may be only an organized way for physicians to view a problem rather than a distinguishable set of symptoms surrounding this period of life. Assessing the effects of socialization and physical development within women may be accomplished by cross-cultural research, but may be complicated by the limited roles available to premenopausal women and shorter life spans in many cultures. Role changes in the postmenopausal years in cross-cultural perspective provide a valuable point of comparison for the study of aging.

Longitudinal studies in which variables are relevant over many years and based on physiological processes are recommended. Minimally, physiological, psychosocial, and nutritional data should be obtained from selected cultural settings. It is important that research be conducted on broad populations, and include women in normal health and those who deviate from it. Such research will be enhanced by a better understanding of personality development in adulthood. It is encouraging that adult development is emerging at a time when a reorientation to theory about women is occurring. There is a need for descriptive studies of the aging experience and to define variables relevant to women's experiences. Variables chosen for their relevance for cross-cultural comparison will further a holistic understanding of aging. At this time we clearly lack descriptive data to validate what aging means to women, and on which to build relevant research. Descriptive research may bring to light mechanisms of successful aging in women and the means by which women adjust to age-related changes in role, family, and physiology.

REFERENCES

Abe, T., and others. 1975. A new method for the screening of unidentified complaints syndrome in pre-, mid- and post-menopausal women. Tohoku Journal of Experimental Medicine 116:81-86.

Altman, N., and others. 1975. Reduced plasma LH concentration in post-menopausal depressed women. Psychosomatic Medicine 37:214-216.

Ballinger, C. B. 1975. Psychiatric morbidity and the menopause; screening of general population sample. British Medical Journal 3:344-346.

Ballinger, C. B. 1976. Psychiatric aspects of the menopause. In S. Campbell (ed.). The management of the menopause and post-menopausal years. University Park Press, Baltimore.

Beard, R. J. 1976. An English viewpoint. In S. Campbell (ed.). The management of the menopause and post-menopausal years. University Park Press, Baltimore.

Beeson, D. 1975. Women in studies of aging: a critique and suggestion. Social Problems 23:52-59.

Bodnar, S., and Catterill, T. B. 1972. Amitriptyline in emotional states associated with the climacteric. Psychosomatics 13:117-119.

Campbell, S. 1976. Double blind psychometric studies on the effects of natural estrogens on post-menopausal women. In S. Campbell (ed.). The management of menopause and post-menopausal years. University Park Press, Baltimore.

Coope, J. 1976. Double blind cross-over study of estrogen replacement. In S. Campbell (ed.). The management of the menopause and post-menopausal years. University Park Press, Baltimore.

Crawford, M. P., and Hooper, D. 1973. Menopause, aging and family. Social Science and Medicine 7: 469-482.

Diers, C. J. 1974. Historical trends in the age at menarche and menopause. Psychiatric Reports 34:931-937.

Flint, M. 1975. The menopause: Reward or punishment? Psychosomatics 16:161-163.

Goldman, L. 1976. A dissident viewpoint. In S. Campbell (ed.). The management of the menopause and post-menopausal years. University Park Press, Baltimore.

Goodman, M. J., and others. 1977. Patterns of menopause of study of certain medical and physiological variables among Caucasian and Japanese women living in Hawaii. Journal of Gerontology 32:291-298.

Greenblatt, R. B., and Bruneteau, D. W. 1974. Menopausal headaches—psychogenic or metabolic? Journal of the American Geriatric Society 22:186-190.

Greenhill, M. H. 1946. A psychosomatic evaluation of psychiatric and endocrinological factors in the menopause. Southern Medical Journal 39:786-793.

Hammond, C. B. 1976. Menopause—an American view. In S. Campbell (ed.). The management of the menopause and post-menopausal years. University Park Press, Baltimore.

Jaszmann, L., and others. 1969. The perimenopausal symptoms: The statistical analysis of a survey. Med. Gynaec. Sociol. 4:268-277.

Kerr, D. 1976. Psychological changes following hormonal therapy. In S. Campbell (ed.). The management of the menopause and post-menopausal years. University Park Press, Baltimore.

Lauritzen, C. 1976. A European viewpoint. In S. Campbell (ed.). The management of the menopause and post-menopausal years. University Park Press, Baltimore.

Lennane, K. J., and Lennane, R. J. 1973. Alleged psychogenic disorders in women—a possible manifestation of sexual prejudice. New England Journal of Medicine 287:288-292.

MacMahon, B., and Worcester, J. 1966. Age at menopause, United States—1960-1962. U.S. Government Printing Office, Washington, D.C.

McKinlay, S. M., and McKinlay, J. B. 1973. Selected studies of the menopause. Journal of Biosocial Science 5:533-555.

McKinlay, S. M., and Jeffreys, M. 1974. The menopausal syndrome. British Journal of Prevention and Social Medicine 28:108-115.

Morantz, R. 1974. The lady and her physician. In M. S. Hartman and L. Banner (eds.). Clio's consciousness raised, Harper and Row, New York.

Neugarten, B. L. 1973. A new look at menopause. In The female experience. From the editors of Psychology Today, Communication Research Machines, Del Mar, California.

Neugarten, B. L. 1975. Personality and the aging process. In F. Rebelsky (ed.). Life the continuous process. Knopf, New York.

Neugarten, B. L., and Kraines, R. J. 1965. "Menopausal symptoms" in women of various ages. Psychosomatic Medicine 21:266-273.

Newton, M., and Odom, P. L. 1964. The menopause and its symptoms. Southern Medical Journal 51: 1309-1312.

Osofsky, H. J., and Seidenberg, R. 1970. Is female menopausal depression inevitable? Obstetrics and Gynecology 36:611-615.

Palmore, E. (ed.). 1974. Normal aging. II. Duke University Press, Durham, N.C.

Ryan, K. J., and Gibson, D. C. 1972. Menopause and aging. U.S. Department of Health, Education, and Welfare, Bethesda, Md.

Saunders, E. B. 1932. Mental reactions associated with the menopause. Southern Medical Journal 25:266-270.

Sheehy, G. 1974. Passages: Predictable crises of adult life. E. P. Dutton, New York.

Showalter, E., and English, D. 1970. Victorian women and menstruation. Victorian Studies 14:83-89.

Stern, K., and Prados, M. 1946. Personality studies in menopausal women. American Journal of Psychiatry 103:358-368.

Wilson, R. A. 1966. Feminine forever. M. Evans and Co., New York.

Wilson, R. A., and Wilson, T. A. 1963. The fate of the nontreated postmenopausal woman: A plea for the maintenance of adequate estrogen from puberty to the grave. Journal of the American Geriatric Society 11:347-362.

Winokur, G. 1973. Depression in the menopause. American Journal of Psychiatry 130:92-93.

Yen, S. S. C. 1977. The biology of menopause. Journal of Reproductive Medicine 18:281-296.

CHAPTER 18

All in the family: the older person in context

William L. Roberts

THE FAMILY BEGINS

The magic words, "I now pronounce you man and wife," have been society's method for giving sanction to the start of a new family. In civil and church ceremonies throughout the Western world, those words are passwords to the larger society—the society of the marrieds. Every tribe in the world provides for a rite of passage to that time when individuals, coming from families, are given approval by the larger society to begin their own families. The man and woman, often young in years, now have multiple roles. They are a part of their own family of orientation, and they are husband and wife prepared to begin the family of procreation.

Marriage may accentuate the development of multiple roles. An individual may be at one time a daughter or a son, a wife or a husband, and a mother or a father. Most people are also members of a larger group, made up of grandparents, uncles and aunts, and cousins, known as the extended family. These form the complex network of kin relationships that parallel both the family of procreation and the family of orientation, usually through the sibling relationship or the marital bond uniting two separate families of orientation.

This chapter is about people in their later years of life and the ways in which they have moved through the family life cycle. It will highlight some of the stages in the life cycle, and will show how family relationships change over time. These relationships have elements that are both positive and negative. Many older persons do not have living families. They have only memories of family. Unmarried or without progeny, or from small families themselves, they are alone. Memo-ries of their families may be accurate and real, or rearranged and distorted in such a way as to best protect the ego of the older individual.

Atchley (1972:272) has provided a listing of the stages of the family life cycle as follows:

Marriage
Birth of first child
Birth of last child
Last child starts to school
First child marries or leaves home
Last child marries or leaves home
Birth of first grandchild
Birth of first great-grandchild
Death of first spouse
Death of second spouse

This classification is sufficiently universal to aid in understanding movement through the life cycle of most people.

Most cultures take special pride in viewing the continuity of the family. The geneological record has deep religious significance for some groups, ethnic significance for others, and pride and curiosity for still others. Some cultures traditionally have living arrangements in which members of the family live together as a unit. Families in India, Old China, and other Asian countries are often comprised of the father and his growing family. After the sons are grown, and after the father has died, the younger sons separate to start their own households and the oldest son becomes the head. The continuity of several family branches is thus assured.

Even in our mobile Western society continuity remains important; however, some authorities see a lessening of close family ties. Bronfenbrenner (1977) has written that there has been a decline in the number of

177

grandmothers, uncles, or unmarried sisters in homes. Nearly 10% of all homes had 3 or 4 adults in 1950 and now only 5% do. The change is even more considerable when compared to 50 years ago. As an example, "In the 1920's half the households in Massachusetts included at least one adult besides the parents; today the figure is four percent" (Bronfenbrenner, 1977:8).

Although there have been a few major and several minor changes in family structure in the past 50 years, Rossi (1972) concludes that the overwhelming majority of Americans seek and contract marriages, desire and have children, and live in independent households of their own. A marriage pattern stressing individual gratification may help explain the high divorce rate. This view of the modern family may not be as "modern" as has been believed. Rosenmayr (1977) cites research on families in rural communities in Austria in the 17th century that indicates that there was an absence of joint living of two married generations in one family-household in several rural communities. Thus the need for privacy and intimacy of the family unit has been evident many years.

The debate about the stability of the American family will continue, and if recent projections are accurate, the number of older persons in our society also will continue to increase. With improved health conditions in most countries, we are witnessing a worldwide increase in the older population.

In 1975 one in every 10 persons in the United States was over 65 years of age, a total of 22.4 million persons. The percentage of the population over 65 years of age was 4.1% in 1900 and 10.5% in 1975, a sevenfold increase (from 3 million to 22 million). If present death rates continue, the older population is expected to increase 40% to 31 million persons by the year 2000.

A recent Department of Health, Education and Welfare (1976) information release reports that of the population aged 65 years and over, slightly fewer than 5% live in institutions. Eighty-three percent (7.4 million) of all men and 50% (7.3 million) of all women live in family settings. The number of women and men in this age group in each of these categories is essentially equal, but the number of women who survive to older ages is much higher. Most older men (70%) are married. Siegal (1972) reports that there is an increase in the proportion of elderly men and women who maintain their own households. Nearly 96% of persons aged 65 years and over are in this category. The majority of older women (53%) are widows. There are more than 5 times as many widows as widowers. Older persons are interested in marriage as a life-style. Eighty-five percent of the brides and 81% of the grooms aged 65 years and over are involved in remarriages. Obviously, the continuation of the family name through one's heirs is not uppermost in the minds of these older persons. Companionship is a significant value for persons in this age group. Having a spouse is the most socially acceptable means of fulfilling that need.

FUNCTION OF THE FAMILY

The family is a social institution that exists as a reality in the interaction of its members rather than in the formalities of the laws that have been made about it. Those functions change over time. The economic function is apparent in contemporary rural societies; the affective and socializing functions in urban and rural cultures are also apparent; the procreative and sexual functions are universally accepted. But family life-styles change and adapt to even broader changes in society. This is evidence of our heterogeneity and societal resilience.

Sussman (1977:5-6) provides a useful set of basic tasks for the family:

1. . . . looking after one's own or another person's physical needs: those associated with activities of daily living such as eating, dressing, and toileting; and those outside the home, school, shopping and visiting.
2. . . . What are the best ways to be a parent? . . . What is the best way to help an aged parent who has been independent all his life and now needs assistance? . . . What criteria should one employ in selecting a mate where remarriage is involved?
3. [Dealing with] infrequent events for which one cannot justify the expenditure of time, energy, or money in preparing to handle . . . such as car accidents, robberies, floods, fires or earthquakes.*

As previously stated, most families begin with a marriage ceremony. What are some

*From Shanas, E., and Sussman, M. B. (eds.). 1977. Family, bureaucracy, and the elderly. Copyright 1977 by Duke University Press.

of the characteristics of people who are married in the United States? Glick (1977) provides us with a review of vital information regarding these characteristics. The median age of women at first marriage in the 1970s is 21.2 years. Their grandmothers, if they married in 1920, married at approximately the same age. Their grandfathers would have been approximately 2 years older than their wives. In 1974, my wife and I (Roberts and Roberts, 1974) studied 50 couples married between 1910 and 1923. In the sample we found that husbands averaged 2½ years older than their wives. Glick (1977) shows that in the 1970s the median age of the wife at the birth of her first child is 22.7 years. This is near the 80-year average for the age of the mother when her first child is born. If trends continue, couples married for the first time in the 1970s will probably have their last child by the time the mother is 29.6 years of age. This age is the youngest for mothers at their last child's birth for the period covered by Glick's review.

The challenges of parenthood and, for many, its accompanying pleasures, require time and attention of parents from their early 20s until their mid to late 40s. The sole responsibility of parents (and other family members) for infants gives way to the sharing of children with the community as they begin school. Children pass through the latency period and into the period of adolescence with its beginning search for independence and allegiance to the peer group. The search continues as they separate from the family for employment, college, or travel. Finally, they marry and begin the cycle again to form another new family.

The period in the family life cycle known by sociologists as "the empty nest" begins with the launching of children. It rarely occurs without strong conflicting emotions. For the mothers there is a release from heavy household chores and the demands of constant attention to the needs of the children. The opportunities for creative activity, employment, or volunteer work are enhanced for mothers who remain unemployed during the child-rearing years. Fathers may feel a release from the financial responsibilities that increase as the children grow older. The following quotes from a National Council on Aging (1975:4) survey demonstrate some typical responses of parents at this time of life:

You no longer have to struggle with a large house or worry about fixing big meals for the whole family, or big washes or lots of housework. It's a more relaxing time. . . . All my twelve kids are grown up and away from home. . . . No teenagers! I am enjoying myself. . . .

The loss of children imposes unfamiliar stresses on the married partners as well. Although neither parent loses his or her status as parent, role changes occur. The stress is magnified when there has been total absorption in the task of parenting to the exclusion of wider interests. This stress comes at a time when physiological and psychological changes occur for both women and men. Mid-life is a crisis time in the family life cycle.

RETIREMENT

The majority of couples survive the empty nest, but they will face other crises, of which retirement is one. Values that affect retirement are set early in life when attitudes toward work and play, responsible and irresponsible behavior are learned. These attitudes stay with individuals throughout life unless conscious attempts are made to change them. Commitment to the work ethic often supersedes commitment to relationships. The loss of the work role and the decrease in income require adjustments for which individuals and their partners are often ill-prepared.

The pattern of the husband-wife relationship determines what involvement the spouse plays in retirement planning. Kerckhoff (1966) measured attitudes toward retirement, preplanning for retirement, current activities, and a number of other variables. He found the experience of retirement differed depending on levels of preretirement occupation of the husband. Upper level (professional and managerial) couples do not welcome retirement, but their experience is comparatively favorable and their reaction to the experience is most often positive. Middle level couples (white-collar and skilled) welcome retirement and seem to have a relatively good experience. Lower level (semiskilled, unskilled, and service) couples are more passive in anticipation of retirement; most do not find the experience pleasant. They tend to respond more negatively than others to the retirement experience.

It is important to realize that personality,

life-style, health, and mobility are other factors that affect retirement (Kerckhoff, 1966). Age at retirement and mandatory versus voluntary retirement are controversial topics. Decisions about these issues affect individuals and families. Consequences are reflected in the national economy, in health planning, in transportation, and in housing; the entire social fabric is affected.

Another crisis for older couples is the death of a spouse. Death is the one inevitable fact of every human existence. Persons may go through life and never marry, and therefore not begin families; persons may have outside wealth and never be employed; but all will die. The majority will marry and one partner will normally precede another in death. For most individuals there is a fear of the circumstances of dying rather than a fear of death itself. In my work I find most older people unafraid because of their years of preparation for death. Fear of death is most typically a youthful phenomenon.

SINGLEHOOD

Although the percentage of persons who marry is higher in America than in any other country, it cannot be assumed that all persons will marry. Some people will not marry because they choose not to. Others who wish to marry may not find a mate. There are two categories of singles: those never married and those widowed or divorced. According to the U.S. Census Bureau, in 1975, 52.2% of women 65 years and over were widows and only 13.6% of the men aged 65 and over were widowers. Fewer than 3% of the older men and women are divorced. Of those never married, 4.7% are men and 5.8% are women.

Widowhood is a difficult time for both men and women. Men are less prepared culturally for widowhood than women and consequently may exhibit more problem behavior following the loss of a spouse. In the United States, suicide and alcoholism are more common for widowers than for widows.

STEREOTYPES OF AGING

There are strong psychological reasons for the maintenance of stereotypes in society. We create myths to permit ourselves the notion of superiority in intellect, physical and sexual prowess, good looks, or youthfulness. Butler (1974:529) notes that:

Those who think of old people as boobies, crones, witches, old biddies, old fogies, pains-in-the-neck, out-to-pasture, boring, garrulous, unproductive and worthless, have accepted the stereotypes of aging, including the extreme mistake of believing that substantial numbers of old people are in or belong in institutions.

But where do these stereotypes originate? Atkin (1976) reports on work by Arnoff who reviewed archival videotape evidence focusing on network television drama from 3 weeks in 1969, 1970, and 1971. Of 2,741 characters, 5% were considered elderly. The sexes were equally represented. Compared with younger age groups, elderly men are more likely to be "bad guys" and less likely to be "good guys." Elderly females are more frequently failures than successes, while other age groups tend to be predominantly successful.

The stereotypes we form in contemporary society derive from countless types of sensory inputs. Although television productions are viewed by groups with special interests to screen for negative portrayals, the general public forms many of its ideas unaware of the effect of cumulative subtle distortions.

Songs, new and old, reflect views of their composers. A recent song, "Old Folks," by Jacques Brel (1968) contains many negative images of old age. So does one ("Old Black Joe") of the songs that follow; the other song, "Put On Your Old Grey Bonnet," gives a more positive view.

Gone are the days, when my heart was young and
   gay,
Gone are my friends from the cotton fields away.

Gone from this earth, to a better land I know.
I hear those gentle voices calling,
"Old Black Joe."

I'm comin', I'm comin'
For my head is bendin' low.
I hear those gentle voices calling,
"Old Black Joe."

Put on your old grey bonnet,
With the blue ribbons on it
While I hitch old Dobbin to the shay.
And through the fields of clover,
We'll drive on to Dover,
On our golden wedding day.

Negative attitudes that are held by society toward older people are confirmed by Lucy in the cartoon by Charles Schulz (Short, 1965:14).

It would be naive to assume that all of our ideas of aging grow out of radio, television, comic strips, or popular songs. Most of us have had experiences with older people that influence our thinking. Older persons unconsciously support some negative stereotypes of aging. They are socialized throughout life to behave in the way it is believed old people are supposed to behave. Artificial separations are maintained in order to isolate older persons from meaningful contact with the rest of the culture.

The National Council on Aging (1975) completed a comprehensive study of attitudes toward aging in the United States. Household interviews were conducted with 4,254 persons who represented a cross-section of the American public 18 years of age and over. Additionally, representative samples from specific age groups, for example, those over age 65, were studied. When asked what are the best years of a person's life, 2% of the public under 65 years of age responded that the 60s are, and fewer than 0.5% believed that the 70s are. Among those who had reached the later years themselves, 8% considered the 60s and 70s the optimal years. Both young and old agreed that the best thing about being aged 65 and over is having more leisure. In terms of how they spent their time, the public at large were far more likely to credit most people over 65 years of age with spending their time at passive, sedentary activities than the older public said they did.

If you have had opportunities to question older people about their attitudes, you have learned as my wife and I did that older persons believe some of the myths about other older people, but not about themselves. Many do not consider themselves old. Some reject other older people. One 84-year-old acquaintance recently told me that she didn't like doing the things most older people do.

The stereotypes described above are of older persons as individuals. What are some common stereotypes of older families? Petranek (1975) reports on couples aged 45 to 64 whose children had left home. Check your own reactions to the following statements. Petranek's (1975) subjects saw each of them as incorrect.

1. The postparental period is a negative phase of life.
2. The couple drifts apart.
3. The postparental period suddenly happens.
4. Menopause happens and the sex drive disappears.
5. There is a loss of health and physical strength.
6. Postparental women seek jobs and involvement in community affairs.
7. Housewives go crazy staying at home.

THE ELDERLY AND THEIR FAMILIES IN OTHER COUNTRIES

Developments in transportation and communication have made it possible for social scientists to explore customs of parent-child interaction in all countries of the world. Some results of these investigations will be reported here.

Shanas (1974) provides data on self-reports of older persons' physical capacity in Denmark, Britain, the United States, Poland, Yugoslavia, and Israel. She reports that there are marked similarities among the aged in these countries. There are 2% to 4% of the elderly population who are bedfast in institutions. More than three fourths of the aged population are ambulatory.

Kamerman (1976) provides somewhat different information than Shanas. Countries compared are Israel, Yugoslavia, Canada, Poland, United Kingdom, France, West Germany, and the United States. The study dealt with social service systems, which varied

PEANUTS®   By Charles M. Schulz

from country to country on the basis of custom and social legislation. Historically, the family is considered to be the primary support of elderly parents, and adult children are legally responsible for their maintenance. Filial responsibility continues to be the law in Yugoslavia but is no longer mandated in most industrialized countries. Policies adopted by governments have strong impact on practice. For example, the British Ministry of Health has a policy that services for the elderly should be designed to help older people remain in their home for as long as possible. It is the belief in Britain, and in most other countries, that older people live longer and more happily when they can remain in their own homes. It is also known that home care services can be provided at less cost than institutional care.

In England a system is designed to monitor the health needs of patients over time by keeping potential long-stay patients in the community with their family supports. Families are able to cope more successfully with their aged relative if they can have a periodic respite from the heavy demands of 24-hour care (Austin, 1976).

Little (1976) describes a study in Samoa, in which she asked elderly subjects who takes care of them when they are sick. Of 64 respondents, 47 indicated a member of the immediate family living in the same village or nearby. The categories "spouse and children" and "daughter" accounted for 22 and 11 responses respectively. There is reluctance to go outside the family. Two respondents indicated they would call on relatives in another village. There is reaction against going to an old age home. In Samoa, the traditional view is that the family takes care of its old people who prefer to stay in their children's hands. The attitude is that if you are sent to an old folks home, others might believe your children do not love you or want you. However, there might be mitigating circumstances, for example, if a family does not have enough help, or if people want to live alone.

Palmore (1975) reports that Japan is an exception to the general rule that modernization and industrialization cause a sharp decline in status and integration of the aged, as seen in many countries. He reports that most Japanese parents live with their children and perform essential tasks in the household. The majority of men over 65 years of age continue to be in the labor force. Clubs and neighborly visits aid older people in their integration into their communities. Palmore also reports that the elders' high status is reflected in many private and public practices that give precedence to older persons. In spite of the change seen in many modern societies, the traditional respect for the aged in Japan demonstrates that high levels of status and integration for older citizens can be maintained.

Rosenmayr (1977) provides data about joint living of the elderly and their children in Austria. He reports that of the agricultural households in Federal State Lower Austria, 26% are three-generational. In urban areas the three-generation households include complete couples (both married parents and grandparents) in 16% of all cases. However, in 34% of farmers' three-generation households both generations are complete. Economic reasons and maintenance of a rational division of labor are seen as reasons for the maintenance of the three-generation household.

SOME AMERICAN ETHNIC PATTERNS

The American Indian is the subject of numerous studies and reports. Wisdom is associated with age and leadership is traditionally in the hands of the elderly. There continues to be conflict in many Indian tribes about changes in life patterns. Maintaining the tradition of revering the elderly seems past in some tribes, while others continue to retain the traditional roles and functions. The patterns of transmission of values, especially in the geographically isolated areas in the western United States, have been altered. Although school transportation is becoming more accessible, many Indian children still attend boarding schools far from home and parents. And in spite of efforts to support cultural learning, teachers are from the majority culture. Interference with the traditional cultural value system is occurring.

I visited an Indian school for retarded children a few years ago. The school was financed through various funding mechanisms, including some funds from the tribal council. I was impressed to see old women employed as foster grandparents, sitting quietly and giving loving attention to the young residents of the school. I was told their purpose was to help the children understand their cultural heritage. Outside, older men were constructing a hogan, the traditional Navajo home. The home contrasted with the adjacent modern brick and glass building. The purpose was identical to that of the employed foster grandmothers—to preserve the cultural heritage.

Kephart (1972) reports his study of Italian immigrants in the United States. They are a large group, nearly 20 million, who are still migrating to this country at the rate of about 25,000 per year. Children are taught to have respect for the aged in Italian families. Older people, whether relatives or not, are addressed as "Uncle" or "Aunt." Aged persons are rarely sent to institutions when they become ill or dependent.

Fandetti and Gelfand (1976) sampled both Italian and Polish residents in Baltimore to ascertain their attitudes toward the care of aged relatives. Regardless of the physical condition of the older persons, over half of those surveyed favored the aged person living with relatives. Respondents from families of second and third generation immigrants tend to favor independent living arrangements for bedridden elderly. Although both groups of respondents tend to favor family living arrangements over long-term institutional care in homes for the aged, Italian respondents expressed stronger preference for family arrangements than did the Polish persons surveyed.

According to Butler (1975), America has over 1 million elderly blacks; and their economic plight is serious. Butler (1975:31) states that:

The percentage of aged blacks living in poverty is twice that of aged whites. Forty-seven percent of all aged black females have incomes under $1,000 . . . elderly blacks tend to have more people dependent on them than do the white elderly. . . .

More elderly black people live with younger people than do white elderly; 28 percent of them live in families with a young head of household compared to 8.9 percent for all elderly regardless of race. There are many reasons why a larger percentage of black elderly live with their children; the importance of the role of grandmother because the mother works or is away; the need for the sharing of income within a family, including the older person's Social Security and public-assistance payments; and the respect and sense of responsibility, said to exist more strongly in black households, in caring for and protecting one's parents, particularly the aged mother.

Protection of one's parent of either sex has also been observed. I recently had occasion to witness first-hand the anguish of a son over the impending placement of his aged black father in a long-term facility. As a practicing social worker one of my tasks is to work with patients and their families for nursing home placement. The son, aged 50, was adamant in his statement, "Blacks don't send their parents to nursing homes!" There seemed to be no alternative at the time; sufficient help and finances were not available for home care. Reluctantly we proceeded with placement plans. "He'll die within a week, I'm sure of it!" the son told me, as before. I completed plans for the placement. The son was right. The father died within 1 week after placement in the nursing home.

Asian-Americans also have severe problems with change. They are traditionally viewed as people who are successful and take care of themselves. Kim (1973) describes the conflict experienced by persons caught between the value systems of American society and those of their parents. It is difficult for both groups.

The pattern of extended relationships has traditionally characterized the Mexican-American family. These relationships include cousins, aunts and uncles, grandparents, and great-grandparents. The extended family may live within one household or in a cluster of homes around its older members, either on a farm or in a barrio (community). According to Maldonado (1975) the important elements are the interpersonal and intergenerational relationships and the interdependence, rather than the strictly physical or geographical proximity of family members. The elderly will not be abandoned by the young for the sake of progress, nor will the elderly cling to the young and demand care. A strong sense of family is being maintained and the young are keeping their respect for the elderly.

I have been privileged to work with many Mexican-American families in which elderly persons were involved. The extended family Maldonado (1975) described has been confirmed in my experience. The pattern of providing personal attention becomes readily apparent at times of serious illness. One time I counted 27 relatives "on-hand." The old lady's hospital room could not accommodate all the family, but 3 or 4 family members usually remained there. The other family members were together, supporting, even by their distant presence in a waiting room; the ill person was part of themselves.

This overview has demonstrated that there are differences in cultural patterns of care for the aged. Increasingly, societies, through their governmental structures, are taking steps on behalf of the elderly. In the United States we are witnessing the development of a political force of elderly. Such groups as The National Council on Aging, the Gray Panthers, and the American Association of Retired Persons are listened to by congressional and administration representatives. Knowledgeable and growing in numbers, the elderly are a force to be acknowledged. The deference to elders seen in many societies has not been especially evident in the United States. It has become incumbent on the elders to press for their own benefits in this society.

INTERGENERATIONAL ATTITUDES AND BEHAVIORS

Patterns of learning social customs are well established. Regardless of the psychological learning theory to which one subscribes, there is general acceptance that parents influence children, and that of all the learning that occurs the lessons taught in the home are probably most influential. One of the problems with much of our learning is that it is not explicit. This is especially true with the values we teach as parents and learn as children. Parents may tell children that they should respect their elders, but if children see the parents being disrespectful to their elders, the double message is clear: "Do not respect your elders."

Lozier and Althouse (1974) describe intergenerational learning in "Social Enforcement of Behavior Toward Elders in an Appalachian Mountain Settlement." They report a study of 270 ninth graders and 142 twelfth graders which found more positive attitudes toward older people than had previously been found. Lozier and Althouse speculate that society may be more accepting of older persons in 1975 than during the 1950s and 1960s. They report that social class has a significant effect, with lower class students having a somewhat less positive attitude than their upper class peers.

Ivester and King (1977) report the number of children who experience grandparents now is substantial when compared with 50 years ago. The average life span was in the range of 40 years in 1900 and now is around 70 years. What do young people say about their grandparents? Two recent studies give some clues. Rowe (1975) reports that the more contact college students have with grandparents through the years, the higher regard they feel for their grandparents at the present time. This relationship is particularly strong with students whose grandmothers had lived in their home for certain periods during their formative years.

Robertson (1976:140) reports generally favorable attitudes from young adult grandchildren between the ages of 18 and 26 years. She says that 90% of the young adults believe their grandparents are not "too old-fashioned or out of touch to be able to help their grandchildren. Seventy-two percent believe grandparents have much influence on grandchildren."

The perception of children toward their parents is also of significance. Culturally, most persons in the United States are affected by Judeo-Christian traditions which teach, "Honor thy father and mother." Individuals are also subject to laws, which began with the passage of the Elizabethan Poor Law in 1601. Those laws gave government responsibility for the welfare of the people of the land for the first time in Western history. The dichotomy between the extremes of those early Biblical teachings and the role of government still affect us. In the United States we are faced with a serious financial crisis in the Social Security system. This crisis demonstrates society's unresolved conflict. Greatly oversimplified, the question is whether we take care of ourselves in old age, through the use of private pension plans and savings that are augmented by employer-employee contributions in the form of payments from the social security fund, or whether payments from general tax revenues bolster the social security fund so that all persons would be adequately provided for in their old age, without reliance on savings. Most industrial nations have been moving toward the latter view.

Johnson and Bursk (1977) examine some of the crucial factors that affect relationships between adult children and their aged parents. They rate these relationships on the basis of health, finances, living environment, and attitude. Children and parents were asked questions about current happiness and general life satisfaction. The trends demonstrated in the study were:

(1) When parents and children share similar values, they give the relationship a higher rating.
(2) Elderly parents tend to rate the quality of the relationship higher than their children.
(3) Elderly parents are satisfied with their living environment.
(4) "Felt" financial security, not level of income, seems important.
(5) There are better quality relationships when the elderly parent is fairly engaged in various activities.
(6) When health is seriously impaired, and when family relationships have been perceived as strained, the parental illness strains the family relationship even more.

Health and attitudes toward aging were found to be the most "important correlates of the affective quality of the relationship between elderly parents and their adult children" (Johnson and Bursk, 1977:14).

Other studies demonstrate that failing health of a parent is stressful to the relationship between parents and their adult children. Simos (1973) has studied 50 adult children and reports on the aging parents of these children. She finds that illness or death of a spouse necessitating the relocation of one parent causes difficulties to surface, particularly if the parent was overly dependent and allowed the adult child no privacy.

There is little question that the problem of *power* is recurrent in the lives of most families. Children are *powerless* to overcome parental strength; adolescents are caught between their own growing power and independence and their child status in relation to parents; young women may begin their careers as wives and mothers with a strong

dependence on their husbands, parents, or significant others to help them in their new roles. Historically, particularly in the rural areas of our country, power has been strongly maintained in the hands of the elderly. Sometimes abusive power can control the entire future of the young, particularly if land ownership and operation are involved. I witnessed this in a dramatic way several years ago while living in a Midwestern state. The 30-year-old son of a 65-year-old father operated one of several farms owned by the father. All decisions relative to planting, harvesting, and marketing of grain and livestock were cleared routinely through the father. The son had the alternative to leave or stay. He continued in a truly subservient role to the detriment of himself and his family.

There are certain groups in this country in which it is accepted that the old move aside but remain in an advisory position. The Amish have this tradition and so do other groups that are agriculturally based.

Karcher and Linden (1974:231), in a study of family rejection and nursing home utilization, postulate that:

(1) Role conflict develops in the family of procreation as its members attempt to assimilate dependent, aged relations; (2) Conflict reduction is necessary for the proper functioning of the family unit; (3) Attempts at conflict reduction are made in accord with societal values.

They conclude that some families reject their parents and that nursing home placement is the socially accepted method for eliminating the conflict-producing stimuli.

Over the past 25 years of social work practice, I have encountered few families who fit Karcher and Linden's (1974) postulates. Observing rejection of older persons by their families has a strong impact on the health care team in a hospital or nursing home. One time, an elderly man was brought to the hospital for care. The patient's wife, totally dominated by a middle-aged son, was initially hesitant but finally adamant that she could no longer care for her husband at home and that other plans would have to be made. Every indication was that the son had threatened his mother with abandonment if she resumed the care of her husband. It appeared that the mother was so frightened by her son's potential rejection that she did, in fact, abandon her husband.

Butler (1975:156) reports an extreme example of victimization of a 67 year-old woman by a son:

. . . widowed eight years, she [the woman] was regularly beaten up by her 35 year-old unmarried son. She had turned her little money and her property over to the son. He stopped working. They subsisted on her $80.00 a month Social Security check. She did some baby-sitting to supplement her income.

Adult protective services are being developed in many communities to aid in such situations.

Older persons are often perceived as powerless, as shown by the two preceding examples. It is likely that powerlessness, some feeling of depression, and withdrawal from some of the roles one has earlier in life are supportive of a portion of the disengagement theory, postulated by Cumming (1975). This theory has been the subject of wide debate by gerontologists. Another theory, widely discussed, is the activity theory, which suggests that persons should continue to maintain the activities that made middle age a good time of life.

One of the most reasonable views of successful aging has been developed by Neugarten and others at the University of Chicago (Neugarten, 1974). They conclude that personality organization or type is an essential factor to aid in predicting which individuals will age successfully. They stress adaptation as the key concept and believe that knowing individuals in middle age helps in predicting patterns of aging.

Currently, many attempts are being made to explore ways of improving the lot of older individuals in need of special services. Attention is being given to kinship ties, which represent "the family" for some persons. These associations may include relatives, but often include neighbors, acquaintances, or good friends. Many older persons are maintained at home because some persons choose to be of help. Persons maintained in this manner have been little studied. During the process of interviewing 50 long-married couples, my wife and I were in the home of an elderly couple in which the husband had been disabled by a stroke and bedridden for

nearly 25 years. They were childless. While we were in the home, a man in his early 20s came in and was welcomed warmly. He was proudly introduced as "our son." Later the wife told us that he was not related to them. After the death of the husband, we received a communication signed, Mrs. _____ and Son.

LIVING ARRANGEMENTS OF THE ELDERLY

Some of the living arrangements of older people have been discussed briefly. Both living with children and living in a nursing home have been mentioned. The majority of older people live with their spouses. Few studies have been made of these couples in their later years. Dressler (1973) reports on a study of 38 retired couples in the New Haven area. The study examines the retirement experiences of these retired couples. Primarily, interest focuses on the marital relationship itself. He also explores interfamilial relationships, leisure time activities, health status, and attitudes toward death and aging. Dressler found that the spouse is of crucial significance in assisting the retired person to adjust to the social stresses of aging.

The retired couples in Dressler's sample tend to live independently of their children, although 90% of those couples with children see them at least once weekly. These couples display a general continuity and stability of life-style. Dressler reports that some persons find the interview stressful fearing that they "would emotionally re-experience traumatic events from their past that often they would have preferred to forget" (p. 347).

My wife and I conducted similar research on 50 couples married 50 or more years in Tucson, Arizona in 1974. The study focused on long marriages rather than on postretirement adjustment. We found that 9 of the 100 subjects were still employed, even though the average age of the individuals was nearly 80 years. The mean number of years married was 55.5 years. Fewer than 50% of the subjects in the study had children living within a day's drive, compared to 90% in the New Haven area (Dressler, 1973). Another difference was that the subjects in this study appeared not to experience the stress referred to in recalling difficult past events. On the contrary, the life review seemed beneficial to some. One subject later wrote, "I've been euphoric for days since you saw us." Recalling the past in a systematic way had been very pleasurable for him. Overall, the 50 marital relationships were characterized by "commitment, companionship, care and concern" (Roberts and Roberts, 1977).

There are undoubtedly large numbers of unhappily married persons, who feel trapped and futile in a relationship that may have been necessary "for the children" but that now has lost even that dubious purpose. Divorce may occur in the older age groups but marriage following widowhood is a more common event. Treas and Van' Hilst (1976) report that marriages contracted in advancing years enjoy considerable success when bolstered by motives of affection, financial security, and children's approval. Four-fifths of the marriages of persons aged 65 and over in 1975 were remarriages. Cleveland and Gianturco (1976) have reports on a study of remarriage probability that indicates that men in the older age groups have less time elapsed between widowhood until remarriage. They find that many factors account for this. Husbands tend to report greater satisfaction with marriage than do wives. Husbands seem less able to handle the loss of a spouse. Our cultural conditioning that encourages men to "stay out of the kitchen" may have something to do with this. Available data suggest that old people who are married experience a more satisfying old age than other groups, yet, many older people are without the comfort of a spouse. Three out of 10 older persons live alone or with relatives. Older men more typically live with family members than do older women.

There is a group of elderly individuals that has been mentioned only briefly. They are the single elderly. They are often without known relatives or are isolated from them. Gubrium (1975) reports on such a group of persons. They tend to be lifelong isolates and they are not especially lonely in old age. Their evaluation of everyday life is similar to married elders in the sense that both are more positive than divorced or widowed aged persons. Compared to other groups, being single is a premium in old age in that it avoids the desolation effect of bereavement following death of a spouse.

For the majority of older persons the definite forecast of the end of the family life cycle is the loss of a spouse and resulting widowhood. Since 95% of Americans marry at some time, it is inevitable that the widowhood experience is a common one. Blau (1973) contrasts widowhood and retirement, and describes the latter as lessening opportunities for social contacts and, therefore, is more demoralizing. She describes widowhood as a natural (expected) event compared to the socially ordered phenomenon of retirement. For all older persons there is some natural preparation for the loss of a spouse because of the number of deaths among peers. In spite of this natural preparation, many psychological and physical symptoms are expected and common. Social role changes following widowhood are difficult for both men and women. Although there are indications that husband-wife roles become blurred with aging, men are often unprepared for domestic tasks and may resort to inappropriate methods to relieve their sense of loss. Women, unaccustomed to certain maintenance tasks in the home, feel ineffective and helpless. It may be in these areas that family supports, children, and extended kinship systems effectively relieve some of the sense of loss and deprivation.

In addition to the living arrangements discussed earlier, there is a relatively small proportion of the elderly (less than 5%), who live in some type of long-term care facility. Butler (1975) reports that 79% of old people in nursing homes are living in "commercial" homes, 14% are in "not-for-profit" homes, and 7% are in federal, state, county, and municipal homes. The experience of nursing home placement is rarely an easy one for the older patient or the family. The public image of long-term care institutions has never been good. Exposés of abuses appear in the public media with regularity. Congressional committees gather testimony in an effort to legislate improved conditions. When an individual is moved to a nursing home, one can witness the greatest intergenerational strife. Many older persons believe they are being sent away to die when placement is planned. Parents who have used guilt as the usual method of social control of their children have the upper hand in this dilemma. Children who have been ambivalent toward their parents since childhood now are in an old conflict situation again. In a study by Kraus (1976), the most common reason for the placement as understood both by the patient and the family was to relieve "the excessive burden" on the family. More than half of the applicants in the study approved of the move.

Alternative systems of care are being attempted in many American communities. Most of these are variations on plans used by European countries to provide more home care services to the elderly and to plan public and private housing so as to minimize the effects of physical handicaps and limitations.

HEALTH-RELATED ISSUES

The pattern of the family life cycle has been traced from the union of two people up to and including a brief discussion of widowhood. Variations in living arrangements and their implications for the family have been considered. It seems appropriate to examine two other factors that affect the satisfaction one finds in life, those of health and illness.

All individuals are subject to "dis-ease" throughout their life cycles. These states of physical "dis-ease" are accompanied by emotional and social implications, which vary according to the age and stage in the life cycle. These implications also vary according to the acceptable methods for response choices exercised in the immediate culture, the nuclear family, and the extended family and/or the kinship system. It may be appropriate to be stoic or agonizing under well-described cultural rules. Ross and Kedward (1977) stress that the importance of the interrelationship between physical and mental illness in the elderly has implications for prevention and treatment. Mental confusion in older people may be caused by infections, disease, fecal impaction, urinary retention, uremia, anemia, and diabetes. Deficiency of an essential nutrient resulting from dietetic deficiency or from malabsorption has been found to cause mental impairment. Kovar (1977) provides information about illnesses of the elderly and some of the treatment alternatives. Health is one of the best indicators of life-satisfaction; however, health as a positive force has received relatively little attention. This is true for the elderly as well as for other age groups.

Although not necessarily tied to marriage, sexual behavior is often associated with it. For most people, sexual interest continues throughout life.

The sexual drives and activities of older people correlate with those of the younger years. Men and women who used to enjoy sex when they were young are likely to still enjoy it when old. This finding disposes of the stereotyped notion that one only has a limited amount of sexual energy, or that by keeping some in reserve one may have more sexual energy later on in life. Actually, the reverse is true; active and regular use of sexual capacities is likely to maintain them in old age. In this respect, sex is no different from other functional capacities, for example, intelligence, that benefit from active and regular use (Verwoerdt, 1976:260).*

In summary, life satisfaction is based on many factors, many purely social in nature, such as those that derive from our closest contacts, nuclear family, friends, and others in the kinship system, as well as psychobiological factors. Individuals' concepts of self stem from their family relationships as well as from the relationships that develop throughout life. Individuals' perceptions are a result of their relationships with other people. The concept of self also comes from the perception of oneself as a physical-biological being. Individuals may view themselves as old, fat, happy, thin, gregarious, solitary, or any of many feeling states. Some individuals are attempting to help older people improve their self-concept and their health by teaching deep breathing, yoga, meditation, and other techniques (Dychtwald: 1977).

DEATH: THE END OF THE CYCLE

According to Atchley (1972) the last two stages in the family life cycle are the death of the spouse followed by the death of the remaining spouse. In the United States and some other Western countries, death is viewed as an unnatural event, something which must be avoided or postponed. Indeed, with our increasing life expectancy, death is being postponed for many of us.

In the 1950s, writers attempted to clarify technical matters that affected the patient's recovery. Some debated whether it was ap-

*From Verwoerdt, A. 1976. Clinical genopsychiatry. Copyright 1976, The Williams & Wilkins Co., Baltimore.

propriate to tell a patient the diagnosis or prognosis. In recent years, Kubler-Ross and others have made major contributions to the well-being of dying patients and their families by discussing death as a normal event rather than a supernatural one. For many people, death has become a part of life rather than the tragic end of it.

Most of the readers of this book will probably think of death in connection with a hospital or nursing home. Over the past half century in our society, rationalizations for "out-of-home" deaths have been developed. Sometimes these include statements such as, "She would get better care there," or "How would we handle her dying with the children here?"

Forty thousand persons die in their own homes in Britain every year:

Dying persons gain much by being cared for by an affectionate family; they are better able to maintain themselves as individuals. Remaining at home, not swallowed up in the possible anonymity of the dying hospital patient, they need not doubt they are still part of the family. While among their family, they do not consider themselves as hulks awaiting the end, as long as they can participate, even in a limited role (Lamerton, 1973:25).

Lamerton (1973) and others have described the efforts that are needed to help not only the dying but also the bereaved. Much has been written about the widow and widower, the physical and psychological problems they face through the anticipation of death and finally the death of their spouse.

The time of death can be, and often is, a painful one for adult children and grandchildren as well. There is a sense of the interruption of the continuity of the family, a pervasive sense of helplessness and often guilt. A sensitive approach to a dying relative is described in a small book entitled *Gramp* (Jury and Jury, 1976). The Jury brothers describe in words and pictures 3 years of caring for their aging grandfather. This story will not be repeated often because we have so many social forces that oppose the care of older persons in homes.

The last remaining spouse is dead; the family life cycle is complete. Some persons may leave a legacy of memories; others may leave legacies of brick and stone. The majority will leave a legacy of children and grandchildren; they are their gift to the future.

• • •

Inherent in working with the elderly and their families is the problem of identification. In other specialties, such as pediatrics, there may be great stress for personnel who give day-to-day care. However, the reluctance to see ourselves as old is strong when working with old patients and, because of it, poor care can result. Burnside (1973:110) notes that:

The staff was often observed as being very protective of "their" patients. It is not uncommon for an individual staff member to attribute his own feelings to patients, or to displace his fears and apprehensions on to his patients. The staff member may be fearful about the patient leaving the hospital because he is protective of the patient.*

Feelings of identification and our defenses against those feelings may interfere with our helping efforts in homes or institutions. Approaches to aid caregivers in understanding their feelings are essential to successful work with older people and their families.

Silverman et al. (1977:133) have offered information "for helping older people and their families develop reliable methods for coping with conflicts and reaching constructive equilibrium between the generations." They state that:

A combination of didactic and therapeutic approaches was blended to achieve the following objectives for the clients who were of the second and third generation:

1. To increase their knowledge about the aging process.
2. To develop awareness of their response to the aging process of their own parents.
3. To increase their understanding of emotional reactions of older people.
4. To initiate group problem solving to cope more effectively with their own and their parents' [patients'] concerns.
5. To provide them with wider access to community supports.
6. To facilitate the development of a support system within the group.

---

*From Psychosocial nursing care of the aged by I. M. Burnside. Copyright 1973, McGraw-Hill Book Co. Used with permission of McGraw-Hill Book Co.

Role-play of many types, including that described by Beatt and Wahlstrom (1976), has the potential for sensitizing those who work with elderly in effective ways. "Life Cycle: A Simulation Game" developed by Chaisson (1976) especially for health care personnel creates an atmosphere for role play and group participation, while providing the opportunity for visual feedback (if equipment is available) as well as practice in the art of giving and receiving feedback from other people.

Consciousness raising with regard to aging for health professionals must continue if there is to be positive impact on care older people receive. The recognition that we are all aging and are potential recipients of mistreatment in old age is powerful. The knowledge that none of us can change our skin color, and thus experience another form of racism, and that few of us can change our sex and experience another kind of sexism, does not hold true for agism. We are all potential victims of this destructive prejudice.

REFERENCES

Atchley, R. C. 1972. The social forces of later life. Wadsworth Publishing Co., Belmont, Calif.

Atkin, C. K. 1976. Mass media and the aging. In H. J. Oyer, and E. J., Oyer (eds.). Aging and communication. University Park Press, Baltimore.

Austin, M. 1976. A network of help for England's elderly, Social Work, March.

Beatt, B. H., and Wahlstrom, B. B. 1976. A developmental approach to understanding families. Social Casework 59(January):3-9.

Blau, Z. S. 1973. Old age in a changing society. New viewpoints, New York.

Brel, J. 1968. Old folks (Les Vieux). Trans. M. Schuman and E. Blau. Hill and Range Songs, Inc., New York.

Bronfenbrenner, U. 1977. The changing American family. AFL-CIO American Federationalist 84(2):7-11.

Burnside, I. M. 1973. Psychosocial nursing care of the aged. McGraw-Hill, New York.

Butler, R. N. 1975. Why survive: Growing old in America. Harper & Row Publishers, New York.

Butler, R. N. 1974. Successful aging and the role of the life review. Journal of the American Geriatric Society 22:12.

Chaisson, M. 1977. Life cycle: A simulation game for training health care personnel in geriatrics. Health Monographs. Johns Hopkins University.

Cleveland, W. P., and Gianturco, D. T. 1976. Remarriage probability after widowhood: A retrospective method. Journal of Gerontology 31:99.

Cumming, E. 1975. Engagement with an old theory. International Journal of Aging and Human Development 6:3.

Dressler, D. M. 1973. Life adjustment of retired couples. International Journal of Aging and Human Development 4:335.

Dychtwald, K. 1977. Bodymind. Pantheon Books, New York.

Facts About Older Americans. 1976. Pub. No. QHD 77 20006, Washington, D.C., 1976 Department of Health, Education and Welfare

Fandetti, D. V., and Gelfand, D. E. 1976. Care of the aged: Attitudes of white ethnic families. The Gerontologist 16:546.

Glick, P. C. 1977. Updating the family life cycle. Journal of Marriage and the Family 39:5.

Gubrium, J. F. 1975. Being single in old age. International Journal of Aging and Human Development 6: 29.

Ivester, C., and King, K. 1977. Attitudes of adolescents toward the aged. Gerontologist 17:85.

Johnson, E. S., and Bursk, B. J. 1977. Relationships between the elderly and their adult children. Gerontologist 17:74.

Jury, M., and Jury, D.: 1976. Gramp. Grossman Press, New York.

Kamerman, S. B. 1976. Community services for the aged: The view from eight countries. Gerontologist 16:532.

Karcher, C. J., and Linden, L. K. 1974. Family rejection of the aged and nursing home utilization. International Journal of Aging and Human Development 5:3.

Kephart, W. M. 1972. The family, society and the individual, ed. 3. Houghton, Mifflin, Boston.

Kerckhoff, A. C. 1966. Family patterns and morale in retirement. In I. H. Simpson, and J. C. McKinney, Social aspects of aging. Duke University Press, Durham, N.C.

Kim, B. L. C. 1973. No model minority. Social Work 18(3):51-53.

Kovar, M. G. 1976. Health of the elderly and use of health services. Public Health Reports 92:9.

Kraus, A. S., and others. 1976. Elderly applicants to long-term care institutions. Part 2. The application process: Placement and care needs. Journal of the American Geriatrics Society 24:165.

Lamerton, R. 1973. Care of the dying. The care and welfare library. London, England.

Little, V. C. 1976. Aging in Western Samoa. Unpublished paper presented to the 39th Annual Scientific Meeting of the Gerontological Society, October, New York City.

Lozier, J., and Althouse, R. 1974. Social enforcement of behavior toward elders in an Appalachian mountain settlement. Gerontologist February.

Maldonado, D., Jr. 1975. The Chicano aged. Social Work 20(3):213-216.

National Council on Aging, Inc. 1975. The myth and reality of aging in America. Washington, D.C.

Neugarten, B. 1974. Successful aging. In M. H. Huyck (ed.). Growing older: Things you need to know about aging. Prentice Hall, Englewood Cliffs, N.J.

Palmore, E. 1975. The status and integration of the aged in Japanese society. Journal of Gerontology 30: 199.

Petranek, C. F. 1975. Postparental period: An opportunity for re-definition. Unpublished paper presented to the National Council on Family Relations, August 23, Salt Lake City, Utah.

Roberts, W. L., and Roberts, A. 1977. Aging with

Grace—and Harry, Hazel and Fred. Scripted video-tape. Copyright Arizona Board of Regents.

Robertson, J. F. 1976. Significance of grandparents; perceptions of young adult grandchildren. Gerontologist 16:2.

Rosenmayr, L. 1977. The family—a source of hope for the elderly? In E. Shanas and M. B. Sussman (eds.). Family, bureaucracy, and the elderly. Duke University Press, Durham, N.C.

Ross, H. E., and Kedward, H. B. 1977. Psychogeriatric hospital admissions from the community and institutions. Journal of Gerontology 42:420.

Rossi, A. S. 1972. Family development in a changing world. American Journal of Psychiatry 128:9.

Rowe, G. P. 1975. College students' perception of their grandparents. An unpublished paper prepared for the National Council on Family Relations Annual Meeting, August 20, Salt Lake City, Utah.

Shanas, E. 1974. Health status of older people: Cross cultural implications. American Journal of Public Health 64:3.

Short, R. L. 1965. The gospel according to Peanuts. John Knox Press, Richmond, Va.

Siegel, J. S. 1972. Some demographic aspects of aging in the United States. In A. Ostfield and D. Gibson (eds.). Epidemiology of aging. National Institute of Child and Human Development. DHEW Pub. No. 77-711, Bethesda, Md.

Silverman, A., Kahn, B. H., and Anderson, G. 1977. A model for working with multigenerational families. Social Casework 33(3):131-135.

Simos, B. 1973. Adult children and their aging parents. Social Work 18(3):78-85.

Sussman, M. B. 1977. Family bureaucracy and the elderly individual: An organizational linkage perspective. In E. Shanas and M. B. Sussman, (eds.). Family, bureaucracy, and the elderly. Duke University Press, Durham, N.C.

Treas, J., and VanHilst, A. 1976. Marriage and remarriage rates among older Americans. Gerontologist 16: 132, 19.

Verwoerdt, A. 1976. Clinical geropsychiatry. Waverly Press, Baltimore, Md.

CHAPTER 19

The phenomenon of selective neglect

Jan R. Atwood

John is dying and he knows it. He is hurting too. His main wish is to spend his last days comfortably, if possible, at home. John's wife, Ann, also wants him to be pain-free and close by. She feels more useful when she is sure he is eating and drinking enough. In their culture, food is love. She keeps nourishments at his bedside and would like to feed him, but John has no interest in eating. Because of his disease process, his swallow reflex is poor, as well. However, he is willing to drink a limited variety of fluids during the time he is awake.

The pain medicine is needed more frequently now. After discussing the matter with John and Ann, the doctor has prescribed enough medication to keep John relatively comfortable. When the medication is most effective, John is very groggy or asleep. The visiting nurse and Ann have found a schedule that allows him comfort plus some time when he is relatively alert. Ann now limits her offers of nourishment to fluids and to times that coincide with John's more alert periods during which he can safely swallow.

John and Ann are not unusual. They typify the growing number of families who prefer to keep a chronically or acutely ill patient with a poor prognosis at home as long as possible. When and if they do admit their family member to an inpatient facility, they prefer a homelike atmosphere that includes homelike care.

This chapter consists of a description of the issue of home care for a chronically or an acutely ill person with a poor prognosis, a metatheoretical delineation of the selective neglect model based on role theory, and a discussion of ways the model can be used by community health personnel.

THE NEED FOR HOME CARE

Most Americans can look forward to some chronic or acute illness prior to death, in-cluding progressive disability and, therefore, progressive dependence on others for care. The leading causes of death (heart disease, cancer, and cerebral vascular disease) in the United States in 1973 are primarily chronic rather than acute illnesses (Department of Health, Education and Welfare 1975). Heart disease is frequently accompanied by chronic hypertension.

Until relatively recently cancer has been an acute disease, which almost invariably ended in death. Annual survival rates indicate that cancer with its after-effects tends to be a chronic illness that may or may not result in death. For example, after having surgery and/or radiation, 70% of the patients with Hodgkin's disease respond to chemotherapy and 40% of the patients survive longer than 5 years; 65% of the patients with acute myeloblastic leukemia respond to chemotherapy with "some prolongation of life"; and 20% to 40% of women with breast carcinoma respond to chemotherapy with "probable prolongation of life" (National Health Education Committee, 1976:61).

As the prime reason for medical care for 20.2 million people in 1973, arthritis and rheumatism lead in causing "prolonged misery to the greatest number of people in the United States" (National Health Education Committee, 1976:15). Of the 20.2 million persons under care, "5.4 million or 26.8 percent are under 45 years of age" (National Health Education Committee 1976:17).

When chronic illness involves acute episodes, the patient is likely to be treated in one or more settings in addition to the home setting. Hospitals are increasingly reserved for acute episodes and for the costly acute care provided within their walls. Sophistication in equipment for care and spiraling labor costs have contributed to the recent national cry for cost containment. Factors such as Medicare provisions and high cost of acute care have stimulated proliferation of extended care facilities that provide a less structured environment than the hospital. However, these facilities still lack homelike features and family activities. After acute episodes are past, some patients receive nursing care in homes. Such facilities typically serve older populations but are rarely preferred by the residents to their own home settings (Melin and Hymans, 1977).

The trend in preference toward a homelike atmosphere for the terminally ill appears to be increasing. Hospices, financed by sources such as hospitals, industrial groups, or proprietary nursing home chains, are springing up nationwide (Traska, 1977). They provide graduated care, according to both patient and family needs. Rooms tend to be decorated like bedrooms rather than hospital rooms. Family members come and go quite freely and are considered a vital part of the treatment program.

During chronic and sometimes terminal phases of illness, home-based services, such as visiting and public health nurses, homemakers, Meals on Wheels, and handicapped transport systems, are available to varying degrees and tend to be cost effective. Colt et al. (1977) have found that supportive home care services save up to two thirds of the costs otherwise needed by chronically ill, elderly people in an institutional setting. In addition, creative combinations of professional, family, and patient resources can provide satisfying days for people with poor prognoses (Epstein, 1975; McEver, 1977; Kubler-Ross, 1975). For example, one hospital staff nurse accompanied a young, terminally ill mother who had nine children to her home for a last day with her family. The staff nurse was asked at the last minute to stay with the patient; however, the nurse had planned a picnic with her own family. Upon discovering the nurse's dilemma, the patient offered a solution: that the families of both women have a joint picnic. Thus the patient saw her home, smelled the special smells, heard the children running and shouting, and spent some time in her own livingroom with each child. The gravely ill cancer patient re-

marked, "This has probably been the nicest day of my life" (Boyd 1977).

Additional examples are found in Martinson's (1977) study of home care for dying children. Typically, the families reported being assisted by the nurse to give care in such a way that they benefited as much as their dying children did.

THE PHENOMENON OF SELECTIVE NEGLECT

Regardless of the setting, the quality of patient care varies. When care is poor, the phenomenon of selective neglect is frequently identifiable. Selective neglect works in two ways (Atwood 1977). First, families selectively attend to patients' needs in order to keep them home as long as possible. They attend well to basic needs such as feeding and nutrition, skin care and bathing, emotional support, and role maintenance in the family. However, they must selectively neglect the medical needs that can be provided only by professional staff. When the medical needs reach the threshold level at home, they can no longer be selectively unattended by the family, and the patient is admitted to the hospital.

Second, the hospital team members' conception of their role as caregivers allows them to attend selectively to some of the needs abdicated by the family—professional medical care represented by IVs, breathing therapy, and so forth. However, the hospital staff selectively neglects the very needs for which the family has been so diligently responsible, such as back care and feeding and nutrition. The family abdicates basic and medical care needs, not just the latter. When the family brings the patient to the hospital, they trade homelike atmosphere and environment, nutrition (feeding), familiar schedule and people—but increasingly marginal medical care—for hospital-type, higher-powered medical care, institutional environment, different feeding and eating patterns, hospital schedule, and many new personnel. However, this trade-off is not satisfactory to many families. The trade-off can occur in the hospital or at home—wherever the family "gives up" some control for the patient's care.

Neglect, itself, is the behavioral outcome of conflict between role concept and role performance. The performer consciously or un-consciously omits an important part of his or her role. This type of neglect is assumed to be negligible. *Selective* neglect pertains to failure to carry out an aspect of a role because it has much lower priority than other aspects. For example, some nurses feel perfectly comfortable not spending a lot of time and effort feeding a terminally ill patient orally, especially if he is kept at least hydrated intravenously. When a patient cannot eat and drink readily, this is a signal that he is to be permitted to pass away peacefully.

Some families seem to view random feeding patterns as selective neglect aimed at permitting the terminally ill patient to die. Thus it becomes a pregnant moral issue (Campbell, 1972).

In a study of families' perceptions of inpatient nursing care prior to and just after death (perimortality care), I recorded the following comments by family members (Atwood, 1975):

ELDERLY WIFE: I come in everyday. By noon. And feed him. They got good meals here. They don't feed him. He doesn't eat so much when I'm not here. They try, but I *tell* him. Then he eats. He *needs* it.

YOUNG HUSBAND: I think it would have been helpful if, when there wasn't someone from the family here, that she would eat all she could eat. I'm not sure that wasn't done, but I don't think it was.

MOTHER OF YOUNG PATIENT: This time they didn't check on her. They just brought the tray in and set it. It seemed none of the nurses came in and checked if she wanted anything. I eventually asked her if she wanted us to feed her. The tray sat there until 2 p.m. The lady that brought the tray in said if she [patient] felt like eating later just to let her know and she would warm the tray up for her. But the *nurses* never came in to see if they could help her. She was so dizzy she couldn't sit up. That didn't seem like too much to expect.

MOTHER OF MIDDLE-AGED PATIENT: He's asleep now. They give him medication for pain. We can't feed him then. I wish they would leave his tray. They took it away.

HUSBAND OF OLDER PATIENT: The food is excellent. I will say that.
INTERVIEWER: Is she eating ok?
SPOUSE: Well, yes. You know three meals a day

is too much. I fed her the last two days when she was home.
INTERVIEWER: Do you feel like they feed her here when you leave?
SPOUSE: (Pause) Let's put it this way. It's best to stay here as long as you can."

Even though the patient is unable to select from the menu, the family still wants to do so because (1) they know the patient's tastes, (2) they know the patient's condition, and (3) they feel the selection may not get done if they don't do it.

CONCERNED HUSBAND OF MIDDLE-AGED PATIENT: I wondered what she should have to eat. We've filled out the food charts. I've ordered things like milk, Jell-o, and custards. I only saw a tray once . . . I was there from 10 AM to 3 PM today. No tray came in there. I gave her sips of water.

Role theory explains a great deal of the behavior in the preceding examples (Bertrand, 1972). Key explanatory elements of the theory are roles and norms. According to Bertrand roles are an "integrated subset of norms and are made up of several norms, all of which are dedicated to the same function" (p. 35). A norm is "required or acceptable behavior for a given interactional situation" (p. 49). For example, one norm about a patient's nutrition is that a patient is to be hydrated and fed. Norms are building blocks for roles. For example, norms regarding health care aspects, such as feeding patients, interacting with families, and giving medications, combine to form the role of "nurse." People use the norms they hold about their roles to determine how they perceive performing those roles. They usually attempt to perform their roles in a manner consistent with their own role perceptions and within cultural and societal expectations.

The performance of the role in toto is evaluated by the role performer and by others according to the degree to which the several norms in the role are implemented. An individual's performance of one or more important norms can result in a negative evaluation by an outsider of the entire role performance and the performer as well.

The process just described is a general one and applies to any patient situation, including both the chronic course of illness and the terminal course. Multiple norms comprise roles. Patients, families, and nurses all have their own norm values, and all evaluate the role performance of the nurse.

When a patient is chronically or acutely ill with a poor prognosis, there are at least three kinds of actors who are concerned about the quality of care the patient receives: the patient, the family (or significant others), and the caregiver. Sometimes the caregiver is an outside person such as a nurse or a neighbor; sometimes the caregiver is a family member; and sometimes the patient is his or her own sole caregiver. In any event, each party has a set of normative expectations that are held for the role of caregiver, and each individual evaluates the performance of the caregiver based on one or more normative aspects of the role. If the norms of the patient, the family, and the caregiver coincide, there is normative consensus, and the actual role performance of the caregiver is likely to be evaluated positively. The outcome of evaluation can be termed attention or neglect, depending on the results of the final analysis. Selective attention is defined as role performance that meets or exceeds the evaluator's expectations. On the other hand, selective neglect is defined as role performance that does not meet the evaluator's expectations. Because selective attention does not present a major

patient care problem, the focus here is on selective neglect.

NUTRITIONAL SELECTIVE NEGLECT

The accompanying figure illustrates the general selective neglect model in the format of Gibbs' (1972) paradigm specifically for nutritional selective neglect. Gibbs' conception is only one of many; his paradigm has been chosen because various conceptual and empirical levels are explicit. The highest level of abstraction is at the top of the paradigm in which partially defined constructs such as consensus on role behavior and internal conflict are linked by axioms. Most fully developed theories have several axioms. Constructs are linked to completely defined concepts by postulates. Concepts such as consensus on nutritional care behavior (CNCB) are linked to empirical referentials or variables by transformational statements. Theorems unite referentials. Each referential, such as the consensus score, can be indexed via an epistemic statement by one or more measures, e.g., CNCB. In highly refined theories, the measures are connected by hypotheses that are actual formulae stating the nature and form of the mathematical relationships. For a complete discussion of the paradigm, see Gibbs (1972).

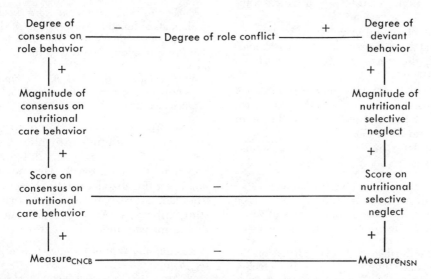

CNCB is an empirically derived number which represents the amount of consensus on nutritional care behavior and is an unspecified function of role expectation and role performance. NSN is an empirically derived number which represents the amount of nutritional selective neglect.

The phenomenon of selective neglect

The model of selective neglect was induced from data. However, it is presented here as a deductive system to permit the reader to follow readily the logic between levels of the model. The figure contains a model of the emergent theory in skeletal form. The upper two levels are hardly earth-shaking or new. They need not be. Grounded theory (Glaser and Strauss, 1966) is frequently begun at a substantive level then developed toward the conceptual levels, either by innovation or adaptation. By the latter approach, the selective neglect phenomenon potentially increases the substantive case on which role theory rests.

The basic axiom is adopted from role theory (Bertrand, 1972):

The greater the degree of consensus on role behavior, the less the degree of role conflict and the greater the degree of deviant behavior.

There are five constructs in the axiom, the last three of which are explicit:

Role expectation: The anticipated performance of a role as viewed by someone in the cultural unit other than the person in the role.

Role performance: The role behavior of an actor (as perceived by another).

Role consensus: The degree to which role expectation and role performance coincide.

Role conflict: The degree of stress within a cultural unit caused by inconsistencies among the norms of the system (Bertrand 1972:173).

Deviant behavior: The degree of negative behavioral deviation from the normative limits of the cultural unit by the actor (Bertrand 1972:173).

The postulates linking the two constructs to concepts are:

The greater the degree of consensus on role behavior, the greater the magnitude of consensus on role-specific care behavior, three types of which are nutritional, environmental, and person-centered care behavior.

The greater the degree of deviant behavior, the greater the magnitude of role-specific selective neglect, e.g., nutritional, environmental, and person-centered selective neglect.

The two concepts in the figure are defined as follows:

Consensus on role-specific care behavior: The degree to which the role-specific care effort made by the nursing team, as perceived by a family member or patient, conforms to the role-specific care expectations held by a family member.

Role-specific selective neglect: The degree of behavioral response by a family member to the perceived omission and/or commission of role-specific or patient behaviors by the nursing team.

In this case the role-specific behavior and neglect are nutritional in nature.

The next level of the model is even more substantive and empirical than the preceding one. The transformational statements assert that each referential is a valid index of its respective concept.

The greater the magnitude of consensus on nutritional care behavior, the greater the score on consensus on nutritional care behavior.

The greater the magnitude of nutritional selective neglect, the greater the score on nutritional selective neglect.

The sample theorem deals with nutritional selective neglect:

The larger the score on consensus on nutritional care behavior, the smaller the score on nutritional selective neglect.

In a completed theory, the referentials are measures and formulae. Here the two referentials are defined as follows:

Consensus on nutritional care behavior: A mathematical function (unspecified) of the family member's or patient's score on the role expectation measure and the perceived role performance measure.

Nutritional selective neglect: The family member's or patient's score on the nutritional selective neglect measure.

The measures may differ from study to study, e.g., magnitude estimations, summed scores on a Likert-type scale, or behavior ratings done by an observer. The measures are not operationalized to date. However, data from families responding to the perimortality study interview (Atwood, 1975) suggest potential measurement parameters:

Amount and kind of feeding effort expected by the family:

a. Meal selection from menu done by patient, by staff with patient, or saved for family to do with or for patient every day.

b. Every time a meal or snack arrives, team takes responsibility for seeing that patient feeds self, is helped by staff safely and patiently, or is helped by a family member.

c. Staff offers patient nutrients unrequested if his nutritional level warrants such (as the family sees it).

Amount and kind of feeding effort made by the team: Could vary from same as above to total absence of all of the above.

Magnitude of nutritional selective neglect: Amount of difference between family's or patient's particular expectations and team's effort.

The bottom level of the paradigm is strictly empirical and contains only numbers. Each measurement is expected to validly and reliably index its corresponding referential. The two epistemic statements that link the referentials and referents or measures are:

The greater the score on consensus on nutritional care behavior, the greater the number labeled Measure$_{CNCB}$.

The greater the score on nutritional selective neglect, the greater the number labeled Measure$_{NSN}$.

In an empirical study, the measures would be scores, such as a magnitude estimation of each measure, in the S. S. Stevens tradition (Hamblin and Smith, 1966; Nunnally, 1967). In a predictive theory, the formula of each measure would specify the form of the resultant curve, as well. The implication here is a simple linear function. The hypothesis in its simplest form is:

The greater the Measure$_{CNSD}$ the less the Measure$_{NSN}$.

When patients have a chronic or an acute illness with a poor prognosis, they bring into play their conceptions of their own patient roles and their perceptions of the roles of the caregivers around them. Perceptions of roles for family members usually differ from those for professional caregivers such as visiting nurses. Caregivers and family also have their expectations of themselves and the patient. The degree of consensus among the various role conceptions and role expectations determines the degree of role conflict among patient, family, and caregivers. The degree of role conflict is positively associated with the degree of behavior labeled as deviant, as illustrated in the theory model, p. 195.

For example, a patient such as John, mentioned earlier, may have the normative value that people in a similar condition do not eat but rather take fluids sparingly. His view of his own behavior (role conception) surrounding his nutritional status may be that *he should* decide what beverages he will consume and that *he should* drink, but needs assistance. His role expectation for caregivers may include facilitating his selection of fluids, providing drink as needed, and giving needed assistance. John's expectations for his wife, Ann, may exceed those for professional caregivers. For example, she is expected to know the fluids he likes best and make them available on request. Professional caregivers, such as the visiting nurses at home or the hospital nurse if he is admitted for care, are likely to be expected to provide the necessities but not attend to a lot of time-consuming individualized aspects of nutrition (e.g., respond to John's request for limited fluids some time during his alert periods but not necessarily at the exact times he would prefer).

The degree to which John's expectations of the caregivers' roles differ from their perceptions of their roles is the consensus on role behavior. The less consensus there is, the more role conflict there will be in the cultural unit comprised of John, Ann, and other caregivers. The greater the stress or conflict, and, therefore, the closer the caregivers' behavior reaches John's limit of normative tolerance, the more likely John is to label the caregivers' behavior as deviant or neglectful.

Previous studies predict that women are slightly more negative toward nurses than men, and older patients more than younger patients (Bergman and Hillman, 1969). Atwood's (1975) review of the data shows that older persons are more likely to be unfed, although one patient was obviously terminal and very young. Relatives have reported more younger patients than older ones being offered interim fluids such as soft drinks. One young spouse said the mate was well fed when no family was there. One middle-aged patient, who did not appear ill, stated in awe:

Here the care and the food are best! When I have my tray, they look at it to see if I've eaten anything. They ask me if I want anything else. If I do, they send right down to the cafeteria and get it for me. That's *unheard* of!!

Diagnosis does not seem to matter. The physical state of the patient and the staff's apparent estimate of life span seem to be the key variables.

Like patients, families have their expectations of caregivers. As the theory model indicates, the degree of agreement between family members and caregivers on the latter's behavior toward the patient, the less conflict there will be and the less deviant behavior will be exhibited by the caregiver, according to the family's norms. For example, if John's wife did not accept his condition and expected the nurses to feed John regularly, but the nurses assessed his condition, noted his unsafe swallow reflex, and respected a patient's right to refuse food and limit fluids, then a great deal of role conflict would have been generated among the parties concerned. The nurses would have been more likely to meet John's role expectations for them, but by so doing would have exhibited negligent behavior as far as Ann was concerned. The more assertive she expected the nurses to be in feeding John, the more conflict there would have been, and the more deviant the nurses' behavior would have appeared to Ann.

ENVIRONMENTAL SELECTIVE NEGLECT

In addition to feeding patterns, two other main theorems emerged in my study. They concern other aspects of the trade-off when a patient is hospitalized: environmental and individualized or person-centered selective neglect. The theorem for the former is:

The larger the score on consensus on environmental care behavior, the smaller the score on environmental selective neglect.

Environmental care behaviors include all efforts made by a caregiver to preserve or enhance the patient's immediate environment and assure privacy; for example, prompt removal of foul-smelling linen or bedpan contents and appropriate screening of the patient during a treatment. Examples that have been reported by patients and their families follow (Atwood, 1975):

RELATIVE OF ELDERLY PATIENT: During the doctor's interview with her roommate, the roommate was asked about [criminal behavior]. Auntie objected to being in with a [criminal label]. A [police official] interviewed Auntie's neighbor during the last time she was here. That neighbor *was* a [criminal label]. Auntie could hear all of the medical interview. The other lady swore at the doctors.

One attractive male patient was helplessly indignant that he had to use a bedside commode and the nurses who assisted him tended to forget to guard the curtains. The spouse of a distraught, ill patient stated:

There is too much excess noise. The TVs are on too much all over. There should be a specific hour to cut off TV. Period. There is a lot of noise in general. Buzzers buzzing, telephones ringing. A lot of noise from a lot of sources.

Another aspect of environmental neglect involves loss of the patient's rights to influence room placement. Three spouses related vivid instances in which patients were moved from one room to the other—bed and all—without advance explanation of the move. Two of the three moves occurred at night and within 48 hours of admission. Patients found this most unsettling, as did their families.

PERSON-CENTERED SELECTIVE NEGLECT

The third type of selective neglect is individualized or person-centered selective neglect. The theorem is:

The larger the score on consensus on person-centered care behavior, the smaller the score on person-centered neglect.

Studies cited earlier predict that younger and male patients are more positive toward nursing care. This was not necessarily the case in my perimortality study. The label "fantastic care" was used by several relatives and patients. Almost all of the interviewees had some very positive comments about the personalized nursing care received by both patient and famiy.

They're all pleasant—it's very noticeable. Wonderful.

In Mexico, I think we have some pretty human service. Here the service is super! The nurses know so much.

The nurses were not rough.

The nurses showed friendliness—an interest in him.

They let her walk around with a mask on after everything was quiet, even though she was on isolation.

They go in and ask how she is. "Would you like me to make your bed now?" or "Would you like to take your shower?" In [city], they *tell* you. If the nurses weren't like they are, she wouldn't have stayed one day. She's afraid. The nurses are concerned. They ask how you are.

There's an overall big improvement from the first time she was admitted here!!

Both male nurses were more concerned than lady nurses. They showed concern for their patients.

I've never seen a place like this! I wish everybody could get this kind of care!

Everybody from the orderly downstairs on up here—the orientation is excellent. I've been in several other places . . .

Where there was family concern it seemed to be chiefly lack of patience and compassion.

If they would have a little more patience with him and let him tell them more what he feels and when he feels bad . . . (Spouse of a patient who did not speak English well.)

Some of the nurses were more abrupt than others.

The younger ones do a better job than the older ones. It's compassion that makes such a difference. Compassion is inborn, you know.

It was the same all the way through. One little gal showed more interest in _____ . That I appreciated. She said things like, "How are you feeling?" "Are you comfortable?" She kept looking for things to make her comfortable. Most of them just gave the shot and got out. They forget everything but the shot. They hardly notice there's a patient there.

In summary, the independent variable is the general category of consensus on care, which has several properties, such as the type of care, the role expectation, and the role perception. The dependent variable is the general category of selective neglect, which contains several properties, such as the type of neglect (nutritional, environmental, and personal selective neglect).

IMPLICATIONS FOR HOME CARE

If there is a lack of normative consensus and role performance results in a discrepant evaluation, there are definite implications for nursing care. If the results of the evaluation show that the caregiver is exceeding expectations of the patient, the family, and/or the caregiver, caregivers can choose to keep doing what they are doing or to give less care. If the results of the evaluation are negative, it means role expectations are not being met. One alternative for remedying the situation is negotiation among the patient, the family, and the professional caregiver. Negotiation is particularly effective in the home where interaction among some of the people involved is common.

There are three sets of norms impinging on caregivers—the patient's, the family's, and their own. Normative consensus is an unspecified function of all three norm sets $C = fx$ (patient, family, caregiver). Buckley (1961:41) indicates the relationships may be "mutual or unidirectional, linear, nonlinear or intermittent." If the function is nonlinear, depending on the nature of the function, a small change in any of the three sets of norms may result in a large change in consensus; for example, the function is exponential.

For example, in John's case, at one time Ann did not recognize that his refusal to accept food was partially the result of his limited swallow reflex. She forced him to eat because she thought he just needed encouragement. John tried in vain to convince Ann he did not want solid food. During one of her visits to the home, the visiting nurse observed John's problem swallowing and discussed the dangers with Ann and her husband. With a little negotiation, John was able to identify several fluids he would like to drink and Ann was satisfied with their nutrient value. A little negotiation goes a long way.

The greatest potential for the selective neglect model is in primary prevention, before conflict occurs. Careful assessment of patient and family norms provides the community health or visiting nurse with a firm information base. Care can be planned with the respective norms in mind. Potential conflict areas can be minimized by advance negotiation. Most important, nursing behavior that is viewed by patient and/or family as neglectful can be minimized.

More often than is generally recognized, patients have a better idea than anyone else how sick they are, how long they will live, and how their last days can best be spent (Kubler-Ross, 1969). When a conflict arises, at a minimum, it is vital to consult the patient, for the patient is the one who is dying.

SUMMARY

An increasing number of people need and desire home care during a chronic or acute illness with a poor prognosis. Home care, as care in any other setting, can be of high or low quality. The phenomenon of selective neglect, based on role theory and delineated here, predicts conditions under which care is likely to be unsatisfactory to the patient or the family and offers the community-based nurse a strategy for preventing nutritional, environmental, and person-centered selective neglect.

REFERENCES

Atwood, J. R. 1977. A grounded theory approach to the study of perimortality care. In M. Batey (ed.). Communicating nursing research. Western Interstate Commission for Higher Education, Boulder, Colo.

Atwood, J. R. 1975. A grounded theory approach to perimortality care and other considerations. Unpublished report to Nursing Department, University Hospital, Arizona Health Sciences Center, Tucson, Arizona.

Bergman, R., and Hillman, G. 1969. Community nursing services as perceived by posthospitalized patients. American Journal of Public Health 59:12:2168.

Bertrand, A. L. 1972. Social organization. A general systems and role theory perspective. F. A. Davis Co., Philadelphia.

Boyd, M. B. 1977. Home for the day. Nursing 77 7:(8): 88.

Buckley, W. 1967. Sociology and modern systems theory. Prentice-Hall, Englewood Cliffs, N.J.

Campbell, A. V. 1972. Moral dilemmas in medicine: A coursebook for doctors and nurses. Churchill Livingston, London.

Colt, A. M., Anderson, N., Scott, H. D., and Zimmerman, H. 1977. Home health care is good economics. Nursing Outlook 25:10:632.

Department of Health, Education, and Welfare. 1976. Health statistics: United States 1975. Pub. No. (HRA) 76-1232, National Center for Health Statistics. Washington, D.C.

Epstein, C. 1975. Nursing the dying patient. Learning processes for interaction. Reston Publishing, Reston, Va.

Gibbs, J. P. 1972. Sociological theory construction. Dryden Press, Hinsdale, Ill.

Glaser, B., and Strauss, A. 1973. The discovery of grounded theory: Strategies for qualitative research. Aldine Publishing, Chicago.

Hamblin, R. L., and Smith, C. R. 1966. Values, status, and professors. Sociometry 29(3):183.

Kubler-Ross, E. 1975. Death: The final stage of growth. Prentice-Hall, Inc., Englewood Cliffs, N.J.

Kubler-Ross, E. 1969. On death and dying. Macmillan Publishing, New York.

Martinson, I. M. 1977. The role of the nurse in home care for the dying child. In M. H. Miller and B. D. Flynn (eds.). Current perspectives in nursing: Social issues and trends. C. V. Mosby, St. Louis.

McEver, D. H. 1977. Death education: An inservice program. Nurse Educator 2(6):7.

Melin, R. C., and Hymans, D. J. 1977. Developing a health care model for long-term care facilities. Journal of Nursing Administration 7(8):12.

National Health Education Committee. 1976. The killers and cripplers: Facts on major diseases in the U.S. today. Davis McKay, New York.

Nunnally, J. C. 1967. Psychometric theory. McGraw-Hill, New York.

Traska, M. R. 1977. Hillhaven negotiates for NCI grant. Modern Healthcare 1(9):40.

INDEX